THE PREHISTORY OF ASIA MINOR

In this book, Bleda S. Düring offers an archaeological analysis of Asia Minor, the area equated with much of modern-day Turkey, from 20,000 to 2000 BC. During this period, human societies moved from small-scale hunter-gatherer groups to complex and hierarchical communities with economies based on agriculture and industry. Dr. Düring traces the spread of the Neolithic way of life, which ultimately reached across Eurasia, and the emergence of key human developments, including the domestication of animals, metallurgy, fortified towns, and long-distance trading networks. Situated at the junction between Europe and Asia, Asia Minor has often been perceived as a bridge for the movement of technologies and ideas. By contrast, this book argues that cultural developments followed a distinctive trajectory in Asia Minor from as early as 9000 BC.

Bleda S. Düring is a postdoctoral research Fellow and lecturer at Leiden University. He has done extensive fieldwork in Turkey and currently directs the Cide Archaeological Project, surveying the western Turkish Black Sea region. The author of numerous articles in edited volumes and journals, such as *Anatolian Studies*, *Journal of Mediterranean Archaeology*, and *Archaeological Dialogues*, Dr. Düring is also the author of *Constructing Communities: Clustered Neighbourhood Settlements of the Central Anatolian Neolithic*.

THE PREHISTORY OF ASIA MINOR

FROM COMPLEX HUNTER-GATHERERS TO EARLY URBAN SOCIETIES

Bleda S. Düring

Leiden University

CAMBRIDGE
UNIVERSITY PRESS

CAMBRIDGE UNIVERSITY PRESS
Cambridge, New York, Melbourne, Madrid, Cape Town, Singapore,
São Paulo, Delhi, Dubai, Tokyo, Mexico City

Cambridge University Press
32 Avenue of the Americas, New York, NY 10013-2473, USA

www.cambridge.org
Information on this title: www.cambridge.org/9780521149815

First published 2011

Printed in the United States of America

A catalog record for this publication is available from the British Library.

Library of Congress Cataloging in Publication data

Düring, Bleda S.
The prehistory of Asia Minor : from complex hunter-gatherers to early urban societies /
Bleda S. Düring.
    p.   cm.
Includes bibliographical references and index.
ISBN 978-0-521-76313-4 (hardback)
1. Prehistoric peoples – Turkey.   2. Antiquities, Prehistoric – Turkey.   3. Excavations
(Archaeology) – Turkey.   4. Turkey – Antiquities.   I. Title.
GN855.T83D87   2010
939'.2–dc22   2010015165

ISBN 978-0-521-76313-4 Hardback
ISBN 978-0-521-14981-5 Paperback

For Marianna

CONTENTS

FIGURES

ix

TABLES

ACKNOWLEDGEMENTS

This book was first conceived of in spring 2007, and the final work on the manuscript took place in early 2010. Looking back, writing this book was a much greater challenge than I had realised when I first started it. However, I hugely enjoyed working on this synthesis and gathering together disparate pieces of knowledge needed for the task. In the course of my work, I became indebted to many colleagues and friends, as well as to a number of institutions.

Archaeology is a cumulative enterprise, and this book builds on the research and publications of countless scholars. Access to this knowledge can be obtained for the most part from well-stocked libraries. The excellent libraries of University College London, the Netherlands Institute for the Near East, the British Institute at Ankara, and the Netherlands Institute in Turkey were of key importance in writing this book.

Throughout my studies on the prehistory of Asia Minor, I have been involved in various field projects and have been inspired and helped by many colleagues. Here I would like to mention Douglas Baird, Ian Hodder, Arek Marciniak, Roger Matthews, Mehmet Özdoğan, Nerissa Russell, Klaus Schmidt, Ulf Schoop, and Sharon Steadman.

This book was written in part during my time at University College London, where Claudia Glatz, Roger Matthews, and Toby Richter made me welcome. For the most part, it was finished in the course of my 'Veni' postdoctoral research, co-funded by the Netherlands Organisation for Scientific Research (NWO) and the Faculty of Archaeology of Leiden University. In Leiden, my gratitude goes to Peter Akkermans, John Bintliff, Gerrit van der Kooij, Diederik Meijer, and Olivier Nieuwenhuyse.

Numerous people granted me permission to reproduce images. They include Erhan Bıcakçı, Isabella Caneva, Altan Çilingiroğlu, James Conolly, Ben Claasz Coockson, Guneş Duru, Refik Duru, Utta Gabriel, Sevil

Gülçür, Carol Hershenson, Ian Hodder, Necmi Karul, Heinrich Müller-Karpe, Marcel Otte, Mihriban Özbaşaran, Mehmet Özdoğan, Aliye Öztan, Andrew Peacock, Jason Quinlan, Jacob Roodenberg, Wulf Schirmer, Ulf Schoop, John Swogger, and Gülsün Umurtak. Joanne Porck prepared the illustrations for this book.

I would like to thank Beatrice Rehl of Cambridge University Press for her support for this book from the start. I also would like to thank the anonymous referees who took the time to read and comment on the first draft of this book. Emile Eimermann proofread Chapter 7 for me.

Lastly, I would like to thank my dear Marianna for her patience and her love.

INTRODUCTION

This book presents a synthesis of the Prehistory of Asia Minor between about 20,000 and 2000 BC.[1] It discusses the transformations of human societies in Asia Minor from small-scale groups engaged in hunting and gathering to complex, hierarchically organised communities with an economy based on agriculture and industry.

The land of Asia Minor sits at a critical junction between the continents of Europe and Asia. For this reason, it has often been seen as a land-bridge through which cultural developments were transmitted. In this book it will be argued, however, that Asia Minor is better understood as a land in which cultural developments followed a distinctive trajectory from as early as 9000 BC. In this regard, the term 'Asia Minor', which implies that we are dealing with a small continent, captures an essential characteristic of this territory.

There are two main motives for investigating the Prehistory of Asia Minor. The first is that an understanding of developments in Asia Minor is of key importance in the study of wider developments in the Prehistory of Eurasia. For example, Asia Minor plays an important role both in the Neolithic transition and in the emergence of metallurgy, developments that have ramifications far beyond Asia Minor. Second, the Prehistory of Asia Minor is a subject worthy of study in its own right. Many phenomena in the Prehistory of Asia Minor are without parallels anywhere, and their study will contribute both to a fuller understanding of the human past in all its diversity and to a fuller appreciation of why things happened the way they did in the Prehistory of Asia Minor. I would argue that these two motives

---

[1] Throughout this book, BC dates are normally used. In older publication BP dates are often encountered, but given the recent extensions of radiocarbon calibration curves, it makes more sense to use BC dates. Wherever possible, the chronology is based on calibrated radiocarbon dates. In a few cases where individual radiocarbon dates are mentioned, they are written as 'cal. BC' in order to avoid confusion.

for investigating the Prehistory of Asia Minor are complementary. Both start from the premise that the Prehistory of Asia Minor should be contextualised within the wider discipline of archaeology and the issues of general anthropological significance it aims to address.

One of the reasons for conceiving this book, in May 2007, is that those who wanted to study the Prehistory of Asia Minor faced a difficult challenge. Despite the fact that a large number of prehistoric excavations are carried out each year in Asia Minor, and that a series of journals are devoted to Turkish archaeology,[2] there were very few synthetic studies of the Prehistory of Asia Minor, and those that did exist were inadequate for various reasons. First, a number of studies of the Prehistory of the Near East were published in the 1970s and are now out of date.[3] Second, there were some more recent edited volumes with papers on the Prehistory of Asia Minor that by default do not provide a synthetic overview.[4] Third, there were a number of publications by Yakar dealing with the Prehistory of Turkey,[5] which, although a valuable resource, are out of date and present a site-by-site summary of the evidence rather than a synthetic overview. Fourth, Joukowsky's book *Early Turkey*[6] provided an overview but is too general in its treatment of the specific periods and sites to be of much use.

Three years later, at the completion of this work, this situation has changed dramatically. Sagona and Zimansky have very recently published a monograph on the archaeology of Turkey.[7] Another book on the Early Bronze Age of Turkey is due to appear in 2011.[8] Finally, an edited volume about Anatolian archaeology is in preparation (Steadman and McMahon personal communication 2009). Thus, there is no longer a lack of synthetic literature on the Prehistory of Asia Minor, and the archaeology of Turkey can finally be compared with that of adjacent regions. Examples that can be mentioned are monographs on regions such as the Balkans, Greece, Cyprus, and Syria.[9]

Nonetheless, the present book constitutes an important addition to the growing literature on the archaeology of Asia Minor. It is more specific in regional and temporal focus than the book by Sagona and Zimansky, which makes it possible to treat data and research problems in depth. At

---

[2] The most important journals are *Adalya, Anatolia Antiqua, Anatolica, Anatolian Studies, Belleten, Istanbuller Mitteilungen, Kazı Sonuçları Toplantısı*, and *Türkiye Bilimler Akademisi — Arkeoloji Dergisi*.

[3] Mellaart 1975; Singh 1976; Redman 1978.

[4] Özdoğan and Başgelen 1999, 2007; Gérard and Thissen 2002; Lichter 2005; Gatsov and Schwartzberg 2006.

[5] Yakar 1985, 1991, 1994.

[6] Joukowsky 1996.

[7] Sagona and Zimansky 2009.

[8] Bachhuber 2011.

[9] Bailey 2000; Perlès 2001; Akkermans and Schwartz 2003; Steel 2004.

the same time, the diachronic discussion of about 18,000 years of occupation hopefully captures some of the most important transformations in human history as they played out in Asia Minor. For such a comprehensive view, a monograph is more suitable than an edited volume.

Research into the Prehistory of Asia Minor has been uneven: Some areas and periods have been poorly investigated, while others are much better known. Further, many excavations and surveys have not been adequately published. Consequently, the synthesis presented in this volume is centred on a limited group of excavated sites for which comprehensive publications are available, although efforts are made to include evidence from recent excavations and sites for which we lack substantial publications.

This book differs in conception from the older publications dealing with the Prehistory of Asia Minor. Rather than presenting a series of sites and their sequences, the aim is to discuss archaeological horizons in a synthetic manner and address socio-cultural developments and relations with surrounding regions where appropriate. In so far as these elements are central to this book, the approach is comparable to that taken by Redman in his *The Emergence of Civilization*[10] and by more recent books on the Prehistory of Egypt and the Balkans.[11] However, unlike these books, my approach here is not programmatic: It is neither neo-evolutionist in outlook nor agency centred. Instead, I draw on ideas from the broad field of the humanities in a much more eclectic fashion. Throughout the book, the aim will be to ground the synthesis in the available data and, where possible, to formulate interpretations in such a way that they can be evaluated in future research.

This book, then, has three aims. The first is to provide a synthetic overview of the Prehistory of Asia Minor that is both thorough and up-to-date. The second is to address issues of general anthropological significance in relation to the unique trajectories of development and phenomena that constitute the Prehistory of Asia Minor and how these bear on wider debates in the discipline of archaeology. The third is to contextualise the Prehistory of Asia Minor within the wider Prehistory of adjacent regions and to assess the nature and importance of contacts between regions.

[10] Redman 1978.
[11] Bailey 2000; Wengrow 2006.

CHAPTER ONE

THE LAND OF ASIA MINOR

'Asia Minor' in this book refers to what today is roughly the western half of Turkey-in-Asia, or 'Anatolia' (Fig. 1.1). Asia Minor consists of a peninsula surrounded by the Black Sea and the Sea of Marmara to the north, the Aegean to the west, and the Mediterranean to the south, and does not include what is presently the easternmost mountainous part of Turkey.

The term 'Asia Minor' developed as a variant of the word 'Asia'. Over the course of millennia, Asia has expanded from a designation for a region in Aegean Turkey to the designation of a significant part of the globe. The word Asia is first documented in Hittite texts, which mention a coalition of small states called 'Assuwa' in western Turkey. Subsequently, a Roman province with the name Asia existed in the same region.[1] Later, Asia was used to refer to all of the Near East, and subsequently expanded to include the entire Asian continent as presently defined. The term Asia Minor came into use to identify the western half of Asiatic Turkey more specifically from about 400 AD, and was mainly used by the Byzantines to describe the part of Asia under their control.[2]

The division between Asia Minor and the rest of the Near East runs along a line approximately connecting the modern towns of Iskenderun and Trabzon (Fig. 1.1). In terms of geography this boundary is not clear-cut, and there is a gradual transition rather than a sharp break. Generally speaking, we are dealing with the division between the Anatolian Plateau to the west, which consists of a wide variety of landscapes at an altitude of about 1000 metres above sea level, and the mountainous highlands to the east. In the south, the coastal plains of Cilicia and Iskenderun are included in Asia Minor, and here the Amanus Mountains mark the separation with the Syrian steppe and the Levant.

---

[1] Cline 1996; Bryce 2005: 124–127.
[2] Hütteroth 1982: 14.

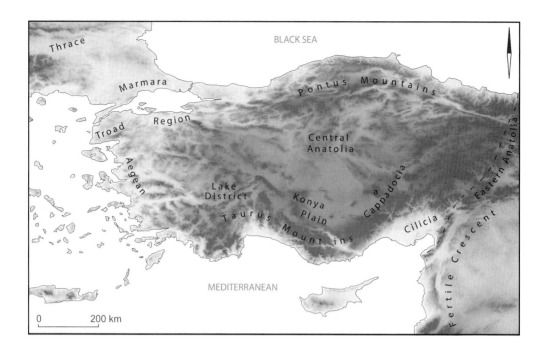

The rationale for adopting the term Asia Minor as central to this book – and by extension the validity of its eastern boundary – is not based primarily on geography, however. Rather, this geographic boundary is relevant to the present study because time and again throughout Prehistory and later periods it constituted an important cultural division between three regions: first, Greater Mesopotamia and the Levant to the south (including Syria and south-eastern Turkey); second, the mountainous highlands to the east where the Taurus, Pontus, Caucasus, Zagros, and Elburz mountain ranges merge; and, third, Asia Minor.

It will be argued in this volume that this cultural boundary existed from about 9000 BC onwards, starting in the Aceramic Neolithic, and continued to exist through the Ceramic Neolithic and Chalcolithic.[3] Subsequently, in the Bronze Ages, there were closer cultural links between the regions mentioned, although in many ways Asia Minor remained distinct in its developments.[4] The same situation continued in the subsequent Iron Age. The cultural division along the eastern boundary of Asia Minor was overcome during the Hellenistic and Roman periods, only to be gradually reasserted in the Byzantine and Ottoman periods.[5] Thus, although there are protracted periods during which strong states managed to unify culture

1.1 Geography and toponyms of Asia Minor. Produced by the author and Joanne Porck.

[3] Yakar 1991; Özdoğan 1996; Thissen 2000.
[4] Efe 2006, 15.
[5] Hütteroth 1982: 14; Yakar 1985; Kozlowski and Aurenche 2005: 88–95.

across the eastern boundary of Asia Minor in later history, this was not the case during most of Anatolian prehistory.

These observations do not amount to geographical determinism. Geography does not structure human interaction and define cultural groups. Instead, cultural practices have an important role to play. For example, regular contacts between Asia Minor and the Fertile Crescent can be firmly documented in the Aceramic Neolithic, but these contacts did not result in the transference of culture in the sense that people took up culturally specific practices from societies on the other side of the mountains. By contrast, during the Early Bronze Age, the desire of elite groups in Asia Minor to set themselves apart from others resulted in a desire for exotic goods and styles that transcended pre-existing cultural and political boundaries and led to the formation of an interregional elite culture.

The boundaries of Asia Minor in directions other than the east are more straightforward in terms of geography. Asia Minor is surrounded by sea to the south, west, and north. Nonetheless, these boundaries are in some cases more permeable than the less self-evident eastern limit of Asia Minor. In the south, contacts between Asia Minor and Cyprus existed throughout Prehistory. In the west, Aegean Turkey constituted a landscape often more integrated with the Aegean islands and Greece than with the central plateau of Asia Minor. Finally, in the northwest, the region surrounding the Sea of Marmara often constituted a cultural whole, which in some periods was affiliated with Thrace rather than with the rest of Asia Minor.

Ultimately, any division of the globe into sub-regions is arbitrary. Nevertheless, I feel that the focus on Asia Minor in this book is appropriate for two reasons. First, handbooks for adjacent regions such as Cyprus, Greece, and the Balkans already exist.[6] Second, there are many periods in which Asia Minor does seem to constitute a coherent cultural entity that can be distinguished from that of adjacent areas.

1.1.1 The Structure of Asia Minor

Asia Minor is a large territory of about 407,700 square kilometres, and is approximately similar in size to Germany and The Netherlands combined. Given this substantial size, it is not surprising that Asia Minor includes a large variety of landscapes. The following description of its main geographical characteristics consists of little more than a sketch. More detailed studies of the geography of Asia Minor are available in other publications.[7]

---

[6] Dickinson 1994; Bailey 2000; Perlès 2001; Akkermans and Schwartz 2003; Steel 2004.
[7] Dewdney 1971; Brinkmann 1976; Hütteroth 1982; Erol 1983; Metz 1996.

On a structural level Asia Minor consists of two large east–west-oriented mountain ranges, the Pontus in the north and the Taurus in the south, that are most formidable in the east and gradually decrease in height towards the west of Asia Minor. To the east of Asia Minor, these mountain ranges merge with those of the Caucasus, Zagros, and Elburz in a large, mountainous highland zone.[8]

In the north, the Pontus Mountains rise steeply out of the Black Sea, with only a few narrow coastal plains. At a few places, rivers from the central plateau break through the Pontus Mountains and have created large alluvial fans on which large-scale agriculture is possible. The most important of these are at Çarşamba and Bafra near modern Samsun. Even today the Pontus Mountains are difficult to breach from the interior, and there are few roads connecting the coast with the hinterland, a pattern that was undoubtedly more pronounced in the past.

To the south of the Pontus Mountains runs the North Anatolian Fault, which can be traced roughly from Erzincan in the east to Izmit in the west. The Anatolian plate south of the fault is pushed west between 1 and 20 centimetres per annum in relation to the Eurasian plate to the north. The enormous pressure that builds up along this fault zone resulted in no less than seven earthquakes with a force above 7.0 on the Richter scale between 1939 and 1999. Apart from this major fault system there are many other fault zones in Asia Minor, as a result of which up to 40 per cent of Turkey is periodically subject to substantial earthquakes.[9]

In the south, Asia Minor is dominated by the Taurus range, running from mountainous eastern Turkey to the region west of Antalya. At both ends the Taurus Mountains reach elevations above 2000 metres above sea level, and like the Pontus, the mountains rise abruptly from the sea. Exceptions are the coastal plains of Antalya, Cilicia, and Iskenderun, and these plains are difficult to reach from the interior. Only a few natural roads cross the Taurus, and these have had great cultural, commercial, and military significance throughout much of history. These are the Göksu River Valley in western Cilicia, the 'Cilician Gates' near Tarsus, and a pass through the Amanus Mountains known as the 'Syrian Gates'.

Set between the mountains of eastern Turkey, the Pontus, and the Taurus are the highlands of Asia Minor, better known as 'Central Anatolia'. These highlands are often described as a 'plateau', but they are neither homogeneous nor level. Instead, we are dealing with diverse landscapes at about 1,000 metres above sea level, which include, first, rugged mountainous terrain interspersed with river valleys – most prevalent in the north

---

[8] See Ilhan 1971a for more details on the structural features of Turkey.
[9] Ilhan 1971b; Yilmaz 2003.

and east; second, large basins in which water drains into large, shallow salt lakes – in particular the Tüz Gölü Basin, the Konya Plain, the Ereğli Basin, and the Seyfe Göl Basin; and, third, the Lakes Region in the south-west between Konya and Denizli.

In the west, the highlands of Asia Minor gradually give way to a series of east –west-oriented river valleys separated by minor mountain chains. The most important are the Gediz and Büyük Menderes river valleys, which form natural roads connecting the interior with the Aegean. Human settlements have clustered in these river valleys throughout most periods in both Prehistory and later periods. In the valleys, a significant amount of alluviation has taken place over the millennia; as a result, prehistoric coastlines and surfaces have by and large been buried under later alluvium.

Finally, along the coasts of the Sea of Marmara in the northwest of Asia Minor another region can be distinguished, with large plains around Bandırma and Adapazarı, and a number of medium-sized lakes, such as Kuş Gölü, Uluabat Gölü, and İznik Gölü.

1.1.2 Natural Resources of Asia Minor

The geology of Asia Minor is complex because several continental plates come together in various folding zones. Related to these folding zones are landscapes formed by volcanism[10] and numerous mountain chains exposing rock formations of great diversity. Consequently, a large variety of minerals and rocks are present in Asia Minor. Many of these have been exploited in Prehistory, only the most important of which will be mentioned here (Fig. 1.2).[11]

The first of these is obsidian, a volcanic glass that was mined and exchanged from the Epipalaeolithic onwards. Two source areas in Asia Minor were exploited in Prehistory, one centred on the Cappadocian relict volcanoes and another on the Galatian volcanic massif, located in North-Central Anatolia (§4.3.1). Both regions contain a number of obsidian sources, which can be distinguished chemically from each other. Several obsidian quarries have been investigated, and it is often possible to trace the material from such quarries to far-removed sites and to date the use of these quarries to specific periods in Prehistory. Obsidian from the Aegean island of Melos is also found in Asia Minor during Prehistory.[12]

---

[10] For more details on the geology of Turkey see Ilhan 1971a; Brinkmann 1976; Erol 1983.
[11] For details on rocks and minerals of economic value see Karajian 1920; De Jesus 1980; Yener et al. 1994; Schoop 1995.
[12] Keller and Seifried 1990; Williams-Thorpe 1995; Balkan-Atlı et al. 1999a; Georgiadis 2008.

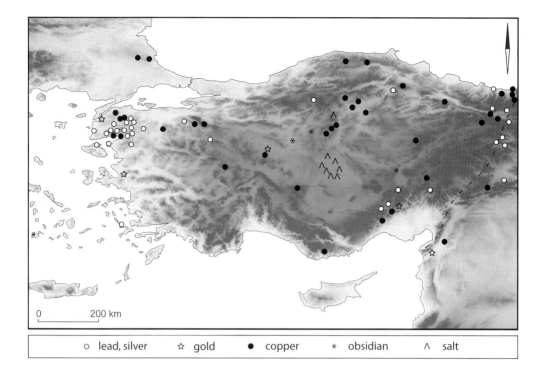

1.2 Rocks and minerals of Asia Minor. Produced by the author and Joanne Porck.

| ○ lead, silver | ☆ gold | ● copper | ∗ obsidian | ∧ salt |

Second, copper ores are available in abundance in Anatolia, and many appear to have been exploited during Prehistory. The earliest copper artefacts are found in Aceramic Neolithic sites, but copper consumption became much more prolific with the rise of metallurgy during the Late Chalcolithic and the Early Bronze Age. Although it is often difficult to date ancient mines, it has been argued that important copper mines were located in the Trabzon Region, in North-Central Anatolia, in the Küre Mountains of the central Pontus, and in the Bolkardağ Region.[13] A number of wooden objects have been found in Anatolian mines – such as a wooden ladder and a shovel – that can be dated to the third, second, and first millennia BC, demonstrating that mining has a considerable, and largely undocumented, Prehistory in Asia Minor.[14]

Third, most of the other metals that were mined in Asia Minor during Prehistory, such as lead, silver, and gold, often came from the same general areas as copper. There is also a notable occurrence of gold in the central Aegean part of Asia Minor, which is reflected in the Greek myth of the golden touch of King Midas of Lydia in the Iron Age. Arsenic can be found

[13] De Jesus 1980; Kaptan 1986; Yener et al. 1994; Schoop 1995.
[14] De Jesus 1980: 110; Kaptan 1986.

across Asia Minor, a circumstance that was of some importance for the production of early copper alloys.[15]

Fourth, there are a number of ores that occur in Asia Minor, but for which it has not been unequivocally demonstrated that they were mined during Prehistory. Iron objects are found from the Early Bronze Age onwards, but it is possible that the origins of this material were almost exclusively meteoric.[16] Further, the debate about whether tin was mined at Göltepe-Kestel is still unresolved and will be discussed at some length in Chapter 7.[17]

Finally, a resource of great importance in Prehistory that was obtained from specific places in the landscapes and exchanged over long distances is salt. Especially well known are salt mining and production at the Tüz Gölü[18] and at the rock salt sources located between the town of Çankırı and the Kizilirmak.[19]

1.2.1 The Ecology of Asia Minor

Asia Minor has four main climates/ecological zones that are largely shaped by the geographical features of the country.[20] Precipitation is highest along the Black Sea littoral, where annual precipitation in many parts exceeds 1,000 millimetres. Precipitation occurs in all seasons, and both summers and winters are temperate, with average summer temperatures of about 25°C, winter averages of about 10°C, and about four frost-days per annum.

Along the western and southern littorals of Asia Minor, the climate is Mediterranean. Although the precipitation can equal that of the Pontus, exceeding 1000 millimetres per year in many areas, rainfall is almost absent during the summer. Winter temperatures average about 11°C, and frost occurs one to three days per annum. Summers are hot, with temperatures averaging around 27 to 33°C. In general, the climate becomes warmer as one moves south and east along the Turkish coast.

The climate of the Marmara Region is intermediate between those of the Pontus and the Mediterranean. Precipitation is about 800 millimetres per annum and occurs in all seasons, although summers are relatively dry. Summers are milder than in the Mediterranean, with average temperatures

[15] De Jesus 1980; Yener et al. 1994; Schoop 1995.
[16] Yener et al. 1994: 383; Pernicka 2006.
[17] Yener and Özbal 1987; Hall and Steadman 1991; Pernicka et al. 1992; Willies 1992; Yener and Goodway 1992; Muhly 1993; Yener and Vandiver 1993a, 1993b; Kaptan 1995; Yener 2000.
[18] Erdoğu et al. 2003a; Erdoğu and Kayacan 2004; Erdoğu and Fazlıoğlu 2006.
[19] Taşman 1937.
[20] For more details see Steinhauer 1970; Alex 1985; Van Zeist and Bottema 1991.

of about 22°C, and winters are about 6°C in the coldest months, with about 12 frost-days per year.

Finally, the central part of Asia Minor is markedly drier than the surrounding regions. Around Tüz Gölü, the great salt lake located in the middle of Central Anatolia, annual precipitation is 300 to 400 millimetres, while in the outer rim of Central Anatolia it is 400 to 500 millimetres. Summer temperatures are 22°C on average but winters are relatively harsh, with temperatures that drop to an average of −3°C, and with about 20 frost-days per year.

These four climatic regions of Asia Minor each have different types of vegetation.[21] In the Pontus Region, vegetation is lush and consists of cold-deciduous trees and shrubs, including beech, hornbeam, hazel, walnut, and oak. In the Mediterranean zone, trees and shrubs are predominantly evergreen, sensitive to frost, and adapted to summer drought. Typical trees include mastic, olive trees, evergreen oak, and pine. These trees do not form a full canopy and are interspersed with herb shrubs. The Marmara Region can be considered an amalgamation of the vegetation found in the Mediterranean and the Pontus. Typical trees often found are pine and oak. Today the Marmara Region is a prime olive-growing region, but citrus trees are not found there. Finally, Central Anatolia at its core can be characterised as a 'dwarf-shrubland steppe'. The relatively dry conditions of this region and the cold winters preclude the development of forests in much of this region, which is dominated by grasslands with shrubs, typically *Artemisia*, and some trees, such as pistachio. According to Zohary and Hillman, this steppe zone was the natural habitat of a number of the wild predecessors of the grains that were domesticated during the Neolithic.[22] Surrounding this steppe vegetation in the core of Asia Minor is a woodland zone with scattered stands of pine, oak, and juniper.[23]

1.2.2 Past Ecologies of Asia Minor

The current climate and vegetation zones of Asia Minor are not necessarily representative of conditions during Prehistory. Ecological systems are complex and dynamic, and it has been argued that change rather than stability is the norm in nature.[24] However, seen from a long-term perspective, climates are more stable in some periods than in others. In particular, the

[21] For more details see Davis 1965–1988; Zohary 1973; Van Zeist and Bottema 1991; Zohary and Hopf 1993.
[22] Zohary 1989: 360–361; Zohary and Hopf 1993; Hillman 1996: 190.
[23] Zohary 1973: 162.
[24] Blumler 1996.

Holocene is much more stable in terms of climate than the preceding Pleis-tocene, which was characterised by very rapid fluctuations between warmer and colder conditions.[25]

There are two main methods for reconstructing past ecological condi-tions. On the one hand, it is possible to use global data for the reconstruction of past climatic trends and ecologies. Here one can think of evidence from ice cores or deep-sea evidence, from which large-scale climatic changes can be reconstructed on the basis of isotope ratios. On the other hand, it is possible to model past climates and ecologies using local proxy data such as pollen cores, diatom analysis, dendrochronology, and the accretion of carbonate coatings.

It has been customary for archaeologists working in the Near East to adopt a global framework towards past climates and ecologies. The liter-ature abounds with references to perceived global climate events such as the 'Younger Dryas', the '8.2 KA event', and the 'Early Holocene Climatic Optimum', and these are often assigned great importance in relation to cul-tural changes in the past such as the emergence and spread of agriculture.[26] What is generally missing from these reconstructions, however, is an aware-ness that postulated global climatic changes may have very different effects in particular regions. Further, most research on past climates has focussed on temperate Europe, reconstructions for which are often extrapolated to other regions, such as the Near East, without the realisation that tra-jectories may have differed markedly. The Near East is situated at the conjunction of various climatic systems, the influence of which may have expanded or shrunk in the past. For example, an expansion of the Indian monsoon into the Arabian Peninsula during the Early Holocene resulted in increased precipitation, creating a very different environment from that of today.[27]

It is clear that the local effects of postulated large-scale climatic changes need to be explored with local datasets. To clarify the issues, it is use-ful to consider the effects of the Younger Dryas in Asia Minor: a cold period immediately prior to the Holocene. On the basis of pollen extracted from the Mediterranean sea bed, this period has been reconstructed as one dominated by steppe plants and followed by an Early Holocene Climatic Optimum between 9000 and 6000 BP (approximately 8000–5000 BC) with more temperate conditions than at present.[28] However, a large number of

[25] Van Andel 2005: 382.
[26] See, for example, Kuzucuoğlu and Roberts 1997; Özdoğan 1997a; Rossignol-Strick 1997; Bryson and Bryson 1999; Weiss and Bradley 2001.
[27] Van Andel 2005: 383–384; Wilkinson 2003: 21–22.
[28] Rossignol-Strick 1993, 1995, 1997.

pollen cores taken across Asia Minor and beyond fail to show such a homogeneous steppe horizon corresponding to the Younger Dryas.[29] Instead, climatic and ecological developments across Early Holocene Asia Minor are diverse and cannot usually be linked to large-scale climatic phenomena, many of which appear to have had little or no impact on pollen sequences.[30] For example, the advance of forests in Asia Minor after the Pleistocene was complex and lasted for several millennia, and the start date and pace of reforestation differed per region.[31] To get at such variable regional trajectories, local proxy data on past climates and ecologies are of key significance.

Fortunately, substantive research has been done on climate proxy data in Asia Minor. The best evidence for the reconstruction of ancient climates and ecologies has been found in lake sediments. These sediments accumulate incrementally, although not necessarily at a constant rate of deposition. Nonetheless, these deposits represent a stratified sequence, and the organic inclusions trapped within the sediments can be analysed to assess changes in past ecologies. Although the chronological resolution of these sediments is often far from ideal, the reconstruction of past environments using lake cores has been remarkably successful. Ecological changes have been reconstructed by analysing, first, pollen: the minute sperm cells of seed plants; second, diatoms: plankton; and, third, stable isotope ratios, or the proportion of elements with an unusual number of neutrons.[32]

Diatoms and stable isotopes are a function of the depth of a lake and its salinity, and will be affected by changes in these conditions.[33] Lake levels and salinity are influenced by factors such as precipitation, the melting of ice and snow, rates of evaporation, and changes in the outlet of a lake. Thus, changes in diatoms or stable isotopes do not always reflect broader climatic trends. For instance, various lakes in the Konya Plain have distinct trajectories of change in diatoms and stable isotopes despite being located in a similar environment.[34] While some have argued for a steppic environment in Central Anatolia during the Early Holocene on the basis of the diatoms of the Tüz Gölü and the Karayazı alluvial fan,[35] other lakes, such as Eski Acıgöl in Cappadocia, show more temperate conditions in the Early Holocene.[36]

---

[29] Bottema 1995: 890; Kuzuçuoğlu and Roberts 1997: 17.
[30] Van Zeist and Bottema 1991; Roberts et al. 2001; Naruse et al. 2002; Kashima 2003; Pustovoytov et al. 2007.
[31] Van Zeist and Bottema 1991; Woldring and Bottema 2001/2002: 25.
[32] See Rosen 2007: 17–31 for an overview of these methods.
[33] Eastwood et al. 1999: 688.
[34] Reed et al. 1999; Roberts et al. 1999: 625.
[35] Kashima 2000; Naruse et al. 2002.
[36] Roberts et al. 2001: 733.

By contrast with the diatom and stable isotope evidence, pollen provide a much more accurate indication of past ecologies. Depending on the size and setting of a lake, the 'pollen catchment area' of a lake can vary from a local to a regional scale. Plants and trees are not necessarily proportionally represented in pollen cores, but with the use of modern reference samples taken near the lakes from which the cores derive, these problems of proportionality can be estimated and controlled for.[37] When analysed within such a framework, pollen cores provide by far the most systematic archive of ancient ecologies. Other types of palaeo-environmental data, such as diatoms, stable isotopes, and geomorphological indicators, are best used to augment pollen data. However, past ecologies as reflected in pollen data do not always correspond directly to climate, given that from the earliest Neolithic onwards, human activities started to affect the landscapes of Asia Minor.

The presence of a large number of permanent lakes and marshy environments in Asia Minor, which have acted as pollen traps over millennia, provides excellent opportunities for reconstructing past ecologies. The most important pollen cores of Asia Minor include, first, Söğüt Gölü, Beyşehir Gölü, Karamik Bataklığı, and Gölhisar Gölü in the Lake District; second, Akgöl Adabağ and Eski Acıgöl in South-Central Anatolia; third, Abant Gölü, Yeniçağa Gölü, Kaz Gölü, Tatlı Gölü, and Ladik Gölü in North Anatolia; and, fourth, Yenişehir in North-West Anatolia (Fig. 1.3).[38]

In a synthetic study of these pollen cores, Van Zeist and Bottema put forward a sequence of vegetation maps for Asia Minor and the wider Near East for the Late Pleistocene, the Early Holocene, and the second millennium BC.[39] This synthesis, augmented with data that emerged after 1991, remains the most solid reconstruction of Prehistoric climates and ecologies of Asia Minor.

For the period at the end of the 'Last Glacial Maximum', between about 18,000 and 16,000 BP (about 20,000–17,000 BC), Van Zeist and Bottema reconstruct forests in the Pontic Region of Asia Minor, woodland and forest-steppe in Mediterranean Asia Minor and the Marmara Region, and steppe and desert-steppe in Central Anatolia. Towards the end of the Pleistocene, in the period directly preceding the Younger Dryas period and dated to about 12,000–11,000 BP (about 12,000–11,000 BC), the reconstructed vegetation belts for Asia Minor were more or less similar to those of the Last Glacial Maximum, although the woodland and forest-steppe

---

[37] Van Zeist and Bottema 1991: 34–35.
[38] Van Zeist et al. 1975; Van Zeist and Bottema 1991; Bottema et al. 1993/1994; Kuzucuoğlu and Roberts 1997; Eastwood et al. 1999; Bottema et al. 2001; Roberts et al. 2001; Woldring and Bottema 2001/2002.
[39] Van Zeist and Bottema 1991.

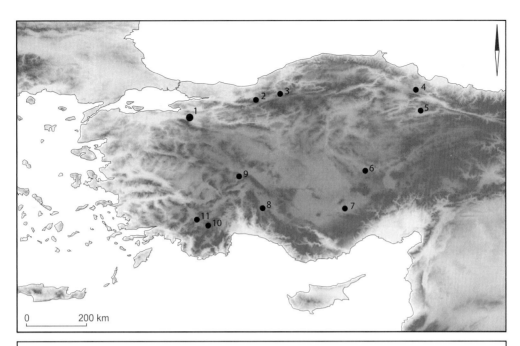

0 ⸻ 200 km

1 Yenişehir; 2 Abant Gölü; 3 Yeniçağa Gölü; 4 Ladik Gölü; 5 Kaz Gölü; 6 Eski Acıgöl; 7 Akgöl Adabağ; 8 Beyşehir Gölü; 9 Karamik Bataklığı; 10 Söğüt Gölü; 11 Gölhisar Gölü.

zone belt had progressed slightly further inland. The subsequent map for the Early Holocene, at about 9000 BC (ca. 8000 BC), differs dramatically from that of the Late Pleistocene. The forest belt has increased to include the Marmara Region and the Mediterranean parts of Asia Minor. A significant part of the highlands of Asia Minor is now characterised as woodland and forest-steppe, and it is only in the core of Central Anatolia that a steppe environment is still present. Finally, in the second millennium BC reconstruction, the steppe zone in Central Anatolia has further diminished and is surrounded by a broad belt of woodland. At this time, the ecology of Turkey would have been roughly comparable to the assumed natural vegetation of the present.

These reconstructions of past ecologies put forward by Van Zeist and Bottema have been largely confirmed in more recent studies of pollen sequences in northern Asia Minor, in the Lake District, and in Cappadocia.[40] A core taken at Yenişehir, in the Marmara Region, has demonstrated that there were virtually no trees in this area at the end of

1.3 Pollen cores of Asia Minor. Produced by the author and Joanne Porck.

[40] Bottema et al. 1993/1994; Eastwood et al. 1999; Roberts et al. 2001; Woldring and Bottema 2001/2002.

the final Pleistocene, however. This means that the woodland and forest-steppe belt reconstructed by Van Zeist and Bottema for this period for the Marmara and Mediterranean regions was probably more marginal than so far assumed. The subsequent rapid forestation of the Marmara Region in the Early Holocene that had been put forward was borne out by this pollen sequence, however.[41]

It has been argued that the climate of Early Holocene Asia Minor was more temperate than at present.[42] One problem with this idea is that the reforestation of many parts of Asia Minor occurred several millennia after the start of the Holocene rather than during this reconstructed early temperate phase.[43] Roberts has posited that the spread of forests might have been delayed by geographical barriers or that people were keeping the landscape open by igniting shrubs and trees.[44] If the latter hypothesis holds true, this would imply that people were leaving their mark on the landscape of Asia Minor from the earliest Holocene onwards. It is difficult to understand, however, why human interference with the landscape would have become less pronounced later in the Holocene, allowing the trees to establish themselves. One would expect the reverse pattern to occur. Thus, the idea that the delay of forestation of interior Asia Minor was caused by human interference is problematic.

More subtle traces of human activities are found in various pollen sequences from the Aceramic Neolithic onwards. At Eski Acıgöl an increase in arboreal pollen can be contrasted with an increase in xeric (drought-tolerant) plants at the expense of the grass steppe. This has been interpreted as possible evidence for herding practices affecting the local vegetation from about 7600 BC onwards. Further, after about 6000 BC, cereal values increase at Eski Acıgöl, which is probably related to farming in the area.[45] During the same period there is evidence for farming in the Ladik pollen sequence in northern Asia Minor, although there are some problems with the dating of this pollen zone.[46]

To summarise this discussion, the following conclusions can be drawn. First, the transition from the Pleistocene climate to that of the Holocene seems to have been relatively abrupt in Asia Minor, although the reforestation of interior Asia Minor took several millennia to complete. Second, throughout the Holocene the climate of Asia Minor was relatively stable, although it is possible that the Early Holocene was somewhat more

---

[41] Bottema et al. 2001.
[42] Rossignol-Strick 1993, 1995, 1997.
[43] Roberts et al. 2001: 732–733; Woldring and Bottema 2001/2002: 26.
[44] Roberts and Wright 1993: 215; Roberts 2002.
[45] Woldring and Bottema 2001/2002: 28–29.
[46] Bottema et al. 1993/1994: 55.

temperate than at present. Third, throughout Prehistory, the human impact on the ecology of Asia Minor as a whole was probably relatively minor. However, in specific places the impact of prehistoric people might have been substantial; here one can think of agricultural fields, pasturing, the exploitation of wood resources, and the hunting of wild animals.

The first major human-induced landscape modification in Asia Minor seems to have occurred during the so-called Beyşehir Occupation Phase, dated to between about 1700 BC and 700 AD,[47] which included a massive deforestation of the uplands that were brought under cultivation during this period, and the cultivation of a range of food-bearing trees, such as olive, sweet chestnut, walnut, manna ash, and plane trees, as well as the vine plant. Although this agricultural transformation falls outside the scope of this book, it does affect the study of the Prehistory of Asia Minor to a significant degree because the cultivation of the uplands during the Beyşehir Occupation Phase led to the massive erosion of those uplands and the formation of enormous deposits in valley floors,[48] and both processes have hampered the preservation and accessibility of prehistoric sites.

1.3.1 Coastal Transformations of Asia Minor

The geography of Asia Minor altered significantly during Prehistory due to changes in sea levels. During the Late Glacial Maximum, between about 25,000 and 18,000 BP (ca. 28,000–20,000 BC), sea levels were 100 to 130 metres below their current level. Subsequently, the rise of sea levels resulting from the melting of land-ice lasted for several millennia in the Late Pleistocene and the Early Holocene.[49] This process was not linear and, as a consequence, reconstructing past sea levels at particular locations is complex. Apart from rising sea levels, land surfaces may also rise or sink due to plate tectonics.[50] During the Middle to Late Holocene, however, the elevation of Asia Minor seems to have been relatively stable, except for the coastal regions around the modern cities of Izmir and Marmaris, which have sunk a few metres.[51]

Most of the southern coastline of Asia Minor consists of mountains rising steeply from the sea, and here the effects of sea level rise in the Early Holocene were probably fairly limited. It is only along the coastal plains of

[47] Bottema and Woldring 1990; Van Zeist and Bottema 1991; Eastwood et al. 1999; Marsh 1999.
[48] Marsh 1999, 2005.
[49] Van Andel 2005: 386.
[50] Flemming 1978; Lambeck 1996.
[51] Flemming 1978: 436.

Cilicia and Antalya that the combined effects of sea level rise and alluviation have strongly affected the morphology of the landscape and the preservation of prehistoric sites, which have been either submerged or buried beneath deltaic formations.[52]

In the Aegean, the coastline of Asia Minor during the Late Glacial Maximum extended significantly westwards, including most of the northern Aegean islands and the northern part of the Dodecanese Islands. Following the rise of sea levels during the Late Glacial and Early Holocene the present coastline came into being, but many of the river valleys were flooded at this point, up to 70 kilometres inland. During the Middle Holocene deltaic formations developed in these valleys, which gave way during the Late Holocene to rivers with a main channel and horizontal alluvial deposition. Over the millennia, these processes resulted in the westward expansion of the coastline and the burial of prehistoric surfaces beneath thick alluvial deposits. The trajectories of individual river valleys vary, of course, but this general pattern does seem to hold true across Aegean Asia Minor.[53]

The reconstruction of the coastal changes along the Sea of Marmara and the Black Sea in the Final Pleistocene and the Early Holocene is more complicated, given that debates are ongoing about how and when the Dardanelles and the Bosporus channels came into being. Both the Sea of Marmara and the Black Sea were lakes during the Late Glacial Maximum. It has been argued that the level of the Black Sea remained about 100 metres below current levels during the Early Holocene, followed by a sudden rise to current levels at about 6000 BC, when water started flowing through the Bosporus.[54] On this basis, it has even been suggested that a submerged Neolithic site had been found 100 metres below the current level of the Black Sea, a claim that has not been borne out by a closer analysis.[55]

The hypothesis of the flooding of the Black Sea around 6000 BC has been challenged on the following grounds.[56] First, the claim that the Early Holocene level of the Black Sea was 100 metres below the present level is problematic given that both precipitation and the melting of glaciers would have created a large inflow in the Black Sea during this period. Second, Ryan and Pitman have dated their flooding event by dating the youngest freshwater molluscs they were able to find on the Black Sea bottom – which could not survive under the anoxic conditions that currently characterise the lower Black Sea. However, these shells do not necessarily date a flooding

---

[52] Özdoğan 1997a: 26; Kuhn 2002: 199.
[53] Özdoğan 1997a; Hakyemez et al. 1999; Kayan 1999; Brückner 2003.
[54] Ryan et al.1997; Ryan and Pitman 1999.
[55] Ballard et al. 2001; Hiebert et al. 2002; Doonan 2004.
[56] Jablonka 2003; Yanko-Hombach 2007.

event of the Black Sea, but rather the onset of anoxic conditions that resulted from the exchange of salt water from the Mediterranean/Sea of Marmara on the one hand and fresh water from the Black Sea on the other.

The following reconstructions for the Sea of Marmara and the Black Sea are most plausible at present. During the Last Glacial Maximum, the level of the 'Marmara Lake' was about 90 metres below that of the present. Around 11,000 BC, water started to flow through the Dardanelles from the Aegean into the Sea of Marmara, which quickly rose to the same level. In the Black Sea, the level during the Late Glacial Maximum was about 110 metres below current sea levels. During the Younger Dryas, this had risen to 43 metres below current levels. At around 7500 BC water started to flow from the Black Sea into the Sea of Marmara, either through the Bosporus or via the Izmit/Sapanca area. At this point, water levels were much higher in the Black Sea, and water flowed westwards only. It was only at around 6000 BC that both seas reached a balance, and at this point salt water from the Marmara Sea started flowing into the Black Sea as an undercurrent. It was this undercurrent of salt water that created the anoxic conditions that put an end to freshwater mollusc communities in the lower Black Sea rather than a flood. At the latest, at about 4000 BC, the Bosporus had become the main connection between the Black Sea and the Sea of Marmara.[57]

1.4.1 Summary

The geography of Asia Minor is an essential element in the study of its Prehistory. It does not amount to geographical determinism to observe that Asia Minor has a very specific geographical configuration that facilitates certain types of activities better than others. For example, much of the coastline of Asia Minor consists of steep mountain ranges rising from the sea. This would have impaired the development of a maritime culture in these regions, as opposed to Aegean Turkey, for instance.

In this chapter, I have argued that Asia Minor can be characterised as a territory in which distinct cultural traditions developed both in Prehistory and in later periods, while acknowledging the fact that cultures are never neatly bounded, and that there were clear connections between Asia Minor and adjacent regions throughout much of Prehistory.

The physical structure of Asia Minor has clear implications in terms of transport and travel, climate, and vegetation. It can be divided into the Pontus, the Marmara Region, the Mediterranean, and Central Anatolia, and each of these regions has different affordances for people both in the

---

[57] Özdoğan 1997a; Aksu et al. 1999; Özdoğan 1999a, 2003; Jablonka 2003.

past and in the present. One of the advantages of the mountainous nature of Asia Minor is the availability of a large number of minerals and rocks, such as obsidian, copper, silver, and gold, many of which were exploited in Prehistory. Finally, the reconstruction of past ecologies of Asia Minor on the basis of local proxy data allows us to establish the ecological context in which prehistoric societies operated.

CHAPTER TWO

ARCHAEOLOGY IN ASIA MINOR

The disciplinary history of archaeology in Asia Minor has affected our understanding of its Prehistory in many respects. For this reason, considering the roots and development of the practice of archaeology in this territory is a central component of any synthesis of the prehistoric past. Here the general disciplinary history will be outlined, something that has often been lacking in synthetic studies on the archaeology of Asia Minor.[1]

2.1.1 The Archaeology of Biblical and Classical Civilizations

Archaeological research has a long history in Asia Minor. Initially, much of the archaeological work that was done was inspired by what were conceived of as the twin roots of Western civilization: the biblical and classical worlds. Much of the earliest work consequently focussed on Hellenistic sites in the Aegean and Hittite sites in Central Anatolia to elucidate these worlds.

Excavations started at a number of Ionian Hellenistic sites as early as the second half of the nineteenth century. The Ephesus excavations started in 1863, those at Miletus in 1873, and those at Pergamon in 1878. From 1906, excavations were also started at the Late Bronze Age site of Hattuša, the capital of the Hittite empire on the central plateau. All of these sites have been excavated more or less continuously since those early campaigns, and some of these projects can boast more than 100 excavation seasons.

---

[1] Mehmet Özdoğan has often discussed the effects of disciplinary history on the Prehistory of Asia Minor, however (1995, 1996, 2001). See also Matthews (2003) for discussion of the origins of archaeology in Mesopotamia.

2.1.2 The Archaeology of Homer

The study of the Prehistory of Asia Minor started in earnest with the large-scale excavations at Troy (Hısarlık) undertaken by Schliemann. Between 1870 and 1890 eight campaigns took place at the mound, in the course of which large parts of it were excavated. Schliemann has often been given a prominent place in histories of the archaeological discipline, but more recently it has been argued that he neither discovered the site of Hısarlık nor pioneered the technique of stratigraphic excavation.[2]

Whatever the flaws of Schliemann may have been, he did manage to give the study of Aegean Prehistory a major impetus that had lasting effects, and to broaden the focus of archaeology in this part of the world beyond the study of the classical and biblical worlds. In so doing, however, he introduced another grand narrative that archaeology served to illustrate. Following Schliemann's excavation projects at Troy and at various sites in Greece, the Aegean Bronze Age became a major research topic that was closely linked to the study of the *Iliad* and the *Odyssey* and the idea that Bronze Age Greece formed the cradle of European civilisation, a notion that was reinforced by the discovery of the Minoan palace at Knossos.[3] This Hellenistic focus of the study of the Aegean Bronze Age is perhaps one of the main reasons why the Troy excavations did not have any further effects on the development of prehistoric archaeology in Asia Minor as opposed to that of Greece.

2.1.3 Ottoman Archaeology

It has been claimed that prior to the 1930s, archaeology in Turkey was done exclusively by foreigners.[4] However, a number of Ottoman scholars were actively pursuing archaeology from the 1880s onwards and into the first decades of the twentieth century.[5] Osman Hamdi Bey, director of the Istanbul Archaeological Museum founded in 1868, excavated at Nemrut Dağ, Sidon, Lagina, and Tralles.[6] Together with his brother Halil Ethem Bey, Osman Hamdi Bey also excavated at Alabanda and Sidamara.[7] Finally, Makridi Bey excavated jointly with Winckler at Hattuša, at Alaca Höyük, at

---

[2] Patzek 1990; Easton 1992; Allen 1999.

[3] Davis 2003; Erciyas 2005; Kotsakis 2005: 8.

[4] Joukowsky 1996: 40.

[5] Von der Osten 1927; Arik 1950; Özdoğan 1998a.

[6] Nemrut Dağ is an Iron Age site situated in Southeast Anatolia; at Sidon, located in Lebanon, Hellenistic levels were investigated; Lagina and Tralles are both classical sites located in southwestern Turkey.

[7] Alabanda and Sidamara are both classical sites located in southwestern Turkey.

Sippar (Iraq), at Akalan, and at two Iron Age tumuli near Ankara.[8] Paradox-
ically, these Ottoman scholars adhered to the research agenda of Western
archaeologists by investigating sites that could be connected with classical
civilisation or the biblical world, while understandably avoiding the study
of the Aegean Bronze Age with its Hellenistic connotations.

Up to the First World War, Turkish archaeology was practiced by a few
well-educated persons who were connected to the Istanbul Archaeology
Museum in one capacity or another. These were the final decades of the
declining Ottoman Empire, during which large parts of its territory were
lost and war was a constant drain on its resources, and it is surprising that in
these circumstances archaeology was practiced at all. However, the interest
in the classical and biblical worlds as the birthplace of Western civilisation
that motivated most Western archaeologists and that had also been adopted
by the Turkish scholars was of no interest to the Ottoman Empire with
its Islamic identity; consequently, archaeology had little to offer Ottoman
society and remained a fringe phenomenon for the educated elite.[9]

2.1.4 Archaeology in the Early Turkish Republic

The founding of the Republic of Turkey in 1923 had profound effects on
the development of archaeology in the country. Following the collapse of
the Ottoman Empire, there was a concerted effort to create a new national
identity for the foundling state. This identity had to be separated from the
cumbersome heritage of the failed Ottoman Empire and Islam. In the very
early years of the Republic, the idea of pan-Turkism held some appeal, but
this was soon abandoned given that unification with Turks in central Asia
was beyond reach. Instead, a thesis known as the 'Turkish History Thesis'
was formulated,[10] consisting of a rather confusing amalgamation of tenets.
It posited that the Turks were a civilised race, whose civilisation in central
Asia came to an end due to climatic catastrophes, which resulted in a series of
migrations that spread civilisation to large parts of the old world, reaching
it highest achievements in Anatolia. Controversially, groups such as the
Sumerians, Hittites, and Greeks were all supposed to have originated in
central Asia and were all considered to have been Turks. It is in this context
that many companies adopted names or logos that referred back to the
past, such as Sümerbank and Etibank (the Sumerian and Hittite Bank) and

---

[8] Hattuša was the Late Bronze Age Hittite capital in Central Anatolia; at Alaca Höyük is an
Early and Late Bronze Age site near Hattuša; Sipar is a Bronze Age site in southern Iraq;
and Akalan is a Late Bronze Age site on the Turkish Black Sea coast.

[9] Özdoğan 1998a: 115; Zürcher 2004: 76–90; Erciyas 2005.

[10] Atakuman 2008: 219–220.

Maltepe cigarettes (displaying an Alaca Höyük standard on its cover), and in which many references to archaeology were used in public architecture, such as the Anıtkabir, the mausoleum of Atatürk, and large reproductions of Alaca Höyük standards (Fig. 2.1).

Most elements of the Turkish History Thesis were dropped after two large symposia in Ankara exposed the flawed reasoning upon which it was based, and it became clear that both inside and outside Turkey, sceptics were winning the argument. Instead, the emphasis shifted increasingly to Anatolia as a cradle of civilisation and to cultural continuity in Anatolia from the earliest Prehistory up to the modern era, although elements of the Turks = civilisation equation persisted for a long time afterwards. In these circumstances, the archaeological research agenda in Turkey became much more inclusive than had previously been the case and archaeology as a discipline gained new prominence. As part of this programme, the Turkish president Mustafa Kemal, better known as Atatürk, sponsored the development of professional archaeology, setting up archaeology departments at various universities, sending young archaeologists abroad for further education, and employing numerous German scholars who had fled persecution from the Nazis.[11]

Between 1923 and the Second World War, a large number of excavation projects were undertaken in Anatolia by both Turkish and foreign archaeologists. Arık estimates that approximately 100 excavations took place between 1922 and 1939, the majority of which were Turkish projects.[12] The most important Turkish excavation projects during this period included those at Alaca Höyük, Ahlatlibel, Dündartepe, Göllüdağ, Karaoğlan, and Gavur Kalesi.[13]

Also during the interwar years, a number of foreign expeditions were granted permits to work in Turkey, a generous decision given the many negative experiences with foreign archaeologists working in Turkey in previous decades and the fact that many of those working in the Turkish Republic came from countries that had occupied parts of Turkey only a few years before.[14] This openness to foreign archaeologists has since become a permanent feature of Turkish archaeology.

Foreign expeditions in Turkey prior to the Second World War of particular importance for prehistoric research include the excavations at Alışar, Mersin-Yumuktepe, Tarsus-Gözlükule, Kusura, and

---

[11] Özdoğan 2001: 33–36; Özdemir 2003; Pulhan 2003; Erciyas 2005; Atakuman 2008.
[12] Arik 1950: 6.
[13] Alaca Höyük is an Early and Late Bronze Age site in Central Anatolia; Ahlatlibel is an Early Bronze Age site near Ankara; Dündartepe is a Chalcolithic and Early Bronze Age site on the Black Sea coast; Göllüdağ is an Iron Age site near Niğde; and Karaoğlan and Gavur Kalesi are Iron Age sites near Ankara. For more details on these projects see Whittemore 1943; Arik 1950: 22–23.
[14] Esin 1993a; Davis 2003.

Kültepe-Kanesh,[15] the renewed excavations at Troy by Blegen, and the Amuq survey and excavations.[16]

2.1
Reproduction
of the Alaca
Höyük standard
at crossroads in
Ankara. Photo by
the author.

2.2.1 The Prehistory of Asia Minor in the 1950s

For one reason or another, all of the prehistoric sites excavated in central, northern, and western Asia Minor before the Second World War dated to the Late Chalcolithic period (4000–3000 BC) and afterwards. During the interwar years, sites dating to the Neolithic and Early Chalcolithic periods had been investigated in the region south of the Taurus Mountains, however, among other places at Mersin, Coba Höyük, Jericho, and Tell Halaf. Given this disparity in the evidence, many scholars concluded that Neolithic sites were absent from Asia Minor north of the Taurus. This was the position taken by Bittel in his *Grundzüge der Vor- und Frühgeschichte Kleinasiens*, in which he argued, first, that Asia Minor became truly settled only from about 3500/3000 BC and, second, that this land was settled so late

---

[15] Alişar dates to the Chalcolithic and Bronze Ages and is located in Central Anatolia; Mersin-Yumuktepe dates from the Neolithic to the Bronze Ages and is situated in Cilicia; Tarsus-Gözlükule is also located in Cilicia, and levels dating to the Chalcolithic and Bronze Ages were excavated; Kusura dates to the Early and Late Bronze Ages and is situated in Central Anatolia; Kültepe-Kanesh dates to the Early and Middle Bronze Ages and is also situated in Central Anatolia.

[16] Whittemore 1943; Arik 1950; Joukowsky 1996: 40.

due to its harsh climate.[17] This hypothesis subsequently became a central tenet of Anatolian archaeology. In 1956 Seton Lloyd, one of the foremost scholars of Anatolian archaeology at that time, famously claimed:

> 'The scene of the Neolithic Revolution seems to have been an area limited to the north by the range of the Taurus and the fringes of the Syrian plain' and 'Climatic conditions at which we can only guess, including perhaps the extreme cold of the Anatolian winter, must indeed be accepted as the most reasonable explanation of the geographic barrier, behind which Neolithic man seems arbitrarily to have confined himself.'[18]

The hypothesis that Asia Minor north of the Taurus became settled only after about 3500 BC was also put forward by Orthmann, one of Bittel's students, in a study of prehistoric assemblages of North-Central Anatolia.[19]

The idea that most of Asia Minor was occupied only from 3500 BC onwards was upheld even after substantial evidence to the contrary started to emerge.[20] For example, Bittel excavated the Neolithic site of Fikirtepe near Istanbul between 1952 and 1954 but assigned it to the Early Bronze Age, a position also adopted by Yakar as recently as 1975.[21] In fact, assemblages predating the Bronze Age deriving from both surveys and excavations had been known since the early nineteenth century,[22] but such was the strength of received wisdom that evidence for Chalcolithic and Neolithic assemblages was routinely dismissed.[23]

The first major critique of the hypothesis that Asia Minor became settled after 3500 BC was put forward by Tahsin Özgüç, who argued for the existence of a Chalcolithic phase in Central Anatolia.[24] It is typical of the debate that Lloyd, while acknowledging the pre–Bronze Age character of some of the assemblages concerned, suggested that they were the remains of originally Chalcolithic settlers who colonised Anatolia from the east, but whose material culture did not develop in the meantime and should consequently be dated after 3500 BC.[25]

2.2.2 The Discovery of the Neolithic of Asia Minor

As a result of new fieldwork from the 1950s onwards, the Prehistory of Anatolia prior to 3500 BC became better known. In his surveys of the Konya

[17] Bittel 1945: 15, fig. 52.
[18] Lloyd 1956: 53–54; Özdoğan 1996: 187–188.
[19] Orthmann 1963.
[20] Schoop 2005a: 69–74.
[21] Bittel 1960; 1969; Yakar 1975.
[22] Ormerod 1913; Todd 1976: 2.
[23] Özdoğan 1995: 49–50; Schoop 2005a: 72.
[24] Özgüç 1945: 357.
[25] Özdoğan 1995: 50.

plain in 1951–1952, James Mellaart found pre–Bronze Age assemblages that were not acknowledged as such by the archaeological community. It was only with the systematic excavations of Mellaart at the sites of Hacılar, between 1957 and 1960, and Çatalhöyük, between 1961 and 1965, and those of French at Canhasan 1 and 3, undertaken between 1961 and 1967, and the regular deployment of the novel technique of radiocarbon dating that the picture of Anatolian Prehistory changed dramatically and decisively.[26] As a consequence, some 5000 years were added to the settled history of Central Anatolia, which has since been recognised as one of the central nodes of the Near Eastern Neolithic.

Although these excavations at the Neolithic sites of Hacılar, Çatalhöyük, and Canhasan were of great scientific importance, they did not leave much of an imprint on the practice of archaeology in Asia Minor. By contrast, the joint excavations of the Chicago and Istanbul universities at the Aceramic Neolithic site of Çayönü in Southeast Anatolia, led by Braidwood and Çambel from 1963 onwards, have been of enormous importance in training a new generation of Turkish prehistoric archaeologists from Istanbul University.[27] Scholars from this university subsequently excavated a large number of prehistoric sites across Turkey.

2.2.3 The Prehistory of Asia Minor: The Status of Research

Despite the efforts of a small number of Turkish and foreign scholars, the Prehistory of Anatolia is poorly investigated relative to that of adjacent regions. For example, in 1995 Özdoğan published a paper on the state of research for the Anatolian Neolithic, in which he demonstrated that whereas in both the 'Near East', defined as the Levant, Syria, and Iraq, and in the Balkans, more than 350 Neolithic sites had been excavated, in Turkey, which is similar in size to these regions, the total was only 38.[28] While a number of additional sites have been excavated since 1995, raising the total to about 50 excavated Neolithic sites, the general picture remains that of a country very poorly investigated.

One explanation for this situation is that Asia Minor has often been seen as a land-bridge – a geographical area that passively transmitted people and ideas from Mesopotamia and the Fertile Crescent, where all new phenomena were supposed to originate, towards Europe – rather than as a large territory in which a variety of not necessarily uniform developments took

---

[26] These sites all date to the Neolithic and are situated in southern Central Anatolia. For more details see Mellaart 1967, 1970; French 1998.

[27] Young et al. 1983; Çambel 1995; Arsebük et al. 1998; *Türkiye Bilimler Akademisi – Arkeoloji Degisi* 7 (2004).

[28] Özdoğan 1995.

place that cannot be reduced to external stimuli.[29] The tendency to treat Asia Minor as an unimportant periphery of the Levant and Mesopotamia continues in much current work in the Near East.[30] One consequence of this bias towards the Fertile Crescent has been that most foreign expeditions have focussed their research there, and that Asia Minor has received relatively little interest, although this situation is now starting to change.

Further, much of the archaeological effort in Turkey has been devoted to rescue archaeology related to the construction of a series of large dams in Southeast Anatolia.

Due to these circumstances, the Prehistory of Asia Minor has been comparatively neglected. For example, in Aegean Turkey, investigations of the Neolithic and Early Chalcolithic started only in the mid-1990s at the site of Ulucak.[31] The Early Bronze Age in this area is much better investigated with the renewed investigations at Troy and a large-scale project at Panaz Tepe/Liman Tepe/Bakla Tepe.

While a number of other regions in Asia Minor are better investigated than Aegean Asia Minor – and here the Lake District, the Marmara Region, and southern Central Anatolia can be mentioned – the investigations have in many cases been executed by relatively few scholars and at a small number of sites. For example, in the Lake District, Refik Duru from Istanbul University has excavated a total of three prehistoric sites – Bademağacı, Höyücek, and Kuruçay – which augment the data from the older Hacılar sequence. Likewise, the Prehistory of the Marmara Region has been mainly investigated by Mehmet Özdoğan from Istanbul University and Jacob Roodenberg from Leiden University.

It is only in southern Central Anatolia that we find a greater diversity of archaeological activities, with teams from various Turkish universities and from a variety of foreign universities investigating a number of sites dating from the Aceramic Neolithic (8500–7000 BC) to the Middle Chalcolithic (5500–4000 BC). An international excavation of particular prominence in this region is the renewed Çatalhöyük project, which started in 1993.

In contrast to the archaeologists from Istanbul University, those working at the University of Ankara and at Hacettepe (also based in the capital, set up in 1982) have focussed most of their work on the Bronze and Iron ages, with some research into the Palaeolithic as well. Their work has contributed significantly to our knowledge of the Early Bronze Age in particular.

---

[29] Özdoğan 1996: 186; 1997b: 2–5.
[30] Bar-Yosef 2001; Simmons 2007.
[31] Çilingiroğlu et al. 2004. In addition, short reports are now available for Ege Gübre (Sağlamtimur 2007), Yeşilova (Derin 2007), and Dedecik-Heybelitepe (Lichter and Meriç 2007).

From the 1960s onwards, the interests of foreign and Turkish archaeologists increasingly started to converge. With the increasing modernisation and consolidation of Turkey, the need for archaeology for nationalistic purposes became less pressing, and archaeologists became more interested in building up knowledge of culture-historical sequences. Western archaeological interests in Asia Minor had by then broadened beyond the investigation of biblical and classical horizons and came to include the developments that occurred in Prehistory.

Both foreign and Turkish archaeologists focussed their research on what has been defined by Gordon Childe as the major transitions in Prehistory: first, the emergence of farming and sedentary life in the Neolithic; second, the development of urban communities, long-distance trade, and elite culture, which started in the Early Bronze Age in Asia Minor; and, third, the formation of states, which dates to the second millennium BC.[32]

This research agenda that foregrounds major transitions in Prehistory has led to a very uneven investigation of the archaeology of Asia Minor. Whereas a lot of research has focussed on the Neolithic and the Early Bronze Age, the Chalcolithic has been largely neglected. As a consequence, the period between 5500 and 4000 BC (the Middle Chalcolithic) is poorly investigated at present. Further, an interest in the westward expansion of the Neolithic across Anatolia and into Europe has meant that some regions, such as North-Central Anatolia, have been largely overlooked in archaeological research. Finally, for a variety of reasons, the Upper Palaeolithic, Epipalaeolithic, and Mesolithic periods have been little investigated in Asia Minor as a whole, with the exception of a number of sites in the Antalya and Amuq regions.[33]

Without a doubt, the archaeological data that are available for Asia Minor are biased in several ways: Specific regions and periods have been much better investigated than others. In some cases, these biases originate from political interests in archaeology; in others, they derive from the dominant frameworks within the archaeological discipline itself and the bodies that supply funding for field and research projects. In this synthesis of the Prehistory of Asia Minor, the aim is to overcome the differences in research intensity where possible. Further, this study aims to go beyond culture-history in the narrow sense – to what period specific types of artefacts can be dated and how large their geographical distribution is – and to address, amongst other matters, issues of subsistence, social organisation, and ritual practices. For these types of topics good-quality data are required, however,

---

[32] Childe 1928, 1936.
[33] Kuhn 2002.

and it is clear that the detailed reconstruction of ancient societies can only take place if and when such data are available.

2.3.1 Conclusion

I have argued in this chapter that the archaeology of Asia Minor initially sprang from the desire to investigate the biblical and classical worlds, which were seen as the twin roots of Western civilisation in Europe and America. Later, in the nineteenth century, researchers such as Schliemann and Evans added the study of the Aegean Bronze Age as another root of Hellenic, and by extension European, civilisation. In the Ottoman Empire a number of gentleman scholars were also practising archaeology, but given that Ottoman society was not interested in archaeology, their activities had little impact. This situation changed dramatically with the foundation of the Turkish Republic in 1923, in which archaeology became part of a nation-building project. It was in this context that the Prehistory of Asia Minor became a topic of interest for Turkish scholars, while archaeologists from other countries also started to explore prehistoric Asia Minor in order to elucidate a more complete culture-history of the region. Between the First and Second Wars, Neolithic sites had not been investigated in Asia Minor, and the absence of this period was held to be a genuine feature of the Prehistory of this region. After the Second World War, investigation of the Prehistory of Asia Minor started in earnest during the 1960s. In Western countries, the old interests in the investigation of biblical sites and classical civilisation were now augmented by the study of the Prehistory of the Near East, in particular the Neolithic revolution. In Turkey, the modernisation and consolidation of the state meant that archaeology could largely free itself from the nation-building purposes it had previously served. The initial spectacular discoveries at Hacılar, Çatalhöyük, and Canhasan were followed by a series of excavation and survey projects, although the Prehistory of Asia Minor on the whole remains poorly investigated. Today the study of the Prehistory of Asia Minor has reached a new threshold, in which we can trace the outlines of the major developments in Prehistory, even if many elements of this picture remain hazy and require further investigation. It is such a sketch of the Prehistory of Asia Minor that I aim to provide in the following chapters.

CHAPTER THREE

HUNTER-GATHERERS OF THE EPIPALAEOLITHIC AND MESOLITHIC (20,000–6000 BC)

This synthesis of the Prehistory of Asia Minor starts at about 20,000 BC, which equates roughly with the end of the Late Glacial Maximum. This starting point is less arbitrary than it may appear at first sight.

First, relatively little is known about the Palaeolithic of Turkey prior to the Late Glacial Maximum, and the data that we do have are best understood in the much larger context of contemporary sites in Europe and Asia, rather than by focussing on Asia Minor. The main sequences have been excavated in a number of cave sites located among the Mediterranean littoral in the Antalya and Hatay regions.[1]

Second, at present there is a hiatus for the later part of the Upper Palaeolithic in Asia Minor, between about 26,000 and 20,000 BC. For the Early Upper Palaeolithic (40,000–26,000 BC) there is good evidence in both the Marmara Region and the Hatay, but the Late Upper Palaeolithic, specifically Gravettian industries, are absent.[2] Özdoğan argues that this Late Upper Palaeolithic hiatus on the Anatolian Plateau may be genuine, given the better-documented Lower and Middle Palaeolithic presence, and that a similar pattern is evident in Greece, which has been more thoroughly investigated.[3] The Late Upper Palaeolithic hiatus has been linked with adverse climatic conditions that also affected human occupation patterns in Europe during this period.[4] Such ecological explanations should be treated with some caution, given that sites dating to the Late Upper Palaeolithic may be discovered in future research or that sites dating to this period have not been recognised.

Third, after the Late Upper Palaeolithic hiatus, there is abundant data for the period between the Late Glacial Maximum and the start of the Holocene, that is, between about 20,000 and 10,000 BC, designated the

[1] Kuhn 2002.
[2] Runnels and Özdoğan 2001; Kuhn 2002; Otte 2008: 907.
[3] Özdoğan 1999b: 226.
[4] Özdoğan 1997a: 32; Bocquet-Appel and Demars 2000; Kuhn 2002: 204; Mellars 2004.

'Epipalaeolithic' in Near Eastern archaeology. The Epipalaeolithic is best documented at a number of sites along the Mediterranean littoral, but it can also be traced on the Anatolian Plateau. Typical of the Epipalaeolithic are microlithic industries that persisted in some parts of Asia Minor during the subsequent Early Holocene. Further, the Epipalaeolithic seems to be characterised, more than earlier periods, by the increasing regionalisation of cultural traditions, which means that discussing the sequences of Asia Minor separately is appropriate for the Epipalaeolithic.

3.1.1 The Epipalaeolithic–Mesolithic Continuum

The traditional distinction between Epipalaeolithic and Mesolithic is based on chronology rather than on the types of societies we are dealing with. 'Mesolithic' is a concept from European archaeology used to describe the hunter-gatherer societies of the Holocene in that region. Some of these European Mesolithic hunter-gatherer-fisher communities were sedentary, while others were more mobile and lived in smaller groups.[5] Sedentary hunter-gatherer-fisher settlements were also found in the Near East, but many of these can be dated to the final millennia of the Pleistocene.[6] These sites were therefore classified as Epipalaeolithic rather than Mesolithic.

Near Eastern archaeologists have focussed primarily on major transitions in the region, including the adoption of agriculture and the emergence of cities.[7] One of the consequences of this orientation has been that, with the exception of the southern Levant, hunter-gatherer communities of the Early Holocene, which must have co-existed for millennia with early farming communities, have been poorly investigated.[8]

In most respects, the distinction between Epipalaeolithic and Mesolithic groups is arbitrary: In both cases, we are dealing with people who obtained their food primarily by collecting wild plants, fishing, and hunting and who produced microlithic chipped stone industries. Some of these groups could have been more or less sedentary for some part of the year, making use of particularly favourable spots in the landscape, but mobility remained an important strategy. Further, the chipped stone assemblages of the Epipalaeolithic and Mesolithic cannot be clearly separated.[9]

---

[5] For example, the Ertebølle culture (Price 1996).
[6] For example, the Natufian culture of the southern Levant (Bar-Yosef and Valla eds., 1991).
[7] Matthews 2003: 28–29.
[8] Sherratt 2004.
[9] A caveat that should be kept in mind is that microliths also occur in later periods, for instance in Chalcolithic sites, and in some cases there does not seem to be continuity with the Epipalaeolithic/Mesolithic (Gatsov 2001: 106–107; Perlès 2001: 31).

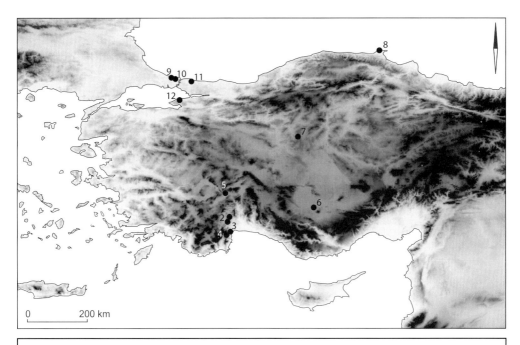

Antalya group: 1 Öküzini; 2 Karain; 3 Beldibi; 4 Belbaşı;
Other: 5 Baradiz; 6 Pınarbaşı; 7 Macun Çay; 8 Tekeköy;
Ağaçlı group: 9 Ağaçlı; 10 Gümüşdere; 11 Domalı; 12 Ibonun Rampası.

The only clear distinction between Epipalaeolithic and Mesolithic groups is that some of the latter could have been in contact with Neolithic groups, and this might have affected their economy and way of life. The degree to which this was actually the case is a matter for investigation, however.[10]

3.1 Epipalaeolithic and Mesolithic sites of Asia Minor, 20,000–6000 BC. Produced by the author and Joanne Porck.

3.2.1 The Epipalaeolithic and Mesolithic of the Antalya Region

Epipalaeolithic and Mesolithic assemblages have been excavated at a number of sites in Asia Minor, and the data from these investigations can be augmented with evidence from surveys (Fig. 3.1).

One region with particularly good evidence for the Epipalaeolithic and Mesolithic is the Mediterranean littoral in the Antalya Region, where a number of cave sites have been investigated. These include the excavated

[10] Zvelebil 1996.

sites of Beldibi, Belbaşı, Karain, and Öküzini.[11] These caves are located in limestone ridges in the vicinity of permanent springs and are not far from the Antalya Plain.[12]

In a comparative evaluation of the sequences from the Antalya sites, it has been concluded that they represent a development that is distinct from the better-studied assemblages from the Levant, but that the sites of the Antalya Region have some affinities with sites in the Zagros.[13]

At a general level, the cave sequences from the Antalya Region can be divided into three periods: Early Epipalaeolithic, Late Epipalae-olithic/Mesolithic, and Ceramic Mesolithic. The key sites for understanding this sequence are Karain and Öküzini, both of which have been excavated and findings published recently.

The Early Epipalaeolithic phase is to be dated between about 17,000 and 13,000 BC.[14] Levels dating to this phase are Karain levels 26 to 15; Öküzini level 17/units XII to VII; and probably Belbaşı III. In these strata shell beads and bone objects, such as points and needles, are commonly found. The chipped stone industries belonging to this phase include a significant component of 'microliths': retouched blade sections or microblades no larger than a few centimetres. The most conspicuous type among the microliths consists of the 'backed blades': microliths of which one of the long edges has been blunted with steep retouches (Fig. 3.2). Other chipped stone tools found include endscrapers, splintered pieces, and some borers. Cores are simple, with a single unprepared striking platform. Towards the end of this phase the striking platforms of the cores are prepared more carefully, resulting in more regular blades and microblades. The backed blades become more standardised, and it has been argued that these were in use as arrowheads for the hunting of wild sheep.[15]

The most common faunal remains retrieved from (the completely sieved) deposits of Öküzini are those of herbivores such as sheep, goats, and fallow deer. Less ubiquitous are the remains of roe deer, red deer, and aurochs. Atici and Stutz have argued, on the basis of the ages of the teeth of the juvenile sheep and goats in the assemblage, that people were present at Öküzini for only a few weeks during spring or summer.[16] The macrobotanical remains likewise suggest occupation of the cave in the (late) summer.[17]

---

[11] Bostanci 1962, 1967; Albrecht 1988; Albrecht et al. 1992; Yalçınkaya et al. 1993; Otte et al. 1995. Additional Epipalaeolithic assemblages are reported for the cave sites of Çarkini and Kızılin (Kartal 2003: 49), but no data are available for these sites.

[12] Yalçınkaya et al. 1993: 101.

[13] Bar-Yosef 1998: 504.

[14] For absolute radiocarbon dates see Albrecht et al. 1992: 130–131; Erdoğu et al. 2003b.

[15] Albrecht 1988: 214.

[16] Atici and Stutz 2002: 105.

[17] Martinoli 2004.

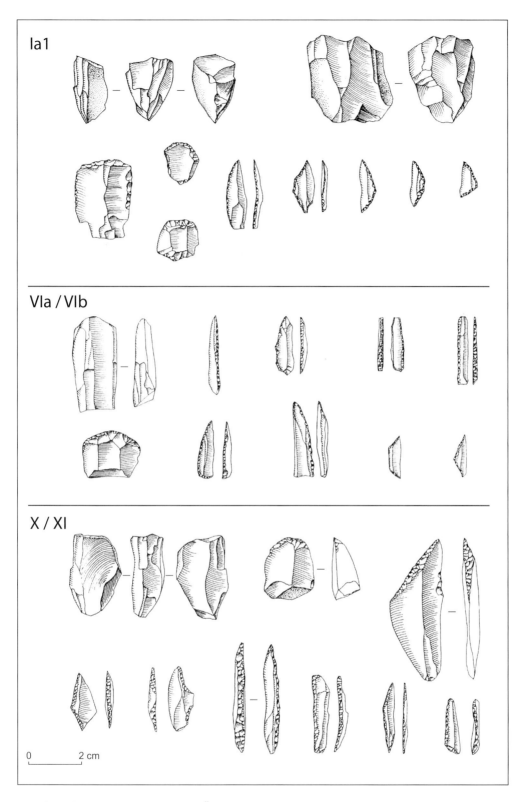

3.2 Chipped stone industries from the Öküzini Cave. Reproduced with permission of M. Otte from Otte, M., Yalcinkaya, I., Leotard, J.-M., Kartal, M., Bar-Yosef, O., Kozlowski, J., Bayon, I. L., and Marshack, A. 1995. 'The Epi-Palaeolithic of Öküzini cave (SW Anatolia) and its mobiliary art'. *Antiquity* 69: 931–944, fig. 8.

During this part of the year various wild plant and tree foods were collected, including hackberry (*Celtis*), grapes/raisins, pears, almonds, pistachios, and possibly olives.[18] Completely absent from the Öküzini deposits are seeds of annual plants such as cereals, and in this respect the Epipalaeolithic of the Antalya Region differs markedly from that of the Fertile Crescent.[19] Analysis of the charcoal at the site has shown that people at Öküzini had access to prime firewood throughout the Epipalaeolithic, again reinforcing the interpretation that occupation was seasonal and did not result in depletion of the local environment.[20]

The Late Epipalaeolithic/Mesolithic horizon of the Antalya Region can be dated between about 13,000 and 7000 BC.[21] To this phase we can assign Öküzini levels 15 to 2/units VI to IA, Beldibi II–IV, and possibly Belbaşı II. In this phase, geometric microliths, such as triangular pieces and lunates, become common (Fig. 3.2). Other tools include endscrapers, retouched blades, and perforators. Backed blades are less frequently found in this phase. Grinding stones also appear in this phase, and it is posited that, together with so-called scapula-knives, these were used for harvesting and processing tubers.[22] Further artefacts associated with these assemblages are bone awls, needles, spatulas, hammer stones, and shell beads.

The faunal assemblage points to a more sedentary, though not necessarily permanent, occupation during the Final Epipalaeolithic and the Early Holocene. The hunting of fallow deer, which had to be done at greater distances from the site, became more common, and the teeth from sheep and goats point to a more protracted hunting period, with possible signs of overexploitation of these species.[23]

Finally, a Late Mesolithic phase with ceramics has been documented in the Antalya cave sites, which can be dated between about 7000 and 6000 BC. Assemblages dating to this phase were found in units O–IB at Öküzini, level I at Beldibi, and level I at Belbaşı. In these stratigraphic units, sherds and polished axes were found together with microliths.

Unfortunately, very little has been published on these assemblages. In older excavations they have often been regarded as unreliable contexts in which artefacts from different periods were mixed rather than as a meaningful whole, and only a very small deposit of this phase was excavated

---

[18] Martinoli 2002.

[19] Martinoli 2004.

[20] Martinoli 2005: 71, 83.

[21] No distinction seems to exist that separates the Epipalaeolithic assemblages from those of the Mesolithic. Distinctions in ecology and subsistence within this phase have been proposed (Albrecht 1988: 222), but the deposits excavated are so limited in volume that these reconstructions should be treated with caution.

[22] Albrecht et al. 1992: 133.

[23] Atici and Stutz 2002: 105.

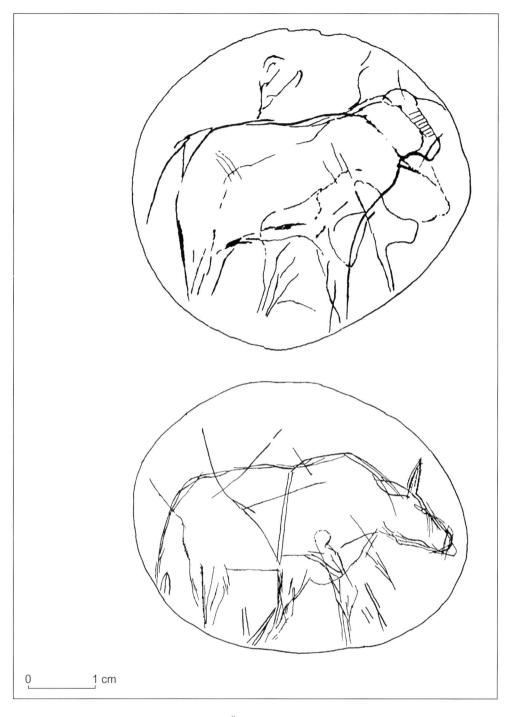

0   1 cm

3.3 Two renderings of a decorated pebble from Öküzini. Reproduced with permission of M. Otte from Otte, M., Yalcinkaya, I., Leotard, J.-M., Kartal, M., Bar-Yosef, O., Kozlowski, J., Bayon, I. L., and Marshack, A. 1995. 'The Epi-Palaeolithic of Öküzini cave (SW Anatolia) and its mobiliary art'. *Antiquity* 69: 931–944, fig. 9.

more recently at Öküzini.[24] Potentially, if excavated and analysed with care, these assemblages could provide evidence of contacts between farming communities and Mesolithic groups and of the exchange of cultural elements between the two.[25]

The study of such contacts is essential if we want to understand how and why Neolithic practices were taken up in a specific region. For example, the botanical remains from this phase differ from those of earlier periods. Apart from the wild plant and tree foods that were found in earlier phases at Öküzini, plant remains also include those of figs, lentils, bitter vetch, peas, and a type of wheat.[26] Given that many of these crops were not native to the Antalya Region, it seems plausible that they were either cultivated or brought from elsewhere. Hopefully, future investigations will shed new light on these levels.

3.2.2 The Art from the Antalya Sites

Various types of artefacts and features have been found in the Epipalae-olithic sites of the Antalya Region that have been classified as 'art' in the broad sense of 'visual communication'.[27]

An interesting artefact category that has been found in both the Early Epipalaeolithic and Late Epipalaeolithic/Mesolithic assemblages consists of decorated pebbles and a decorated bone object.[28] At both Karain and Öküzini incised pebbles were found, some of which have geometric decoration, whereas others carry figurative depictions of humans or animals. The most interesting of these objects from Öküzini shows a large animal, possibly a bovid. It has been argued that the animal is being attacked by a human with a spear,[29] but the image could be read in other ways (Fig. 3.3). Further, at Karain, a bone hook was found with a schematic human face modelled on it and a pebble with a geometric decoration executed in red paint.

The incised and painted pebbles found at Karain and Öküzini can be linked with rock art on the walls of some of the Antalya caves. While rock

---

[24] For example, in a recent overview this layer is dismissed as a mixture resulting from Neolithic burials, and it is argued that there is a clear gap between the two periods (Kartal 2003: 50–51). This interpretation is somewhat surprising given the clear association of ceramics with microliths in numerous sites discussed in this chapter.

[25] Perlès 2001: 50–51; Zvelebil 2001.

[26] Martinoli 2002.

[27] Corbey et al. 2004: 358. The problem with such a broad definition is, of course, that it includes such things as road signs under the rubric of art. On the other hand, this lack of specificity may actually be an advantage when discussing Prehistory given that we know so little about the nature of that imagery.

[28] Bostanci 1967; Anati 1968; Mellaart 1975: 92–93; Albrecht et al. 1992: 133, 135; Otte et al. 1995: 942–943.

[29] Otte et al. 1995: 942–943; see also Anati 1968: 26–29.

art is notoriously difficult to date,[30] the juxtaposition of 'art mobilier' found in dated layers with rock art executed with similar technologies and showing similar motives allows for a more satisfactory way of dating than is usually possible in this case.

At Beldibi, rock art includes stylised animal figures and geometric shapes such as crosses executed with red paint on the rock.[31] Further, an incised schematic depiction of a bovid has been reported.[32] Likewise, at Öküzini, there are incised images on the rock surface of a bovid and a human.[33] Further incised and painted rock art of similar appearance has been reported at five more sites in the region, including geometric motifs, depictions of animals, and a rendering of a human.[34] None of these images has been adequately published.

A point that is remarkable in this imagery is that bovids are prominently depicted in the art, while bovid bones are almost completely absent from the faunal remains. By contrast, sheep, goats, and deer, which make up most of the faunal assemblages at Karain and Öküzini, are apparently completely absent from the imagery. This emphasis on symbolically important animals such as bovids and leopards, rather than those that were important to the subsistence economy such as sheep, goats, and deer, has also been documented in the context of Neolithic Çatalhöyük.[35] Although the art from the Antalya sites precedes the art of Çatalhöyük chronologically, it is not possible at present to argue that one developed out of the other. Perhaps such links could be made if the art from the Antalya sites were more systematically investigated, however.

There is another reason why the bovid depictions of the Antalya sites are of importance. In an influential book, Cauvin has argued that the worship of bovids, and in particular bulls, was associated with the Neolithic revolution in the Near East, manifestations of which occurred in the Levant first and then spread along with agriculture to adjacent regions.[36] The prominent depictions of bovids in the Antalya sites are problematic in this model and suggest that bovids were also symbolically important in pre-Neolithic societies of Asia Minor.

---

[30] For example, Peschlow-Bindokat (1996a, 1996b) has dated a series of rock paintings in the Latmos Range of the Aegean to the Neolithic on the basis of a few stylistic elements, but this dating should be considered problematic.

[31] Bostanci 1967: 57, fig. 1; Anati 1968: 27; Balkan-Atlı 1994b: 196.

[32] Otte et al. 1995: 943.

[33] Anati 1968: 22; no illustrations have been published of this image.

[34] Anati 1972: 24; Taşkıran 1996: 103–104.

[35] Russell and Meece 2006.

[36] Cauvin 1997: 50–54, 170–172.

3.3.1 The Epipalaeolithic/Mesolithic of the Marmara Region

Apart from the evidence from the Antalya Region, the Epipalaeolithic and Mesolithic of Asia Minor are relatively poorly known. Sites with a component of microlithic artefacts have been documented in the Marmara Region, in the Black Sea Region, and in Central Anatolia.[37] Of these, the sites in the Marmara Region have been the most systematically investigated.

At present, there is a complete absence of Late Upper Palaeolithic sites in the Marmara Region.[38] By contrast, a significant number of Epipalaeolithic/Mesolithic sites have been found in the region. In particular, a group of sites known as the 'Ağaçlı' group date to this period.[39] All of the Ağaçlı sites are located near the seashore, some on fossil dunes facing the Black Sea in the vicinity of Istanbul, others on various terraces overlooking the Sea of Marmara, and still others on terraces adjacent to various lakes in the Marmara Region. From these settings, it can be concluded that marine resources were important to the communities concerned. In the absence of excavated sites, it is not possible to determine whether these sites were more or less permanently occupied or whether they were only seasonally used.[40] If the latter is true, we have yet to find inland sites that also date to the Epipalaeolithic/Mesolithic and can be connected to this horizon.

The assemblages that have been published for the Ağaçlı sites are quite distinct from those in the Antalya Region.[41] For example, the conical cores of the Ağaçlı group are much more carefully prepared, and the bladelets struck from them are much more standardised than those found in the Antalya sites (Fig. 3.4). While this difference in chipped stone industries could relate in part to the availability of better-quality material for knapping in the Marmara Region, the tool kit also differs from that of the Antalya sites. Circular and semi-circular endscrapers are very common in the Ağaçlı sites, whereas geometric microliths are virtually absent. Backed bladelets, with both straight and arched backs, are fairly ubiquitous. According to Gatsov and Özdoğan, the Ağaçlı sites have assemblages that are similar to Epipalaeolithic sites found in Bulgaria, Romania, and Ukraine.[42]

An element of great interest with regard to the Ağaçlı assemblages is their relation to the later Fikirtepe assemblages that are generally associated with

---

[37] Esin and Benedict 1963; Gatsov and Özdoğan 1994; Özdoğan 1997a: 32; Kuhn 2002: 206; Kartal 2003; Baird 2006a.

[38] Runnels and Özdoğan 2001: 71.

[39] Gatsov and Özdoğan 1994.

[40] Nor can the Ağaçlı sites be dated with any degree of accuracy.

[41] Özdoğan 1999a: 210.

[42] Gatsov and Özdoğan 1994: 109–110. Confusingly, however, in a more recent paper, Gatsov (2001) argues that the Ağaçlı assemblages are technologically distinct from those of Epipalaeolithic Bulgaria.

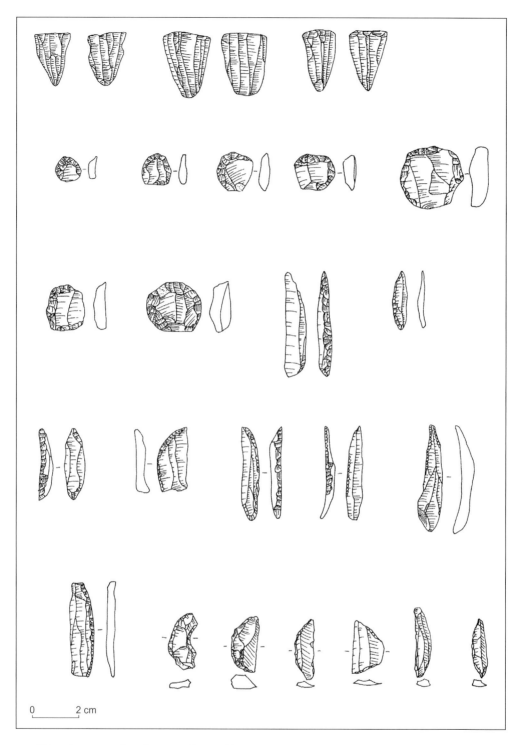

0   2 cm

3.4 Chipped stone artefacts from Ağaçlı assemblages. Reproduced with permission of M. Özdoğan from Özdoğan , M. 2007. 'Marmara Bölgesi Neolitik çag kültürleri'. In *Anadolu'da Uyğarligin doğuşu Avrupaya yayılımı. Türkiye'de Neolitik dönem, Yeni kazılar, yeni bulgular*, edited by M. Özdoğan and N. Başgelen, pp. 401–426, fig. 2. Istanbul, Turkey: Arkeoloji ve Sanat Yayınları.

the neolithisation of the Marmara Region. Like the Ağaçlı sites, Fikirtepe sites are almost exclusively located near the shores of a sea or lake, suggesting a similar focus on marine resources. Further, Fikirtepe sites have a microlithic component in their assemblages that is less prominent in early farming sites in the Marmara Region, and their chipped stone industries are almost identical to those of the Ağaçlı sites.[43] The discussion of the Fikirtepe sites will be taken up later in this book (Chapter 5), as they exist alongside the earliest sedentary farming settlements of the region.

For now I would like to point out, however, that the close cultural relations between the Ağaçlı and Fikirtepe sites point to the existence of well-established Epipalaeolithic/Mesolithic groups in the Marmara Region, something that could have easily eluded us on the basis of the rather ephemeral Ağaçlı assemblages alone, especially given that their documentation and investigation is mainly the work of a single scholar: Mehmet Özdoğan.[44]

3.4.1 The Epipalaeolithic/Mesolithic of Central Anatolia

In Central Anatolia only a handful of sites have been dated to the Epipalaeolithic/Mesolithic. Furthermore, the dating of a number of these sites is problematic. In particular, the dating of the sites of Macunçay (near Ankara), Tekeköy (on the Black Sea), and Baradiz (in the Lake District), all of which were assigned to the Epipalaeolithic/Mesolithic and were reported to have held microliths,[45] has recently been questioned. With the exception of a single microlith from Baradiz, none of the drawn objects that have been published can be designated as such, and the collections from these sites have not been preserved.[46] Consequently, these three sites are best disregarded in any discussion of Epipalaeolithic/Mesolithic sites in Asia Minor.

Fortunately, new evidence for sites dating to these periods has been obtained from the Konya Plain. In the Konya Plain Survey, a substantial number of sites with a microlithic component were found. At least three, and more likely five or six, sites predating 8000 BC were found.[47]

One of these sites is Pınarbaşı, which has been excavated in recent years.[48] Layers dating to the ninth millennium BC were excavated in a

[43] Özdoğan 1983; 1999: 215; Gatsov 2001. It is unfortunate that levels 7 and 6 at Yarımburgaz, which could potentially have bridged the Ağaçlı and Fikirtepe assemblages, are poorly known due to the nature of the rescue excavations that took place at the site (Kartal 2003: 48).

[44] Gatsov and Özdoğan 1994; Runnels and Özdoğan 2001.

[45] Kansu 1944, 1945, 1947; Kansu and Ozansoy 1948; Kökten 1952; Esin and Benedict 1963.

[46] Kartal 2003: 46–47.

[47] Baird 2002; 2006a: 64.

[48] The site was excavated first in 1994 and 1995 and then again in 2003 and 2004.

small exposure in Area A. The site was located near a shallow lake. There is some evidence of fishing and fowling, but primarily it is the hunting of large animals, such as aurochs and equids, which presumably would have drunk at the lake, that is in evidence, augmented by the consumption of nuts.[49]

Seven burials were found, including men, women, and children. Some were complete and primary, others not. Several large curvilinear structures were found that were sunk into the ground and plastered repeatedly, in one case up to seven times, and in some cases these plasters were painted with ochre. Judging from the building debris, consisting of mud with impressions of reeds and twigs, these buildings probably had wattle-and-daub superstructures. There was also evidence of activity areas in these structures in the form of a grinding stone, a hearth, a basin, and a platform. These buildings have many similarities to those of later Neolithic sites in the region, which will be discussed later in this book, such as Aşıklı Höyük, Boncuklu, and Çatalhöyük, in terms of subdividing rooms into smaller special-purpose spaces, frequent replastering of surfaces and in some cases painting of these surfaces.

The chipped stone, 80 per cent of which consists of obsidian, included many microliths, in particular scalene triangles. Although irregular bidirectional cores are typical, the assemblage also included two naviform cores, normally not found in the region (§4.3.2). There is evidence for the conversion of large blades into microliths, which are the dominant tool type.[50] Other common artefact types include grinding stones and arrow shaft straighteners, often decorated with geometric patterns.

Earlier microlithic assemblages at Pınarbaşı were found in Area B, beneath layers dating to the Ceramic Neolithic. Associated with these layers are three, possibly four, burials. Burial 14, an adult man, had 114 shell beads associated with him. Another young man, burial 13, had his skull removed some time after initial burial. Also found were a possible hearth and stone shaft straighteners. Microliths constitute the predominant element amongst the chipped stone tools. These are made primarily from obsidian and include a large number of lunates. The microliths seem to have arrived on site ready made, as there is no evidence of production. The faunal remains suggest that fishing and fowling in the nearby wetlands were of great importance in this period, along with hunting.[51]

The latest radiocarbon dates from these layers point to a date prior to the Holocene, at about 12,000 BC (Baird personal communication 2006).[52] If

[49] Baird 2007.
[50] Watkins 1996: 55; Baird 2007.
[51] Watkins 1996: 55; Baird 2004: 2; 2007.
[52] Yildirim and Gates 2007: 279.

this date is reliable, it clearly demonstrates that an Epipalaeolithic horizon existed on the Anatolian Plateau that remains virtually uninvestigated at present.

According to Baird, there are few links between the Epipalaeolithic of Pınarbaşı and that of the Antalya sites. The chipped stone industries are held to differ between the two regions, and obsidian, which constitutes 90 per cent of the assemblage at Pınarbaşı, is almost absent at Öküzini. Instead, it is suggested that cultural links and exchange relations existed with Natufian groups in the Levant.[53] Such contacts need not surprise us. For the European Palaeolithic it has been postulated, on the basis of raw material distributions, that people were seasonally moving hundreds of kilometres from the Middle Palaeolithic onwards,[54] while sea-crossings to Cyprus and Melos during the Epipalaeolithic[55] provide evidence of mobility that is probably also representative of contemporary groups in Asia Minor.

The results of the Konya Plain Survey and the Pınarbaşı excavations demonstrate how much remains to be discovered of the Prehistory of Asia Minor, and how even small-scale projects can alter our understanding of this period dramatically and add thousands of years to our archaeological sequences. In these circumstances, arguments for a plausible absence of specific periods of occupation for particular regions of Asia Minor should be treated with extreme caution.[56] At present, there are large parts of Asia Minor, such as North-Central Anatolia and the Aegean, that lack any evidence of Epipalaeolithic/Mesolithic sites. It is plausible, however, that microlithic assemblages will be found in such regions in future research.

3.5.1 Residual Evidence for the Epipalaeolithic/Mesolithic in Asia Minor

The situation described earlier for the Marmara Region, in which poorly documented Epipalaeolithic/Mesolithic groups can be substantiated by the characteristics of the assemblages of (later) Mesolithic/Neolithic sites, is one that also occurs on the central plateau of Asia Minor.

The presence of Epipalaeolithic/Mesolithic groups in Central Anatolia can be postulated on the basis of the persistence of microlithic traditions in early Aceramic Neolithic sites, which can be dated between about 8500 and 7500 BC. Examples include Aşıklı Höyük and Boncuklu.[57] After 7500

---

[53] Baird 2007: 293–294.
[54] Féblot-Augustins 1993; Slimak and Giraud 2007.
[55] Broodbank 2006: 210.
[56] Düring 2008.
[57] Balkan-Atlı 1994a; Baird 2006a: 60–61.

BC, microliths are no longer found in Aceramic Neolithic sites in Central Anatolia at sites such as Canhasan 3 and Musular.[58]

It is remarkable that the earliest Neolithic assemblages seem to include a microlithic component in both Central Anatolia and the Marmara Region and possibly in the Antalya Region. Given that the moment when microliths fall out of use is different for each region, it would appear that they derive from older Epipalaeolithic/Mesolithic traditions rather than arriving in these regions as part of a Neolithic package.

For example, in early Aceramic Neolithic sites in Southeast Anatolia such as Demirköy Höyük, Çayönü, and Boytepe, microliths have been documented, but these disappear later on, from about 8500 BC at sites such as Nevali Çori and the upper levels at Çayönü,[59] which is when the earliest Neolithic in Central Anatolia starts. Likewise, in the Marmara Region microliths persist until 6000 BC, by which time they had fallen out of use for 1,500 years in Central Anatolia. Such patterns suggest that the microliths in early Neolithic sites in Asia Minor inform us about otherwise poorly documented Epipalaeolithic/Mesolithic predecessor groups.[60]

3.6.1 Conclusion

Some have argued that there is no Epipalaeolithic in Asia Minor except for that of the Antalya Region[61] and that the Epipalaeolithic tradition ends with the start of the Holocene.[62] Here I take issue with both of these positions. Although the evidence is far from satisfactory, the combined data from the Antalya Region, the Ağaçlı group in the Marmara Region, the Konya Plain Survey, Pınarbaşı, and the Early Aceramic Neolithic sites with microlithic assemblages clearly demonstrate that Epipalaeolithic/Mesolithic groups were present across Asia Minor prior to the start of the Neolithic. The advent of these Epipalaeolithic/Mesolithic traditions remains poorly defined, although the new early dates from Pınarbaşı may indicate that this occurred prior to the Holocene.

Second, evidence from various sites across Asia Minor, including Aşıklı Höyük, Beldibi, Belbaşı, Boncuklu, Öküzini, Pınarbaşı, and Pendik, clearly

---

[58] Baird 2006a: 61. The microliths found in the Çatalhöyük deep sounding are generally held to be residual (Baird 2002: 143).

[59] Balkan-Atlı 1994b; Rosenberg and Peasnall 1998.

[60] Not all microliths necessarily date to the Epipalaeolithic and/or Mesolithic. For example, at Aşağı Pınar, microliths were dated to after 5500 BC (Gatsov 2001: 106). At Franchti microliths were abundant in the Epipalaeolithic, are almost absent during the earliest Holocene, and regain their importance in the Upper Mesolithic (Perlès 2001: 31).

[61] Balkan-Atlı 1994b: 143.

[62] Kartal 2003: 51.

indicates that microlith traditions persisted in the early Holocene, in some regions up to about 6000 BC, and that we should understand these later microlithic assemblages as being produced by groups similar to those who created earlier Epipalaeolithic assemblages. In subsequent chapters it will be argued that some of these groups had a pivotal role to play in the transition to a Neolithic way of life in Asia Minor.

CHAPTER FOUR

EARLY FARMERS OF THE SOUTHERN PLATEAU (8500–6500 BC)

The Near Eastern Neolithic is of enormous culture-historical significance. Although Neolithic 'revolutions' also occurred in several other regions of the world, the Near Eastern Neolithic was both the earliest and eventually had the most far-reaching impact on the global development of humanity due to the domestication of a comparatively productive suite of domesticated plants and animals that allowed for a swift and vast expansion of agriculture outside the Near East.[1]

After hundreds of thousands of years during which human groups obtained their nourishment from a combination of hunting, gathering, and fishing, and in which groups were, with a few exceptions, both small and mobile, the transition to a settlement-based existence founded on an agricultural economy in the Near East occurred within a relatively brief span of time that may not have lasted more than a few centuries.[2]

The effects of these processes on prehistoric societies were enormous and affected almost every aspect of people's lives. Among these effects were the following: Changes in subsistence and bodily routines affected the stature and health of people;[3] sedentary life in relatively close quarters created conditions in which diseases could spread much more easily than before and in which a variety of animals, such as mice and dogs, associated themselves with human settlements, some being more welcome than others;[4] a new dependency on the seasons and climatic events brought about a changed perception of humans' place in the cosmos;[5] and the close and permanent agglomeration of relatively large groups of people altered the ways in which people interacted with each other and created the need to categorise people

[1] Harris 2002.
[2] Nesbitt 2002, 2004; Colledge et al. 2004.
[3] Larsen 1995; Pinhasi and Pluciennik 2004.
[4] Tchernov 1991; Vigne and Guilaine 2004.
[5] Hodder 1990; Cauvin 1997; Watkins 2004; Lewis-Williams and Pierce 2005.

in various ways.[6] These changes occurring in human societies in the Near Eastern Neolithic are at the root of later complex societies both in the Near East and in adjacent regions.

4.1.1 The 'Where' of the Near Eastern Neolithic

It has long been thought that the (southern) Levant was the main area in which the Neolithic transition occurred in the Near East. In this reconstruction the Late Epipalaeolithic Natufian culture in the southern Levant, with its sedentary hunter-gatherer-fisher groups heavily dependent on wild cereal resources, constituted the basis from which the Neolithic emerged when confronted with the cold spell of the Younger Dryas (about 10,600–9200 BC). In these circumstances, people would have started to experiment with cultivating cereals in the PPN-A (Pre-Pottery-Neolithic-A), between 9500 and 8700 BC, culminating in the formation of full-scale farming in the subsequent PPN-B, between 8700 and 7000 BC.[7] This model of the Neolithic transition has become entrenched in much of the synthetic literature on the Near Eastern Neolithic.[8]

There are a number of problems with this dominant model, however. First, wild cereals, which constituted the main subsistence base in this period, did not become scarce during the Younger Dryas; consequently, there was no climatically induced need for experiments in cereal cultivation.[9] Second, the first domesticated crops appear in the Early PPN-B period, to be dated between about 8700 and 8200 BC, and are found predominantly in sites in southeastern Turkey rather than in the PPN-A in the Levant proper.[10]

Although some archaeologists now argue for a primacy of the central parts of the Fertile Crescent, consisting of northern Syria and Southeast Anatolia, sometimes designated the 'golden triangle',[11] most researchers now agree that the domestication of plants and animals took place in a much larger region, which includes the Taurus and Zagros foothills and perhaps Cyprus.[12]

Apart from the issue of *where* domestication took place, it has become increasingly clear over the last few decades that a Levant-centred model of

---

[6] Redman 1978; Düring and Marciniak 2005; Düring 2006.
[7] Henry 1989; Bar-Yosef and Meadow 1995; Cauvin 1997; Bar-Yosef and Belfer-Cohen 2002; Hole 2004.
[8] Colledge et al. 2004; Barker 2006; Simmons 2007.
[9] Bottema 2002: 37.
[10] Nesbitt 2002.
[11] Aurenche and Kozlowski 1999; Kozlowski and Aurenche 2005.
[12] Nesbitt 2002; Peltenburg and Wasse, eds., 2004; Rollefson and Gebel 2004.

the Near Eastern Neolithic is no longer tenable from a culture-historical perspective and that this model is to a significant degree biased by the greater intensity of archaeological research in the southern Levant. In particular, a series of discoveries in northern Syria and Southeastern Anatolia have demonstrated that the Early Neolithic in that region had its own distinctive traditions.[13] From the Early PPN-B onwards, Early Neolithic horizons with distinctive traditions have also been documented in the Zagros foothills,[14] in Central Anatolia,[15] and on Cyprus.[16]

With the growing realisation that the Early Neolithic was a dispersed phenomenon that unfolded over a vast area of the Near East and developed along path-dependent trajectories in each region, it has been argued that a 'polycentric' model is best suited to further our understanding the Near Eastern Neolithic.[17] In this model there are several core regions, such as the southern Levant, Central Anatolia, and Upper Mesopotamia, each of which developed along its own culture-historical trajectory. Such a perspective does not deny that there were significant interactions and commonalities between regions or that what happened in one region could affect what happened in others.

It remains to be seen whether what are perceived as 'core regions' in Near Eastern Prehistory at present reflect factors of research intensity and site preservation and to what degree the boundaries of such core regions will become diffuse when sites in intermediate regions are excavated. For example, one reason that the Central Anatolian Neolithic appears as a distinct entity from that of the Fertile Crescent may be that no Early Neolithic sites intermediate between Southeast Anatolia and Central Anatolia have been investigated to date which could fill this spatial and cultural gap.[18]

On the other hand, clear differences between the Neolithic of the Konya Plain and the Lake District,[19] which are located adjacent to one another and both of which have been systematically investigated, exist, indicating that cultural boundaries do exist in the Near Eastern Neolithic. I will argue in this chapter that a similar cultural boundary also separated the Fertile Crescent and Central Anatolia in the Neolithic.

One advantage of the polycentric model of the Near Eastern Neolithic is that it allows us to comprehend the Central Anatolian Neolithic in ways other than as an offshoot of the Neolithic in the Fertile Crescent, which is

---

[13] Özdoğan 1995; Hauptmann 1999.
[14] Watkins 1990; Balossi Restelli 2001; Kozlowski 2002.
[15] Özdoğan 2002; Düring 2006.
[16] Swiny, ed., 2001; Peltenburg and Wasse, eds., 2004.
[17] Özdoğan 1995; Rollefson and Gebel 2004.
[18] The earliest layers at the site of Mersin are dated to about 7000 BC and were excavated in a very small sounding (Garstang 1953; Caneva and Sevin, eds., 2004).
[19] Duru 1999; Thissen 2000: 154–156; Umurtak 2000: 695–696.

how it has often been portrayed. Another advantage of this model is that it allows us to better understand both the specific features of the Neolithic in this region and the nature and effects of the frequent contacts and exchanges with the Fertile Crescent.[20]

4.1.2 Neolithic Revolution versus Neolithisation

The term 'Neolithic revolution' was coined by Gordon Childe to describe what he conceived of as a process analogous to the more recent Industrial Revolution: a relatively quick transformation of the means of production that made more complex and populous societies possible.[21] At a general level Childe's model continues to be valid, in the sense that the transition to an agricultural economy, which was the foundation for a settlement-based existence in the Near East, occurred within a relatively brief span of time that may not have lasted more than a few centuries in a specific region.

However, on a more detailed level, it is clear that the transition to a Neolithic way of life was more gradual. For example, sedentary villages existed in the Near East several millennia prior to the emergence of farming,[22] and early farming communities continued to rely on wild plant and animal resources for much of their subsistence.[23] Further, many plants and animals were domesticated millennia after the initial domestication of a number of cereals. For instance, olives do not seem to have been cultivated before the Late Bronze Age.[24] It could even be argued that the Neolithic never really ended because the process of the domestication of plants and animals is ongoing today.[25]

In this study, the Neolithic is defined as a sedentary way of life in which agriculture provided the staple subsistence resource. It was this combination that retrospectively turned out to be of great cultural importance, because it allowed for the expansion of sedentary settlement-based life outside the optimal habitats to which it had been confined up to that point.

Defined in this manner, the transition to the Neolithic occurred fairly rapidly, although the processes of sedentarisation and domestication that are associated with the Neolithic started millennia earlier and continued for a long time after this transition. In light of these circumstances, it is unlikely that the emergence of sedentism on an agricultural foundation was

[20] Özdoğan 1996, 2005.
[21] Childe 1928, 1936.
[22] Tchernov 1991; Bar-Yosef and Meadow 1995.
[23] Özdoğan 1997b; Esin 1998; Colledge 2001; Fairbairn et al. 2005: 183–184.
[24] Runnels and Hansen 1986; Bottema and Woldring 1990; Roberts et al. 2001: 733.
[25] Higgs and Jarman 1972: 13.

perceived as a major threshold by people living in Near Eastern Prehistory, given that sedentary life had an extended history and changes in the subsistence economy would have appeared relatively minor. To draw attention to these extended processes and to capture the arbitrariness of the division between the Neolithic and the periods preceding and postdating it, many scholars now prefer the term 'neolithisation' when discussing the Neolithic transition.[26]

4.2.1 The Roots of the Central Anatolian Neolithic

The roots of the Central Anatolian Neolithic remain obscure in the sense that we know very little about the transition between Epipalaeolithic/Mesolithic and Neolithic societies in this region.[27] This transition has now been documented with various degrees of detail in the southern, central, and western reaches of the Fertile Crescent.[28] Some archaeologists have argued that given the absence of an incipient Neolithic, Central Anatolia might have been colonised by farmers from the Fertile Crescent.[29]

Here I argue against the colonisation from the Fertile Crescent hypothesis and in favour of an autochthonous take-up of the Neolithic way of life. This argument is based on two observations: First, the Central Anatolian Neolithic is culturally distinct from that of the Fertile Crescent, a point further explored in this chapter; and second, there is cultural continuity between the recently documented Epipalaeolithic groups in Central Anatolia and the earliest Neolithic in the region.

In the previous chapter, evidence for Epipalaeolithic/Mesolithic sites in the Konya Plain has been discussed. At Pınarbaşı B, assemblages and features dating to 12,000 BC have been excavated.[30] Several sites dating to the Early Holocene have been found in the Konya Plain, including the excavated strata at Pınarbaşı A.[31] Thus, we have lithic assemblages that can be dated to the final Epipalaeolithic and Mesolithic in the southern part of Central Anatolia, a sequence that mirrors that in the Antalya Region at sites such as Öküzini and Karain.

There is no a priori reason to assume that these pre-existing groups living on the Anatolian plateau played a role in the neolithisation of the region. However, there is one element in the earliest Neolithic sites that

---

[26] Cauvin 1989: 4; Balkan-Atlı 1994a; Watkins 2006.
[27] Esin 1999: 17; Özdoğan 1999b: 226.
[28] Watkins 1990; A. Özdoğan 1999; Bar-Yosef and Belfer-Cohen 2002; Kozlowski 2002; Stordeur and Abbès 2002.
[29] Yakar 1994: 25, 337; Cauvin 1997: 218; Binder 2002.
[30] Baird 2007; Yildirim and Gates 2007: 279.
[31] Watkins 1996; Baird 2003, 2004.

suggests that they were involved. At sites such as Aşıklı Höyük and Bon-cuklu, to be dated to about 8500–7500 BC, microliths are common in the chipped stone industries in the earliest layers.[32] By contrast, after 7500 BC microliths are no longer present, for example at Canhasan 3 and Musular. One possible exception is Çatalhöyük pre-level XIIA–D, which will be discussed later (§4.8.4). Given that at 8500 BC microliths had already fallen out of use in the Fertile Crescent, at sites such as Nevali Çori and the upper levels at Çayönü,[33] it seems plausible that the microliths in the earliest Aceramic Neolithic sites of Central Anatolia derived from local Early Holocene chipped stone traditions, with which they share many characteristics.[34]

4.3.1 The Exchange of Obsidian from Asia Minor in Prehistory

Obsidian is a volcanic glass that is formed by the sudden cooling of molten, generally acidic, magma with a high water content.[35] It is generally found in areas with other types of volcanic deposits and can vary in colour from black to red and green. In terms of mineral composition each obsidian source, and in some cases each individual flow within a source, is unique. The unique chemical 'fingerprint' of obsidian sources and their age of formation make it possible to distinguish among obsidian sources and to trace obsidian found elsewhere back to its source.[36] Further, because obsidian is a glass, it possesses conchoidal fracture properties that make it very useful for producing chipped stone artefacts. This amenability of obsidian, in combination with its transparent and shiny appearance, were probably the reasons why this material was widely used in Prehistory in many regions of the world.

There are a substantial number of obsidian sources in Asia Minor, but their suitability for making chipped stone artefacts and their accessibility vary considerably; it is probably due to such factors that many of the known sources do not seem to have been exploited in Prehistory (Fig. 4.1).[37] At some sites, such as Demircihüyük, obsidian artefacts cannot be linked with any known source at present, however, and many obsidian sources in Asia Minor await further investigation.[38] Amongst the most important

---

[32] Balkan-Atlı 1994a; Baird 2006a: 60–61.
[33] Balkan-Atlı 1994b: 143. It should be noted, however, that at Cafer Höyük microliths are found until much later (ibid.). Perhaps a similar case of persistent local chipped stone traditions applies in the Taurus uplands as in Central Anatolia.
[34] Compare Balkan-Atlı (1994a) and Baird (2006a) with Léotard and López Bayón (2002).
[35] Ercan et al. 1994: 505.
[36] Willams-Thorpe 1995; Yeğingil et al. 1998.
[37] Yeğingil et al. 1998, 825–826.
[38] Wagner and Weiner 1987; Özdoğan 1994.

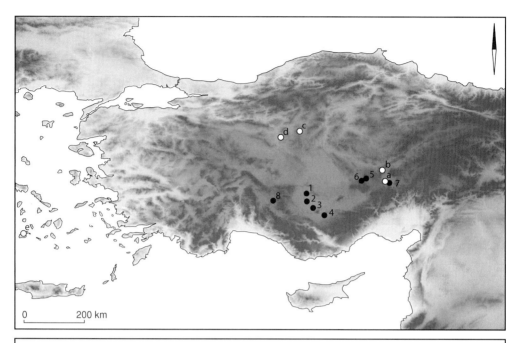

Obsidian sources: a Göllüdağ; b Nenezidağ; c Sakaeli; d Yağlar; e Melos;
Early Neolithic sites: 1 Boncuklu Höyük; 2 Çatalhöyük; 3 Pınarbaşı; 4 Canhasan; 5 Aşıklı Höyük; 6 Musular; 7 Kaletepe; 8 Suberde.

investigated sources of Asia Minor that were exploited in Prehistory are, first, those in Cappadocia, in particular the sources at Göllüdağ (including the flows of Kayırlı-village, Kayırlı-East, Kömürcü, Gösterli, Bozköy, and Sirça Deresi), Nenezidağ, and Acıgöl (including the flows of Kalecittepe, Göldağ, and Acıgöl-crater); and, second, those in the Galatean Massif, including sources at Sakaeli, Yağlar, and Galatia-X.[39]

Outside Asia Minor, a number of obsidian sources were exploited in Prehistory both in eastern Turkey and on the Aegean islands of Melos and Giali.[40] Apart from the rare occurrence of some Melian obsidian in Aegean sites in Asia Minor, such as at Morali and Aphrodisias, and the sporadic find of East Anatolian obsidian in Asia Minor, most of the obsidian found derives from the Galatean and Cappadocian sources already discussed.[41]

Obsidian from the Cappadocian sources, in particular Nenezidağ and eastern Göllüdağ, has been found at many sites in the Fertile Crescent. From the Epipalaeolithic onwards, obsidian from Göllüdağ is found in

4.1 Early Neolithic sites and obsidian sources in Asia Minor, 8500–6500 BC. Produced by the author and Joanne Porck.

[39] Keller and Seifried 1990; Yeğingil et al. 1998
[40] Williams-Thorpe 1995; Yeğingil et al. 1998; Kobayashi et al. 2003.
[41] Renfrew et al. 1965: 238; Renfrew et al. 1966: 37; Blackman 1986; Ercan et al. 1990; Bigazzi et al. 1998; Herling et al. 2008.

the Levant at sites such as Mureybet, Abu Hureyra, and Ain Mallaha.[42] During the subsequent PPN-A period (9500–8700 BC), artefacts produced from Göllüdağ obsidian are found at sites such as Jericho, Netiv Hagdud, Tell Aswad, Mureybet, and Jerf el Ahmar,[43] but obsidian becomes much more common in the Early and Middle PPN-B (8700–7500 BC), and it has been found at sites such as Abu Hureyra, Tell Aswad, Beidha, Dja'de, Tell Halula, Nahal Lavan, Munhata Mureybet, Ras Shamra, and Shillourakambos, among others.[44] In the subsequent Late PPN-B and throughout the sixth and fifth millennia BC, Cappadocian obsidian continued to be exported to the Fertile Crescent. It is not clear at what point in Prehistory the volume of obsidian brought to the Levant and Syria decreased substantially, but from the Bronze Age onwards the material seems to have been used primarily as an exotic material for the production of vessels, seals, and the like, rather than for chipped stone tools.[45]

The distances over which obsidian is exchanged in these periods range up to 900 kilometres. Up to about 300 kilometres from the obsidian sources, this material constituted the major component of the lithic assemblages at Neolithic sites. Beyond this threshold, the percentages of obsidian in the chipped stone assemblages decreases rapidly.[46] In sites further removed from the source, the exotic nature of obsidian and its scarcity probably added to its perception as a desirable commodity, and obsidian could easily become a prestige good or acquire symbolic significance. By contrast, in the vicinity of obsidian sources the material was generally used more prosaically.[47] Given such mechanisms, the uses to which obsidian was put, in terms of the artefacts created and the industries used, may differ quite substantially with the distance from the source.

4.3.2 The Obsidian Mining Workshops of Cappadocia

The obsidian sources of Cappadocia have been the subject of systematic investigations.[48] A variety of obsidian extraction and processing workshops were found in the vicinity of outcrops at Göllüdağ and Nenezidağ. These workshops can be dated to specific periods in Prehistory and can be linked

[42] Cauvin and Chataigner 1998.
[43] Renfrew et al. 1966, 1968; Chataigner 1998;.Carter et al. 2005b.
[44] Renfrew et al. 1966; Chataigner 1998; Gratuze 1999; Binder 2002, 80; Carter et al. 2005b. During these periods a minority of the Cappadocian obsidian in the Fertile Crescent came from Nenezidağ, but most of it derived from Göllüdağ.
[45] Cauvin and Chataigner 1998; Chataigner 1998; Coqueugniot 1998.
[46] Renfrew et al. 1968; Wright 1969; Cauvin 1998.
[47] Robb and Farr 2005: 37.
[48] Cauvin and Balkan-Atlı 1996; Balkan-Atlı and Der Aprahamian 1998; Balkan-Atlı et al. 1999a, 1999b; Balkan-Atlı and Binder 2000, 2001.

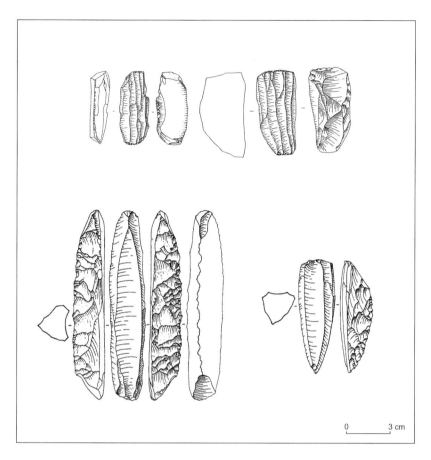

4.2 Cores from Aşıklı Höyük (above) and Kömürcü-Kaletepe. Reassembled with permission of N. Balkan-Atlı from Balkan-Atlı, N. 1994. 'The typological characteristics of the Askılı Höyük chipped stone industry'. In *Neolithic Chipped Stone Industries of the Fertile Crescent*, edited by H. G. Gebel and S. K. Kozlowski, pp. 209–221, fig. 1. Berlin, Germany: Ex Oriente, and Balkan-Atlı, N., Binder, D., and Cauvin, M.-C. 1999. 'Obsidian, sources, workshops, and trade in Central Anatolia'. In *Neolithic in Turkey: The Cradle of Civilization*, edited by M. Özdoğan, pp. 133–145, fig. 1. Istanbul, Turkey: Arkeoloji ve Sanat Yayınları.

with particular sites or regions where obsidian from these sources has been found.[49]

Besides compositional analysis to trace obsidian in exotic regions back to its source, another clue for the reconstruction of obsidian exchange patterns consists of the knapping industries employed at the obsidian workshops. Investigations at several Cappadocian workshops have revealed that apart from the knapping technologies known from early Neolithic sites in Central Anatolia, such as Aşıklı Höyük, Canhasan 3, and Çatalhöyük, there

[49] Cauvin and Balkan-Atlı 1996; Balkan-Atlı and Der Apramian 1998; Balkan-Atlı et al. 1999a.

are also 'alien' knapping technologies at these workshops that are without counterparts in Asia Minor.

In particular, at the excavated Kömürcü-Kaletepe workshop, cores and core reduction strategies are identical to those of chipped stone industries known from the Fertile Crescent. More specifically, the 'naviform' cores of Kaletepe, a type of core with two striking platforms that resembles a boat in shape, and the unipolar pressure cores at Kaletepe have direct parallels in Syria and the Levant (Fig. 4.2).[50]

The exotic chipped stone industries of Kaletepe are more efficient than those used in Central Anatolia in the sense that both more and more standardised blades were obtained from a block of obsidian than was possible with local technologies. However, the exotic knapping strategies used at Kaletepe also required a higher level of skill to achieve a more controlled knapping sequence.[51] Given that identical knapping technologies were used in the Fertile Crescent on flint and that the knappers at Kaletepe could dispose of almost limitless supplies of obsidian, it is probable that it was the need for standardised blades that was the rationale behind the technology rather than the efficient use of raw materials.

The exploitation and export of Cappadocian obsidian to the Fertile Crescent has received by far the most attention from scholars, but most of the obsidian was consumed locally, that is, in Asia Minor. Within Asia Minor some interesting shifts in exchange patterns have begun to be documented.

One site for which this topic has been thoroughly investigated is Çatalhöyük East (§4.8.1), where a shift in chipped stone industries occurs around level VII, after which prismatic blades derived from unipolar pressure cores started to be produced on site, a technique that requires a substantial amount of skill.[52] Interestingly, this technological shift coincided with a change in the obsidian source that supplied Çatalhöyük: Whereas in earlier levels the obsidian was derived from Göllüdağ, from level VII onwards most material came from Nenezidağ.[53] Given that the obsidian from both sources has essentially the same physical properties, a technical explanation for this shift is hard to find. It is possible that the two sources were controlled by different groups and that the allegiance of people living at Çatalhöyük shifted from one group to the other. Accompanying this shift was the transfer of the production of prismatic blades to Çatalhöyük, whereas previously they had only arrived as end-products.

Interestingly, a similar type of link between obsidian sources and knapping technologies has also been documented at Musular (§4.7.1), where

[50] Balkan-Atlı and Der Aprahamian 1998; Balkan-Atlı et al. 1999b; Binder and Balkan-Atlı 2001.
[51] Abbes et al. 1999; Binder and Balkan-Atlı 2001.
[52] Conolly 1999a, 1999b.
[53] Carter et al. 2005a; Carter and Shackley 2007: 443.

obsidian from both the Göllüdağ and Nenezidağ sources was present, but each was used for different industries: Whereas the Nenezidağ obsidian was used for large, thick blades, the Göllüdağ obsidian was used for more fragile, sharper, and smaller blades.[54] In the later Aceramic levels of Musular the amount of Nenezidağ obsidian increases at the expense of that from Göllüdağ,[55] which is probably related to a shift in chipped stone industries.

The cases of Çatalhöyük and Musular need not be representative of the situation at other sites, such as Aşıklı Höyük, Boncuklu, the Canhasan sites, and Çatalhöyük West, but they do provide previously unexpected hints of the dynamics of past exchange systems that require further investigation.

4.3.3 The Nature of Obsidian Exchange

A topic that has been debated is how obsidian exchange and extraction were organised.[56] Here I will focus on the nature of the activities at Kaletepe, which is the best-investigated obsidian mining site of the Near East. The question is whether we are dealing with, first, the use of foreign technologies by local people for the purpose of export; or, second, knappers from the Fertile Crescent producing artefacts for their region of origin.

If the former was the case, it was presumably the standardisation of the blades produced that was important. Moreover, local and foreign technologies might co-occur in the same workshops because they were used by the same knappers, depending on the consumers they were targeting. In the second scenario, it might be that the 'PPN-B technologies' used at Kaletepe were part of the 'habitus', or the standardised bodily practices, of the knappers rather than a conscious choice, and a spatial segregation of local and exotic knapping traditions might occur.

The Kaletepe excavators argue for the second scenario: that the people knapping at the site came from the Fertile Crescent in organised expeditions in order to obtain obsidian. Their argument is that the PPN-B chipped stone technologies were highly sophisticated and difficult to master.[57] Further, along the same lines, they propose that these obsidian expeditions played a major role in the neolithisation of Central Anatolia.[58] Domestic crops and farming technologies would have arrived in the wake of these expeditions from the Fertile Crescent, inducing local groups to adopt sedentism and farming.

---

[54] Özbaşaran et al. 2007: 276.
[55] Kayacan 2003: 7.
[56] Renfrew et al. 1968; Wright 1969; Cauvin 1996; Cessford and Carter 2005.
[57] Binder and Balkan-Atlı 2001; Binder 2002.
[58] Binder and Balkan-Atlı 2001; Binder 2002.

However, the idea of putting obsidian expeditions at centre stage in the neolithisation of Central Anatolia is problematic. The distances concerned are considerable, minimally about 400 kilometres, and include difficult mountainous terrain. Expeditions over such long distances suggest complicated exchange systems, whereas much simpler modes of exchange between local groups could have achieved similar effects with much less effort.[59] It has been calculated that a single journey from Çatalhöyük, located some 190 kilometres from the Cappadocian sources, would have lasted 10 to 13 days; thus, a return journey would have taken 20 to 26 days.[60] By the same reckoning, an expedition from the Fertile Crescent would have taken twice as long, 40 to 52 days of travelling, to which we have to add the work at the obsidian quarries. Expeditions of such duration seem implausible in the context of the Near Eastern Neolithic.

It is probably this factor – that there is a limit to the distance from which expeditions could be effectively mounted – that best explains Renfrew's boundary of 250 to 350 kilometres of the 'supply zone', within which obsidian constituted more than 80 per cent of the chipped stone assemblage, while groups further removed would have obtained smaller amounts of obsidian through exchange with intermediate groups. A related issue is how people from the Fertile Crescent first became aware of the Cappadocian obsidian sources. It is not plausible that the export of obsidian to the Fertile Crescent could have operated without local partners. Considering that, it is probably significant that at the Kayırlı-Bitlikler workshop, local Central Anatolian core types are found alongside the exotic naviform and unipolar pressure cores.[61] Further, naviform cores have been found in the ninth millennium BC hunter-gatherer settlement of Pınarbaşı, and blades struck from these cores were found at Çatalhöyük.[62]

4.4.1 Introducing Aşıklı Höyük

Aşıklı Höyük, about 30 kilometres away from the obsidian sources of Nenezidağ and Göllüdağ (Fig. 4.1), is of key importance for our understanding of the Aceramic Neolithic of Central Anatolia. It is located along the Melendiz River in a fertile landscape with abundant water sources. The site has a substantial size even after considerable erosion on its northern, eastern, and southern edges, stands at least 15 metres high and measures about 4 hectares, or 230 by 240 metres.

---

[59] Renfrew et al. 1966: 54.
[60] Cessford and Carter 2005: 310.
[61] Balkan-Atlı and Der Aprahamian 1998.
[62] Conolly 2003; Baird 2007.

Aşıklı Höyük was first investigated in the 1960s by Todd, who collected chipped stone artefacts, radiocarbon samples, and faunal remains, which were published in various reports.[63] The construction of the Mamasın Dam beginning in 1988, projected to flood the site, led to large-scale rescue excavations. Large horizontal exposures totalling some 4200 square metres were obtained, providing important evidence of the spatial organisation of the settlement.

Three layers have been distinguished at Aşıklı Höyük, which are further subdivided into phases designated with letters. Layer 1 comprises the disturbed features and deposits located in and just below the mound surface. Layer 2 consists of the well-preserved buildings and deposits beneath, and was subdivided into ten phases (2A–2J). In the sounding 4H/G, layer 2 continued until about 7 metres below the mound summit, below which a flood horizon of 70 centimetres was encountered. Beneath this flood horizon building remains have been assigned to layer 3, which has been divided into phases 3A–3C.

Forty-seven radiocarbon samples have been published for Aşıklı Höyük, which date between 8200 and 7400 BC.[64] The vast majority of these samples were taken from the large horizontal 2A–C exposures on the mound summit, and five samples were taken from the earlier phases G–D of layer 2.[65] No samples are available at present to date the earliest layer 3, which means that it is difficult to estimate when the Aşıklı Höyük sequence began. Given that more than 7 metres of deposits remain undated, it is argued that the site was occupied from at least 8500 BC.

Aşıklı Höyük has often been presented as a site in which domesticated foods were of minor importance to the subsistence economy, with the majority of the diet deriving from wild plants and animals.[66] This view has come under attack from botanists, who argued that domestic crops, in particular cereals, did form the staple food resource and that wild plants, such as hackberry stones, are overrepresented in the assemblage because they are preserved better than seeds.[67] Amongst the botanical remains found at Aşıklı Höyük are domestic einkorn, emmer wheat, naked barley, and a free-threshing wheat. Pulses were also important and included bitter vetch, lentil, and pea. Amongst the wild plants used, hackberry, pistachio, and almond seem to have been of considerable importance,[68] which

[63] Todd 1966, 1968a, 1980: 59–61; Payne 1985.
[64] Esin 1998; Thissen 2002.
[65] Esin and Harmankaya 1999: 123.
[66] Esin et al. 1991: 132; Esin 1998: 98–99; Esin and Harmankaya 1999: 126–127; Esin and Harmankaya 2007: 266.
[67] Asouti and Fairbarn 2002.
[68] Van Zeist and De Roller 1995; Asouti and Fairbarn 2002.

is reminiscent of Epipalaeolithic consumption practices documented for
Öküzini.[69]

None of the animals identified in the Aşıklı Höyük faunal assemblage are
domesticated. More than 84 per cent of the faunal remains belong to sheep
and goats, however, demonstrating that these animals played an important role in the economy. Other species found at the site include cattle,
pigs, equids, and deer. It has been argued that the sheep and goats have
a kill-off pattern that is characteristic of herded populations. Further, on
the basis of the age and sex profiles of the sheep and goat assemblage at
Aşıklı Höyük, Buitenhuis posits a 'proto-domestication' stage at the site in
which animals were kept and exploited but did not yet differ morphologically from wild populations.[70] If this interpretation is accepted, most of the
meat at Aşıklı Höyük derived from a managed resource rather than from
hunting.

The chipped stone industries of Aşıklı Höyük consist almost entirely
of obsidian that was obtained from the nearby Göllüdağ (Kayırlı) and
Nenezidağ sources.[71] It seems to have been brought to the site in blocks,
where it was further processed. Two types of cores were found. The more
common is the opposed platform core with two striking platforms on opposite sides; the other type of core has a single striking platform and a pyramidal shape. The opposed platform cores were employed for blade production
using direct percussion and produced relatively few blades for each core.[72]
The pyramidal cores were used to obtain flakes. Blades, flakes, and core
preparation/rejuvenation flakes were all used for producing tools, which
were often retouched on the dorsal face. The most common tools are
scrapers, followed by retouched blades, whereas projectile points are rare.
Microliths are most common in the early phases of layer 2 and decrease
in phases 2A–C.[73] The chipped stone industries from Aşıklı Höyük are
distinct both from those used in the Fertile Crescent[74] and from the later
industries of Canhasan 3 and Çatalhöyük, although for the latter, affinities
can be demonstrated.[75]

Very little has been published on other artefact categories found at Aşıklı
Höyük. Mention is made of clay figurines, mostly depicting animals that
cannot be identified because the heads and legs are missing. Beads are

---

[69] Martinoli 2002.
[70] Buitenhuis 1997; Vigne et al. 1999; Martin et al. 2002. At the more or less contemporaneous
site of Nevalı Çori domestic sheep have been documented, but unlike the domestic crops,
these were not brought to Central Anatolia (Peters et al. 1999: 39).
[71] Gratuze et al. 1994; Balkan-Atlı et al. 1999a.
[72] Abbès et al. 1999: 125.
[73] Balkan-Atlı 1998: 87; Abbès et al. 1999: 119.
[74] Todd 1966: 162; Abbès et al. 1999: 127; Balkan-Atlı et al. 1999b: 241.
[75] Todd 1966: 162; Balkan-Atlı 1994a: 221; 1998: 87.

common, some of which are made from copper.[76] Other conspicuous find categories are bone hooks and buckles. Also common are ground stone artefacts produced from volcanic rocks such as basalt.[77] Polished stone tools, such as celts, are rare.

4.4.2 The Aşıklı Höyük Settlement

Due to large-scale excavations, the spatial organisation of Aşıklı Höyük is exceptionally well documented. The buildings that were exposed on the relatively flat summit of the mound, which are dated to layers 2A–C, constitute a remarkably consistent plan despite some stratigraphic problems.[78]

Aşıklı Höyük is the oldest example of a 'clustered neighbourhood settlement', also documented at other Central Anatolian Neolithic sites such as Çatalhöyük, Canhasan 1 and 3, and Erbaba. The clustered neighbourhood settlements are characterised by, first, a lack of streets within neighbourhood blocks, in which structures are built directly adjacent to one another; second, the absence of doors communicating directly with open spaces; and, third, a large degree of building continuity in which buildings remain true to their location, dimensions, and orientation over long periods of time and through many phases of redevelopment.[79] This type of settlement is unique to the Central Anatolian Neolithic.

The settlement at Aşıklı Höyük consists of four components (Fig. 4.3). First, there are a number of streets and alleys within the settlement that divide the settlement into blocks of buildings. These streets vary greatly in their width and elaborateness. On the one hand, there are narrow alleys (like 'CP') that are less than 1 metre in width, with a winding course and an earthen surface. On the other hand, there is the broader street 'GA', which is up to 4 metres wide, has a straight course, and is paved with pebbles. Street GA is spatially associated with a monumental complex to its south, and this may have been one reason why it is grander. Interestingly, it has been shown that street GA has a series of equally elaborate predecessors, suggesting that the purposes it served were important over several centuries at least.[80]

Second, there are a number of open midden areas at Aşıklı Höyük, the largest of which is 'JA'. These consist primarily of domestic refuse, including ashy deposits and faunal remains. According to the excavators, these

---

[76] Esin 1995.
[77] Güldoğan 2003.
[78] For a discussion of the stratigraphical problems in these exposures see Düring 2006: 73–74.
[79] Düring 2005: 3. Also Özbaşaran 2000: 135; Düring 2006: 23–24.
[80] Esin and Harmankaya 1999: 124.

spaces were used for the production of bone antler and obsidian artefacts, butchering activities, and the processing of plant foods, besides the disposal of refuse.[81] Thus, many of the activities that tend to occur in a domestic context at other sites took place in such communal open areas at Aşıklı Höyük.

Third, two large monumental complexes have been found at Aşıklı Höyük (one around courts HV and T, the other around court MI; see Fig. 4.3). These complexes differ from other buildings in various respects. First, they are much larger than the normal buildings. Second, stone is uniquely used as a building material in these complexes. Third, distinct building techniques are used in their construction, such as walls built of multiple parallel mud slabs.[82] Fourth, features are found that are not present in other buildings, such as round hearths and elaborate painted floors.

Finally, there are a large number of small mud buildings that make up the clustered neighbourhoods at Aşıklı Höyük. These neighbourhoods have a continuous façade along the streets and alleys but open up towards the large midden area JA. Within the individual neighbourhoods there are some open areas, but these are not continuous and could not have been streets. Most likely, these open spaces served as additional midden areas.

4.4.3 Domestic Buildings at Aşıklı Höyük

The Aşıklı Höyük domestic buildings were constructed from mud slabs up to 1 metre in length.[83] Slab sizes are not standardized, and they might have been cut rather than shaped in a mould. The slabs contain vegetal inclusions, which suggests some form of preparation prior to extraction, however. On the walls and floors a base plaster about 1 centimetre thick was applied, on which finer plaster layers were regularly added. Up to 13 floor levels have been recognised.

The buildings at Aşıklı Höyük can be clearly distinguished due to the absence of party walls. Some buildings contain two or three rooms, whereas others have only one. The rooms are only 6.5 square metres on average but range considerably in size. The total interior sizes of buildings at Aşıklı Höyük ranges between 2 and 26 square metres and clusters at 6 to 12 square metres.[84] The buildings are commonly reconstructed with flat roofs.

---

[81] Esin and Harmankaya 1999: 125; Esin and Harmankaya 2007: 264.
[82] In this book 'mud' refers to the mixture of sand, silt, clay, and chaff used in building vernacular buildings in the Near East (Christensen 1967: 91–94; Peters 1972: 173–174; Facey 1997: 83–84).
[83] Esin and Harmankaya 1999: 125.
[84] Düring 2006: 80–83.

4.3 Composite plan of Aşıklı Höyük layers 2A–C. Produced by the author and Medy Oberen-dorff after fig. 3 in Esin, U., and Harmankaya, S. 1999. 'Aşıklı'. In *The Neolithic of Turkey*, edited by M. Özdoğan and N. Başgelen, pp. 115–132. Istanbul, Turkey: Arkeoloji ve Sanat Yayınları. Reproduced with permission of M. Özbaşaran and G. Duru.

Architects have calculated that the load-bearing capacities of the walls were sufficient only for single-storey structures.[85]

Some buildings with multiple rooms have interior doors, but exterior doors are absent.[86] The buildings appear to have been accessed from above by means of a ladder, something for which we have good evidence at the later site of Çatalhöyük (§4.8.6). For buildings with multiple rooms a single

[85] Esin et al. 1991: 149–153.
[86] Özbaşaran 1998: 555; Esin and Harmankaya 1999: 125.

ladder would probably have provided access, and other spaces were then accessed via interior doors.

The buildings at Aşıklı Höyük contained few *in situ* remains or features that could hint at activity patterns or abandonment practices. There appear to be only 3 rooms that contained silos and bins out of a total of 400. By contrast, hearths appear in 50 per cent of the buildings at Aşıklı Höyük.[87] These are large rectangular features typically measuring about 1.4 by 0.8 metres and usually located in a corner of a room. They were constructed with flat stones lining the pavement and along an upstanding edge, which was then covered with plaster.[88]

Given the characteristics of the Aşıklı Höyük buildings, the question arises how and by whom they were used. At first sight, it would appear that each building served a household group: a social unit of economic and social cooperation commonly defined on the basis of shared residence and the pooling of economic resources.[89] However, at Aşıklı Höyük there are two problems with this idea. First, the buildings are relatively small, with average sizes of 6–12 square metres. Numerous cross-cultural estimates suggest that these buildings are too small to have served household groups of at least four to five people.[90] However, there is, of course, the possibility that the cross-cultural estimates may not be valid for this particular case. Second, ethnographical studies of the Near East suggest that the best index for households consists of 'living rooms' characterised by superior plaster, regular upkeep, and the presence of hearths. At Aşıklı Höyük, only half of the buildings have a hearth. This also suggests that many buildings might not have served as discrete household residences. Instead, the use of the buildings may have been fragmented, with household groups using various rooms that were not necessarily in the same building and were centred on one of the rooms with hearths. Further, there is little evidence for economic pooling at Aşıklı Höyük, and it could be the case that much of the production and consumption of goods took place on the roofs of buildings or in large open spaces.

4.4.4 Building Continuity at Aşıklı Höyük

A remarkable aspect of the Aşıklı Höyük buildings is their development over time. In the deep sounding 4H/G this diachronic dimension of buildings

---

[87] Düring 2006: 85–86.
[88] Özbaşaran 1998.
[89] Wilk and Rathje 1982: 619–621; Bernbeck 1994: 28; Robin 2003: 308; Düring and Marciniak 2005.
[90] Naroll 1962; Cook and Heizer 1968; Casselberry 1974.

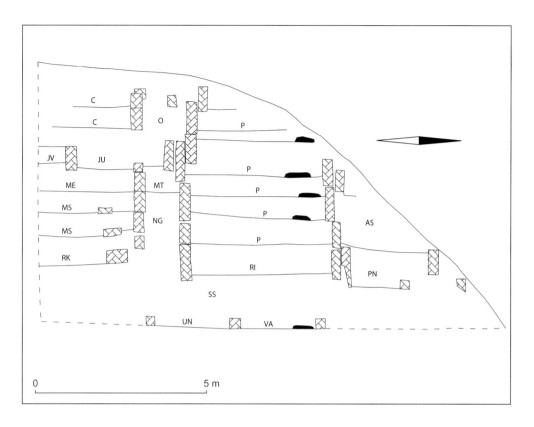

is best documented (Fig. 4.4). What can be observed is that buildings were continuously reconstructed on the same spot, with the same dimensions and orientations as older buildings, using existing walls as the foundation upon which a new structure was raised. Most of the buildings in sounding 4H/G can be traced through a long sequence of rebuilding episodes, up to eight of which can be documented, amounting to some 5 metres of archaeological deposits, before the sequence is cut short by erosion. A typical use life of these buildings can be estimated at 30 to 60 years, which would mean that the 4H/G sequence represents between 240 and 480 years!

This type of building continuity can also be documented at a number of other Neolithic sites in Anatolia, but to the best of my knowledge, it has no parallels elsewhere in ethnography and archaeology.[91] It is common to find the haphazard use of older walls for foundations,[92] but the long-lasting building continuity encountered at Aşıklı Höyük and at other Central Anatolian Neolithic sites, is unique. The default pattern in vernacular building traditions and in archaeology is that buildings are continuously altered to

4.4 Schematic section of deep sounding 4H/G at Aşıklı Höyük. Produced by the author and Medy Oberendorff after fig. 9 in Esin, U., and Harmankaya, S. 1999. 'Aşıklı'. In *The Neolithic of Turkey*, edited by M. Özdoğan and N. Başgelen, pp. 115–132. Istanbul, Turkey: Arkeoloji ve Sanat Yayınları. Reproduced with permission of M. Özbaşaran and G. Duru.

[91] Düring 2005.
[92] Aurenche 1981: 104; Peters 1982; Horne 1994; Facey 1997.

adjust them to the changing needs and fortunes of their inhabitants, and building spaces are regularly transferred between households in exchange for money or goods. The result is a picture of constant and unpredictable change in the built environment.[93] Set against this background, it is clear that the building continuity seen at Aşıklı Höyük is exceptional.

What is the rationale behind this cultural practice? It has been argued that building continuity was a means for creating secure foundations and that the closely built-up settlement restricted alterations in building size.[94] However, given that the building continuity is unique to the Anatolian Neolithic, other factors might also be at play. It is plausible that the exact reproduction of buildings was socially sanctioned and that building continuity was important to the social order.[95]

This idea can be supported with evidence pertaining to the interior arrangements of buildings, in particular the location of hearths. Their locations vary from one building to the next for reasons that are elusive. In contrast to the seemingly random locations of hearths in the synchronic settlement plan, from a diachronic perspective hearth locations are very regular. In deep sounding 4H/G, hearths tend to be rebuilt on the exact same spot in successive buildings. There is no functional reason why they should consistently remain in the same place within a room over many rebuilding phases. We know little about other interior arrangements, such as where food was stored or where people slept, but it is plausible that such uses of space were also reproduced when buildings were reconstructed.

To move beyond the idea that the exact reproduction of Aşıklı Höyük buildings, including interior arrangements, was important to people at the site, for reasons that do not seem to be exclusively functional, is difficult. One set of ideas that I find useful for conceptualising the possible meanings of building continuity at Aşıklı Höyük, however, is the opposition between 'hot' and 'cold' societies put forward by Lévi-Strauss.[96] In this distinction, hot societies embrace change as an essential part of their identity, whereas cold societies ideologically reject change and relate the present to a changeless originary past through myths. Hot societies have histories, whereas cold societies have a fixed and immutable past. An example of such a view of the past is provided by Bloch in a study dealing with the official history of the Zafimaniry in Madagascar that takes on a particular form, called 'Tantara', which

> tends to reduce events to exemplary tales where the moral structures of the society win against the requirement of transmitting information. Tantara does not abolish time but in it the passage of time is not cumulative, it does not

---

[93] Peters 1982: 226; Düring 2006: 63–64.
[94] Esin et al. 1991: 130; compare also Mellaart 1967: 67.
[95] Düring 2005.
[96] Lévi-Strauss 1973: 39–42; Gell 1992: 23–29; Bloch 1998.

lead to a succession of new unique events, rather in Tantara the past is seen as precedent.[97]

This kind of relation to an immutable past might explain why building continuity was important to people at Aşıklı Höyük if these buildings were indeed a manifestation of the past as a precedent for the present.

4.4.5 Aşıklı Höyük Burials

About 70 burials have been found at Aşıklı Höyük, all located beneath building floors. They were placed in cuts dug through the floors that were subsequently patched, most likely during the occupation of buildings. All burials seem to be primary. Most graves contained single inhumations, but some double burials were also recovered. The bodies were in a variety of postures and had diverse orientations. Some burials contained necklaces or bracelets made up of beads produced from shell, stone, deer teeth, and copper.[98] Remarkably, about half of the burials show signs of burning.

Given a total of 400 rooms excavated at Aşıklı Höyük, it is clear that the 70 burials found represent a sample of the people who lived at the site.[99] Many rooms were excavated only to their uppermost floors, and it is possible that more burials await discovery. However, in sounding 4H/G burials were also scarce: Only four burials were found in the 65 rooms dating to levels 2J–B. While many of these rooms were not completely excavated, it is clear that only a minority of the buildings had burials associated with them.[100] About 80 per cent of the rooms with burials also contained hearths,[101] suggesting that such rooms were considered more appropriate than others for interring the dead. If these were indeed living rooms on which household groups were centred, there might have been a symbolic link between burials and households, a social group otherwise weakly articulated at Aşıklı Höyük. Further, about half of the burials show signs of burning and must have been exposed to fire at some point during or prior to the burial, reinforcing a symbolic link with hearths.

The criteria operating behind the selection of people to be buried on site are elusive. The burial record at the site includes all age categories and

---

[97] Bloch 1998: 108
[98] Heat-treated copper has likewise been found at the Aceramic Neolithic site Çayönü, in southeastern Turkey, and in Çatalhöyük, dating to the Ceramic Neolithic (Esin 1995; Schoop 1995). Such finds show that the later period designation 'Chalcolithic' has become problematic, and should be understood as a period designation rather than as a stage when copper is first worked.
[99] Esin and Harmankaya 1999: 126; Esin and Harmankaya 2007: 265.
[100] Düring 2006: 86–89.
[101] Özbaşaran 1998: 560.

both sexes.[102] It might be the case that people were buried on site primarily
to represent a particular social group, and that the reason for burying a
specific person may have had more to do with the season of death and the
social needs of a household or other group than with the particular person
being buried.

4.4.6 Neighbourhoods at Aşıklı Höyük

The buildings at Aşıklı Höyük were constructed in tight clusters, without
streets or alleys separating the structures. Although buildings were mostly
rectangular, many buildings were modified to fit the specific conditions of
their location. This explains why many structures are trapezoidal in outline
or have rounded walls.

The neighbourhoods were densely occupied, and in many areas every
available parcel of land was used. However, the building density is greatest at the outer edges of the neighbourhoods at the interface with streets
and alleys, where buildings were constructed in a solid façade, whereas the
neighbourhoods are much more open at the interface with midden area JA
and in their centres (see Fig. 4.3). These characteristics shed some light on
the genesis of these neighbourhoods, which seem to have been constructed
as a more or less closed outer rim first, whereas the core of the neighbourhood developed subsequently in a more haphazard way. This path of
development may indicate that, first, the plot inhabited by a neighbourhood
was fixed rather than shifting from one period to the next – a point borne
out by what little diachronic evidence there is, which shows that the streets
separating these neighbourhoods were continuously in the same place;[103]
and, second, that the groups of people inhabiting these neighbourhoods
felt that creating a continuous outer edge was a priority.

Despite the fact that very large areas have been excavated at Aşıklı Höyük,
no complete neighbourhoods have been exposed. Nevertheless, is it possible
to make an estimate of the size of these neighbourhoods. For the most
complete neighbourhood excavated we can estimate about 90 rooms, of
which 30 were living rooms. If we correlate the latter with small households
groups of about five people, we arrive at an estimated 150 people for this
particular neighbourhood.[104]

Why were people at Aşıklı Höyük living in such spatially discrete neighbourhoods without streets? It is plausible that this form of spatial organisation was related to and reinforced a particular type of social association: that

[102] Özbek 1998.
[103] Esin and Harmankaya 1999: 124.
[104] For more details see Düring 2006: 97–101.

of the neighbourhood community. This argument can be based on, first, the uses to which the roofs were put and how these affected social interaction; and, second, the fact that people would have traversed the neighbourhood roofscape regularly on their way to and from their houses.

We know very little about the roofscape at Aşıklı Höyük. No collapsed roofs with possible features and/or artefacts on top have been reported for the site. Nonetheless, we can be confident that many activities occurred on these roofs for two reasons. First, relatively few features and artefacts were found within houses, and the roofs would have provided a convenient nearby venue where domestic activities could take place. Second, the thermal properties of mud buildings are such that buildings heat up slowly and subsequently retain their heat longer than their surroundings.[105] The effect of these thermal properties is that people across the Near East living in mud buildings spent a large part of the afternoon and early evening outside during the hot, dry part of the year. Commonly, the spaces used most intensively were those located closest to houses, such as courtyards and flat roofs.[106]

The Aşıklı Höyük roofs probably would have been more like courtyards than what we normally think of as roofs, featuring the entrance to the building below, with various goods and features present on the roofs and with people performing a range of activities on them during the hotter part of the year. Further, people moved across these roofs on their way to and from their houses. The pattern of movement probably would have been influenced by factors such as age and gender, as well as climatic factors. Children, for instance, might have moved around the roofscape constantly, whereas elderly people and infants would have been more restricted in their movements.

Taking these two factors together – the use of the roofs at Aşıklı Höyük and the movement of people across the roofscape – it is clear that interaction within these neighbourhoods would probably have been intense. It can be posited that people inhabiting these roofscapes formed a social collectivity grounded in shared activities and built upon personal relations, shared experiences, and face-to-face interactions.

Keeping this pattern in mind, we can return to the question of why buildings were constructed in streetless neighbourhoods at Aşıklı Höyük. The spatial organisation of the neighbourhoods deterred non-residents from entering them, making the neighbourhood a communal rather than a public arena. At Aşıklı Höyük and other sites of the Central Anatolian Neolithic this is achieved by the complete abolishment of streets and exterior

---

[105] Aurenche et al. 1997: 79; Facey 1997: 70–74.
[106] Peters 1982: 223; Friedl and Loeffler 1994: 33; Van Beek 2008.

doors, but there are other ways of achieving a separation of resident and outsiders.

In particular, I would like to refer to traditional Arab-Islamic settlements, in which a distinction can be drawn between wide, straight public streets, open to the public at large and dominated by men, and narrow, winding streets within neighbourhoods that were not accessible to non-residents, in which women could roam more freely.[107] Another feature often associated with Arab-Islamic settlements is a division into relatively autonomous neighbourhoods. It has been noted that the groups living within these neighbourhoods often defined themselves as a corporate group.[108] People were often deeply involved with each other and closely monitored the behaviour of other residents, and outsiders were barred from entry unless invited.[109] For this system to work it is essential that neighbourhoods do not become too large, in which case such social control can no longer function.[110]

This model of a neighbourhood community living in a spatially segregated part of the settlement and policing their neighbourhood from outsiders is one that seems to fit the evidence at Aşıklı Höyük and provides a good explanation for the particular settlement form encountered there.

4.4.7 The Local Community at Aşıklı Höyük

Estimating populations of prehistoric settlements is problematic because key data, such as the settlement size at any one point in time, are usually not available. A Neolithic tell such as Aşıklı Höyük could accumulate as the result of shifting occupation, which would mean that the settlements might have been much smaller than the mound.[111] At Aşıklı Höyük, however, the building continuity documented in sounding 4H/G and elsewhere indicates that a pattern of shifting occupation probably does not apply. Thus, during the prime period of the settlement, most of the mound might have been occupied.

Aşıklı Höyük measures about 40,000 square metres,[112] about 10 per cent of which has been excavated. In the excavated area nearly 60 per cent was taken up by the clustered neighbourhoods, and approximately 60 living rooms were exposed. If we take these figures as representative for the

---

[107] Antoun 1972; Abu-Lughod 1987: 167–168; Wirth 2000.
[108] Antoun 1972; Wirth 2000.
[109] Abu-Lughod 1987.
[110] Antoun 1972: 111; Wirth 2000: 377–381.
[111] Hole 2000: 194–195; Akkermans and Schwartz 2003: 59–60; Verhoeven 2006.
[112] Esin et al. 1991: 126.

settlement as a whole, and assuming that living rooms index household groups of about five people, we would arrive at a maximum population of about 3,000. If we reconstruct 25 to 50 per cent of the site as not in use even during the period of maximum occupation, the estimates would fall to 1,500–2,250 people.[113]

This is a surprisingly large population for the earliest Neolithic settlement documented in Asia Minor. In neighbouring regions, the earliest Neolithic communities are often estimated to have been no larger than about 300 people: Such a figure has been put forward for Neolithic Cyprus, Greece, the Balkans, and the Marmara Region.[114] Large parts of the Fertile Crescent seem also to have been dominated by such villages, although there are larger communities there as well.[115]

That the Aşıklı Höyük community ran into the thousands is therefore notable. Further, the site does not seem to be part of a local settlement system. No contemporary settlements seem to have existed in the Aşıklı Höyük region. There are a number of 'satellite' settlements a few kilometres from the site, including the sites of Musular, Yellibelen, Acıyer, Sırçan Tepe, and Gedikbaşı/Kızılkaya, but these seem to either complete postdate Aşıklı Höyük or overlap with its latest occupation only.[116] It is possible that these sites were the results of a breakup of the Aşıklı community.

A settlement such as Aşıklı Höyük, with a large number of clustered neighbourhoods, might represent the contraction of a regional system of small settlements into a single large community.[117] In this respect, each neighbourhood is similar to the settlements with fewer than 300 people typically found in the early Neolithic in adjacent regions.

The question is, what held all these neighbourhood communities together? A variety of factors might have played a role, ranging from place-bound ideologies to sodalities crosscutting neighbourhoods, but there is one phenomenon at Aşıklı Höyük in particular that seems to relate to this level of social interaction.

In the southwestern part of the excavated area at the site, a large, monumental complex was found organised around courtyards HV and T (see Fig. 4.3). This complex is differentiated from the domestic buildings at the site in its scale: It is about 20 times larger than the normal buildings; in the use of distinct building materials and techniques; and in form: It contains both large open courtyards and narrow roams sandwiched between massive

---

[113] See also Düring 2006: 101.
[114] Halstead 1999: 89; Roodenberg 1999: 197; Peltenburg et al. 2001: 53; Perlès 2001: 178–180.
[115] Akkermans and Schwartz 2003: 58–60.
[116] Gülçur 1995; Balkan-Atlı 1998: 81; Özbaşaran 2000: 129.
[117] Düring 2006, 2007.

walls, which are not found elsewhere on the site. Apart from the complex associated with courts HV and T, there is a second possible complex of a similar nature, albeit significantly smaller in scale, in the northwest of the excavated area, centred around court MI, and due south of another broad street, MH (see Fig. 4.3). It is not clear how these two complexes related to each other and whether they were contemporaneous or not.

The most important components of these monumental complexes are their courtyards. These were elaborated in various ways: Court T was painted in various colours over the course of several rebuildings, and had a large, round hearth of a type not found elsewhere in the settlement and benches along its edge; court HV was paved with mud slabs and probably had some sort of colonnade.

It is highly plausible that gatherings of some sort took place in these courtyards. Given that the complexes do not appear to be associated with any one particular neighbourhood, it seems likely that these gatherings included participants from various neighbourhoods and thus helped to create links that crosscut the neighbourhood communities. It can be estimated that up to 340 people could have participated in gatherings in court HV, whereas meetings in courts T and MI would probably have included 30 to 40 people.[118] However tentative these estimates may be, it is clear that the courts are too small to accommodate the entire local community and that only select individuals could take part in the gatherings that occurred there. Further, all these courts are surrounded by massive walls without doors, suggesting that access to them was restricted.

In Aceramic Neolithic sites of the upper Fertile Crescent such as Çayönü, Jerf el Ahmar, and Nevali Çori, public buildings have been found that are in some respects similar to the monumental complexes found in Aşıklı Höyük: They are distinct from domestic buildings in location, type, and construction techniques. These buildings consist primarily of a large rectangular room or court and they probably hosted gatherings of selected people, perhaps an elite.[119] Many of these buildings abound with stone sculptures depicting both animals and humans. At Çayönü the so-called skull building contained a large amount of assorted human skeletal remains. Other public buildings had stone slabs with blood residues on them, suggesting that offerings might have taken place.[120] Whatever the merits of these interpretations, it is clear that they cannot be transferred to the monumental complexes of Aşıklı Höyük, which differ in many respects from those in the Fertile Crescent. In particular, there is no clear link with burials or stone

[118] Düring 2006: 105–106.
[119] Hole 2000: 205; Verhoeven 2002: 245–248.
[120] Schirmer 1983; Loy and Wood 1989; Hauptmann 1993; Downs 1995; A. Özdoğan 1999.

sculptures at Aşıklı Höyük, and there is little to suggest that the monumental complexes were used primarily for ritual purposes. Nor is there any
evidence for elites at Aşıklı Höyük, although their existence also cannot be
excluded.

At the Aşıklı Höyük complexes, different groups might have gathered for
various purposes; for example, they could have served as a ritual nexus for
the community, a men's house, or a place devoted to initiation rituals or for
the celebration of festivals. Which of these functions are most appropriate
is impossible to determine. What seems clear, however, is that these meetings would have been important for linking the different neighbourhood
communities together.

4.4.8 Aşıklı Höyük and the Neolithisation of Central Anatolia

Aşıklı Höyük is the only systematically excavated Neolithic site of Asia
Minor dating to the early Aceramic period. For this reason, it is important for our understanding of the neolithisation of Central Anatolia. The
Central Anatolian Neolithic is often presented as an offshoot of that of
the Fertile Crescent.[121] However, the idea that Aşıklı Höyük represents a
transplanted cultural tradition is unconvincing for various reasons. First,
Aşıklı Höyük is culturally distinct from the Neolithic of the Fertile Crescent, differing in its chipped stone industries, its spatial organisation of the
settlement, and the form that public buildings take. In theory, some of these
differences could result from a 'bottle-neck effect' in which colonisation by
a small group can lead to the adoption of novel practices. However, the
completely distinct chipped stone industries are less plausibly explained in
such a model, given that these technologies are part of bodily practices that
are performed without much reflection. Further, there is good evidence
for continuity between local Epipalaeolithic and Mesolithic chipped stone
industries in the earliest levels at Aşıklı Höyük in the form of microliths.[122]
The situation at Aşıklı Höyük can be contrasted with the colonisation of
Cyprus during the Early PPN-B at around 8100 BC, when groups from the
Fertile Crescent colonised this previously unoccupied island, bringing with
them their material culture traditions and a suite of animals and plants.[123]

The originality of the Aşıklı Höyük assemblages and settlement and
the continuity of chipped stone industries with earlier lithic traditions do

[121] Yakar 1994: 25, 337; Cauvin 1997: 218; Binder 2002; Bar-Yosef 2007.
[122] Balkan-Atlı 1994b; Baird 2006a: 60–61.
[123] Peltenburg et al. 2001; Peltenburg and Wasse, eds., 2004.

not support a colonisation model, in which people from the Fertile Crescent moved to Central Anatolia to set up a new life there. On the other hand, there is little doubt that many of the domesticated plants found at Aşıklı Höyük ultimately derived from the Fertile Crescent, and the evidence from the obsidian sources demonstrates that there were frequent contacts between the two regions. Given these contacts, the distinctive nature of the Aşıklı Höyük settlement is all the more apparent, and it can be suggested that a cultural difference was consciously created and maintained by people in Central Anatolia.[124] In my reading of the evidence, local groups were stimulated by encounters with foreign goods and technologies and played a crucial role in the neolithisation process, although we cannot exclude the possibility that people from the Fertile Crescent opted into this alternative Neolithic, choosing to abandon their previous affiliation. Whatever the composition of the Aşıklı Höyük population, it is clear that this early Neolithic culture in Central Anatolia is highly original and cannot be seen simply as an offshoot of that of the Fertile Crescent.

4.5.1 The Central Anatolian Neolithic and Proto Indo-European

In a series of publications, it has been argued that there is a relation between the spread of farming from the Near East to surrounding regions and the spread of the Indo-European languages.[125] Indo-European languages include, amongst others, Germanic, Slavic, Latin, Iranian, and Baltic languages, as well as Celtic, Greek, Hittite, and Sanskrit. The oldest attested Indo-European language is Hittite, which was spoken from at least 2000 BC in Anatolia.[126] It is thought that all Indo-European languages originate from a common source labelled 'Proto Indo-European' (PIE).

The traditional consensus amongst scholars studying PIE is that it was spoken sometime around 4000 BC somewhere on the Eurasian steppe stretching from the Ukraine to Mongolia, and that it spread out of this zone in a series of waves over the course of several millennia and resulted in the known distribution of Indo-European languages.[127] By contrast, Renfrew and Bellwood have argued that Central Anatolia was the region where PIE was spoken around 8000 BC and that it spread with the Neolithic economy, which led to a demographic explosion of this group and an expansion to surrounding regions. Thus, if Renfrew and Bellwood are correct in their

---

[124] See also the discussion following Binder 2002.
[125] C. Renfrew 1987, 1996, 2000; Bellwood 2001, 2005.
[126] Mallory 1989.
[127] Mallory 1989: 143–185; 1997; Nichols 1998.

hypothesis, Aşıklı Höyük would be the first site inhabited by PIE speakers, and the cultural differentiation between the Fertile Crescent and Central Anatolia would also have been linguistic.

At first sight, this thesis seems to hold great promise because a powerful mechanism operating behind the spread of Indo-European languages is provided: a demographic explosion of a relatively small group resulting in the widespread distribution of their language. Further, it may appear that this model – in which PIE was spoken in Neolithic Central Anatolia, whereas Semitic languages originated in the Fertile Crescent – fits nicely with the cultural differences between these two early Neolithic regions that can be deduced from their archaeological remains and suggests that language was yet another cultural phenomenon in this distinction.

Nonetheless, I am sceptical of the thesis put forward by Renfrew and Bellwood for various reasons. First, language spread does not necessarily involve the colonisation of landscapes following a demographic expansion of its speakers. There are a large number of historically documented language spreads, including those of Latin, Turkish, Mongolian, and Arabic, in which the number of people actually migrating was rather limited but in which various circumstances made the adoption of the new language advantageous.[128] While these 'imperial' examples may not be appropriate to Prehistory, they do show that language spreads do not necessarily involve large-scale demographic changes and that domination by foreign elites can effect language spreads.

A second problem with the Renfrew–Bellwood model is that it does not fit the available linguistic data: "Most Indo-Europeanists insist on a number of independent movements scattered over centuries to account for the distribution of Indo-European languages."[129] To take one example, it is clear that Armenian established itself as the major language of East Anatolia only in the first millennium BC, replacing Urartian, about five millennia after the emergence of farming.[130] From this single case, and from many more that could be listed,[131] it is clear that, at least in some cases, factors other than the farming dispersal were at play in the spread of Indo-European languages.

A third problem with the Renfrew–Bellwood model is the documentation of non-Indo-European groups in Anatolia and Greece that appear to be more autochthonous than Hittites, Greeks, and other groups. Renfrew argues that these languages either co-existed with Indo-European or

---

[128] Nichols 1998; Campbell 2002.
[129] Campbell 2002: 52.
[130] Mallory 1989: 178.
[131] For example, the case of the Tocharians in central Asia.

entered these regions later. However, on the basis of names of places and people, the precedence of these languages can be clearly established.[132]

Finally, there are problems with the thesis that PIE can be dated to the Early Holocene.[133] On the basis of 'glottochronology', that is, the rate of language change, it has been estimated that PIE dates to about 4200–2400 BC.[134] This compares well with a study of PIE vocabulary, which included words such as 'wagon', 'horse', 'wool', 'yoke', and 'plough', indicating a date no earlier than the fourth millennium BC, given that both domesticated horses and wagons first appear at sites dating to that period.[135]

On balance, the hypothesis that Indo-European originated in Central Anatolia and spread along with the dispersal of farming is not convincing. The model can only be upheld if important components of the PIE puzzle are either ignored or misrepresented. More fundamentally, we should ask if archaeologists should try to correlate archaeological phenomena, such as the spread of farming or particular types of artefacts or burials, with language distributions. I concur with the view put forward recently: "Linguists cannot associate an archaeological culture with words, syntax, and grammar, and archaeologists cannot make their sherds utter words."[136] While the origins of Hittite-speaking groups (and those speaking related languages such as Luwian and Palaic) around 2000 BC in Anatolia remains an enigma, it is doubtful that archaeology can shed much light on this topic, which will be taken up further in Chapter 7 (§7.1.2).

4.6.1 Boncuklu Höyük

Apart from the Aşıklı Höyük evidence, we know surprisingly little about the earliest Neolithic in Central Anatolia due to a lack of research. In 2006, however, excavations began at the site of Boncuklu, in the Konya Plain, with occupation levels probably dating to about 8500–7500 BC. Although only a few preliminary reports have been published,[137] it is clear that the site will be of great importance in the study of Anatolian Prehistory.

At Boncuklu Höyük, mud buildings were found with rounded corners, and in some cases with posts along the interior edge of the wall. These buildings were typically constructed over an older predecessor: In one case, six buildings in sequence have been documented. Thus, building continuity,

---

[132] Mallory 1989: 180.
[133] Renfrew 2000; Bellwood 2005.
[134] Mallory 1997; Nichols 1998: 255.
[135] Mallory 1989: 158; Nichols 1998: 255.
[136] Lamberg-Karlovsky 2002: 75.
[137] Baird 2006b, 2007, 2008, 2009.

as in other Neolithic sites in Central Anatolia, such as contemporary Aşıklı Höyük and later Çatalhöyük, was also significant at Boncuklu. The dead were interred in these buildings during their occupation, after which the buildings were patched. Inside the buildings at Boncuklu, floors seem to have been regularly replastered, and some were painted red or had remains of mats on them in the form of phytoliths. Reminiscent of later Çatalhöyük buildings is evidence for the partitioning of the interior of houses into compartments, some of which were associated with hearths and cooking, and were relatively dirty, whereas other were kept much cleaner and replastered more often. There are some indications that there were also plastered mouldings and wall paintings at the site.

In contrast to other excavated Neolithic sites, however, the buildings at Boncuklu were not organised in clustered neighbourhoods but appear to have been more or less free-standing. Likewise, midden areas seem to be much less circumscribed in their locations at Boncuklu. It is conceivable that settlement was more open because the community residing at Boncuklu was much smaller in scale, and that clustered neighbourhoods only occur in larger agglomerations.

Lithic industries at Boncuklu are reported to be similar to Pınarbaşı 'Mesolithic' industries dating to the ninth millennium BC. A common category of artefacts at Boncuklu consists of stones with incised decorations.

Although investigation at Boncuklu Höyük have only recently begun, it is already becoming apparent that this site differed in many respects from Aşıklı Höyük, which has so far been the typical site for the earliest Neolithic in Central Anatolia, suggesting that the Aceramic Neolithic might have been more diverse than is thus far evident.

4.7.1 The Later Eighth Millennium BC in Cappadocia

The later eighth millennium BC has been investigated both in Cappadocia and in the Konya Plain. As mentioned before, there are a number of satellite settlements surrounding the site of Aşıklı Höyük, including the sites of Musular, Yellibelen, Acıyer, Sırçan Tepe, and Gedikbaşı/Kızılkaya.[138] According to Balkan-Atlı, who analysed the chipped stone assemblages from these sites, Sırçan Tepe and Acıyer are probably contemporary with the latest occupation of Aşıklı Höyük, whereas Musular and Yellibelen probably postdate the Aşıklı sequence.[139] Given that all these sites seem to either completely postdate Aşıklı Höyük or overlap with its latest occupation only,

[138] Gülçür 1995; Özbaşaran 2000: 129.
[139] Balkan-Atlı 1998: 87.

it is possible that these sites were related to the breakup and dispersal of the Aşıklı community. Alternatively, they could have been special-purpose sites rather than settlements.

Musular is the only one of these sites that has been excavated.[140] It is located on a spur opposite the river from Aşıklı. Musular has relatively shallow archaeological deposits of about 80 centimetres, which are located in an ovoid depression in the bed rock. Generally speaking, the preservation of features is poor, and in many cases only parts of structures were found. Further, the site contains both strata dating to the Chalcolithic[141] and levels dating to the later eighth millennium BC, and the two are difficult to distinguish. As a result of these circumstances, much at Musular remains tentatively understood.

One of the most interesting structures at Musular consists of 'building A' (Fig. 4.5). This is a small square structure of about 6.5 by 6.5 metres, with a red-painted floor, raised benches, and post stands. The excavators compare these features with those at court T at Aşıklı Höyük and argue that building A served ritual purposes. However, building A also differs in many respects from court T at Aşıklı: It is not part of a large complex; it is not surrounded by stone walls, and the hearth found in building A is similar to the hearths in domestic buildings at Aşıklı Höyük. Nonetheless, there are other reasons for interpreting Musular as a special-purpose site. Botanical remains included both cultivated and gathered plants. Unlike at Aşıklı Höyük, where sheep and goats provided the staple meat source, the faunal assemblage at Musular is dominated by the remains of wild cattle. The abundant bovid bones have been interpreted as feasting remains. Further, there are differences in the chipped stone assemblages, with a relatively large proportion of arrowheads and scrapers when compared to Aşıklı Höyük. This has been interpreted as related to the hunting, slaughtering, and processing of cattle.[142]

A number of other structures have been found at Musular. Many of these take the form of stone walls, presumably foundations for mud architecture, but in all cases the buildings were incompletely preserved and no coherent plans could be obtained.[143] As a rule, these structures had only fragmentary floors preserved, and features such as hearths seem to be lacking.

A total of seven burials were found at Musular and a lower mandible. These burials include males, females, and one child. Two of the skeletons

[140] Özbek 1998; Özbaşaran 1999, 2000; Kayacan 2003; Duru and Özbaşaran 2005; Özbaşaran et al. 2007.
[141] A single radiocarbon date has been obtained from these Chalcolithic deposits, which dates to 5890–5770 BC (Özbaşaran et al. 2007: 278).
[142] Duru and Özbaşaran 2005; Özbaşaran et al. 2007.
[143] Özbaşaran 2000: 142.

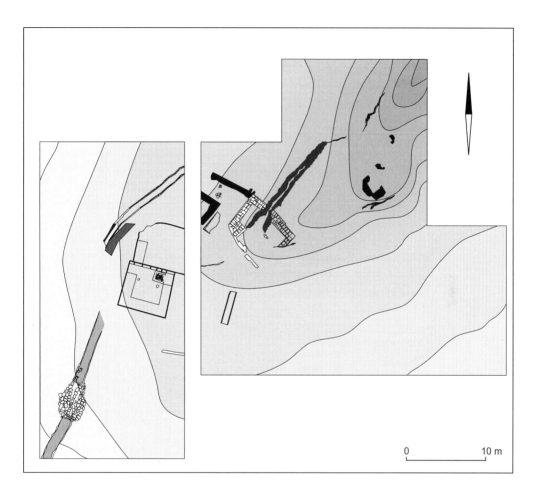

4.5 Plan of Musular. Reproduced with permission from Duru, G., and Özbaşaran, M. 2005. 'A "non-domestic" site in Central Anatolia'. *Anatolia Antiqua* 13: 15–28, fig. 2.

were buried in a stone wall, which was disturbed in the process, and subsequently the burials were covered with stones. Given that none of the burials have an associated burial pit or burial goods, it is uncertain to what period these graves date.[144]

Another class of features consists of a number of drains, some of which were flanked with walls and/or covered with flat stones on top (see Fig. 4.5). Finally, 'feature Z' consists of a linear bedrock ridge on each side of which the bedrock has been cut away approximately 40 centimetres. In the middle of this feature the ridge has been removed, and there is an oval stone pavement (see Fig. 4.5). It has been argued that this was an entrance of sorts to the settlement,[145] but this explanation is not very convincing. In truth,

---

[144] No signs of burning on the skeletons, often seen at Aşıklı Höyük, have been reported for Musular.

[145] Duru and Özbaşaran 2005: 18.

many of the features at Musular remain poorly understood, beyond the fact that many of them seem to have something to do with managing liquids of some sort.

4.7.2 The Later Eighth Millennium BC in the Konya and Karaman Plains

In the Konya Plain Survey, an increase from two to six sites has been noted from the Early Aceramic Neolithic to the Late Aceramic Neolithic, approximately 7500–7000 BC, and site sizes also increase in the late eighth millennium BC.[146]

A number of Late Aceramic Neolithic sites have been excavated. These include Canhasan 3, Suberde, and the deep sounding at Çatalhöyük. At the sites of Suberde and Çatalhöyük we know relatively little about this period. Suberde was excavated with a series of small test pits, so the overall structure of the settlement remains difficult to grasp. Only a few short publications have appeared,[147] and little is known about the artefacts found. Although Suberde was originally held to be a site used by hunters, more recently it has been argued that sheep and goats, comprising some 85 per cent of the faunal remains, were in fact herded.[148]

The more recent excavations at Çatalhöyük (see the next section) have been much more satisfactorily published. However, at this site, our understanding of the Late Aceramic period also remains limited. The area excavated, in a deep sounding on the southwestern slope of the mound, consists of a midden area. This sounding measured about 5.2 by 1.5 metres at the bottom and is 3.8 metres deep. A series of deposits and features predating the earliest building level XII were excavated and labelled pre-level XII-E to A.[149]

Pre-XII-E consists of a series a pits that had been cut through the natural surface for the extraction of clay or marl. Pre-XII-D consists of the predominantly alluvial fill of these pits. Pre-XII-C to A were midden deposits of various compositions. The most interesting features were found in level pre-XII-B: a number of areas with evidence of lime burning. These were probably for the production of lime floors, fragments of which were found in the same deposit. Lime floors are found at many Aceramic Neolithic sites in Anatolia, including Çayönü and Aşıklı Höyük.[150] At Çatalhöyük

---

[146] Baird 2006a: 65.
[147] Bordaz 1965, 1966, 1968, 1973.
[148] Perkins and Daly 1968; Arbuckle and Özkaya 2008.
[149] Cessford 2001, 2007a.
[150] Esin et al. 1991; Schirmer 2000; Cessford and Near 2006.

they have also been reported in an older deep sounding.[151] In later levels of Çatalhöyük lime floors became rare: Only one building with a red-painted lime floor was found.[152] In other respects that particular building was not exceptional, and this should serve as a reminder that buildings with 'elaborate' lime floors need not be interpreted as ritual buildings.

In terms of subsistence economy, the Aceramic Neolithic levels at Çatalhöyük are similar to later levels at the site. A range of domestic cereals and pulses have been documented alongside wild plant and tree food resources of various sorts.[153] Further, almost all animal remains found in these layers derived from wild animals, with the exception of sheep, which were domestic from the start.[154] Thus, it appears that the domestication of sheep occurred sometime between 7600 and 7400 BC – that is, between the end of the Aşıklı Höyük sequence, where sheep were herded but morphologically wild, and the start of the Çatalhöyük sequence – and that the transition remains to be documented.[155]

In the chipped stone industries a distinction has been drawn between the assemblages from pre-XII-C to B, on the one hand, and pre-XII-A, on the other, in which pre-XII-C to B have clear affinities with other Aceramic Neolithic sites in the region, such as Canhasan 3, Musular, and Suberde, whereas in pre-XII-A more local industries not identified elsewhere are found.[156] Examples of technologies similar to those at other sites include opposed platform and unipolar prismatic blades, large flake scrapers, stemmed points, and, more controversially, microliths.

Unfortunately, these claims are difficult to evaluate on the basis of the published data. The claim that the microliths at Çatalhöyük were *in situ* is especially questionable. These artefacts disappear from other sites in Central Anatolia after about 7500 BC and have not been documented at either Musular or Canhasan 3.[157] A total of 77 microliths were found in pre-XII-D and C.[158] It is possible that microliths were either residual, in which case they derive from older periods;[159] that these artefacts remained in use longer in the Çatalhöyük region than elsewhere; or that they were briefly taken into use again. Possible support for this last explanation is that

---

[151] Mellaart 1964: 73.

[152] Mellaart 1966a: 180–181.

[153] Fairbarn et al. 2005.

[154] Russell and Martin 2005: 69.

[155] A similar problem exists for the introduction of domestic cattle around 6000 BC, which will be discussed in Chapter 5.

[156] Carter et al. 2005a: 277. Here it should be noted that there are no other excavated sites contemporary with this part of the Çatalhöyük sequence, which makes this claim somewhat problematic.

[157] At both sites, dry sieving was a standard procedure.

[158] Carter et al. 2005a: 273.

[159] Baird 2002: 143; 2006a: 61.

the pre-XII microliths share few characteristics of the geometric, carefully produced, and standardised artefacts more typical of earlier periods, and they are much more haphazard in their shapes, production techniques, and retouches.[160]

The most comprehensive evidence for the Late Aceramic Neolithic in Central Anatolia derives from the site of Canhasan 3, despite that fact that investigations there were very limited in scope. An area of 20 by 30 metres was scraped, complemented by the excavation of a number of soundings to obtain a stratigraphic sequence.[161] Various domesticated cereal crops were documented, as well as wild plant and tree foods such as walnut, hackberry, grape, and prune.[162] Fauna remains included sheep, goats, cattle, deer, and others. Assemblages were too small to assess whether or not animals were domesticated.[163]

The chipped stone assemblages of Canhasan 3 have been differentiated from the industries at earlier Aşıklı Höyük and later, post pre-XII, Çatalhöyük.[164] In general, the chipped stone industries seem to be haphazard in nature, with little standardisation of core types, relatively few blades, and little standardisation in the tool categories. Some retouched bladelets (blades shorter than 5 centimetres) are present, but these do not show any clear types or geometries and are therefore not to be considered as microliths.[165] Of special interest among the chipped stone artefacts are about 30 points with incised geometric patterns, which are so far without parallels elsewhere. It is tempting to interpret this 'individualisation' of what appear to be arrowheads as evidence for group hunting practices, facilitating the distinction of stray arrows, but other interpretations could be put forward with equal validity.

The settlement at Canhasan 3 consisted of mud buildings usually no larger than 25 square metres in size and containing one or two rooms (Fig. 4.6). Given that these spaces were not excavated, we know little about the uses to which they were put. The buildings were located adjacent to one another, and many were surrounded by neighbouring buildings. Thus, like the buildings at Aşıklı Höyük, they must have been accessed by ladders from roofs.

Within the scraped area at Canhasan 3 there are two narrow alleyways that connect to large square courtyards. It is plausible that these courts served as points of entry to the roofs, where ladders would have been

---

[160] For Canhasan 3 see Ataman 1988: 155.
[161] French 1970a; French et al. 1972; Payne 1972; Hillman 1978.
[162] French et al. 1972; Hillman 1978.
[163] Payne 1972.
[164] Ataman 1988: 255.
[165] Ataman 1988: 155.

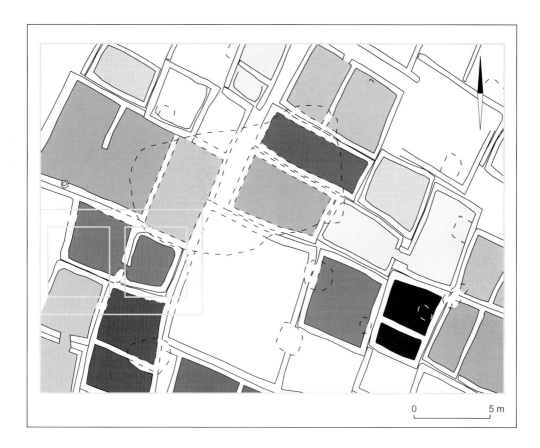

positioned that gave access. Buildings that were located along open spaces also seem to have been accessed via their roofs rather than through doors, mirroring the situation at Aşıklı Höyük and Çatalhöyük, although without excavations we cannot be confident about this.

Little is known about the overall spatial organisation of the Canhasan 3 settlement and whether, as at Aşıklı Höyük, it was subdivided into clustered neighbourhoods. With its size of about 1 hectare, the site is about four times smaller, and its population probably ran into the hundreds rather than the thousands.[166]

To summarise this section, it is clear that due to a combination of circumstances, we know frustratingly little about the Later Aceramic Neolithic in the Konya and Karaman plains. The prime reason for this situation is that archaeological research has been limited to small excavation areas or scraped surfaces, although better publications of the data obtained would also have been helpful. Notwithstanding this paucity of data, it is clear that this is an

4.6 Plan of Canhasan 3. Produced by the author and Medy Oberendorff with permission of D. French. In French, D., Hillman, G. C., Payne, S., and Payne, R. J. 1972. 'Excavations at Can Hasan III, 1969–1970'. In *Papers in Economic Prehistory*, edited by E. S. Higgs, pp. 181–190. Cambridge, England: Cambridge University Press, fig. 4.

[166] Düring 2006: 124–125.

important period in the Neolithic of the area in which domestic sheep and goats first appear on the scene; settlements continue to take the form of close clusters of buildings accessed from the roof; and the antecedents of the better-known main occupation of the site of Çatalhöyük, to which we now turn, are to be sought.

4.8.1 Introducing Çatalhöyük

Çatalhöyük was initially recognised during a survey of the Konya Plain in 1958 by Mellaart, French, and Hall. They were surprised that this large mound, measuring approximately 275 by 450 metres and standing 17 metres above the plain, dated exclusively to the Neolithic.[167]

Mellaart began excavations at Çatalhöyük in 1961, and successive excavations took place in 1962, 1963, and 1965. Large areas and a substantial number of buildings were excavated (approximately 4,300 square metres and 400 rooms). Mellaart produced a series of articulate reports for both the general public and the academic community. A monograph on the site was published in 1967, only two years after the last campaign. Çatalhöyük became one of the most famous archaeological sites in the world due primarily to the spectacular discoveries made there. These include, first, a corpus of vivid imagery in the form of wall paintings, mouldings applied to interior wall surfaces, and figurines; second, a large number of well-preserved intramural sub-floor burials, some of which were buried with valuable grave goods; and third, a large settlement of a type that seemingly lacked a public domain.

In 1993 a second project was started at Çatalhöyük, directed by Ian Hodder, and is scheduled to last for 25 years. This project differs in many respects from the earlier excavations. It is a large-scale project involving a substantial field team, often numbering over 100 participants, and with great financial resources. The financial resources of the Çatalhöyük Research Project allow for meticulous excavation practices involving elaborate documentation and sampling procedures and employing a suite of analytical methodologies, such as micro-morphology, heavy residue analysis, and chemical analysis, that allow for the extraction of a wealth of fine-grained contextual data to a degree that would have been inconceivable in the 1960s.

Excavations have been undertaken in a number of areas across the site, including the southwestern flank where Mellaart had worked before (Fig. 4.7). The new excavations at Çatalhöyük have largely confirmed and augmented the site stratigraphy developed earlier by Mellaart, who

[167] Mellaart 1967: 27.

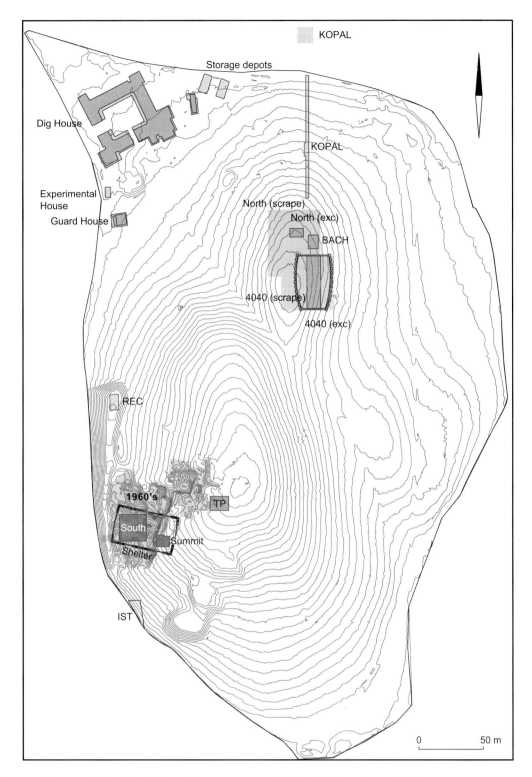

4.7 The mound of Catalhoyuk East with excavation areas. Produced by the author and Medy Oberendorff after fig. 5.2 in Pollard, T., Shell, C. A., and Twigg, D. R. 'Topographic survey of the Çatalhöyük mounds'. In *On the Surface: Çatalhöyük 1993–95*, edited by I. Hodder, pp. 59–72. Cambridge, England: MacDonald Institute. With permission of the Çatalhöyük Research Project.

distinguished 15 building levels, numbered from top to bottom O–XII. Level VI was later subdivided into VIA and VIB, VIA being more recent. To these we can now add the pre-XII E–A levels. Levels XII to VI are usually assigned to the Early Ceramic Neolithic and can be dated between roughly 7000 and 6400 BC. Levels V–O belong to the Late Ceramic Neolithic, to be dated between about 6400 and 6000 BC.[168]

The Early and Late Ceramic Neolithic at Çatalhöyük differ in many respects.[169] Changes occur in lithic industries,[170] figurine typology and gender,[171] and ceramic traditions.[172] Further changes can be noted in the wall painting motifs,[173] in the moulded features and installations,[174] in the configuration of settlement space,[175] and in the value attached to building continuity.[176] In this chapter the focus is on the evidence from levels XII to VI at Çatalhöyük; the later levels will be discussed in the next chapter.

4.8.2 The Ecology of Çatalhöyük

Çatalhöyük is situated on the Konya Plain, along the eastern bank of the former Çarşamba River. Opposite the now dry riverbed is another mound, known as Çatalhöyük West, which was occupied in the Early Chalcolithic period.

The Konya Plain is one of the most arid environments of Anatolia, with precipitation of 200–300 millimetres per annum. It is a marginal zone for rain-fed agriculture. At present, the area is irrigated in order to secure continuous productivity.[177] The general climatic history of Central Anatolia suggests that the climate was more or less similar to that of the present in the Neolithic, although it is possible that between 10,000 and 6000 BC the climate was somewhat more temperate, which could have made a marked difference for rain-fed agriculture in this landscape.[178]

Geomorphologists working on the reconstruction of the surroundings of Çatalhöyük have concluded that the site was located at the centre of an active alluvial fan and was flooded on a regular basis, most likely in spring following

---

[168] Özbaşaran and Buitenhuis 2002; Cessford 2005a.
[169] Düring 2001; 2002.
[170] Conolly 1999b.
[171] Hamilton 1996: 225; Voigt 2000: 287.
[172] Mellaart 1966a: 170; Last 1996: 118.
[173] Mellaart 1967: table 13; Voigt 2000: 287; Düring 2006: 192–195.
[174] Todd 1976: 50; Düring 2006: 195–201.
[175] Düring 2001; 2006: 235–245.
[176] Düring 2005; 2006: 218–229.
[177] Roberts 1990.
[178] Zeist and Bottema 1991: 124–125; Bryson and Bryson 1999; Woldring and Bottema 2001/2002: 16–18.

the melting of snow in the Taurus Mountains.[179] In the surroundings of the site, stagnant marshes would have formed. Indeed, salt-loving plants and marsh plants have been documented on site,[180] and fish, frog, and waterfowl bones have also been found.[181] In this marshy landscape there were some hummocks on which riparian tree stands could be found. To the north of the river fan, a steppe zone existed that supported some dispersed shrubs, and to the south, along the Taurus foothills, oak-park woodlands could be found.[182] An important landscape element is a sandy ridge located approximately 12 kilometres south of Çatalhöyük. Historically, this ridge was one of the first to be used for rain-fed farming because it is suitable for agriculture.

By contrast, it has been argued that the back swamp soil surrounding Çatalhöyük in the Neolithic was ill suited for farming.[183] Some researchers have suggested that the people at Çatalhöyük were mainly using the sandy ridges located 12 kilometres away for farming[184] rather than the more immediate surroundings. It appears from the phytolith morphology of *Triticum dicoccum* that this crop was grown, at least in part, on dry land, which has been interpreted as possible proof for this hypothesis.[185]

The idea that Çatalhöyük was located in an area unsuitable for agriculture is not completely convincing. Although it is clear that at least some of the cereals were grown on dry lands, it does not follow that they were grown on the sandy ridges. It is possible that water management was practiced in the surroundings of the site, creating dry patches suitable for farming. Further, cereals might have been of secondary importance, with tubers and pulses being more prominent.[186] These species tend to preserve less well but are nonetheless documented in considerable quantities.[187] Pulses in particular could have been suited to the wet environment, as they could be planted in late spring after the floods had receded.[188]

Whatever the precise characteristics of the agriculture practiced at Çatalhöyük, many specialists are convinced that the site was in a sub-optimal location.[189] Nor is it possible to explain the positioning of the site on the

---

[179] Roberts et al. 1996; Baird 2002: 145; Asouti 2005: 245; Boyer et al. 2006.
[180] Helbaek 1964: 123; Fairbarn et al. 2005.
[181] Martin et al. 2002; Russell and McGowan 2005.
[182] Asouti 2005: 249.
[183] Roberts et al. 1999; Asouti and Hather 2001: 27–28; Fairbarn et al. 2002: 49.
[184] Asouti and Fairbarn 2002: 188, note 19; Fairbarn et al. 2005: 183; Rosen 2005: 210–211; Rosen and Roberts 2006.
[185] Rosen 2005: 210–211.
[186] Molleson and Andrews 1996.
[187] Asouti and Fairbarn 2002: 185; Fairbarn et al. 2002: 44–45; Fairbarn et al. 2005: 173–174.
[188] Asouti and Fairbarn 2002: 188, note 19; Fairbarn et al. 2002: 49.
[189] Asouti and Fairbarn 2002: 188, note 19; Fairbarn et al. 2005: 183; Rosen 2005: 210–211; Rosen and Roberts 2006.

basis of landscape morphology: There are no distinct morphological features that might have given the site special prominence or meaning.[190]
Thus, the location of Çatalhöyük in the landscape is somewhat enigmatic.

The initial reasons for settling at this particular spot most likely differed from later motives for maintaining the settlement. The history of the
site is of some importance here.[191] During the Late Aceramic Neolithic,
Çatalhöyük was one of many small settlements in this region. In the subsequent Early Ceramic Neolithic, the site seems to have grown at the expense
of other pre-existing sites in the region, which disappeared altogether.
Given these circumstances, it could be suggested that social and ideological
factors, as well as economic and ecological factors, may have been important
for the formation of this Neolithic community.[192]

4.8.3 Botanical and Faunal Remains at Çatalhöyük

Through a programme of comprehensive sieving and analysis, a large range
of botanical remains have been recognised at Çatalhöyük.[193] These relate
to a variety of activities, including the production of mats, ropes, clothes
and baskets, building practices, and firing pottery, as well as subsistence and
heating. Dung was in use along with wood as a source of fuel, and through
the charred remains of dung, much information about the environment and
the grazing of animals can be obtained.[194]

One category of macro-botanical remains consists of wood and charcoal.
In exceptional cases complete beams were preserved,[195] but small charcoal
fragments are more ubiquitous. The most common species are juniper,
oak, pistachio, and elm.[196] Various plants were used for the production
of mats and baskets.[197] In addition, it is plausible that flax was grown to
produce some of the textiles found in the 1960s.[198] Another interesting plant
that should be mentioned is the date palm (*Phoenix dactyliferan*), of which
phytolith remains were found in no fewer than nine different samples.[199]

---

[190] Roberts et al. 1996: 39.
[191] Baird 2002: 149; 2006a.
[192] Hodder 2005: 6–12; Baird 2006a.
[193] Fairbarn et al. 2005.
[194] Fairbarn et al. 2005: 180–181. Given the fact that sheep and goats were the only domestic
      herd animals kept by people at Çatalhöyük, it is probable that this dung derived from
      sheep. See Anderson and Ertug-Yaras (1998) for a recent example from Central Anatolia
      of using sheep dung for fuel.
[195] Mellaart 1963a: 52.
[196] Asouti and Hather 2001.
[197] Fairbarn et al. 2005.
[198] Mellaart 1964: pl. 24; Ryder 1965; Vogelsang-Eastwood 1988; Fairbarn et al. 2005: 174.
[199] Rosen 2005: 207.

These were probably part of basketry or cordage imported from Syria or beyond.

Agriculture was of prime importance in the subsistence economy of Çatalhöyük. About 75 per cent of the calorific value of the charred seeds derived from domestic crops,[200] which include various species of wheat, naked barley, domestic rye, bitter vetch, lentil, pea, and chickpea.[201] It has been suggested that pulses and tubers may have been the major food source at Çatalhöyük.[202] Apart from agricultural crops, the collecting of a variety of wild plant resources, including hackberry, almond, plum, acorn, and fig, played a substantial supplementary role at Çatalhöyük.[203]

Recent research on the Çatalhöyük faunal remains has substantially altered the interpretations put forward on the basis of the earlier Mellaart excavations. For instance, in the 1960s work, the predominant species represented in the faunal assemblage were cattle.[204] By contrast, the recent data show that sheep and goat bones are far more common than those of cattle.[205] This difference probably reflects different sampling methods: In the older excavations, hand picking by workers resulted in a bias towards larger cattle bones, whereas at present, all excavated soil is sieved in order to retrieve the full spectrum of macro-botanical, faunal, and artefactual inclusions.

On the basis of the 1960s faunal remains, Perkins[206] argued that bovines were domesticated at Çatalhöyük. At that time, these were the earliest domesticated cattle known from the Near East, and Anatolia became the 'centre' for cattle domestication in secondary sources. Although this interpretation was challenged by Ducos,[207] the new research has been instrumental in discrediting the domestic status of cattle at least in the early levels XII to VI.[208] This issue is also of importance given the role cattle play in the symbolic imagery of the site.

Faunal remains from a large range of animals have been recognised at Çatalhöyük, including, first, domestic species such as sheep, goat, and dog; second, large hunted mammals, including cattle, pig, deer, ass, horse, and bear; and, third, a large variety of remains from small animals, including eggs, turtle shell, fish bones, and bones of various birds.

[200] Asouti and Fairbarn 2002: 187.
[201] Asouti and Fairbarn 2002: 183; Fairbarn et al. 2002: 44–45; Fairbarn et al. 2005: 141.
[202] Molleson and Andrews 1996.
[203] Asouti and Fairbarn 2002: 184; Fairbarn et al. 2002: 45; Fairbarn et al. 2005: 141–143
[204] Mellaart 1967: 223; Perkins 1969: 178.
[205] Martin et al. 2002: 200–201; Richards et al. 2003: 69; Russell and Martin 2005.
[206] Perkins 1969.
[207] Ducos 1988.
[208] Russell and Martin 2005.

Whereas sheep and goats were most common amongst the faunal remains, they do not represent the greatest calorific value. A bovid provides about 30 times more meat than a sheep or goat, and it is clear that the amount of cattle meat consumed was greater than that of sheep and goats. In some levels, equids also provide greater amounts of meat than sheep and goats.[209] Cattle bones are often found in large clusters in particular contexts – for instance, on the floor of a building subsequently abandoned and sealed. For that reason, and given the large amount of meat provided by butchering cattle, it has been posited that cattle meat consumption was primarily a feasting activity. The same was probably true for equids. By contrast, the more amenable sheep and goats seem to have been a part of the more ordinary diet.[210]

4.8.4 Çatalhöyük Assemblages

The chipped stone industries of Çatalhöyük consist almost entirely of obsidian (usually more than 95 per cent). This material was obtained primarily from two Cappadocian sources: Nenezidağ and Göllüdağ.[211] A considerable complexity in the chipped stone industries has been reconstructed, with up to six distinct industries in operation at any one time.[212] However, from a typological perspective, the Çatalhöyük chipped stone industries appear to be much simpler, with relatively irregular multi-platform cores in the early levels, and highly standardised bullet cores for the production of long prismatic blades, with pressure flaking appearing from level VI onwards (Fig. 4.8). These cores were used for the production of flakes and blades, respectively, and were in part reworked into oval or shouldered points, often completely retouched, and large, finely retouched daggers. Other tools include scrapers on large flakes, large retouched obsidian flakes used for cutting, and obsidian mirrors.[213]

Both in the Çatalhöyük buildings and in the midden areas debitage was rare, suggesting that much of the knapping took place elsewhere. Conolly has distinguished a major change in lithic industries in the Çatalhöyük assemblage. In levels XII to VII, most artefacts were produced on flakes struck from irregular multi-platform cores, using direct percussion. From level VI onwards, most artefacts were produced from pressure-flaked prismatic blades deriving from 'bullet' cores. This technique requires

---

[209] Russell and Martin 2005: 46.
[210] Russell and Martin 2005: 96.
[211] Carter et al. 2005b.
[212] Carter et al. 2005a.
[213] Conolly 1999a: 33–57.

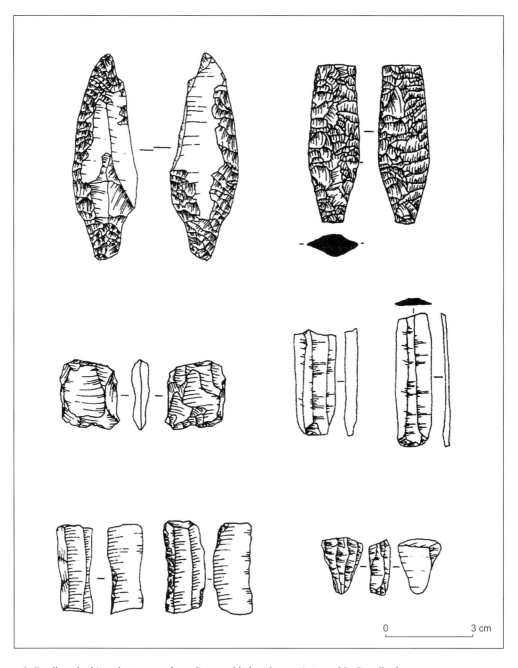

4.8 Çatalhöyük chipped stone artefacts. Reassembled with permission of J. Conolly from Conolly, J. 1999. *The Çatalhöyük Flint and Obsidian Industry: Technology and Typology in Context.* Oxford, England: Archaeopress, figs. 3.4, 3.8, 4.1, 4.8, and 4.11.

considerable skill and is interpreted by Conolly as evidence for craft specialisation.[214]

A peculiar type of deposit often encountered in the Çatalhöyük excavations is obsidian caches, consisting of small pits below floors containing large amounts of obsidian. These caches contained large flakes and blades that were struck from opposed platform cores of the naviform type, a type of core not found at Çatalhöyük. It appears plausible that the caches contained imported half-fabricates awaiting further processing. However, some of the caches were never retrieved, and it has been argued that these were placed in buildings for symbolic reasons and were closely associated with hearths and cooking, hence the transformation of natural resources into cultural products.[215] Along with objects found in graves, these caches represent one of the few contexts at the site in which objects are regularly found *in situ*.

The Çatalhöyük pottery is amongst the oldest of the Near Eastern Neolithic.[216] Pottery has been found at Çatalhöyük from level XII onwards, which can be dated to about 7000 BC. What is particular about the Çatalhöyük pottery is its relative scarcity when compared to other find categories. *In situ* pottery is rare at Çatalhöyük. It is occasionally found in buildings and is absent from burials.[217] With a few exceptions, all the pottery derives from midden areas and is fragmented. These circumstances make it extremely difficult to assign functions to pots.[218]

Last distinguished four wares (groups) in the pottery and sees a technological shift around level VII; after that point, mineral temper becomes more common and sherds become thinner and better fired, and there is an associated shift from vegetal to mineral temper.[219] In the upper levels more complicated vessel shapes start to appear, such as rectangular box-shaped forms on legs. On the whole, pottery shapes are relatively simple and consist mostly of round bowls and oval jars. Carinated rims, feet, or handles are absent, but pierced lugs and ledge handles are sometimes present. Apart from some burnishing, decoration is absent in the pottery assemblage.

Hundreds of figurines have been found at Çatalhöyük in both excavation projects. These were made of both stone and clay and include a variety of motifs. Only a selection of the figurines found in the 1960s have been published, mostly of females with large breasts and buttocks, but these constitute only a small proportion of the figurines. Figurines capture a

---

[214] Conolly 1999b: 798.
[215] Conolly 2003: 71–74.
[216] Le Mière and Picon 1998: 11–22.
[217] Mellaart 1967: 208; Last 2005: 101.
[218] But see Hodder 2005: 12.
[219] Last 1996, 2005.

variety of human figures and animals, some human–animal combinations, and geometric shapes.[220] Some of the humanoid figurines are marked as female, while others lack such sexual characteristics and should perhaps not be gendered.[221] Sexless humanoids seem to have been made predominantly of stone and disappear after level VI. Clay figurines marked as females derive almost exclusively from the upper levels.[222] These female figurines are depicted in a variety of positions: squatting, standing, or lying on their stomach. Some were painted with geometric motifs; others seem to be wearing clothes. The faces of the figurines are highly stylised, and in most cases the hair of these women seems to have been done up in a kind of pigtail on top of the head.

A number of figurines are combinations of humans and animals. In most cases the humans seem to be sitting on top of an animal, but in some they are standing behind one. The latter combination seems to be particularly common with animals resembling leopards. These figurines also occur in some of the wall paintings – for instance, those of building F.V.1 (1960s).[223] Undoubtedly the most famous figurine of Çatalhöyük is the unique one found in building A.II.1 (1960s) of a female figure sitting on a sort of throne, with both arms resting on felines, possibly leopards. Between her legs is a vague protruding 'blob', which has been interpreted by Mellaart as a baby in the process of being born.[224] Another equally interesting female figure found more recently has large breasts and a large belly on the front and a skeleton on the back, seemingly representing both life and death (Fig. 4.9).[225]

Many of the humanoid figurines are headless. Some of these heads may have been deliberately broken, given that many were made of stone.[226] Other figurines were found intact, however. Animal figurines were not treated in the same manner: They were generally found complete, although they sometimes had signs of other forms of mutilation, such as stabbing.[227] Animal figurines represent mainly bovids, boars, dogs, and felines.[228] They

---

[220] Hamilton 1996, 2005a; Meskell et al. 2008.
[221] Kuijt and Chesson 2005.
[222] Hamilton 1996: 226; Voigt 2000: 287; Düring 2002: 221; Hamilton 2005a. Stone figurines do not disappear altogether (Mellaart 1963a: 93; 1964: 45), but they do become rare in the upper levels.
[223] The 1960s building designations will be distinguished by '(1960s)' from those more recently dug '(ÇRP)', and consist of area designations (in some cases omitted), followed by the level, followed by the building number.
[224] Mellaart 1963a: 95.
[225] Hodder 2006a, colour fig. 22.
[226] Hamilton 1996: 220; Talalay 2004; Verhoeven 2007.
[227] Mellaart 1962a: 51; Hamilton 1996: 223.
[228] Hamilton 1996: 223.

4.9 Figurine 12401.X7 from Çatalhöyük. Reproduced with permission. © Çatalhöyük Research Project. Photo by Jason Quinlan.

0   1 cm

are often produced with much less care than the human figurines, and it is possible that they were part of a completely different set of practices.

Like ceramics, figurines were completely absent from the Çatalhöyük burials. The figurines in all categories seem to have been found predominantly in midden areas and in buildings fills; most were broken, and *in situ* figurines are rare.[229] The interpretation of these items remains a difficult challenge in the absence of primary contexts.

Thirty-five clay stamp seals have been found at Çatalhöyük. The large majority of these seals have geometric motifs, the most common being meanders, waves, lozenges, and spirals. In 2003 a leopard-shaped figurine was found,[230] and in 2005 a bear-shaped figurine was located. The function of these seals is difficult to determine. No seal impressions have been found so far, and it is often thought that they were used to decorate textiles. The seals were found mainly in graves, building fills, and middens, and most derived from the upper levels (VII–I) at Çatalhöyük. In the cases of the leopard and bear figurines, the stamp motifs can be related to mouldings occurring on walls in earlier levels.

A large range of small finds has been encountered at Çatalhöyük. Personal adornments are an important category, including beads and bracelets made

---

[229] Hamilton 1996, 2005a.
[230] Türkcan 2005.

of stone, bone, and copper.[231] A variety of artefacts were made of bone, including awls, needles, spoons, belt fasteners, and even vessels.[232] A final category to mention here are clay balls, which have been found in large numbers at the site. These have various size and shapes and often show indications of having been used near fireplaces. Atalay argues that these objects were used for cooking, being placed in a hearth and subsequently in containers with liquids or roasting pits, and states that their importance declined with the development of pottery that was suitable for cooking on a fire in the upper levels (from level VII onwards) of Çatalhöyük.[233]

A remarkable group of objects found at Çatalhöyük consists of a number of burial goods made of organic materials. These were included in burials below a number of level VI houses. An intense fire that ravaged these buildings charred and preserved a range of objects that would normally have decomposed. Included are wooden vessels and boxes, textiles, and baskets. The woven textiles were most likely produced from linen.[234] Baskets of various shapes and sizes were also preserved, some of which ended up as

4.10 Reconstruction of the Çatalhöyük settlement. Reproduced with permission. © Çatalhöyük Research Project. Drawing by John Swogger.

---

[231] Mellaart 1964: 114; Hamilton 2005b; Russell 2005.
[232] Mellaart 1964: 84–85; Russell 2005.
[233] Atalay 2005.
[234] Helbaek 1963: 43; Burnham 1965; Ryder 1965: 176; Vogelsang-Eastwood 1988.

containers for burials.[235] In other contexts, baskets can often be recognised in fragile silica skeletons encountered during excavations.

One of the enigmatic characteristics of the Çatalhöyük domestic spaces is the near absence of querns and mortars at the site. In the 1995–1999 excavation seasons 359 pieces were found, but most of these are small curated fragments,[236] and Mellaart mentions only 10 of these objects in his reports. The main source for the production of ground stone artefacts seems to have been Karadağ, some 40 kilometres from the site. Compared to other materials brought to the site, this distance is not great, and it is possible that the role of grinding in food preparation was not as important as it was at other Neolithic sites.[237] Interestingly, a grinding feature was recently found in building 1 (ÇRP) and contained traces of ochre rather than food.[238]

4.8.5 The Çatalhöyük Settlement

In the early levels XII–VI the Çatalhöyük settlement consists of three types of spaces: first, buildings; second, enclosed open areas; and, third, unbounded open spaces (Fig. 4.10). As at Aşıklı Höyük, the buildings were generally built next to one another, so many structures could only be reached via adjacent roofs. Buildings generally have a large main room with a suite of domestic features, and some buildings have one or more subsidiary rooms, which are smaller and have different kinds of features.

Interspersed between the mud buildings are enclosed midden areas. The deposits in these middens seem to consist mainly of fine ashy deposits and domestic refuse, although occasional penning deposits are also encountered. The overwhelming majority of both artefacts and ecofacts found at Çatalhöyük come from the midden deposits. The following activities can be associated with midden areas:[239] first, the dumping of oven and hearth rake-outs; second, the dumping of other types of domestic refuse; third, dogs seem to have been kept in some of the middens; fourth, coprolites of humans have been found; fifth, in some midden layers there is evidence of animal penning.

Middens generally show evidence of a fairly rapid build-up of loose deposits with little disturbance by trampling. Thus, these midden areas would have been breaks in the settlement texture – sunken areas in which

---

[235] Mellaart 1964: pls. 22-a and 23-a; Wendrich 2005.
[236] Baysal and Wright 2005.
[237] Baysal and Wright 2005: 323–324.
[238] Cessford 2007b.
[239] Martin and Russell 2000; Bull et al. 2005; Matthews 2005; Russell and Martin 2005; Farid 2007a.

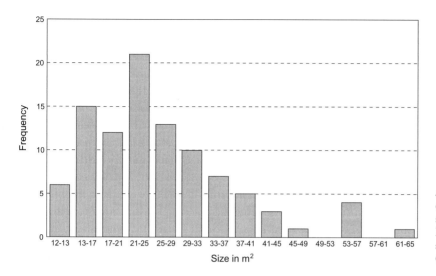

4.11 Spread of house sizes at Çatalhöyük. Produced by the author and Medy Oberendorff.

refuse was thrown and faeces were deposited and in which dogs were kept – and were not used much for domestic or group activities.

In contrast to these enclosed midden areas, there are continuous open spaces that separate the different neighbourhood clusters from one another at Çatalhöyük. These spaces vary in width from narrow alleys of only 1 metre to stretches more than 3 metres in width.

4.8.6 Domestic Buildings at Çatalhöyük

At Çatalhöyük buildings can be easily distinguished by the fact that they had their own sets of outer walls. Buildings differentiated in this manner are remarkably standardised and fall into a restricted size range of about 10 to 40 square metres, with an average of about 27 square metres (Fig. 4.11). The standardised dimensions could mean that these buildings all served similar purposes, most likely as household residences.

A few buildings at Çatalhöyük are much larger than the average. These are visible on the right-hand side of Figure 4.11. Such buildings contain many more rooms than is normal and their walls may have been poorly preserved, precluding accurate documentation. However, the exceptional nature of those larger-than-average buildings is clear, and as such, they emphasise the overall standardisation of building sizes at Çatalhöyük.

At the room level we can distinguish three categories at Çatalhöyük: first, 'living rooms', which contain fire installations (hearths and ovens), have one or more platforms, and average 21 square metres in size; second, 'ante-rooms', which do not have the combination of features found in living rooms and are contained within the same buildings as a living room, averaging 5 square metres in size; and, third, all rooms falling outside these categories, which have been classified as 'indeterminate', and unlike living rooms and anterooms have a size range beyond that of a normal distribution.[240]

The buildings at Çatalhöyük normally contain either a single living room or a single living room with one or two anterooms. There are, however, interesting exceptions to this norm. Among a total of 105 Çatalhöyük buildings analysed by me there are at least three cases of 'twin buildings', with two living rooms in the same structure, in some cases connected by interior doors or sharing an anteroom.[241] It seems, then, that although single-household residences were the norm at the site, there were some clear exceptions.

The interior furnishings of the buildings at Çatalhöyük form a consistent set of features, including hearths, ovens, compartments, and storage features, with a standardised spatial configuration and orientation of elements.[242] At the south end of the living rooms one typically finds hearths, ovens, the ladder entrance, storage features, and a relatively dirty compartment with remnants of cooking, heating, and craft practices.[243]

The fact that the buildings at Çatalhöyük each contained a living room with a standardised set of domestic features and sometimes additional anterooms would seem to suggest that they were economically independent entities and that economic pooling was focussed primarily on the household. Thus, in terms of both residence and economic pooling, the available evidence at Çatalhöyük points to relatively autonomous households.

The size of these households can only be estimated tentatively. Matthews has estimated the average household size at four.[244] If we apply cross-cultural estimates for roofed space per person[245] to the normal buildings at Çatalhöyük, it appears that they were probably large enough to have housed a nuclear family, with some potentially housing larger extended families.[246] Such cross-cultural estimates are problematic, however.[247] For example, Horne found that in Iran houses can have a more or less standard size, regardless of considerable variability in the size of the associated household.[248] Given these problems, what other light can be shed on household size at Çatalhöyük?

[240] Düring 2006: 166–170.
[241] Düring and Marciniak 2005: fig. 7.
[242] Mellaart 1967: 56–63; Hodder 1990.
[243] Matthews 2005; Düring 2006: 180–192.
[244] Matthews 1996: 86.
[245] Naroll 1962; Cook and Heizer 1968; Casselberry 1974.
[246] Düring 2006: 211–214.
[247] Byrd 2000: 80–81.
[248] Horne 1994: 158–159.

The average household size at Çatalhöyük can also be modelled on the basis of the number of compartments found within buildings. Mellaart postulated that some of these functioned as beds and estimated that the sleeping compartments would have accommodated a maximum of eight residents, while noting that the normal size of the group would have ranged from three to four.[249] A closer analysis of these platforms has demonstrated that those in the northeast and east were the most standardised in dimensions and would have been most suitable as beds.[250] Accordingly, it may be suggested that in the average living room, there would have been space for four to six people in the clean compartments on the north and east sides of the building.

4.8.7 Wall Paintings, Moulded Features, Installations, and Incorporations

The fame of Çatalhöyük rests to a large degree on the presence of, first, wall paintings and, second, moulded features and installations. Some of these features appear out of place in domestic buildings, and have led Mellaart to interpret buildings containing elaborate mouldings and wall paintings as 'shrines' rather than houses, a distinction I will return to later (§4.8.9).

Classifying the Çatalhöyük imagery is problematic. For example, some moulded features were also painted, blurring the distinction between wall paintings and mouldings. Likewise, it has been argued that moulded features with inset bone elements, on the one hand, and faunal elements incorporated into walls and floors, on the other, are difficult to distinguish.[251] Therefore, any classification of the Çatalhöyük 'art' is at most a heuristic tool for ordering the data.

The Çatalhöyük imagery has been the subject of many interpretative essays focussing on Neolithic symbolism and religion. In these studies, motifs and scenes from Çatalhöyük were interpreted using sources describing Aegean and Near Eastern mythology from the Bronze and Iron Ages;[252] as an example of the religion of the 'Mother Goddess';[253] as imitations of slit-tapestry weavings similar to 'kilims';[254] as depictions of hunting scenes or death rituals;[255] as representing the symbolic structures of the

[249] Mellaart 1967: 60.
[250] Düring 2006: 181–182.
[251] Last 2006; Russell and Meece 2006.
[252] Mellaart 1963a, 1964; Dietrich 1967; Mellaart 1967; Urbin-Choffray 1987; Cauvin 1997.
[253] Gimbutas 1991; Meskell 1998; Rountree 2001; Wunn 2001.
[254] Mellaart 1963a: 48–49; 1984; Mellaart et al. 1989.
[255] Mellaart 1964: 64; 1966a: 184–191; Clamagirand 2004.

Neolithic;[256] in a structuralist vein, representing a series of linked oppositions centring on male–female and nature–culture dichotomies;[257] and as
an example of shamanistic practices.[258]

All of these studies, except where specific motifs are treated in isolation, are based on two problematic assumptions concerning the Çatalhöyük
imagery. First, the Çatalhöyük imagery is held to constitute a unified, inter-
connected, and coherent corpus. Second, the images are often seen as a
direct and relatively straightforward reflection of the symbolism and religion of people at Çatalhöyük or even that of the Near Eastern Neolithic as
a whole. In such a perspective, the images represent a coherent code that
needs to be cracked by the annalist. This was most often done either by
comparison to later religions and myths in the Eastern Mediterranean or
through a structuralist analysis in which the aim was to identify a series of
linked oppositions in the various images of the site.

It not difficult to expose both of the basic assumptions on which these
studies rest as erroneous. Even a preliminary acquaintance with the material
suffices to show that the images are extremely diverse in terms of motifs and
that these motifs do not recur in fixed configurations. Instead, most motifs
occur during a restricted time span, and some can be linked to specific
buildings. Consequently, the idea that these images are a type of coherent text can be questioned.[259] Second, the comparison to later religions
and myths in the Mediterranean is problematic, because there is a temporal gap between about 6200 and 2000 BC separating the Çatalhöyük
imagery from myths and religion documented in historical sources, and such
long-term continuity in symbolic thought is highly implausible. Finally,
the methodology by which the structuralists have arrived at their series of
linked oppositions in their analysis of the Çatalhöyük imagery has been
criticised for ignoring certain configurations and relations and stressing
others.[260]

A more promising approach to the imagery of Çatalhöyük was proposed
by Last,[261] who argues that these images are best understood in the context of the practices and spaces in which they were embedded. In this view,
the focus should be on the ways in which images were produced and consumed rather than on some abstract symbolic system. For instance, many
paintings were plastered over not long after their production and became
embedded in the walls. Paintings were not primarily objects for display, but

---

[256] Hodder 1990; Cauvin 1997; Watkins 2004.
[257] De Jesus 1985; Hodder 1987, 1990; Forest 1993.
[258] Lewis-Williams 2004; Lewis-Williams and Pearce 2005.
[259] Last 1998: 359.
[260] Ellen 1986: 25; Carsten and Hugh-Jones 1995: 23.
[261] Last 1998, 2006.

they might have been produced to celebrate particular occasions, such as festivals or rites of passage,[262] in a manner akin to a Christmas tree. Both Last and Hodder have argued that wall paintings at Çatalhöyük may have been related to burial episodes.[263] While this model seems promising, much analytical work remains to be done to flesh out the argument.

The Çatalhöyük imagery was not ubiquitous. As Mellaart put it: "the idea of Çatal Hüyük presenting a picture gallery at any chosen time is clearly erroneous. Blank walls were the rule."[264] For example, the 187 wall paintings documented up to 1999 derive from a total of 437 rooms. Further, wall paintings were only briefly visible given that rooms typically had about 60 thick annual plasters and many additional washes applied in between.[265] By the same token, it is clear that only a sample of wall paintings are retrieved in excavations: It is physically impossible to peal off these plaster layers discretely.

The most common paintings are wall panels or floor compartments painted in a single colour. The next most common class is geometric motifs. These include rows of stylised hands, crosses, and squares, honeycomb motifs, and the so-called kilim motifs, consisting of triangular patterns superficially resembling woven fabrics.[266] Up to 1999, only 24 figurative scenes (about 13 per cent of the total) were found. These include two clearly defined motifs recurring in various buildings: 'vulture scenes' and 'hunting scenes'. The vulture scenes depict large vulture-like birds pecking at headless humanoids that are represented on a much smaller scale. The hunting scenes show a multitude of humans wearing leopard skins teasing wild animals represented on a much larger scale, such as bulls, stags, and wild boars. This motif was only encountered in buildings assigned to levels V to III. Other figurative motifs that have been reported include the so-called city plan;[267] an animal in silhouette; an abstract animal head; birds; various

---

[262] Boivin 2000.

[263] Hodder 1998; Last 1998: 371.

[264] Mellaart 2000: 38.

[265] Matthews 2005.

[266] Mellaart has argued that these paintings actually represent kilims: slit-tapestry weaves, and were a cheap alternative for the real thing, which he suggested was commonly produced and used at the site and hung on pegs along the walls (Mellaart 1962a: 59; 1963a: 48; 1964: 57; 1966a: 166; 1967: 152–155; 1984). This interpretation linked recent practices in Anatolia to those of the distant past and suggested a considerable antiquity for the tradition of producing kilims (Mellaart 1984). This interpretation raised a lot of interest amongst kilim dealers (Eiland 1993) but does not seem to be borne out by the evidence. The oldest evidence for slit-tapestry from Anatolia stems from the first millennium BC, from a Phrygian tomb that can be dated to ca. 735 BC (Maréchal 1985: 11), and the technology required for weaving kilims cannot have been in place before the Bronze Age. Moreover, the paintings interpreted by Mellaart as kilims often fail to make sense, because they cannot be produced without a kilim technology (Eiland 1993: 861).

[267] Mellaart 1964: 55, pls. 5-b and 6-a; Meece 2006.

Table 4.1 Occurrence of wall painting motifs in relation
to the levels at Çatalhöyük

Motifs	VIII	VII	VI	V	IV	III
Vulture	x	x				
Kilim	x	x	x			
Hands and honeycombs		x	x			
Hunt				x	x	x

human figures; stylised humans; goats; scenes with humans and animals; and finally, a possible 'splayed figure' (see below).[268]

Wall painting motifs at Çatalhöyük appear to be clustered in time and space (Table 4.1).[269] First, some motifs were present only in levels VIII–VI, whereas the hunting scenes were found only in the upper levels of the site. Second, some of the motifs seem to be spatially clustered. For instance, the rows of stylised hands and honeycomb motifs all occur within a few neighbouring buildings in the South Area. By contrast, the kilim motif is more widespread, and the hunting scenes do not show any clear spatial clustering. Third, there is a more than random pattern in which painted motifs recur in buildings in sequence. For instance, stylised hands arranged in horizontal rows occur in building VII.8 and its successor, building VI.8; kilim motifs occur in building VII.1 and its successor, building VI.1; and vulture scenes appear in building VIII.8 and its successor, building VII.8.[270] It is thus possible that some motifs might have been associated with particular buildings.

Paintings are found predominantly in living rooms at Çatalhöyük and are normally located in the northeast corner of the buildings. On the whole, paintings do not show a clear correlation with the presence of either burial or moulded features. Many paintings have been found in rooms lacking subfloor burials.[271] Thus, the link between burials and paintings postulated by Hodder and Last might work for particular motifs of wall paintings but not at a general level. Likewise, wall paintings do not correlate with the presence of moulded features in buildings: Only a quarter of the wall paintings occur in rooms with mouldings. Instead, more than half of the living rooms excavated in the 1960s at Çatalhöyük have evidence of wall paintings,[272] and in the new excavations wall paintings are even more common. It seems plausible that wall paintings are part of the normal set of practices that

[268] Mellaart 1962a: 59–60, pls. 12 and 13; 1963a: 49, 54, pls. 5-a, 5-b, and 8-b; 1964: 42, 70, pl. 14-b, figs. 4 and 24; 1966a: 176–177, pls. 35 and 36; 1967: table 13, 150.
[269] Russell and Meece 2006.
[270] All these buildings were excavated in the 1960s.
[271] Düring 2006: 201–210.
[272] Düring 2001; 2006: 192–195.

occur in every building at the site. In this respect, they can be contrasted to the moulded features and installations and the sub-floor burials at the site.

Some buildings at Çatalhöyük contained vivid three-dimensional sculptures and installations made from materials such as plaster, horns, and teeth. Most famous are animal figures in profile, animal heads with inset horns, and benches and pillars with inset horns. Cattle horns and teeth are often prominent in these features, but there are also many examples of faunal elements that were hidden rather than displayed.

Unlike the wall paintings that were visible only for a short while, many of the moulded features seem to have been present in the rooms for an extended period of time. Evidence for this consists of multiple layers of plaster and paint on many of these features. At present, similar evidence of reconstitution is lacking for the installations, such as horned pillars. Evidence of the dismantling of a horned bench has been found in building 44 (ÇRP), which was then replastered and converted to a normal bench.[273] Similarly, there is evidence of the removal of moulded features in some cases.[274]

The fact that some moulded features and installations were removed, combined with issues of preservation of walls and wall plaster, makes it difficult to estimate the number of these features. In the 1960s publications, 45 are documented in photographs or slides but many more are reported.[275] In the recent excavations, moulded features and installations have been found mainly in buildings 52 and 77.[276] The richest assemblages of moulded features and installations are found in burned buildings. An interesting question is whether these buildings are so rich in these features because they were burned, or whether these buildings had to be burned because they had been charged with so many of these features.

The moulded features at Çatalhöyük can be divided into, first, leopards in high relief; second, animals in profile in sunken relief; third, splayed figures; fourth, moulded animal heads; fifth, embedded horns and installations; sixth, round plastered protrusions containing faunal elements; and, seventh, incorporated bones.

A number of leopards depicted with their bodies in profile and their heads twisted towards the room have been found, often occurring in juxtaposed pairs.[277] These leopards often had many layers of plaster, and their spots were regularly repainted. Thus, these figures were probably present for a

[273] Jónsson 2004, 'South Summit Area, Excavation of Building 10' at http://www.catalhoyuk. com.
[274] Hodder and Cessford 2004.
[275] Düring 2006: 195–196.
[276] See 2008 Archive Reports at http://www.catalhoyuk.com.
[277] In buildings VIII.27; VII.44, which had a third, single leopard, on its east wall; its successor, VI.44; and, finally, VI.80 (Mellaart 1964: 42, pl. 2, fig. 5; 1966a: 176–177, 180, pls. 37–40; 1967: pls. 18–21).

considerable period of time. There is a second group of animals with their bodies in profile. These are two large animals in sunken relief on the north walls of buildings VII.8 (1960s) and VI.8 (1960s).[278] It is not clear whether these animals were carved or whether they were plastered differentially. The animal in building VI.8 was frequently replastered and was painted red in one episode; the one in building VII.8 was painted black.[279]

Amongst the most famous moulded features are the splayed figures,[280] often referred to as the 'Goddess'.[281] These figures are depicted with 'arms and legs' extending horizontally from the body and with the lower limbs bending up 90 degrees. The 'heads', 'hands', and 'feet' of these figures are invariably mutilated, which makes identification difficult. In one instance the head had rounded ears on top, which suggests an animal figure.[282] Another marked element in these figures is a navel-like feature on the stomach. Female organs such as breasts and vulva are absent. Thus, there are no features that suggest that these were human figures or, more specifically, females. A find of a figurine resembling the splayed figures throws a new light on the nature of this motif. This figurine clearly depicts a bear, complete with the prominent navel and the pointed ears that are typical of the moulded splayed figures (Fig. 4.12).

Another category of moulded features attached to walls at Çatalhöyük consists of plastered animal heads, with or without inset horns. They may occur in isolation or in horizontal or vertical configurations. Often these animal heads were repeatedly replastered and painted with geometric motifs.[283] Where horns were inserted into these moulded heads and have been identified, they are aurochs horns.[284] Given that cattle remains at Çatalhöyük are commonly found in feasting deposits,[285] it is possible that these cattle heads commemorated feasts in which these animals were consumed.[286]

A link can be postulated between the horned installations at Çatalhöyük and the moulded animal heads with inset horns, and they might have been part of very similar practices. Not dissimilar are plastered protrusions that

---

[278] Mellaart 1963a: 67, pl. 9-b, figs. 9–12; 1964: 57, pl. 7-a, fig. 18; 1967: pls. 12 and 14.
[279] Mellaart 1967: pls. 11–14.
[280] Following Russell and Meece 2006.
[281] It has recently become popular to compare the splayed figures with similar animal figure types from Göbekli Tepe (Beile-Bohn et al. 1998: 70; Schmidt 1998: 29; Voigt 2000: 289–290). However, this comparison is problematic. The two sites are separated by a geographical distance of some 500 kilometres, are some 2,000 years apart in chronology, and are part of completely different cultural horizons with distinct iconographical traditions.
[282] Mellaart 1964: pl. 4-b.
[283] Mellaart 1963a: fig. 13.
[284] Russell and Meece 2006.
[285] Russell and Martin 2005.
[286] Adams 2005.

4.12 Stamp seal 11652.X1 from Çatalhöyük. Reproduced with permission. © Çatalhöyük Research Project. Drawing by John Swogger.

often contain faunal elements, sometimes referred to as 'breasts'.[287] Perhaps these breasts are simply the result of an act of covering up as part of the abandonment of a building.[288] They occur singly, in pairs, and in more complicated horizontal or vertical configurations. Faunal elements within them include boar mandibles and tusks, skulls of griffon vultures, a fox skull, and a weasel (or badger) skull.[289] Finally, there are 'incorporations': highly particular faunal elements that are intentionally placed in the fabric of walls, floors, and features. Incorporations require careful excavation to be recognised and are known predominantly from the recent excavations. Bones placed in walls and floors are scapulae, feet bones, and rare bones such as a wolf ulna or a bear's claw.[290] In general, there seems to be a concern with horns, teeth, jaws, and claws from dangerous animals such as cattle, boars, bears, and wolves. In some cases these animal parts protruded from the walls or features, but in other cases they were incorporated without being visible, and these are best understood as a continuum.[291]

The occurrence of categories of moulded features and installations over the stratigraphical levels at Çatalhöyük is patterned (Table 4.2). First, these

[287] Mellaart 1967: pl. 27; Hodder 1987; 1990: 5.
[288] Russell and Meece 2006.
[289] Mellaart 1963a: 67–70; 1967: 106; Russell and Meece 2006.
[290] Russell and Martin 2005: 80; Russell and Meece 2006.
[291] Last 2006; Russell and Meece 2006.

Table 4.2 Occurrence of the classes of moulded features and installations in relation to the levels in the South Area at Çatalhöyük

Motifs and installations	X	IX	VIII	VII	VI	V	IV	III
Animal heads	x			x	x			
Leopards			x	x	x			
Deep-relief animals				x	x			
Splayed figures				x	x			
Clay protrusions				x	x			
Horn pillars					x			
Horn benches					x	x		

features become rare in the later levels V–I at the site.[292] Similar to the wall paintings and figurines, the later levels at Çatalhöyük have different types of imagery.[293] Exciting new discoveries are geometric decorations applied with fingers in wet plaster that have been found in the 'TP Area' and on an oven in the '4040 Area', both of which date to the Late Ceramic Neolithic, a technique not found in the earlier levels.[294] The moulded features and installations cluster in levels VII and VI, with only a few dating to earlier levels. While these earlier levels have been less comprehensively investigated, it is possible that moulded features and installations, like wall painting motifs, were associated with changing fashions. This is the reverse of the unchanging structuralist symbolic systems that many have reconstructed on the basis of the Çatalhöyük imagery.

Second, in some instances, we see a recurrence of similar moulded figures in a building and its successor. For instance, leopards were found both in building VII.44 (1960s) and in building VI.44 (1960s), and an animal figure in profile in deep relief was found on the north wall of building VII.8 (1960s) and building VI.8 (1960s), echoing an earlier painted animal in profile in building IX.8 (1960s). However, most of the types of moulded features and installations seem to be dispersed across the settlement rather than being specific to any part of it.

The large majority of the features are found in living rooms. They are located along the west, north, and east walls but are rare in the south.[295] On present evidence, about a quarter of the living rooms at Çatalhöyük might have contained moulded features and installations. Although some

[292] One exception is a level V horned bench in building 44 (ÇRP).
[293] Hamilton 1996: 225–226; Voigt 2000: 278; Düring 2002.
[294] A 4040 example found in building 57 and discussed in Farid, Yeomans, and Krotchek in 2005 Archive Reports; TP example found in space 327, discussed by Marciniak and Czerniak in 2007 Archive Reports (both at http://www.catalhoyuk.com).
[295] Düring 2006: 200.

of these features may have been removed in the Neolithic,[296] they were probably not a normal component of the Çatalhöyük buildings, especially given the scarcity of these features in the new excavations. If moulded features and installations were present in only some buildings, they may relate to activities that were not centred on the house and household but might have linked several households. In the following section I will explore the sub-floor burials, in which a similar type of patterning can be observed.

4.8.8 Çatalhöyük Burials

The Çatalhöyük excavations have provided one of the largest datasets on intramural burial practices in Near Eastern Prehistory.[297] In the 1960s excavations at Çatalhöyük approximately 685 burials were excavated, and hundreds more have been uncovered in recent years.[298] About half of the burials are adults, with both sexes represented in equal measure. In the recent excavations comparatively more juveniles, including neonates and children, were recovered than in the 1960s,[299] undoubtedly due to more careful methods of excavation.

Burials normally occurred in a pit dug through the floor during the occupation of a building, after which the burial site was closed and the floor was patched. Given that floors were often plastered, the precise location and extent of a burial were not permanently marked. There are also graves that are associated with foundation deposits of buildings or that were placed during their abandonment.

Most burials at Çatalhöyük seem to have occurred as single primary internments, although in some cases double or triple burials have been found. New burials often disturbed the remains of earlier burials, which were sometimes pushed aside or re-arranged. This practice regularly resulted in chaotic mixtures of skeletons in which there seems to be little concern for the integrity of the individual deceased person.

The burials were often, but not exclusively, found beneath the compartments located in the northeastern part of the living room. These compartments most likely served for sitting and sleeping.[300] Thus, the association of the living and the dead seems to have been particularly intimate

---

[296] Hodder and Cessford 2004.
[297] Düring 2003: 1–4.
[298] See Düring 2003 for details.
[299] Molleson et al., 2005: 281, table 12.3.
[300] Mellaart 1962a: 47; Düring 2006: 180–184.

at Çatalhöyük: a relation in which some group members were resting tem-
porarily, whereas others 'rested' on a more permanent basis.[301]

The general perception of Çatalhöyük burial practices has been greatly
influenced by Mellaart's imaginative interpretations of the treatment of the
deceased and the ways in which males and females were differentiated in
death. These views were first challenged by Hamilton, who problematised
the gender differentiation that Mellaart perceived in the burial record.[302]

Mellaart had suggested that specific compartments were used to bury
specific categories of people. For instance, he argued that adults were
placed mainly below the northeast compartment, whereas juveniles could be
buried anywhere in a building, or that particular compartments were associated with males or females.[303] Mellaart also suggested that grave goods
were gender specific. Male grave goods, he stated, included weapons, such
as stone maces, obsidian daggers, and points, as well as bone belt-hooks,
whereas grave goods deposited with women consisted of items of jewellery,
such as necklaces, rings, and bracelets, as well as obsidian mirrors and spatulas (interpreted as make-up applicators).[304] No physical anthropologists
were present during the 1960s excavations to determine the sex of the skeletons, however. Thus, Mellaart's distinction of gender- or age-specific burial
practices seems suspect. In the recent excavations, no such age- or gender-
related spatial differentiation of burials or gender-specific burial goods have
been found.[305]

Another issue concerns the treatment of the dead prior to burial. Because
many skeletons were incomplete, Mellaart argued that they were secondary
burials.[306] Furthermore, he interpreted an enigmatic painting from building VI.1 (1960s) as a depiction of charnel houses,[307] in which the bodies of
the deceased were excarnated, a process supposedly depicted in the vulture
scenes.[308] Again, it has become clear from the new excavations that excarnation was not the normal practice at the site. The large majority of the
skeletons were primary burials, and evidence pointing towards excarnation
is absent, although there are a few cases of secondary burial.[309]

Was everyone buried on site at Çatalhöyük? The average number of
burials per living room is about 3.8. On the basis of the number of plaster
layers in buildings and radiocarbon dates, the average use life of buildings

[301] For a close parallel among the Maya see Gillespie (2000: 146–151).
[302] Hamilton 1996.
[303] Mellaart 1962a: 52; 1964: 93.
[304] Mellaart 1963a: 94–95; 1967: 208–209.
[305] Hodder 2004; Hamilton 2005c: 301–302.
[306] Mellaart 1962a: 52.
[307] Mellaart 1963a: pl. 26-a.
[308] Mellaart 1963a: 97–98; 1964: 93; 1967: 166, 204.
[309] Andrews et al. 2005: 274–275.

Level VIB Burials

40

20

4

7   Building n

0   10 m

4.13 Distribution of sub-floor burials in level VIB in the South Area at Çatalhöyük. Produced by the author and Medy Oberendorff after fig. 2 in Mellaart, J. 1964. 'Excavations at Çatal Hüyük: Third preliminary report, 1963'. *Anatolian Studies* 14: 39–119.

can be estimated at approximately 60 years.[310] Assuming that at least four people lived in each building, this would imply some 240 man-years spend in these buildings. If four people were buried in such a building, this would presuppose an average life expectancy of approximately 60 years.[311] Such a life expectancy is not realistic for Çatalhöyük, given that only half of the burials belong to adults. This means that not everyone was buried on

[310] Mellaart 1964: 64; 1967: 50–51; Cessford 2005b; Matthews 2005: 368; 2006.
[311] Note that this life expectancy would be even more substantial if the average group of people associated with a living room is set at a higher number.

site beneath the building floors.[312] The presence of both sexes and all age categories implies that these were not criteria for determining who got buried in the settlement.

How are the Çatalhöyük burials distributed over the settlement? In both projects, the burials found were not spread evenly across the rooms. Mellaart associated the burials with the domestic sphere of life, with each household burying its deceased beneath its floors.[313] However, about half of the buildings had no sub-floor burials. Further, there are many examples of buildings with a large number of burials, such as building 1 (ÇRP), with 64 burials. Such burial 'populations' are much too substantial to encompass only the deceased of a single household: It would imply a death in a nuclear household every one to two years. It is plausible that non-resident people were also preferentially buried in such buildings.

As an example of the variability in burial density, we can look at level VIB at Çatalhöyük (Fig. 4.13). Most rooms contained no sub-floor burial at all. There are some buildings with a small number of burials. However, burials are found primarily within the main rooms of buildings VIB.1, VIB.7, VIB.10, and VIB.34 (all 1960s), each with more than 25 burials. These four rooms together contained more than half of the level VIB burials.

How can we understand the link between burials and buildings? Two hypotheses have been put forward. The first is that we are dealing with some form of ancestor veneration.[314] A lot of attention has been given to the few examples of skull removal from burials, and the curation and embellishment of those skulls, as practices involving ancestor veneration.[315] However, on the whole, skull removal and curation constitute an exceptional rather than a common practice at Çatalhöyük, in contrast to the PPNB in the Levantine region, where the removal of skulls from graves and the plastering of skulls were more widespread.[316] At Çatalhöyuk, the examples of skull removal and curation, along with other secondary burials, which tellingly do not include young people,[317] may well have been connected to ancestor cults, but there is no reason to extend this interpretation to the Çatalhöyük burial practices at large.

An explanation for the asymmetrical distribution of Çatalhöyük burials over the settlement, with concentrations in specific buildings, is to regard those as burial sites used by a larger kin group, or 'lineage'. Communal

---

[312] Hamilton 1998; Düring 2003.
[313] Mellaart 1964: 92–93; 1967: 205.
[314] Macqueen 1978; Wunn 2001.
[315] Hodder and Cessford 2004: 35; Hodder 2006a.
[316] Bienert 1991; Kuijt 2000; Talalay 2004. Plastered skulls have also been found at the Middle Chalcolithic site of Köşk Höyük (see Chapter 5).
[317] Andrews et al. 2005.

tombs for collective burials of lineage members are well documented in anthropology.[318] Further, there are some examples of societies where houses serve as a communal burial site, in which lineage members, not all of whom are resident in that specific house, may be interred.[319] Particularly appropriate as a parallel for the case at Çatalhöyük seems the practice in pre-colonial Roti society, in Indonesia, described by Waterson:

> 'Identification of the living and the dead with the house is particularly marked in Roti. Here the dead were buried under the house floor, while their spirits took up residence in the loft' and 'One is not necessarily buried in the house one has lived in, but in a clan house already designated as an uma nitu or "spiral house", that is, one in which other burials have already taken place and which has therefore accumulated ritual power and is regarded as a sort of temple.'[320]

There is much in this example of the Roti that seems relevant for understanding the practices at Çatalhöyük. I will argue in the next section that the buildings with large groups of sub-floor burials were central to social collectivities that included several households.

4.8.9 Building Differentiation and Building Continuity at Çatalhöyük

Confronted with the spectacular moulded and painted imagery found in the buildings at Çatalhöyük, Mellaart argued that many of the buildings he excavated should be interpreted as shrines rather than houses and that these spaces were devoted to cultic practices, which could be recognised by the presence of features such as "wall paintings of an elaborate nature, plaster reliefs, horns of cattle set into benches, rows of horn-pillars, the presence of cult statuettes, and human skulls set on the floors."[321]

The distinction Mellaart made between shrines and houses was found wanting by a number of scholars, who argued that Mellaart did not rigorously apply his own criteria for distinguishing between the two.[322] Ritchey made a survey of all the buildings excavated by Mellaart in order to explore the variability amongst them. A large range of architectural features was tabulated to measure the 'complexity scale' of these buildings, and Ritchey concluded that "the demarcation between 'shrine' and 'non-shrine' as proposed by Mellaart cannot be substantiated."[323] Hodder has also argued that

---

[318] Metcalf and Huntington 1991; Waterson 1995; Chesson 2001.
[319] Waterson 1990: 221; Gillespie 2000; Kirch 2000.
[320] Waterson 1990: 221.
[321] Mellaart 1967: 77–78.
[322] Heinrich and Seidl 1969: 116; Hamilton 1996: 226.
[323] Ritchey 1996: 7.

all buildings were homologous household residences imbued with symbolism, in which the same symbolic structures were celebrated and played out, as exemplified in his 'domus' concept.[324] More recently, however, he has acknowledged some degree of ritual differentiation amongst buildings.[325]

It is plausible that all buildings at Çatalhöyük served as household residences, given that they all possess features such as hearths and ovens and are alike in their spatial layout. In recent investigations, it has become clear that the buildings that Mellaart interpreted as shrines were used for domestic activities on the same regular basis as other buildings.[326] In short, the idea that some buildings were used primarily for cultic rather than living purposes finds little support in the evidence. It does not follow, however, that there is no significant degree of ritual differentiation amongst buildings.

This differentiation of buildings is best demonstrated in the uneven distribution of sub-floor burials, rather than in features such as wall paintings or mouldings. Unlike the paintings and moulded features, the burial data are both abundant and reliable: In contrast to wall paintings, they are easy to find and they were not intentionally removed, as is the case with installations and moulded features. The burials were not used by Mellaart or Hodder when discussing building status differentiation, and they constitute an independent dataset to assess the issue.

Given that burials were preferentially performed in specific buildings by social groups that must have included several households, the question is why these buildings were preferred. Part of the answer can be found in the diachronic development of buildings. In the South Area a number of buildings can be traced from level V down to level VIII, and in some cases to level X (Fig. 4.14). We are dealing with a substantial depth here. If we take 60 years as an estimate of the average use life of the buildings at Çatalhöyük, the sequence represented in Figure 4.14 lasted for approximately 420 years. The vertical displacement of floors that occurred over the course of these seven building levels ranges up to 7.5 metres.

This pronounced building continuity is similar to that documented for Aşıklı Höyük (§4.4.4) and is characteristic of the Central Anatolian Neolithic. It has been suggested that building continuity was the result of building practices in which older walls were used for foundations or resulted from the congested nature of the settlement.[327] While these factors were certainly important, building continuity at Çatalhöyük cannot be reduced to these functional parameters.[328]

---

[324] Hodder 1990; Hodder and Cessford 2004.
[325] Hodder and Cessford 2004: 30–31; Hodder 2006a: 151–163.
[326] Matthews 2005.
[327] Mellaart 1967: 67.
[328] Düring 2005.

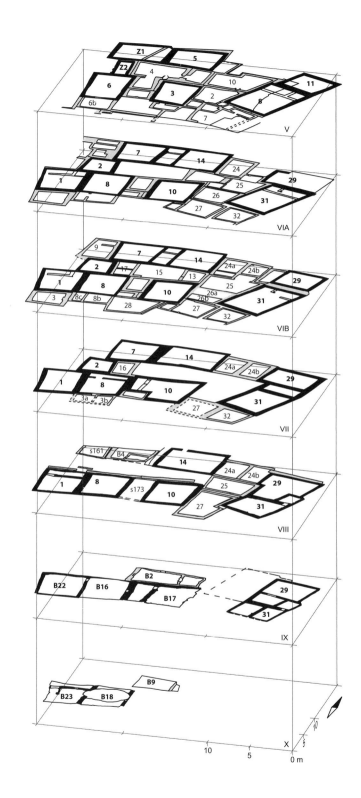

4.14 Diachronic overview of the development of buildings in the South Area at Çatalhöyük. Produced by the author and Medy Oberendorff.

The degree of building continuity is not similar for all structures in the South Area. Some buildings can be traced over a number of building levels, whereas others are more short-lived, existing for one or two building levels, and were abandoned afterwards. Buildings can be classified as either continuous or non-continuous.

Most non-continuous structures are associated with the central midden in the South Area (in grey in Fig. 4.14). These buildings often have unusual proportions and shapes. Best documented is building 2 (ÇRP) of level IX,[329] which after its initial use as a domestic structure, as is evident from features such as floors, ovens, and bins, was converted into an animal pen. No burials, moulded features, or installations were found within this building, but it did contain two geometric wall paintings. Overall, this seems to have been a building of low status. Other non-continuous spaces likewise have few burials below their floors.

The continuous buildings at Çatalhöyük (in black in Fig. 4.14), differ in several respects from the discontinuous structures. Examples include buildings 1, 8, 10, 29, and 31 (all 1960s), that are present in all excavated building levels. These buildings remain true to their location and dimensions over several phases of reconstruction and over the course of centuries. They were as a rule infilled with clean material upon abandonment, and were generally immediately redeveloped into new successor buildings.[330]

In a way these buildings were not novel structures, but reproductions of pre-existing buildings. Elements of the internal configuration of buildings and the embellishment of buildings at Çatalhöyük show continuities that cannot be related to function. For example, internal division walls tend to recur in the same location over many phases of the redevelopment of a building. Of course, it could be argued that these spatial configurations were simply the outcome of cultural preferences, for instance a preference for a storage room to the north. There are also more specific continuities at Çatalhöyük, however. Both painted and moulded motifs tend to recur in the same buildings in different levels, often in the same spot within buildings (§4.8.7). From this it would appear that buildings might have had some form of identity that was appreciated and reproduced.[331] Building continuity, it seems, was more than just a practice of foundation and was meaningful to people associated with these buildings.[332]

An interesting pattern at Çatalhöyük for continuous buildings is an increase of their ritual elaborateness over time. Put simply, we can follow buildings that started out as more or less average domestic units and

[329] Farid 2007b.
[330] Matthews 2006; Farid 2007a.
[331] Düring 2006: 221–223; Hodder 2006b.
[332] Düring 2005; Matthews 2006.

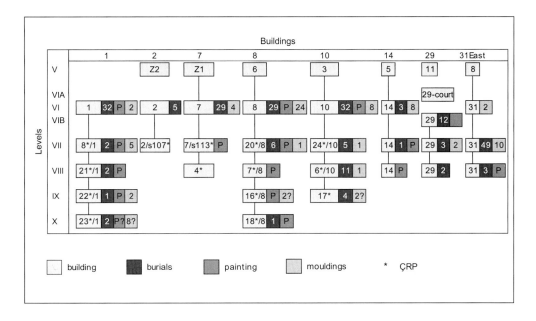

see how they gradually became invested with symbolism. This can be done by tabulating the occurrence and frequency of mouldings, wall paintings, and burials (Fig. 4.15). In this manner, we can note a clear increase in these 'ritual features'. For instance, most buildings have either no or only a few burials in level VIII, but these numbers rise substantially in later levels. Second, the diversity of ritual features present in buildings becomes greater over time. In level VIII many buildings contained only a single type of ritual feature, but by levels VII and VI, most of them contained the full set of features.

The differential distribution of burials, moulded features, and installations that has been interpreted as a differentiation in building statuses could be a function of 'building pedigrees': that is, the circumstances of building origins (the mythical identity of the founders of the house and the relation to pre-existing houses) and their trajectory of development. Such trajectories of development, involving transformations from inconspicuous buildings to buildings with great ritual significance, can be best understood in the context of the 'house' concept proposed by Lévi-Strauss.[333]

The situation described by Lévi-Strauss[334] is one in which people define themselves in relation to specific high-status houses in which they can claim membership. These houses are named entities that legitimate their domination of other houses of less status by claims of precedence and continuity.

4.15 Overview of the diachronic development of continuous South Area building inventories at Çatalhöyük. Produced by the author and Medy Oberendorff.

[333] Düring 2005; 2007.
[334] Lévi-Strauss 1983; 1991.

Such houses tend to form hierarchical systems in which wealth, status, and prestige are concentrated in a few 'lineage houses'. Lineage houses serve as a focal point for a group of people beyond the household group residing in them. Many of the rituals of this larger group are centred on the lineage houses.

In many ethnographic studies, a relation can be demonstrated between the pedigree of a building and its status.[335] In these examples, a building can increase in status over time, and its pedigree is essential in a system where building status and ancestry are intertwined. Given a shared awareness of building histories, the past cannot be rewritten at will. These characteristics of lineage houses seem to fit with the evidence at Çatalhöyük. On the basis of these parallels, it is possible to understand the buildings at Çatalhöyük that contain many sub-floor burials as lineage houses: buildings that were important for supra-household social collectivities.

4.8.10 Neighbourhoods at Çatalhöyük

One of the striking aspects of the Çatalhöyük settlement in the early levels XII–VI is the way in which the buildings were constructed in streetless neighbourhood clusters that could be accessed only from the roof level. Streets and larger open spaces did exist at the site,[336] but they served mainly to differentiate neighbourhoods from one another. A ladder from one of these open spaces would have given access to these neighbourhood roofscapes, and further traffic would have taken place on the roof level. In this form of spatial organization, Çatalhöyük can be compared with other excavated settlements of the Central Anatolian Neolithic such as Aşıklı Höyük, Canhasan 3 and 1, and Erbaba.

We have a fair idea of the sorts of places these roofscapes constituted. In some parts of Çatalhöyük there would have been vertical steps between roofs, given that the settlement was constructed on sloping surfaces. Although there is increasing evidence that some buildings had small structures, such as wooden lofts, on their roofs,[337] the idea that the Çatalhöyük buildings had substantial upper storeys[338] can be dismissed because the buildings could not have supported them.[339]

A range of activities seems to have been performed on the roofs. The best data derive from the collapsed roof of building 3 (ÇRP).[340] A fire installation

---

335 Waterson 1990: 142; Kirch 2000; Waterson 2003.
336 Matthews 1996.
337 Hodder 2009.
338 Cutting 2006.
339 Düring 2006: 241.
340 Matthews 2005: 373.

was found on top of this roof and clean and dirty roof areas were recognised, suggesting that activities similar to those in the living rooms took place on the roofs. The use of flat mud roofs in the summer for a range of activities is well documented in Near Eastern ethnographies,[341] and it is probable that this was also the case at Çatalhöyük, where open spaces were rare in the settlement and were used mostly as garbage dumps.

The Çatalhöyük roofs, then, gave access to the buildings below, contained various goods and features, and enabled people to carry out a range of activities during the hotter part of the year. People would have regularly moved across these roofs on their way to and from their houses. Taking these factors together, it is clear that interaction within these neighbourhoods must have been intense. As at Aşıklı Höyük, it can be posited that people using these roofscapes formed a social collectivity grounded in shared activities and built upon personal relations, shared experiences, and face-to-face interaction. It is not unlikely that we are dealing with a corporate community controlling the access of non-residents to their neighbourhood. The model of neighbourhood communities living in spatially segregated parts of the settlement and policing their neighbourhood from outsiders is one that seems to fit the evidence at Çatalhöyük.

In relation to the boundedness of neighbourhoods, the clearest evidence comes from the scrape area on the northern summit of the mound, which has been tentatively assigned to level VI.[342] In the scrape plan is a linear open space running from the northwest to the southeast and clearly separating a neighbourhood to the northeast. This feature seems to suggest that at least some of the Çatalhöyük neighbourhoods were clearly bounded.

The scale of the neighbourhoods is difficult to establish. The most complete excavated exposure is level VIB in the South Area. Although large, this exposure does not include a complete bounded neighbourhood. In the VIB neighbourhood we have about 30 buildings with living rooms. If we take these as indices of households with about 5 people, we can estimate the neighbourhood population at minimally 150 people. This estimate is comparable to that proposed earlier for Aşıklı Höyük (§4.4.6).

The Çatalhöyük neighbourhoods might have varied considerably in size, but it is likely that there was an upper limit. If it is accepted that neighbourhoods depended on personal contacts amongst members, there are other studies that might give us a clue about their possible maximum size. Here I am referring to studies that have investigated 'face-to-face communities'. The idea that humans can engage directly with only a finite number of other people has been posited on the basis of observations in various disciplines.[343] The thresholds arrived at in these studies are remarkably consistent,

[341] Peters 1982: 223; Friedl and Loeffler 1994: 33.
[342] Conolly 1996; Last 1996.
[343] Forge 1972; Birdsell 1973; Kosse 1990; Dunbar 1992; Bintliff 1999.

averaging about 150–250 people for close personal relations and 400–600 people for more casual relations. These figures represent a selective amalgamation of disparate phenomena, but taken together, they suggest that face-to-face communities normally would have been no larger than about 250 people. Tentatively, then, it can be suggested that the normal neighbourhoods at Çatalhöyük ranged between 150 and 250 people, although it is theoretically possible that they included as many as 600 people.

4.8.11 The Local Community at Çatalhöyük

With its estimated size of 13 hectares, Çatalhöyük is amongst the largest sites of the Near Eastern Neolithic.[344] This size may be deceptive, because we could be dealing with the cumulative effect of a much more limited occupation shifting over the site.[345] At Çatalhöyük, however, this shifting occupation scenario seems less plausible, given the marked building continuity documented at the site, with evidence of uninterrupted sequences spanning centuries.[346] On the basis of the excavated sequences and surface assemblages, the maximum expansion of the Çatalhöyük settlement seems to have occurred in level VI at about 6400 BC.[347]

Various calculations for the maximum population size of Çatalhöyük have been proposed, with estimates ranging between 3,500 and 10,000 people and centring on 5,000 to 8,000 people.[348] While the older estimates were calculated with population density figures per hectare derived from ethnographic studies, the more recent ones are based on an evaluation of the building density of the site, with an allowance for large open areas so far undetected. Calculations were then performed by multiplying the number of domestic buildings by the assumed household size. There is some consistency in the population estimates, despite the fact that they were calculated in different ways. It is clear from these estimates that Çatalhöyük was a sizeable community that included thousands of people during levels VIII to VI.

The fact that the population of Çatalhöyük, like that of Aşıklı Höyük, ran into the thousands has important implications for how we understand the site. Whereas a small local community is a very concrete entity to people grounded in shared activities, larger local communities are more

---

344 Moore et al. 2000: 5.
345 Hole 2000: 194–195; Akkermans and Schwartz 2003: 59–60; Verhoeven 2006.
346 Düring 2005; Cessford 2007b.
347 Matthews 1996: 85; Baird 2006a: 67.
348 Mellaart 1965: 202; Cohen 1970: 122–123; Angel 1971: 82–83; Mellaart 1975: 99; Matthews 1996: 86; Cessford 2005b: 326; Düring 2006: 234; Düring 2007: 158.

ideational in character. Kosse writes that in communities of up to 2,500 inhabitants, people will still be able to monitor each other on the basis of gossip.[349] The maximum population of Çatalhöyük probably exceeded this threshold.

Here the distinction between 'natural' and 'imagined' communities drawn by Isbell becomes relevant.[350] A natural community is a real and bounded entity, whereas the imagined community is primarily about identification with specific categories and is not based on face-to-face interaction. It is plausible that people at Çatalhöyük had social identities more inclusive than those of people living in face-to-face communities. One such identity we can postulate is that of being a member of the Çatalhöyük community.

So, how did people living at Çatalhöyük interact with one another and with people living in other settlements? Both Birdsell and Wobst have argued that a group of some 500 people constitutes the minimum necessary for human biological reproduction.[351] On the basis of a cross-cultural comparison, Adams and Kasakoff have shown that completely endogamous groups do not exist in the ethnographic record, but that local communities in the range of 850–10,000 people will typically be about 80 per cent endogamous.[352] On the basis of such estimates, Baird posits that the advantage of Çatalhöyük growing as large as it did was that the settlement could have become largely endogamous.[353] A preference for marriages within the local community could explain in part why people at Çatalhöyük might have preferred to live in one large settlement rather than in smaller dispersed communities.

The Çatalhöyük settlement can be contrasted with the contemporary site of Erbaba, located near Lake Beyşehir. Erbaba is a small site with a diameter of about 80 metres. On the basis of building density at the site, the local community has been estimated at around 250 people.[354] Settlements of this size, with populations not exceeding 300 people, are the norm for the Neolithic in many of the regions surrounding Central Anatolia.[355] The Erbaba community would not have exceeded a face-to-face community in which everybody knew each other firsthand, and it appears very similar in scale to the neighbourhoods at Çatalhöyük.

[349] Kosse 1990: 284.
[350] Isbell 2000: 245.
[351] Birdsell 1973; Wobst 1974.
[352] Adams and Kasakoff 1976: 155–158.
[353] Baird 2006a: 67.
[354] Düring 2006: 256–267.
[355] Halstead 1999: 89; Roodenberg 1999: 197; Peltenburg et al. 2001: 53; Perlès 2001: 178–180; Akkermans and Schwartz 2003: 58–60.

Interestingly, Erbaba is one of a larger group of relatively small Ceramic Neolithic sites often only a few kilometres apart.[356] None of the sites appears to be larger than the others, and functional differentiation is unlikely. It is probable, however, that people from Erbaba participated in marriage networks with other small sites in its vicinity.

Such a comparison suggests that, as at Aşıklı Höyük, each Çatalhöyük neighbourhood was not unlike the village community at Erbaba, and that the Çatalhöyük settlement represents the contraction of a regional settlement system into a single site. It can be estimated that in its heyday, Çatalhöyük would have incorporated between 27 and 53 of these neighbourhoods/villages.[357]

Indeed, Baird has argued that the initial formation of Çatalhöyük represents the clustering of a group of previously dispersed small local communities.[358] Given this development, the contraction of the population of Çatalhöyük could be explained in part by some form of place-bound ideology similar to that operating at the level of the houses. We might think of a corporate identity tied to a settlement. Such a place-bound identity might help to explain why the people at Çatalhöyük remained in their growing settlement for some 800 years.

Another reason why people first became interested in living in larger associations may have been social: the chance to engage with a large number of other people and the attraction of communal events, such as feasting and dancing.[359] Indeed, there is some evidence for social gatherings with regard to burials, moulded features and installations, and feasting deposits.[360] At many Neolithic sites, such as Göbekli Tepe, Nevali Çori, and Çayönü in Southeast Anatolia and Aşıklı Höyük in Central Anatolia, we have evidence of large communal structures where such events could have taken place, but at Çatalhöyük these functions seem to have been taken over by houses.[361]

Finally, the 'compartmentalisation of society' seems to have been important at Çatalhöyük. Johnson has offered one model that could help us understand how this might have worked.[362] According to him, large groups of people can be integrated in two ways: first, by developing social hierarchies; and, second, by subdividing society into more or less egalitarian sub-units of a restricted size, the delegates of which can then negotiate amongst themselves on the basis of equality. The clustered neighbourhoods of Çatalhöyük might be considered as such units engaging in decision-making processes.

---

[356] Mellaart 1961.
[357] Düring 2006: 235.
[358] Baird 2006a: 67.
[359] Hayden 1990; Garfinkel 1998.
[360] Russell and Martin 2005.
[361] Hodder 2006a: 164.
[362] Johnson 1982.

4.9.1 Early Farmers of the Southern Plateau: A Conclusion

This chapter has presented the evidence of a handful of Neolithic sites dating to the period between about 8500 and 6500 BC in the southern part of Central Anatolia. While much more research is needed to understand this cultural horizon, a picture is starting to emerge that significantly affects our understanding of the Near Eastern Neolithic as a whole.

While it is clear that people in Central Anatolia were in frequent interaction with the Fertile Crescent, exemplified by Cappadocian obsidian at Jericho and date palm leaves at Çatalhöyük, it is clear that the Neolithic in this region developed along a distinct trajectory from the start. The adoption of crops from the Fertile Crescent is in marked contrast to the development of a cultural model that differed fundamentally from that in the Fertile Crescent, and is most clearly manifested in the ways people constructed their settlements and buried their dead, both of which were very different from practices in the (upper) Fertile Crescent. In this respect, it is of interest that some degree of continuity with earlier groups of the Epipalaeolithic and Mesolithic can be documented in the microlithic industries and in the prominence of wild plant resources.

It is remarkable that the clustered neighbourhoods accessed through the roofscape and the building continuity first documented in Aşıklı Höyük can be documented in a series of other sites and persisted for at least two millennia. It is equally apparent that hidden beneath these ways of building and living were very different types of societies, as best exemplified in the cases of Aşıklı Höyük and Çatalhöyük. Both of these sites were very large in comparison to the normal Neolithic sites in adjacent regions and seem to represent the contraction of a regional settlement system into a large settlement, with each neighbourhood representing the equivalent of a village. The reasons for this type of agglomeration remain poorly understood, but factors of demographic pressure or economy do not seem to be at the root of these large sites, and we have to assume that these agglomerations were held together primarily by social and ideological factors. This conclusion – that the Neolithic of this region was probably not the result of demographic pressure or resource stress, but seems to have been above all a socio-ideological phenomenon – is of great importance for our understanding of the Near Eastern Neolithic as a whole and for our understanding of how societies beyond face-to-face communities first took shape.

CHAPTER FIVE

NEOLITHIC DISPERSALS (6500–5500 BC)

The period between 6500 and 5500 BC is a period of profound transformations in the Prehistory of Asia Minor with ramifications far beyond the peninsula. In particular, this is the stage during which the Neolithic way of life expanded out of the steppe region of the southern interior of Asia Minor, in parallel with similar developments in the Fertile Crescent, and towards the adjacent regions of the Lake District, Aegean Turkey, and the Marmara Region, and ultimately towards Greece and the Balkans.

In this chapter, the evidence from this crucial period will be discussed for the regions to the west, northwest, and southeast of Central Anatolia in which the Neolithic way of life was taken up during this period. The transformations that occurred within Central Anatolia itself are also considered. Apart from the traditional questions – whether, first, the spread of the Neolithic was the result of a demographic expansion of farmers; or, second, should be seen as the transformation of local hunter-gatherer groups; or, third, was a combination of the two – we should also ask why the expansion of the Neolithic way of life occurred at around 6500 BC.

5.1.1 The Second Neolithic Revolution

The initial domestication of plants and animals has been the subject of a massive amount of research, often by researchers with a background in biology.[1] This research focus is understandable, given that the processes of domestication of plants and animals and the sedentarisation of humans are at the root of complex societies worldwide. However, the focus on the initial domestication of cereals and mammals has erroneously condensed

[1] Hillman 1996; Tchernov 1998; Vigne et al. 1999; Colledge 2001; Nesbitt 2002; Colledge et al. 2004; Nesbitt 2004; Colledge and Conolly, eds., 2007.

the Neolithic transition into a threshold event occurring within a relatively brief period of time, that is, the early Neolithic, during which it is generally thought that the Neolithic package effectively took shape. It is probably because of this threshold view of the Neolithic, in which the main developments are held to occur in the ninth and eighth millennia BC, that the later Neolithic has been relatively poorly researched and has been regarded as a period with little change to the way of life that had developed earlier in the Neolithic.[2]

In this regard, it is interesting to note that Sherratt's thesis of a 'secondary products revolution', in which animals started to be exploited for dairy products, wool, and traction, as well as for their meat,[3] has been influential in European archaeology but has had relatively little impact in the study of Near Eastern Prehistory. As a consequence, there is a whole range of agricultural developments, not necessarily occurring in concert, such as the domestication of cattle, the introduction of dairy products, and the development of woolly sheep, that remain poorly investigated.

The initial domestication of cereals, which formed the mainstay of the Near Eastern Neolithic economy, occurred at around 8700 BC and formed the basis for the subsequent emergence of Neolithic societies. However, Neolithic sites rarely occur outside the steppe zone of the Near East until the seventh millennium BC.[4] The present picture suggests that after an early uptake of the Neolithic way of life in South-Central Anatolia at around 8500 BC, it lasted until 7000 BC before it was taken up elsewhere in Asia Minor, and that it was only at around 6500 that this expansion gained the momentum to colonise comprehensively the landscapes of West Anatolia, Greece, and the southern Balkans. This expansion of cultivation practices out of the habitats resembling the natural habitat zone of early crops could be labelled the 'second Neolithic revolution', and it can be argued that its effects were more profound than the initial domestication of crops and animals.

Given that the steppe environments of Central Anatolia and the Fertile Crescent are ecologically very similar, and that they constitute the natural habitats of most domesticated crops and animals, it is perhaps not surprising that the earliest Near Eastern Neolithic is concentrated in these habitats.[5] This is not to argue that the earliest Neolithic was homogeneous: Different crops and weeds have been found in various regions, and animal husbandry was quite diverse. A recent analysis of the agricultural crops and associated

[2] Bogaard 2005.
[3] Sherratt 1983.
[4] Schoop 2005b; Düring 2008.
[5] M. Özdoğan 1999a; Schoop 2005b.

weed taxa in early Neolithic sites in the Near East has demonstrated significant similarities between the steppe zones of the northern Fertile Crescent
and Central Anatolia, which differ from agricultural crops and weeds found
in the southern Levant, on the one hand, and those of the Taurus foothill
sites, on the other.[6]

In general, it has been argued that early farming was quite varied and that
an integrated set of crops and animals, as well as optimal farming strategies
in which these were linked, first emerged in the seventh millennium BC.[7]
In terms of new domesticates there are crops such as barley and bread wheat
(*Triticum durum/aestivum*),[8] and in Asia Minor there is the addition of cattle to the suite of domestic animals.[9] Bogaard has argued that increasingly
managed and artificial growing conditions made the cultivation of a standard range of crops (cereals, pulses, flax) possible. Further, she argues that
this took the form of 'intensive mixed farming', a form of farming in which
small garden plots were cultivated intensively, on which a range of crops
were grown, and on which manure from small animal flocks was used to
replenish soil nutrients.[10]

These changes in agricultural practices occurring in the seventh millennium BC remain tentatively understood and require further study, but they
do point to one mechanism that could help us understand why the Neolithic
expanded out of the Fertile Crescent and Central Anatolia at approximately
6500 BC. It might have been the case that changes in agriculture made
farming an attractive option outside the steppe zone.[11]

Another element that has recently been connected with this phase of
agricultural expansion is the climatic fluctuation known as the '8.2 KA
event', between about 6400 and 6100 BC, during which there were lasting
droughts in many parts of the world; it is possible that these droughts also
occurred in parts of the Near East and had effects on Neolithic societies.[12]
Some researchers have suggested that the Neolithic expansion in the seventh millennium BC was triggered by this climatic event.[13] While the 8.2

---

[6] Colledge et al. 2004, 42–47; Coward et al. 2008.

[7] Kislev 1999; Perrot 2001; Bogaard 2005; Zeder 2009: 40.

[8] Kislev 1999.

[9] Russell et al. 2005.

[10] Bogaard 2004, 2005.

[11] Schoop (2005b) has suggested that the Central Anatolian Neolithic was based on optimal
resources in the form of large flocks of wild mammals, and for this reason remained 'stuck'
on the steppe, and that growing crops also required little effort in this habitat. This view
is demonstrably too simple: At Aşıklı Höyük sheep were probably tended, and cultivated
crops formed the mainstay of subsistence (§4.4.1), whereas at Çatalhöyük domestic sheep
were most numerous among the faunal remains, and agriculture was probably relatively
labour intensive (§4.8.2/3).

[12] Weiss and Bradley 2001; Wagner et al. 2002; Akkermans 2004; Budja 2007.

[13] Bar-Yosef 2001; Budja 2007.

KA event could have been a factor contributing to the Neolithic expansion in the seventh millennium, it has sometimes been seen erroneously as a prime mover, an idea that can be discounted for three reasons. First, without agricultural technologies allowing for expansion into other ecological zones, farming elsewhere simply wouldn't have been a feasible option. Second, in the climate proxy record of Asia Minor, in particular the pollen records, the 8.2 KA event has yet to be recognised (§1.2.2), and it remains to be seen whether this period was as disruptive as is often thought. Third, as will emerge in this chapter, the agricultural expansion into adjacent regions precedes the 8.2 KA event by at least a century, meaning that the 8.2 KA event could have accelerated this process but did not cause it.

Third, social factors might also have played a role in the Neolithic expansion of the seventh millennium. Changes can be demonstrated in the social organisation of communities during this time period, with a general pattern of large aggregate communities giving way to more dispersed smaller groups living in more modest settlements and with a new prominence for households.[14] Such developments, in which small groups operated more independently, could have facilitated the expansion of the Neolithic into adjacent regions.

5.1.2 Preludes to the Second Neolithic Revolution

After the start of the Central Anatolian Neolithic, at around 8500 BC, it took two millennia, until 6500 BC, for the Neolithic way of life to spread to the Pisidian Lake District,[15] Aegean Turkey,[16] and the Marmara Region,[17] where the earliest good evidence for Neolithic villages can be dated to around 6500 BC (Fig. 5.1).[18] The only substantially earlier date is that of 'Aceramic Hacılar', dated to 8000 BC, but this is a single date that could well be erroneous.[19] The date of 6500 BC also seems to be the baseline for the start of the Neolithic in Greece and the Balkans.[20]

There are some indications, however, that the Neolithic might have spread west somewhat earlier than 6500 BC. First, a new radiocarbon date from Bademağacı, in the Lake District, suggests that this site was occupied from 7000 BC onwards.[21] Unfortunately, apart from a limestone plaster

[14] Düring and Marciniak 2005.
[15] Duru 1999.
[16] Çilingiroğlu et al. 2004.
[17] M. Özdoğan 1999a.
[18] Schoop 2005b; Düring 2006: 12.
[19] Duru 1989; Thissen 2002.
[20] Perlès 2001; Thissen 2005.
[21] Duru 2004.

floor that could not be associated with any walls and a few small shards,[22] nothing has been published for the 'Early Neolithic I' at this site. In these circumstances, it is difficult to judge how reliable this single radiocarbon date is (we could potentially be dealing with old wood, for instance). At the site of Ulucak, recent radiocarbon dates also suggest that the site was first occupied in the early seventh millennium BC.[23]

Second, Özdoğan and Gatsov[24] have argued for the existence of an Aceramic Neolithic phase in the Marmara Region, to be dated from about 7000 BC onwards. The evidence on which they base this conclusion consists of two survey sites, Çalca and Musluçesme, with chipped stone assemblages that are distinct from those found in Ağaçlı and Fikirtepe sites, but without ceramics. No absolute dates are available; consequently, the assignation of these sites to the Aceramic Neolithic is tentative and needs to be confirmed through excavations. The chipped stone finds published from these sites would not be out of place at the Ceramic Neolithic sites of Ilıpınar and Menteşe, even if some artefact classes, such as bullet cores and blades converted into perforators, are absent. It is conceivable that we are dealing with special-purpose sites dating to the later Ceramic Neolithic or Early Chalcolithic.

Finally, new evidence from Aceramic Knossos on Crete has confirmed that its occupation started in the first half of the seventh millennium BC, for which there are now a number of radiocarbon dates.[25] Here, although the excavated area is small, there is solid evidence for a Neolithic settlement, with domestic sheep, pigs, and cattle, as well as domestic cereals and pulses. For the early seventh millennium the Knossos Neolithic remains without parallels elsewhere on Crete.[26] It is plausible that the true expansion of Neolithic settlement in the Aegean only occurred at around 6500 BC, when evidence for it emerges at many sites simultaneously.[27] The question of whether the Knossian Neolithic came from inland Anatolia or from the Levant via Cyprus, where Neolithic sites dating to the ninth millennium have been found, and from coastal Anatolia has been the subject of some debate,[28] but given the extremely limited evidence from the earliest levels, the answers are highly hypothetical and need not concern us here.

From this brief discussion of three possible Neolithic sites outside the steppes of the Fertile Crescent and Central Anatolia that may date to the

---

[22] Duru 2002, 2004, 2007: 344, 349.
[23] Çevik personal comment May 2010.
[24] Özdoğan and Gatsov 1998.
[25] Evans 1964; Efstratiou et al. 2004.
[26] Tomkins et al. 2004; Thissen 2005.
[27] Perlès 2001; Reingruber 2005; Thissen 2005: 33.
[28] Comment of Peltenburg on page 52 following Colledge et al. 2004; Perlès 2005; Broodbank 2006: 214–215.

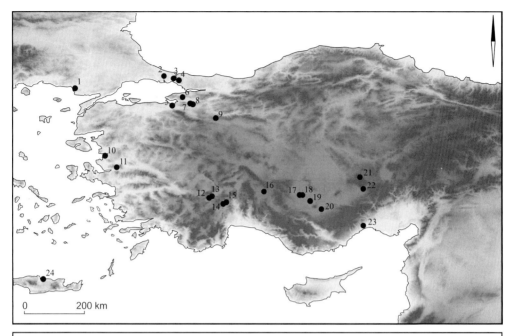

1 Hoca Çeşme; 2 Yarımburgaz; 3 Fikirtepe; 4 Pendik; 5 Aktopraklık; 6 Ilıpınar; 7 Menteşe; 8 Barcın Höyük; 9 Demircihüyük;
10 Ege Gübre; 11 Ulucak; 12 Hacılar; 13 Kuruçay; 14 Bademağacı; 15 Höyücek; 16 Erbaba; 17 Çatalhöyük West;
18 Çatalhöyük East; 19 Pınarbaşı; 20 Canhasan 1; 21 Tepecik-Çiftlik; 22 Köşk Höyük; 23 Mersin-Yumuktepe; 24 Knossos.

first half of the seventh millennium BC, the following conclusions can be drawn. First, all four cases can be problematised: Only a few radiocarbon dates are available, and these could potentially be flawed. Excavated areas are very limited, making it difficult to evaluate the nature of these sites. Second, even if early seventh millennium BC dates are accepted for these sites, it is clear that these sites are exceptional rather than representing the full-blown emergence of a Neolithic way of life in their respective regions, which seems to occur by about 6500 BC.

5.1 Late Neolithic sites of Asia Minor, 6500–5500 BC. Produced by Joanne Porck and the author.

5.2.1 Chronology and Terminology

As in most other regions, the periodisation of prehistoric Asia Minor developed in the early stages of the discipline and subsequently became entrenched in the literature. This means that period designations are often no longer meaningful in their original sense and that period boundaries are often incongruent with cultural developments. In Asia Minor, the problems are further compounded by the fact that the Neolithic spread across the area in at least two waves: one at around 8500 BC for southern Central

Table 5.1 Periodisation of Central Anatolia

Early Bronze Age	3000–2000 BC
Late Chalcolithic	4000–3000 BC
Middle Chalcolithic	5500–4000 BC
Early Chalcolithic	6000–5500 BC
Late Ceramic Neolithic	6500–6000 BC
Early Ceramic Neolithic	7000–6500 BC
Aceramic Neolithic	8500–7000 BC

Anatolia and one at around 6500 BC, during which it spread to the Lake District, the Aegean, and the Marmara Region.

The traditional chronology of Central Anatolia during Prehistory is presented in Table 5.1. It is based on a modified version of the three-age system developed in European archaeology (with its Stone, Bronze, and Iron ages). For example, it became necessary to define a new Stone Age without ceramics: the Aceramic Neolithic. Another such development was the introduction of the term 'Chalcolithic' to identify a period in which copper artefacts were used but bronze had not yet become common.

Over time such terms took on meanings that were different from the circumstances they were originally based on. For example, it is clear that heat-treated and hammered copper artefacts were in use as early as the Aceramic Neolithic,[29] which means that there is no longer a link between the appearance of copper artefacts and the start of the Chalcolithic. Instead, the start of the Chalcolithic in Central Anatolia became linked with the emergence of painted pottery assemblages, following a similar older linkage in Mesopotamian archaeology.[30] The problem with this way of defining the Chalcolithic, however, is that painted pottery is largely absent in the subsequent Middle Chalcolithic and Late Chalcolithic periods, and that even in the Early Chalcolithic painted pottery is found only in some regions of Asia Minor.

Archaeological periodisations can easily take on a life of their own, in which specific features are held to be typical for each period and in which different periods are contrasted with each other.[31] However, where we have enough evidence, it is clear that the past was heterogeneous; in other words, different ways of living co-existed in any one period. For example, hunter-gatherers co-existed with farmers for millennia following the introduction of farming and sedentary lifeways. Further, developments in Prehistory were not monolithic: For example, while at some sites we can document

[29] Esin 1995; Schoop 1995.
[30] Schoop 2005a: 14–17.
[31] See Özbaşaran and Buitenhuis 2002 and the following discussion.

the decline of clustered neighbourhoods, at others they continue to exist or might even have been adopted in the same period. Finally, periodisations may not always agree well with cultural developments. For example, it is clear that there is continuity between the Late Ceramic Neolithic and the Early Chalcolithic, and that the introduction of painted ceramics would probably not have been perceived by prehistoric people as a matter of great importance in the scale of things. By contrast, at the start of the Middle Chalcolithic, many sites seem to have been abandoned. Culturally, this transition was probably of much greater significance than the introduction of painted ceramics.

A final problem with periodisations is the differential development of regions and the archaeological periodisations applied to them. During the Late Ceramic Neolithic period, regions such as the Aegean and the Marmara Region first took up farming and a sedentary way of life. Researchers often designate such sites as Early Neolithic, following conventions in adjacent regions such as Greece and Bulgaria, where the Neolithic is dated between 6500 and 3000 BC, without an intermediate Chalcolithic period.

In view of these problems, the use of period designations will be kept to a minimum in this chapter, and the following discussion will focus on the evidence at hand on a region-by-region basis. Ultimately, periodisations are only useful as a shorthand for referring to specific time spans in particular regions, and efforts to devise new periodisations that fit the data more closely often suffer from the mistake that periods are perceived as homogeneous and monolithic, and consequently fail to advance synthetic work.

5.3.1 Southern Central Anatolia in the Later Neolithic

In the period between 6500 and 5500 BC many profound, if often poorly understood, transformations occur in southern Central Anatolia within earlier cultural traditions best documented at the sites of Aşıklı Höyük and Çatalhöyük East, which had been extremely stable for many centuries. Among the characteristic practices at these sites were a preference for living in large, agglomerated communities rather than in smaller dispersed settlements and a subdivision of the large settlements into clustered neighbourhoods, which probably constituted the main arena for daily social interaction and bonding among people. Another significant factor in these settlements was the importance of buildings and their exact reproduction for the constitution of social groups, although the ways in which this mechanism operated differed at Aşıklı Höyük and Çatalhöyük East.

This understanding of the early Neolithic in the southern highlands of Asia Minor is probably erroneous because of its bias towards large settlements: Both Aşıklı Höyük and Çatalhöyük East were selected for investigations because of their large size, and we know far too little about smaller sites from this period. However, at least some characteristics, such as building continuity, are also seen at smaller settlements such as Boncuklu, Pınarbaşı, and Canhasan 3. Further, Canhasan 3 also appears to have clustered neighbourhoods.

In the period between 6500 and 5500 BC large 'stand-alone settlements', such as Aşıklı Höyük and Çatalhöyük East, disappear from the record and are replaced by settlement systems, in which most settlements are small and evenly distributed over the landscape, although some larger sites are also documented.

This overview of events occurring between 6500 and 5500 BC on the southern plateau of Asia Minor starts with a discussion of the Çatalhöyük East to West transition, followed by a consideration of the evidence from Erbaba, Canhasan 1, and the Cappadocian sites of Köşk Höyük and Tepecik-Çiftlik.

5.3.2 Çatalhöyük: From East to West

Çatalhöyük is the only site in Central Anatolia with substantial evidence of the Late Ceramic Neolithic and a sequence that includes the transition to the Early Chalcolithic. This sequence is therefore important for our understanding of developments in these periods. Two problems in this Çatalhöyük sequence need to be pointed out, however. The first is that both the upper levels V–I at Çatalhöyük East and the complete sequence of Çatalhöyük West remain relatively poorly understood. The second is that there is some evidence to suggest that the Çatalhöyük sequence is not representative of the wider developments in this area during these periods.

At Çatalhöyük a series of significant changes took place in the upper levels. These did not all occur as coherent package, with some starting earlier than others, but generally the changes do seem to concentrate roughly around 6500 BC.[32]

Conolly saw a change in the chipped stone industries after level VI, with a sharp increase in the use of prismatic blades produced with pressure flaking, a technique requiring substantial skill, leading Conolly to suggest that the blades were produced by specialists.[33] Interestingly, this technological shift

[32] Düring 2002.
[33] Conolly 1999a, 1999b.

coincided with a change in the obsidian source that supplied Çatalhöyük: Whereas in earlier levels the obsidian had derived from Göllüdağ, from level VII onwards most material came from Nenezidağ.[34]

In the ceramic assemblages Last sees a technological shift at around level VII, after which mineral temper becomes more common and vessels become thinner and better fired.[35] Atalay has argued that this was accompanied by a decrease in the use of clay balls in cooking, thus arguing for changes in cooking practices and technologies.[36]

Further changes can be observed in various types of imagery found at the site. It has been observed that changes occurred in the figurine motifs. For example, the clay figurines depicting large females occur mainly after level VI, while figurines that are clearly male disappear; it has been argued that this could reflect changes in the way gender was perceived.[37]

Changes also can be seen in wall paintings, with some motifs appearing in the upper levels V–I, such as the hunting scenes depicting large wild animals such as bulls and deer surrounded by a crowd of people engaged in a dance of sorts. Changes also occur in moulded features, with installations and animal sculptures disappearing after level VI and with the introduction of geometric relief decoration in wall plaster (§4.8.7). Given that wall paintings, moulded features, and installations at Çatalhöyük seem to be episodic, in that they occur over a restricted period in a fashion-like manner, it is prudent not to read too much into these changes.

Hodder and Last have argued that motifs occurring in wall art in the Early Ceramic Neolithic were transposed in the Early Chalcolithic to portable seals and to the painted pottery of the latter period.[38] This idea is problematic, however. Although there are some seals with motifs recalling earlier wall paintings or mouldings, such as a bear and a leopard figurine, most of the primarily geometric motifs on seals and painted ceramics have no parallels in earlier art at Çatalhöyük.[39] Instead, in recent campaigns, geometric patterns applied to wet plaster have been documented in the upper levels at Çatalhöyük East that are both highly comparable to motifs on seals (less so with painted ceramics) and contemporary with them. By contrast, fragments of painted plaster found in Early Chalcolithic levels at the site of Canhasan 1 do have clear parallels in ceramic decoration patterns (§5.3.5).

---

[34] Carter et al. 2005a; Carter and Shackley 2007: 443.

[35] Last 2005: 101.

[36] Atalay 2005.

[37] Hamilton 1996: 225–226; Voigt 2000; Hamilton 2005a.

[38] Hodder 1990: 21; Last 1998: 375; Last and Gibson 2006; Marciniak and Czerniak 2007.

[39] The recent suggestion that the Hacılar fantastic style is the missing link between the Çatalhöyük East wall paintings and the Çatalhöyük West painted pottery (Last and Gibson 2006: 47) is unconvincing in the absence of such pottery from the Konya Plain.

The most dramatic changes in the Çatalhöyük sequence occur in relation to the built environment. The marked building continuity that had been of central importance to the constitution of society in the early building levels (§4.8.9) is abandoned at around level V. The exact reconstruction of buildings in the same place that was important in the linked articulation of building pedigrees and lineage houses is abandoned. The use of older walls for the foundation of new structures continues, but this is more haphazard than was previously the case.[40] Some buildings continue to be used as burial sites for supra-household groups – for example, F.V.1 (1960s), which contained 33 burials – but such buildings are no longer defined by a strong pedigree. After level V, buildings containing large populations of sub-floor burials are no longer attested. Given these developments, it is plausible that we are looking at the demise of the house society format of social organisation in the Late Ceramic Neolithic at Çatalhöyük (§4.8.9).

Another change occurring in the upper levels at Çatalhöyük is the breakup of the clustered neighbourhoods that were typical of the earlier phases of the settlement. Instead, all buildings seem to be adjacent to open spaces, and we see the appearance of streets and alleys between buildings and possibly doors.[41]

Both the breakup of the clustered neighbourhoods and the fact that building continuity was no longer important for the social fabric suggest that households were no longer as firmly embedded in larger collectivities. It is likely that households became more independent in their social relations. The demise of the clustered neighbourhoods meant that social interaction became less intense and monitoring the behaviour of others more difficult.

It is probably no coincidence that with the demise of the clustered neighbourhoods, which had previously been the main arena for social interaction, the Çatalhöyük settlement started to shrink in size. The maximum expansion of the settlement occurred at around level VI, the remains of which are in evidence across most of the mound, and the level V–I occupation is much more restricted.[42]

In these upper levels buildings became less standardised, both with regard to dimensions and the number of rooms and with regard to interior arrangements, which are more varied in the configuration and orientation of furnishings in the buildings.[43] A good example of these changes are the buildings found in the 'TP Area' on the summit of the east mound, where three buildings were found that belong to levels I and 0 and date to about 6000 BC. These structures were irregular and of varying dimensions and did

[40] Düring 2001; 2006: 226–228.
[41] Düring 2001; 2006: 236–243.
[42] Last 1996; R. Matthews 1996: 85; Baird 2006a: 67.
[43] Düring 2001.

not have predecessors.[44] One feature observed in the upper levels is the appearance of large hearths located in the centre of the room,[45] a feature also documented in the Early Chalcolithic at Çatalhöyük West.

The mound of Çatalhöyük West is located on the opposite side of the former Çarsamba River. With its size of 8 hectares and its height of about 7 metres, the site is smaller than the east mound. However, the Chalcolithic mound is one of the largest of its period in Asia Minor.[46] The west mound was first excavated in 1961 by Mellaart. From 1998 onwards new excavations started, but apart from notes, no substantial publications have appeared.

It has become increasingly clear that there are considerable similarities between the final occupation of the east mound and that of the west mound. For example, the so-called pot stands from Çatalhöyük West are considered characteristic of the Early Chalcolithic (Fig. 5.2): These are L-shaped clay objects, often with geometric incised decoration. These objects have now also been found in the TP Area of Çatalhöyük East.[47] Further, in a new deep sounding at the west mound, basal layers were excavated that contained monochrome pottery comparable to that of the east mound.[48] Finally, recent radiocarbon dates have closed the chronological gap between Çatalhöyük East and West, with both the upper east mound and the west mound producing dates of about 6000 BC.[49] Thus, there may have been an extended period of overlap during which there was occupation on both sites.[50]

Given the gradual transition between Çatalhöyük East and West, it appears that some major shifts took place during the west mound sequence, changes that at present remain poorly understood. These include a massive increase in the use of pottery,[51] much of it painted with geometric motifs; changes in the form and construction of buildings; and new animal husbandry practices.

The Early Chalcolithic is marked by the appearance of painted pottery, most often reddish brown motifs on a buff body (see Fig. 5.2). The painted motifs are in most cases geometric, usually taking the form of chevrons, lozenges, and wavy lines. The pottery is tempered with small grits and

[44] Marciniak and Czerniak 2007.
[45] Mellaart 1967; Marciniak and Czerniak 2007: 119.
[46] Baird 2006a.
[47] Czerniak and Marciniak 2003.
[48] Biehl and Rosenstock 2007: 128–129.
[49] Gökturk et al. 2002; Marciniak and Czerniak 2007.
[50] The radiocarbon calibration curve has considerable wriggles around 6000 BC cal (Kuniholm and Newton 2002), however, and further dates are necessary to obtain better chronological control of this transition.
[51] Last 1996.

mica and in some cases a little chaff. The firing conditions in which these vessels were produced must have been carefully controlled.[52] The painted decoration varies in colour from orange to light brown. Typical shapes are carinated bowls with feet and jars with everted necks, some of which have handles on the shoulder or basket handles.

Mellaart distinguished two ceramics wares, labelled Early Chalcolithic I (EC I) (older) and Early Chalcolithic II (EC II).[53] Most of the mound is covered with EC I pottery; EC II pottery was found only in a few places.[54] The EC II material published by Mellaart is similar in vessel shapes and fabric to the EC I ware and differs only in the painted decoration,[55] but even this distinction is not very clear, and both EC I and EC II have parallels in Canhasan I level 2B (§5.3.5).[56]

The buildings of Çatalhöyük West are much more poorly understood than those of the east mound. Unlike at the east mound, the bricks at Çatalhöyük West were very similar in texture and colour to the mound matrix and buildings are irregular in plan, negatively affecting their retrieval. Mellaart found a poorly preserved building with internal buttresses. Building 25, the best-understood structure excavated in recent years, consists of small cell-like rooms surrounding a central plastered room with a large hearth. The unplastered and featureless small rooms could have been basements, mirroring the situation at Canhasan I (§5.3.5).[57] Another building with large internal buttresses also resembles level 2B buildings at Canhasan I.[58] Overall, buildings at the west mound appear to be haphazardly constructed, with few large spaces or features that can be linked with domestic activities. This situation, in combination with the often massive walls, seems to suggest that we are dealing mostly with basement spaces.

The subsistence economy at Çatalhöyük West seems generally similar to that at the east mound, with mixed food procurement strategies. Sheep and goats dominate the faunal assemblage and appear larger than in the preceding period.[59] Spindle whorls are absent, suggesting that wool was not important. The cattle at Çatalhöyük West appear to have been smaller than in the Neolithic, which could indicate domestication.[60] The tentative

---

[52] Mellaart 1965; Last 2000.
[53] Mellaart 1965.
[54] Mellaart 1965; Last 1996.
[55] Schoop 2005a: 129.
[56] French 1967a: 172.
[57] Gibson and Last 2003; similar small cell-like rooms were found in trench 5 (Biehl and Rosenstock 2007).
[58] Erdoğu 2007.
[59] Frame 2001.
[60] Gibson et al. 2002.

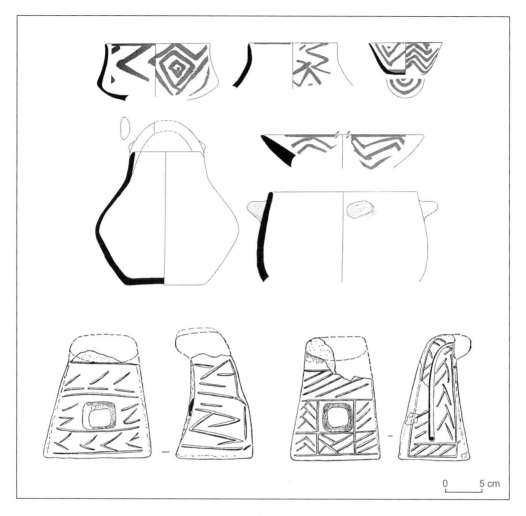

5.2 Pottery and pot stands from Çatalhöyük West. Pot stands drawn by the author and Joanne Porck after fig. 10 in Mellaart, J. 1965. 'Çatal Hüyük West'. *Anatolian Studies* 15: 135–156. Pottery drawn by the author and Joanne Porck after fig. 1 in Last, J., and Gibson, C. 2006. 'Ceramics and society in the Early Chalcolithic of Central Anatolia'. In *Prehistoric Pottery: Some Recent Research*, edited by A. Gibson, pp. 39–49. Oxford, England: Archaeopress.

evidence at Çatalhöyük West of domestic cattle is mirrored at other sites in Central Anatolia postdating 6000 BC, such as Köşk Höyük and Tepecik-Çiftlik (§5.3.6).

Summarising the sequence of Çatalhöyük East–West, settlement size decreases significantly concomitant with the disappearance of the clustered neighbourhoods in the Late Ceramic Neolithic. Instead of the social collectivities of the neighbourhood and lineage houses, we can document increasing household autonomy and the differentiation of house sizes and interiors. In the subsequent poorly investigated transition to the Early Chalcolithic, houses were transformed in ways that remain poorly understood and painted ceramics were introduced.

5.3.3 Erbaba

The site of Erbaba is located on the shores of Lake Beyşehir, in a region that receives about 500 millimetres of rain per annum, and in close proximity to wooded uplands (see Fig. 5.1). Erbaba is thus in an environmentally rich and varied setting. The site measures about 80 metres in diameter and has 4 metres of archaeological deposits. The site dates to the Late Ceramic Neolithic, with radiocarbon dates of 6700–6400 BC.[61] Unfortunately, the Erbaba excavations have been poorly published.[62] Nonetheless, the site is of some importance because it is one of only a few excavated Late Ceramic Neolithic sites in Central Anatolia.[63]

A large amount of pottery was found at Erbaba, all of which is monochrome, predominantly grey to brown in tone. Much of the pottery is tempered with crushed shell from Lake Beyşehir. Forms are simple, although some handles, lugs, and feet have been noted. The faunal spectrum is dominated by sheep and goats and to a lesser degree by cattle.[64] Botanical remains include emmer and einkorn wheat, barley, pea, and lentil.[65]

In four seasons between 1969 and 1977 about 1,100 square metres of Erbaba was excavated, amounting to some 20 per cent of the mound (Fig. 5.3). Buildings were constructed from stone, judging from extant wall heights and wall collapse. In some cases, walls were constructed over earlier walls, but whether building continuity was important at the site cannot be assessed. Few floors were exposed in the excavations and were of poor quality. Up to 10 refloorings were documented in one of the rooms. Plaster benches, painted plastered embellishments, and ovens were found, but no details have been provided. Most of the rooms encountered at Erbaba are very small; in combination with the sturdy walls, this can be interpreted as evidence that these were basement spaces supporting an upper storey.[66]

At Erbaba we appear to be dealing with a more or less fully built-up settlement, without streets separating the buildings. Although the plan is not

---

[61] Thissen 2002: 326.
[62] Bordaz 1969, 1973; Bordaz and Bordaz 1976, 1977a, 1977b, 1978a, 1978b, 1982.
[63] In recent years rescue excavations have been undertaken at Gökhöyük, a site similar to and near Erbaba, but nothing seems to have been published so far.
[64] Martin et al. 2002.
[65] Van Zeist and Buitenhuis 1983.
[66] Düring 2006: 253–254.

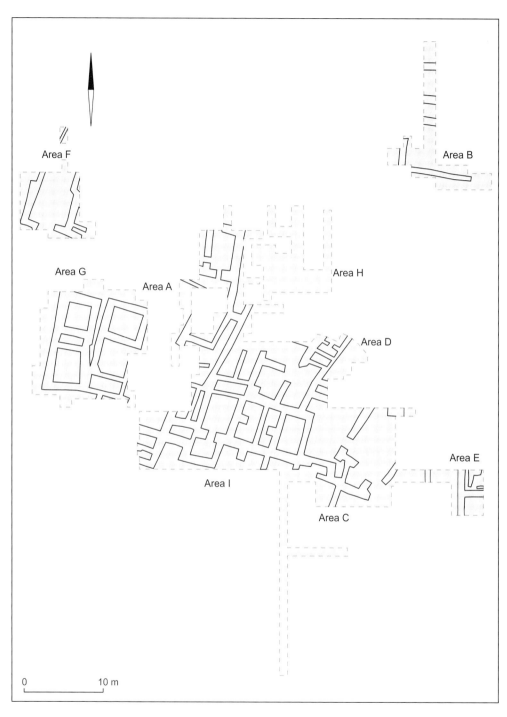

5.3 Plan of Erbaba. Produced by the author and Medy Oberendorff after fig. 1 in Bordaz, J., and Bordaz, L. A. 1982. 'Erbaba: The 1977 and 1978 seasons in perspective'. *Türk Arkeoloji Dergisi* 26: 85–92.

as clear as one would like it to be, this seems to be a clustered neighbourhood settlement. From the limited size of the mound it can tentatively be
estimated that the settlement probably encompassed only a single neighbourhood, with a local population of probably fewer than 300 people.[67]

5.3.4 Settlement Evidence in Central Anatolia

The small size of the Erbaba community is best understood in relation to
the local settlement system. Erbaba is one of a group of relatively small
Late Ceramic Neolithic sites located on the shores of Lake Beyşehir and
Lake Suğla often only a few kilometres apart.[68] None of the sites is larger
than the others, and any form of functional differentiation seems unlikely.
Little is know about the settlement pattern in the Beyşehir/Suğla Region
in the subsequent Early Chalcolithic,[69] and I assume that this is the result
of research biases rather than a reflection of past realities.

   In the Konya Plain Survey data, the number of sites rose between 6500
and 5500 BC from 1 Ceramic Neolithic site to 15 Early Chalcolithic sites,
and this increase is mirrored in the aggregate site area. It is possible, however, that many of the Early Chalcolithic sites may have been occupied only
during part of the Early Chalcolithic.[70]

   Similar data are not available for surveys in other areas of Central Anatolia, where reports typically take the form of an annual list of sites visited. In
the CANeW period maps of Central Anatolia there are 10 Early Ceramic
Neolithic (ECN) sites (but 4 of these actually predate the ECN: Aşıklı
Höyük, Canhasan 3, Suberde, and Musular), 35 Late Ceramic Neolithic
sites, and 17 Early Chalcolithic sites.[71] While these figures should not be
taken at face value, it does appear that there is a substantial increase in
settlement numbers after 6500 BC, and that most of these settlements are
relatively small and part of a larger network of settlements.

   While the Late Ceramic Neolithic settlement evidence from the
Beyşehir/Suğla Region suggests a network of small equivalent sites, more
differentiated settlement systems appear in the Early Chalcolithic on the
Konya Plain. Çatalhöyük West, with its 8 hectares, is much larger than
other sites and Baird has argued that it was a central site, also because
obsidian appears to be more common at Çatalhöyük West than at other

---

[67] Düring 2006: 256–257.
[68] Mellaart 1961; Thissen 2002: 18.
[69] Kuzucuoğlu 2002: map for ECA IV.
[70] Baird 2002, 2006a.
[71] Kuzucuoğlu 2002: 55–57.

mounds.[72] With its size of 9 hectares, Canhasan 1 is similar to Çatalhöyük West. Although we do not have settlement evidence from the Canhasan Region, it is plausible that Canhasan 1 was also a central place serving a network of smaller settlements.

Summarising the settlement evidence in Central Anatolia: At first, we have large communities in stand-alone settlements, as at Aşıklı Höyük and Çatalhöyük; in the Late Ceramic Neolithic, we witness the rise of networks of undifferentiated small settlements in some regions; and for the Early Chalcolithic, we can postulate functionally differentiated settlement systems with central places. These observations have implications for how large settlements such as Aşıklı Höyük and Çatalhöyük are interpreted. They have often been labelled 'towns' or 'cities', concepts that are better reserved for central settlements with a hinterland of smaller villages or hamlets.[73]

5.3.5 Canhasan 1: Bridging the Neolithic and the Chalcolithic

Canhasan 1 is a key site for the Early Chalcolithic and has a sequence spanning the transition with the preceding Neolithic. The site is situated near Karaman on the eastern bank of the former Selereki River, in a flat landscape that receives about 300 millimetres of precipitation per annum. The assumed natural vegetation is open steppe with some shrubs, and prior to the recent irrigation agriculture the area was mainly used for pasturing flocks.[74] The site measures approximately 9 hectares and rises some 5 metres above the plain.

Excavations at Canhasan 1 took place between 1961 and 1967. Recently, two volumes of the final publications have been published.[75] The sequence spans the Late Ceramic Neolithic (layers 7–4), Early Chalcolithic (layers 3, 2B, and 2A), and Late Chalcolithic (layer 1). There is some controversy over the layer 2B/2A chronology at Canhasan 1. French[76] assigned layer 2B to the transition between the Early and Middle Chalcolithic and 2A to the Middle Chalcolithic. As Thissen[77] has pointed out, however, radiocarbon dates from layers 2B and 2A give a range of 6000–5500 BC, and therefore they date to the Early Chalcolithic. Additional radiocarbon dates on beams

---

[72] Baird 2002: 150; 2006a: 72–73.
[73] Düring 2007.
[74] Hütteroth 1968; Van Zeist and Bottema 1991: 24–25; French 1998: 2.
[75] French 1998, 2005.
[76] French 1998: 20.
[77] Thissen 2000: 90–95; also Schoop 2005a: 146.

found in layer 2 B produced dates as early as 6700 BC, and these suggest that the older layers 7–4 may date to the second half of the seventh millennium BC.[78]

Botanical remains at Canhasan 1 include hulled six-rowed barley and field pea.[79] Sheep seem to dominate the faunal assemblage. According to Perkins and Daly, bovids were domesticated at Canhasan 1.[80] Pottery wares from layers 7–5 are described as burnished and dark brown to reddish in tone.[81] Some of these have incised decorations, most commonly zigzag patterns with rows of dots in between. Simple shapes such as globular vessels and open bowls predominate, but some carinated forms do occur. Most vessels have out-turned rims, and developed bases are common. French dates this assemblage to the final Ceramic Neolithic.[82] Little has been published on other artefact categories at Canhasan 1. Finds include a group of carved shell pendants, figurines, pendants, and spindle whorls. Bone was used for beads, armlets, and awls. A copper mace head was also found. The chipped stone industry is described only as being 'simple'.

Layers 7 and 6 at Canhasan have been investigated only over an area of 2 by 3 metres. Consequently, little of interest is known about these layers. In layer 5, exposed over 4 by 4 metres, a confusing array of walls was found. The features in this layer were constantly modified: Doors were opened and blocked, a wall was constructed over a pre-existing bench, and hearths were shifted in location in the room.[83]

The remnants of the layer 4 buildings show characteristics similar to those of layer 5. Walls were constructed over those of the preceding layer. The floor surfaces consisted of multiple high-quality plasters and rested on wooden beams. On the floors various domestic features were found, including two hearths, a series of six bins, and two embedded querns. Further, floor compartments with plaster ledges were found similar to those documented at Çatalhöyük East. Finally, one element of particular interest was a double burial of two dogs located below a raised threshold separating two rooms.[84]

Subsequent layer 3 was excavated over 10 by 10 metres, and in this exposure one poorly preserved structure was found.[85] In this layer the first

[78] http://www.canew.org/data.html.
[79] J. Renfrew 1968.
[80] Perkins and Daly 1968: 104. However, given that Perkins (1969) reached similar conclusions for the Çatalhöyük bovids that have since been disproved (Ducos 1988; Russell and Martin 2005: 55), these conclusions should be treated with due caution.
[81] French 2005: 16–17.
[82] French 1967a: 176; 1998: 16.
[83] French 1998: 23–24.
[84] French 1998: 25, pls. 4–2 and 5–1.
[85] French 1998: fig. 10.

mould-made mud bricks occurred and walls became more massive. Another innovation in layer 3 is the use of internal buttresses. The walls of the layer 3 structures were plastered with red clay and white clay, but no features other than a possible bench were found, nor could a floor be distinguished. The pottery originally assigned to layer 3 was described as transitional: It included both monochrome and painted sherds but has more recently been reassigned to layer 2B.[86]

The most extensive exposure at Canhasan 1 is that of layers 2A and 2B. A neighbourhood of approximately 15 buildings was exposed (Fig. 5.4) in which buildings were completely surrounded by other structures. It is clear that Canhasan 1 is an example of the clustered neighbourhood settlements that are well known from the Central Anatolian Neolithic.

The persistence of this type of settlement form at Canhasan 1 in the Early Chalcolithic demonstrates that developments in Central Anatolia were not homogeneous and that changes probably occurred along different trajectories amongst various local communities. At Çatalhöyük the clustered neighbourhoods disappear in the Late Ceramic Neolithic, but at Late Ceramic Neolithic Erbaba a clustered neighbourhood settlement is well attested, housing a local community radically smaller in scale than that of Çatalhöyük. Thus, we cannot draw the scattered evidence from the various Central Anatolian Neolithic and Early Chalcolithic settlements into a single grand narrative. Rather, various local developments took place, some of which might have contradicted one another.

The buildings exposed in layer 2 at Canhasan 1 were initially interpreted as constituting one layer but were later subdivided into layers 2B (older) and 2A, both of which encompass several building levels. This sequence is in many ways problematic and difficult to conceptualise.[87] From the outset of the excavations at Canhasan, French recognised a 'Middle Chalcolithic' 2A layer with distinctive pottery that was found in a variety of deposits, including pits and deposits of debris and ash. Many of these deposits were found over and within buildings of the earlier layer 2B buildings, but no substantial structures that could be associated with layer 2A. In 1966 French noted for layer 2A: "The problem which still remains unsolved after five years of excavation over an area of more than 1100 square metres is: where was this settlement?"[88] The problem was partly solved in the following season, when it was realised that some of the structures that had been assigned to layer 2B could in fact be assigned to layer 2A, and this brought about the transfer of a whole series of structures located on the western edge of the

---

[86] French 1968: 48; 2005: 18.
[87] Düring 2006: 261–264.
[88] French 1966: 115.

plan to layer 2A. It appeared that all these layer 2A structures were super-imposed on layer 2B buildings.[89] In the final report on the stratigraphy and structures of the site, French explains the rationale behind these re-assignments. He argues that some of the layer 2A buildings were 'inserted' into existing layer 2B structures. This insertion was achieved by construct-ing new structures within extant older buildings, although in some cases this procedure involved removing some of the earlier walls and features. The inserted structures that were built in this way did not damage the sur-rounding buildings and follow the alignment of the settlement in general.

The prime problem that French does not solve in his final publication on the stratigraphy and structures of Canhasan 1 is the relation between the building remains of layers 2A and 2B. The issue is whether the 2B buildings that were not replaced by 2A insertions continued to be in use alongside those of layer 2A or whether they were no longer inhabited. French opts for the latter position.[90] This interpretation has one important problem. If it was indeed the case that the buildings of layer 2B were already in disuse and falling apart, why were the layer 2A buildings inserted carefully into the older settlement structure? The insertion procedure described by French would make sense only if the 2A structures replaced some of the older 2B structures while co-existing with others. If this is true, the division between the two layers is less rigid than that envisaged by French. Rather than a wholesale reconfiguration of the settlement, this would fit with the piecemeal fashion in which ethnographically documented mud built villages have been documented to change.[91] Buildings were renovated by inserting a new set of walls in front of the existing walls of a building, possibly because a particular building was no longer structurally sound.

Many of the 2B and 2A buildings were preserved up to a considerable height, facilitating the reconstruction of individual structures and the set-tlement. Mould-made mud bricks were now standardised in size. The use of buttresses first evidenced in layer 3 continued in layer 2B. In order to further enhance the load-bearing capacities of walls, bricks are laid in the header-and-stretcher pattern. Finally, in some buildings, evidence of posts is found. These posts are placed in the axis between two buttresses, and this positioning suggests that these posts supported beams resting on the buttresses.

Why are the Canhasan walls thus reinforced? There is a strong case that these changes in building practices are related to the construction of upper storeys. The plan obtained of level 2B/2A at Canhasan 1 appears to

[89] French 1968: 169.
[90] French 1998: 65.
[91] Peters 1982: 226.

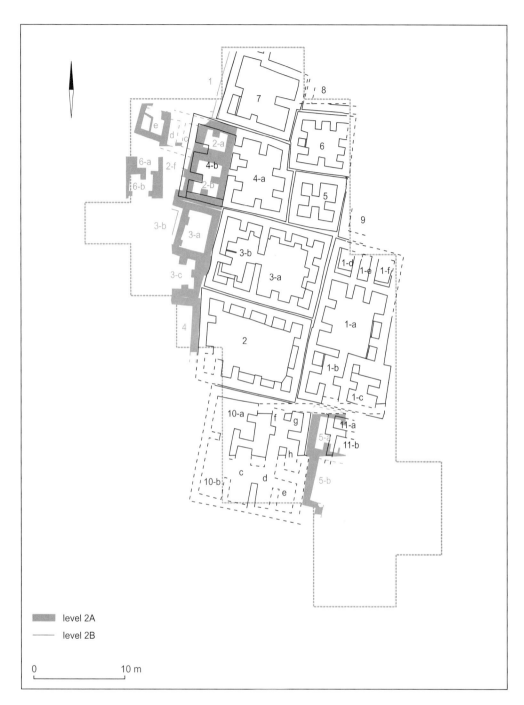

level 2A

level 2B

0   10 m

5.4 Plan of layers 2B and 2A at Canhasan 1. Produced by the author and Medy Oberendorff after figs. 11 and 12 in French, D. 1998. *Canhasan Sites I: Stratigraphy and Structures*. Ankara: BIAA. Reproduced by permission of D. French and the British Institute of Ankara.

represent the basements of the settlement only. Apart from the changes in building technology, this argument can be supported by contextual data.

Unlike the buildings at Çatalhöyük East and Canhasan layers 5 and 4, the Canhasan 2B/2A buildings do not have good plasters, and they have few interior features to suggest that they were domestic spaces. Many buildings do not seem to have been plastered at all; others have a white mud plaster. There is also a notable lack of good floors. Few features were found in the structures, most of which can be placed into two general categories: benches and bins. The 'benches' are often irregular in shape and most likely served as shelves rather than seats. Ovens and hearths are absent altogether.

At Canhasan 1 there are also data pertaining to the upper storeys. Fragments of collapsed upper storeys with painted plaster were found, and in buildings 3 and 10 of layer 2B, painted wall plaster was found on standing remains of the upper storeys. Painted plaster appears to have been fairly common in the upper storeys, and the qualitative difference from ground floor plasters is a good argument for reconstructing the living quarters on the second storey.

The shift of living quarters to the first floor documented at Canhasan 1 is also relevant for the reconstruction of less well understood buildings at Erbaba and Çatalhöyük West, where spaces are often small, lack plastered floors and wall surfaces, and contain few *in situ* features or floors. For archaeology, the consequences of this development are that the preservation of living quarters becomes far less likely, and that we have less information from which to reconstruct the social uses of spaces.

Both Hodder and Last have argued that motifs occurring in wall paintings in the Ceramic Neolithic were transposed in the Early Chalcolithic to portable pottery.[92] However, from the evidence at Canhasan 1, it is clear that wall plaster continued to be painted in the Early Chalcolithic but that this occurred on the upper storeys. Thus, wall painting does not disappear in the Early Chalcolithic; it simply becomes less visible archaeologically.

The really interesting question is why people started to construct two-storey structures at Canhasan 1. Various reasons could be put forward for introducing two-storey buildings, but the relevance of none of them can be demonstrated. These include a scarcity of good building locations in a settlement where people wanted to live in a specific neighbourhood; matters of prestige; and the need to create non-domestic spaces that could be used for storage purposes or as workshops. That Canhasan 1 might have been a central place in a wider network of dependent smaller settlements could have been important in this development.

---

[92] Hodder 1990: 21; Last 1998: 375.

In layers 2B and 2A fine buff burnished pots with incised decoration, also present in the earlier levels, continue to be found. The vessels consist predominantly of carinated bowls, and many are decorated with meander motifs that have clear parallels in the fragments of painted wall plaster found at Canhasan 1 (Fig. 5.5). Further, the incised ceramics often have knobs below the rims in the form of stylised cattle heads.

The pottery of layers 2B and 2A is characterised by geometric painted wares (see Fig. 5.5). The colour of the paint is brown to red and is applied on buff-brown to cream-beige pots. Many of the painted surfaces were prepared with a wash or slip. Some were burnished after painting. There is a bewildering variety of painted motifs on vessels, but with a few exceptions, all are geometric designs consisting of zigzags, lattices, lozenges, and crosshatches arranged in various configurations. Pots were often subdivided into various horizontal bands to enable further elaboration of decoration. The repertory of vessel shapes is dominated by jars with S profiles, many with small lugs or handles on the shoulder. Necked jars and bowls are also common. Most vessels have flat bases, and elements such as feet, carinations, or handles seem to be rare.

Some of the layer 2B/2A vessels are of considerable size, with diameters of up to half a metre, attesting to considerable skill of the potters in both creating and firing these vessels. The elaboration of surfaces with painting and burnishing points to the importance of the visual appearance of the pots. The context in which some of the vessels were found, on top of the collapsed remains of the upper storeys,[93] suggests that they were placed centrally in living rooms. Considering these find contexts and the effort put into producing these vessels, it seems clear that these were objects for domestic display, and they might have played a role in the articulation of households in the wider community, for instance through feasts. In such a model, both the diversity of decoration on vessels of the same type and the efforts put into their production make sense.

Considerable efforts have been devoted to subdividing the Canhasan 1 painted ceramics into chronological groups and linking these groups with assemblages from other sites. These subdivisions were created primarily on the basis of the style of painting on these vessels rather than changes in vessel shapes or pottery technologies. Over time, these subdivisions have become increasingly problematic and untenable.

The first subdivision created was between layers 2B and 2A. This distinction was not based initially on stratigraphic considerations, since 2A building levels were only defined later in the excavations, but on a desire to link the Canhasan assemblages with those of Mersin-Yumuktepe. Thus, 2B

---

[93] French 2005: 18.

was held to parallel levels 21–20 at Mersin and 2A to parallel levels 19–17 of that site. At Yumuktepe, levels 19–17 showed Halaf influences and were labelled 'Middle Chalcolithic' for that reason; it is on this basis that French placed his layer 2A in the Middle Chalcolithic. However, the link between Canhasan 2A and Yumuktepe 19–17 is not particularly strong.[94] Further, there is no convincing stratigraphic break between layers 2B and 2A at Canhasan, and the same is true for the ceramics. Many of the secure 2B vessels are very similar to 2A ceramics, and French even discusses a group of 2B/2A pots.[95]

In his 1965 report on Çatalhöyük West, Mellaart distinguished two phases, EC I and EC II.[96] EC II was apparently found only in a number of pits and remained elusive in later excavation seasons. Again, the distinction between EC I and II was not based on changes in vessel forms or pottery technology, but on rather subtle changes in painted decoration. Mellaart argued that his EC I assemblages bridged the gap between the Ceramic Neolithic and the Chalcolithic, whereas his EC II assemblage paralleled Canhasan 2B.

In response to this proposal, French argued that both Canhasan 2B and 2A had three subphases, each with distinctive ceramics, and that Mellaart's EC I assemblage paralleled the second subphase of 2B, whereas EC II could be linked to the third subphase of Canhasan 2B.[97]

While French is correct in arguing that good parallels for both EC I and EC II of Çatalhöyük West can be found at Canhasan 2B, the sub-division of Canhasan 2B and 2A each into three subphases with distinctive ceramics is problematic. Both in the stratigraphy and in the ceramic assemblages there is little to justify these subdivisions, which seem to have been proposed mainly to facilitate correlation with published sequences from other sites and the desire to fill chronological gaps. In the final report on ceramics the tripartite subdivision of layers 2B and 2A does not resurface, nor is it mentioned. Instead, it is argued that most of the sherds that were found are unreliable to date the associated levels and/or features.[98]

Summarising the situation of Canhasan 1, the site provides good evidence of the transition between the Ceramic Neolithic and Early Chalcolithic, which is characterised by architectural changes and a shift of living quarters to the second storey. A further element is the increasing elaboration of ceramics, which appear to have become important in the definition and articulation of households in the wider community. Unfortunately, we

---

[94] Schoop 2005a: 126, 130–131.
[95] French 2005: 26.
[96] Mellaart 1965.
[97] French 1966: 121; 1967a: 172.
[98] French 2005.

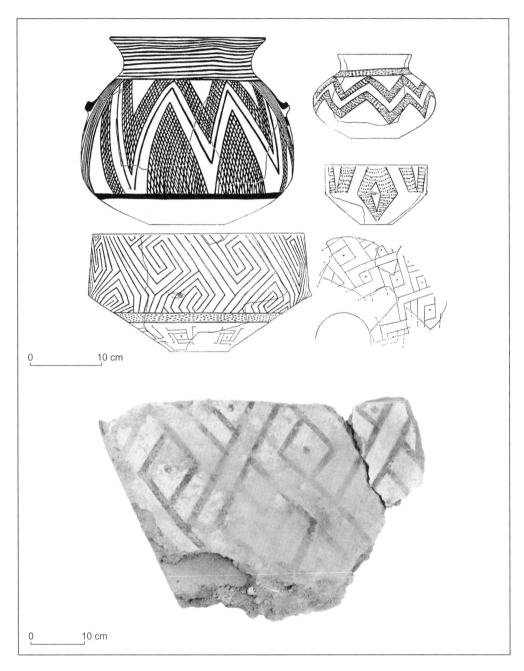

5.5 Painted and incised ceramics and painted plaster from layer 2 B at Can hasan 1. Reproduced with permission of D. French and the British Institute of Ankara from French, D. 1962. 'Excavations at Can Hasan: First preliminary report, 1961'. *Anatolian Studies* 12: 27–40, plate 2 and fig. 9.

know little about accompanying changes in the community or in the economy at Canhasan 1, although the site might have been a central settlement catering to a hinterland of smaller settlements.

5.3.6 Köşk Höyük and Tepecik-Çiftlik

In the fertile landscape of Cappadocia a series of Chalcolithic sites have been recognised. These sites were first surveyed by Todd in the 1960s.[99] Subsequently, small-scale excavations took place at Niğde-Tepebağları in 1972, Pınarbaşı-Bor in 1982, and Gelveri-Güzelyurt in 1990,[100] and more systematic investigations have been undertaken at Köşk Höyük and Tepecik-Çiftlik. The remains from Musular dating to this period are less well understood[101] but are compatible with the assemblages found at Tepecik-Çiftlik and Köşk Höyük.

What is remarkable about the Cappadocian sites is that the assemblages found are completely different from contemporary assemblages at Çatalhöyük West and Canhasan 1, although the distance between the latter site and the Cappadocian sites is only about 130 kilometres. Köşk Höyük and Tepecik-Çiftlik are approximately 40 kilometres apart and have assemblages that are almost interchangeable.

Tepecik is about 6 hectares in size and stands 9 metres above its surroundings. The site is located in a fertile valley that profits from high groundwater levels. Excavations were initiated in 2000 and are ongoing. Five main levels have been identified: Levels 5 and 4 have been assigned to the Neolithic; level 3 has been dated to the Early Chalcolithic; layer 2 has been dated to the Middle Chalcolithic, but it will be argued that it is most likely Early Chalcolithic as well; and layer 1 consists of Late Roman and Byzantine remains.[102]

Relatively little is known about levels 5 and 4. Level 5 was excavated in a sounding that contained midden deposits and a few poorly preserved hearths or ovens. Level 4 contained 16 extramural burials, which included adults, juveniles, and infants. Some of the burials were fully articulated, whereas others were secondary and incomplete, for example including only the long bones and skulls. Some burials contained objects such as beads or a celt.

The best-preserved building remains of level 4 consist of a partially excavated rectangular room with stone walls: probably the base for a mud

---

[99] Todd 1968b, 1980.
[100] N. Özgüç 1973; Silistreli 1984; Esin 1993b.
[101] Özbaşaran et al. 2007: 278–280.
[102] Bıçakcı et al. 2007.

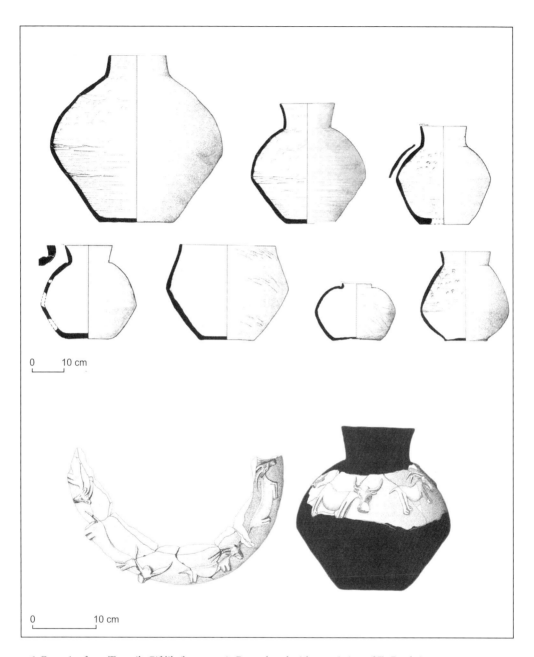

5.6 Ceramics from Tepecik-Çiftlik (layers 2–3). Reproduced with permission of E. Bıçakçi from Bıçakçi, E., Altınbilek-Algül, C., Balcı, S., and Godon, M. 2007. 'Tepecik-Çiftlik'. In *Anadolu'da Uygarlığın doğuşu Avrupaya yayılımı Türkiye'de Neolitik Dönem, Yeni Kazılar, yeni Bulgular*, edited by M. Özdoğan and N. Başgelen, pp. 237–254, figs. 30 and 35. Istanbul, Turkey: Arkeoloji ve Sanat Yayınları.

superstructure. It had a central fireplace, and both this and the associated floors were renovated several times. Under the floor, an infant burial was placed in a ceramic vessel.

Many of the ceramic vessels found in layers 5 and 4 are quite large (up to 30 centimetres high) and have a red slip, and some have geometric decorations, such as zigzags, or loops hanging from the rim (Fig. 5.6).

Early Chalcolithic layer 3 at Tepecik has been the most extensively investigated. Building remains consisted of the stone bases for mud superstructures and associated floors and features. Two types of buildings have been distinguished. First, there are buildings with a single large room measuring up to 5 by 5 metres. These contain a range of domestic features, including hearths, ovens, and silos, and often have compartmentalised floors. Some floors were paved with stones. Second, there are buildings consisting of small cell-like spaces, often measuring less than 1 metre in width and breadth. A building of this kind has also been found at Musular.[103] The cells might have been used for storage; they are too small for any other purpose. Alternatively, the floors of these buildings could have been constructed at a higher level, with the cells supporting the raised floors.

The buildings at Tepecik were constantly modified, extra rooms were added to buildings, or interior furnishings were altered.[104] The dynamic development of buildings fits with the default pattern documented in ethnographic studies. In this pattern, buildings are continuously adjusted to the changing fortunes of their inhabitants[105] and can be contrasted with the extreme degree of building continuity in sites such as Aşıklı Höyük and Çatalhöyük.

Relatively few burials were found in level 3, and all appear to be in open spaces. Many burials were secondary, consisting of skulls and long bones only, sometimes accompanied by objects such as obsidian points, stone celts, or ceramic vessels.

Köşk Höyük, 40 kilometres to the south, is highly comparable to Tepecik-Çiftlik. It is situated next to a spring on a limestone outcrop and in a fertile region. The site measures about 4 hectares and stands 6 metres above its surroundings. Excavations took place between 1982 and 1990 and from 1995 onwards. The first synthetic reports on these new excavations have started to appear.

In the latest report five levels are distinguished, of which levels 5–2 are assigned to the Ceramic Neolithic and level 1 is dated to the Early Chalcolithic.[106] This chronology is problematic, however, and is not

---

[103] Özbaşaran et al. 2007: 278–279, fig. 24.
[104] Bıçakcı et al. 2007: 238–239, fig. 5.
[105] Peters 1982: 226; Düring 2006: 63–64.
[106] Öztan 2007: 224.

accepted here. Level 1 has been radiocarbon dated to between 5200 and 4800 BC, and wriggle matching produced a best fit around 4911 BC for the beam from which these radiocarbon dates were taken.[107] This clearly puts level 1 into the Middle Chalcolithic (5500–4000 BC). The ceramics and buildings found in level 1 of Köşk Höyük match those of nearby Güvercinkayası, another site that can be firmly dated to the period between 5200 and 4800 BC (§6.2.4).

Öztan reports finding Canhasan 2B–style ceramics in level 1,[108] which would imply an Early Chalcolithic date for this level. Very few sherds were found, however. They might have been displaced from earlier deposits, given that these ceramics date from at least half a millennium earlier than level 1.

For levels 5 to 2 at Köşk Höyük a single radiocarbon date has been published, from level 3 with a date of 5600–5380 ± 38 cal BC. This radiocarbon date indicates that levels 3 and 2 probably date to the Early Chalcolithic, while levels 5 and 4 remain undated at present. The material culture found at Köşk Höyük also supports a date in the Early Chalcolithic. It seems that the site has been dated to the Ceramic Neolithic on the basis of postulated cultural continuities with Çatalhöyük East and even with the Levantine PPN-B, which cannot be substantiated at present.

Levels 5 and 4 have been investigated in small exposures, and little is known about them. By contrast, levels 3 and 2 have been exposed over large areas. As at Tepecik, the building remains consist of stone bases for mud walls, often with remnants of plaster on the interior surface that link up with the plastered floors, upon which a range of features and artefacts have been found. Another feature in common with Tepecik is the dynamic nature of buildings, which are constantly altered, enlarged, subdivided, renovated, and so on. Buildings were accessible through doors but were constructed closely adjacent to each other, which meant that they could only be accessed through a haphazard system of small alleys.

Buildings contained between two and four rooms, but in each building there is one large room that can be identified as the main room (Fig. 5.7). It contains a compartment or bench raised about 50 centimetres above the floor, usually in one of the corners opposite the entrance. Other features commonly found in the buildings are ovens and silos. In many buildings, grinding equipment was found in the smaller rooms.

Some of the floors were painted orange or white, and one wall painting has been found in level 3. It is poorly preserved, but according to the excavators it depicts a large deer surrounded by a multitude of small humans engaged

---

[107] Kuniholm and Newton 2002; Thissen 2002.
[108] Öztan 2002: 58; 2003: 72; also Silistreli 1985.

in either hunting or dancing. This scene has some parallels in the relief decorated pottery of Köşk and Tepecik, but it has also been linked with the hunting scenes of the upper levels at Çatalhöyük East (§4.8.7), and this has been one argument for dating the site to the Ceramic Neolithic.

Burials at Köşk were usually placed beneath buildings, either below the benches or beneath walls. All these burials are those of neonates, infants, or children. Some were buried in a pit; others were placed in a ceramic container. Objects such as ceramics with relief imagery, figurines, seals, arm rings, and necklaces were commonly found in these burials.

In addition, a number of plastered skulls were found on top of, or buried in, the raised compartments of the Köşk buildings. Sixteen of these skulls have been found so far. Some were plastered on the face only; the rest of the skull originally might have been covered by a hat or wig. The eyes are often carefully executed and are sometimes inlaid with stones. The plastered skulls include those of women, infants, and children. Interestingly, one level 3 adult burial was found in an open space, with the skull missing and accompanied by various ceramic vessels. The plastered skulls have been interpreted as representing the tail end of a tradition of skull plastering well known from the PPN-B in the Fertile Crescent.[109]

Little has been published on the chipped stone industries of Tepecik and Köşk, which appear to be almost exclusively obsidian. Conspicuous are tanged arrowheads often covered with flat retouche on one side. These oval objects were made both from highly standardised blades struck from a double platform core in alternating fashion and from less standardised flakes. Oval scrapers on flakes are common. Both double and single platform cores have been found at Köşk Höyük. In very general terms, the objects found at these sites may be compared to the objects found at Çatalhöyük East, although they appear to have been produced with different technologies. At Köşk, obsidian mirrors have also been found; this is the only site other than Çatalhöyük East where they seem to occur.

In terms of subsistence at Köşk, the remains of wheat, barley, lentils, beans, and chickpea have been documented. The faunal analysis at Tepecik and Köşk demonstrates that domestic sheep, goats, pigs, and cattle were present.

One very exciting find of relief-decorated pottery from Köşk shows what appears to be somebody milking a cow.[110] The question of when dairy products started to be used for human consumption has been pursued in recent years by analysing residues in pot sherds. Recently, it has been argued in a brief paper that dairy consumption started in the seventh millennium across

[109] Öztan 2002: 57–58; 2007: 226.
[110] Öztan 2007: 29, fig. 16.

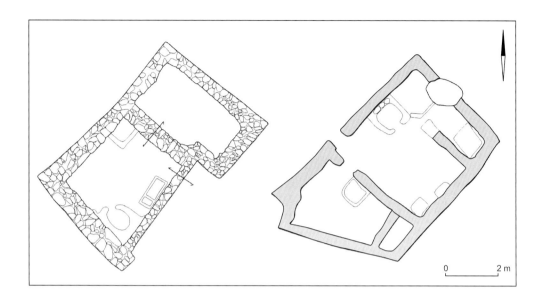

5.7 Two level 3 buildings from Köşk Höyük. Reproduced with permission of A. Öztan from Öztan, A. 2007. 'Köşk Höyük: Niğde-Bor Ovasında Bir Neolitik Yerlesim'. In *Anadolu'da Uygarlığın doğuşu Avrupaya yayılımı Türkiye'de Neolitik Dönem, Yeni Kazılar, yeni Bulgular*, edited by M. Özdoğan and N. Başgelen, pp. 223–236, figs. 4 and 5. Istanbul, Turkey: Arkeoloji ve Sanat Yayınları.

the Fertile Crescent and in Anatolia.[111] In this study a marked increase was noted in dairy residues in the Marmara Region. Another study of Neolithic sherds from the Balkans dating to between 5900 and 5500 BC also provided evidence of dairy product residues in ceramic vessels.[112] Thus, in terms of the time frame, the Köşk depiction would fit. The addition of cattle dairy products to the diet would have significantly altered the menu of people in Prehistory.

Apart from the domestic species, bones of deer, bears, wild boars, wild horses, wild donkeys, hares, and foxes were also found, and it appears that hunting played an important role at the site, whether for subsistence, symbolic reasons, or both. It has been argued that the Early Chalcolithic was characterised by increased reliance on farming, and that hunting and gathering were no longer significant during this period.[113] In particular, the faunal evidence from Tepecik and Köşk clearly contradicts this idea.

Further, wild animals such as cattle, deer, and donkeys also feature prominently on the relief decorated ceramics of level 3 at Tepecik and of levels 3 and 2 at Köşk. Vessels in this level have a red slip and complex forms also appear, including necked and carinated jars and carinated holemouth vessels (Fig. 5.6). Their lower parts were produced in baskets, while their upper parts were slab built. Some box-shaped vessels have also been found, as well as forms resembling large wine cups, which are known as 'fruit stands'.

[111] Evershed et al. 2008.
[112] Craig et al. 2005.
[113] Gérard 2002: 108; Marciniak and Czerniak 2007.

Pottery is well fired. Firing was probably done in kilns rather than in open fires. Some of the carinated necked jars, vessels with diametres of up to 40 centimetres, are decorated with figurative scenes of humans and animals in high relief, some of which are also painted. Depicted motifs include processions of wild animals; animal heads moulded onto the shoulder of vessels; what appear to be hunting scenes – for example, human figures with bows and arrows juxtaposed to wild animals, and others where humans seem to be dancing next to wild animals rather than hunting them; scenes in which stylised female human figures appear to be dancing; and others in which people appear to be harvesting wheat or milking cows. The women depicted in figurines and on the vessels are wearing their hair in a long cone upwards, or perhaps this is a hat of some sort. The men on the ceramic vessels seem to be wearing a kind of hat and a skirt with a back flap that is also visible in figurines as a hanging piece of cloth, which is sometimes shown horizontally on the vessels, possibly to indicate that the person is moving fast.[114]

Much of this extremely rich imagery is reminiscent of wall paintings found in the upper levels at Çatalhöyük East, and the two have been explicitly linked.[115] However, as has already been discussed, there is no evidence that either Tepecik or Kösk dates to the Ceramic Neolithic, and both the radiocarbon dates and the assemblages found suggest a date in the early sixth millennium BC. There are several specific parallels that can be adduced here. At Köşk, as has already been discussed, Canhasan 2B ceramics were found. Conversely, there is a small amount of figurative relief decorated pottery at Canhasan layer 2B and at Çatalhöyük West[116] that matches the pottery found at Tepecik and Köşk.

Finally, recent excavation seasons at Köşk have finally solved the problem of where pottery of the 'Gelveri style' should be dated. Pottery from the site of Gelveri-Güzelyurt consists of monochrome burnished material often decorated with incised and impressed patterns in the form of spirals bands and triangles, in which spaces between incised lines were marked with rows of dots originally filled with a white material. Gelveri-style ceramics have often been compared to Gumelnitsa and other Balkan assemblages and dated to the Middle Chalcolithic, between 5500 and 4000 BC.[117] By contrast, Schoop has argued on stylistic grounds that Gelveri assemblages date to the Early Chalcolithic.[118] At Köşk in levels 4–2, sherds have been found that are clearly similar to those of Gelveri, thus produced in the Early

[114] Godon 2005; Bıçakcı et al. 2007; Öztan 2007.
[115] Bıçakcı et al. 2007: 248; Öztan 2007: 229.
[116] French 2005: 105; Biehl et al. 2006: fig. 105.
[117] Esin 1993b; Özdoğan 1996.
[118] Schoop 2005a: 134–136.

Chalcolithic.[119] Further, on the same vessels, previously unknown meander motifs are present. Both the traditional curvilinear Gelveri patterns and
these meanders have counterparts at Canhasan 2B,[120] and the curvilinear
sherds are also found at Çatalhöyük West.[121] Given these data, there can
be little doubt that Gelveri dates to the Early rather than the Middle Chalcolithic. At Tepecik-Çiftlik, level 2 was dated to the Middle Chalcolithic
because of its Gelveri-type ceramics; this level can be reassigned to the
Early Chalcolithic instead.

Summarising this section on Kösk and Tepecik, it is clear that culturally these sites have much in common with earlier Neolithic sites. We are
dealing with what appear to be relatively substantial communities com-
posed of a large number of households occupying discrete houses. In terms
of subsistence, hunting wild animals continues to play an important role.
Thus, the earlier suggestions that in this period we are dealing with small
village communities relying almost exclusively on farming are no longer
tenable. In terms of imagery and burial practices, it is also possible to draw
links with earlier Neolithic sites – for example, in terms of how prominent
wild mammals are in the imagery and in the practice of intramural burials.
However, these parallels can be juxtaposed with other elements that are
dissimilar – for example, that only children are buried in houses at Kösk or
scenes of harvesting at the same site – that are unparalleled. Finally, what
is interesting about the Early Chalcolithic is the apparent fragmentation of
culture in this period. In the Neolithic, sites can often be compared over
long distances and over long time periods, yet Kösk and Tepecik are completely different from contemporary Canhasan 1 in terms of buildings and
ceramic industries, although they are only about 130 kilometres apart. This
cultural fragmentation can be contrasted with the large cultural horizon of
the Halaf emerging in the early sixth millennium of the Fertile Crescent,[122]
and it seems to suggest that communities in Central Anatolia were much
more local in their outlook.

5.3.7 Central Anatolia in the Later Neolithic: A Conclusion

There are many transformations occurring in Central Anatolia between
6500 and 5500 BC. These include the gradual replacement of clustered
neighbourhoods, as a key social institution facilitating very large local communities living in a landscape devoid of other nearby settlements, by more

[119] Öztan and Özkan 2003.
[120] French 2005: 94, 103, 155–162, 195.
[121] Franz 2007.
[122] Nieuwenhuyse 2007.

distributed settlement patterns, and in some areas settlement hierarchies may have developed during this period. In the communities of this horizon households seem to have been more autonomous, and there would have been more options for people to move to other settlements. At some sites, such as Köşk and Tepecik, we see a much more dynamic way of building, with buildings continuously altered and adjusted instead of the fixed, immutable building continuities documented in earlier periods. It is argued that such changes would have facilitated the expansion of groups of people into other areas; this movement may be connected in part to the agricultural expansion out of the steppe zone.

A second clear change is in animal husbandry, with the introduction of cattle and pigs as domestic animals and the intriguing possibility that cattle may have been kept in part for dairy products. Finally, the fragmentation of cultural practices that we can document in Central Anatolia during the Early Chalcolithic is surprising given the earlier existence of shared traditions in the Neolithic.

5.4.1 Cilicia during the Later Neolithic

Through the ages, the region of Cilicia has occupied an intermediate position geographically and culturally between Central Anatolia and the Fertile Crescent. As a result, cultural links with both regions seem to exist in many periods, and sites from this region have often been used to link the chronologies of both areas, especially before the emergence of radiocarbon dating methods.[123] However, the region also has its own distinctive archaeological sequences. In the words of Garstang:

> the fertile plain in Cilicia in southern Turkey, shut of as it was by the great ranges of Taurus from the Anatolian plateau and by bold Amanus from northern Syria while open to the Mediterranean Sea, seemed designed by nature for a history of its own.[124]

At present, nothing is known about the Aceramic Neolithic in Cilicia, a factor that some authors have argued is linked to marked alluviation taking place in the area.[125] With new evidence for the Aceramic Neolithic in Cyprus colonisation in which apart from people a range of mammals, including large species such as deer, were brought to the island by boat, it is plausible to assume that the coastal areas of the Levant and Cilicia, which are more amenable to a farming economy than Cyprus, were also occupied in

[123] Schoop 2005a: 14–17.
[124] Garstang 1953: 1.
[125] Yakar 1991: Özdoğan 1997a: 26.

the Aceramic Neolithic and that the island was colonised by coastal groups familiar with seafaring.[126] Here, it seems, an important cultural horizon awaits further investigation.

Cilicia was the first region of Asia Minor for which the Ceramic Neolithic was systematically investigated. Garstang, one of the pioneers of Near Eastern Prehistory, directed excavations at the site of Mersin-Yumuktepe in four seasons between 1937 and 1947 and established a sequence of key importance to Anatolian Prehistory. From 1993 onwards, new excavations have been taking place at Yumuktepe.

The Garstang excavations were expediently published, but given that excavation methodologies were still in their infancy, there are many problems with the stratigraphy. As a result, many buildings remain poorly understood and many of the published assemblages appear mixed.[127] By contrast, the more recent excavations were better executed, but relatively small exposures were dug.[128] Thus, the sequence of Yumuktepe remains problematic.

Yumuktepe is located at the western end of the Cilician plain, on the banks of the Efrenk River. In Prehistory the site was probably not far from the coast. The surroundings of Yumuktepe consist of fertile land on which rain-fed agriculture is feasible. The nearby Taurus Mountains would have provided other resources such as timber and game. Yumuktepe stands about 25 metres above the surrounding plain and measures about 5 hectares, but much of the site dates to periods later than Prehistory.

The relevant part of the sequence at Yumuktepe can be subdivided into two phases: first, levels 33 to 27, dating to the Ceramic Neolithic (7000–6000 BC) and excavated only in soundings; and, second, levels 26 to 20, dating to the first part of the Early Chalcolithic (6000–5800 BC).

The Ceramic Neolithic, from about 7000 BC, at Yumuktepe is best known from Garstang's trench 'A', which measured about 1 by 2 metres at the bottom,[129] and from the more recent sounding 'SA', immediately adjacent to it. The Ceramic Neolithic sequence in these soundings overlies virgin soil.[130]

Botanical remains include domestic crops, such as cereals and pulses, as well as wild tree foods such as pistachio, almond, olive, and fig.[131] The faunal remains include some fish, relatively few wild animals, and four domestic mammals: sheep, goat, pig, and cattle.[132] Interestingly, domestic cattle are

---

[126] Peltenburg et al. 2001; Swiny ed. 2001; Peltenburg and Wasse eds. 2004.
[127] Breniquet 1995: 14.
[128] Caneva and Sevin, eds., 2004; Caneva 2007.
[129] Garstang 1953.
[130] Caneva 2004a: 33.
[131] Fiorentino 2004.
[132] Buitenhuis 2004.

in evidence at Yumuktepe almost a millennium before they appear in Central Anatolia.

In the Ceramic Neolithic levels (33–27) at Yumuktepe, obsidian is more common than flint in the chipped stone assemblages. The obsidian artefacts are mainly regular bladelets, produced by pressure flaking from unidirectional cores. No debitage or cores have been found, and it is possible that bladelets were obtained rather than cores. Characteristic tools include retouched perforators made on bladelets and points that were completely covered with flat retouche that are similar to points found in Neolithic sites in Central Anatolia.[133]

The ceramics are either dark grey or brownish in colour and are generally burnished. Some vessels have a wash. Some decoration is present, taking the form of rows of often crescent-formed impressed lines and rows of impressed dots. Shapes are simple, including open and closed bowls and simple jars. Some knobs and handles have been documented. Many of the vessels were unevenly fired. Some coarse unburnished wares with vegetal temper have also been found, and soot on their surfaces indicates that they might have been used for cooking.[134]

The ceramics of levels 33–27 fall into the class known as 'dark-faced (burnished) wares' that are found in sites in Cilicia and northern Syria such as Judaidah, the Rouj basin, and Ras Shamra, and frequent cultural interactions between sites in these regions can be postulated.[135] This ceramic evidence ties in well with the presence of domestic cattle at Mersin, which are documented in the Fertile Crescent at this time but are absent from Central Anatolia.[136]

Little is known about the buildings of the seventh millennium BC at Yumuktepe. In the Garstang project various stone walls were found, some with associated earthen floors, but no coherent plan was obtained.[137] In the new excavations a sequence of wattle-and-daub buildings was recognised, but the buildings could not be reconstructed due to the small size of the exposure.[138]

Towards the end of the seventh millennium, mud buildings on stone foundations appeared. One small cell and a building assigned to level 27 were found. The building contained two hearths and appears to have had a narrow room, perhaps used for storage, and a larger room possibly used as a living room.[139]

[133] Garstang 1953; Zambello 2004.
[134] Garstang 1953: 18–24; Balossi Restelli 2004; 2006: 17–43; Caneva 2004a: 37–39.
[135] Balossi Restelli 2006: 203–211.
[136] Peters et al. 1999; Buitenhuis 2004.
[137] Garstang 1953: 14–15.
[138] Caneva 2004a: 34.
[139] Caneva 2004a: p. 37 and fig. 9.

In Early Chalcolithic levels at Yumuktepe (levels 26–20) the chipped stone industries appear little changed. Retouched points and perforators become less common, and some obsidian cores are found.[140] By contrast, the ceramics at Yumuktepe change considerably in this period (Fig. 5.8). The dark-faced (burnished) wares gradually disappear from the assemblage. Vessel shapes become more elaborate, with necked jars and handles making their appearance. The first painted ceramics appear in this level, generally in the form of parallel chevrons arranged either horizontally or vertically. Incised variants of the same geometric patterns also occur. In levels 21 and 20 lattices are also found, and both chevrons and lattices are applied in horizontal bands.[141] Some parallels for the painted vessels of Yumuktepe levels 21/20 can be found in the Canhasan 2B ceramics.[142]

From level 24 onwards, spindle whorls of clay are commonly found at Yumuktepe, often decorated with geometric motifs. While not in itself a spectacular find category, these whorls probably hint at the importance of wool for the production of textiles and clothes from about 5900 BC onwards and seem to indicate that sheep were no longer kept exclusively for their meat.

In terms of buildings, we know little about levels 26–20 at Yumuktepe. Building remains appear to consist of the stone foundations for mud super-structures. Some structures consist of a number of small cell-like spaces (level 26); other may have been large single-room buildings (levels 24/23). Little is known about the associated floors and features, but in some cases burials appear to have been placed beneath building floors. One common feature is a large number of silos, which were dressed with stones and plastered with clay and lime on the interior. Some are very large and are carefully constructed. Their functions are unclear.[143]

To summarise, our current understanding of the Yumuktepe between 7000 and 5800 BC is mainly culture-historical in that we can compare the ceramic assemblages with those from other regions. In the seventh millennium these ceramics resemble those found in sites of the Levant and Syria. In the early sixth millennium, painted ceramics appear that do not have strong parallels either to the east or in Central Anatolia. The most remarkable difference between Yumuktepe and contemporary sites in Central Anatolia concerns animal husbandry. Domestic cattle were present up to a millennium before they are first in evidence on the Anatolian plateau, and from the Early Chalcolithic onwards, there is good evidence for spinning

[140] Garstang 1953: 30, 50–52; Zambello 2004.
[141] Garstang 1953: 34–40, 54–63, 78–99; Caneva 2004b; Balossi Restelli 2006: 43–46.
[142] Schoop 2005a: 126.
[143] Garstang 1953: Caneva 2004b.

at Yumuktepe, whereas contemporary evidence for wool industries is so far scant in Central Anatolia.

Such elements demonstrate that Cilicia developed along trajectories distinct from those of Central Anatolia during the Ceramic Neolithic and the ensuing Early Chalcolithic, and in some periods it appear to be more in synchrony with the Fertile Crescent.

5.5.1 The Lake District Neolithic

The Lake District is probably the only region in Asia Minor where the Neolithic has been systematically investigated, in the sense that a series of contemporary sites have been investigated, providing an understanding at a regional rather than a site level. The excavations at Hacılar directed by Mellaart between 1957 and 1960 first uncovered Neolithic levels in the region. The Hacılar project was followed by excavations at Kuruçay directed by Duru (1978–1988), and at Höyücek (1989–1992) and Bademağacı (1993–2005), both co-directed by Duru and Umurtak (see Fig. 5.1).

The Lake District consists of a series of relatively isolated but well-watered intermontane valleys and lakes that can be contrasted with the vast expanses of Central Anatolia. Frost is less common than on the central plateau, and rainfall is sufficient for agriculture. In addition, the region is attractive for its landscape diversity, providing various resources such as game and timber.

In the nearby Antalya Region there is good evidence of the Epipalae-olithic and Mesolithic (§3.2.1), and it is plausible that similar groups were operating in favourable environments within the Lake District. If so, these groups could have played an important role in the transition to agriculture in the region. Unfortunately, our knowledge of the start of the Neolithic in the Lake District remains unsatisfactory. Thus, the genesis of farming communities in the area and the relative contributions of local groups versus those of people from elsewhere cannot be evaluated. Seventh millennium contexts in which 'Mesolithic' artefacts co-occur with pottery and domestic crops in the Antalya Region, such as Öküzini 0–1B, level 1 at Beldibi, and level 1 at Belbaşı, have not been published in detail, and have often been regarded as unreliable and mixed rather than as potentially coherent and informative on the transition to the farming economy.[144]

The earliest evidence of Neolithic sites in the Lake District is likewise problematic. The so-called Aceramic Neolithic of Hacılar, dated by a single

---

[144] Kartal 2003: 50–51.

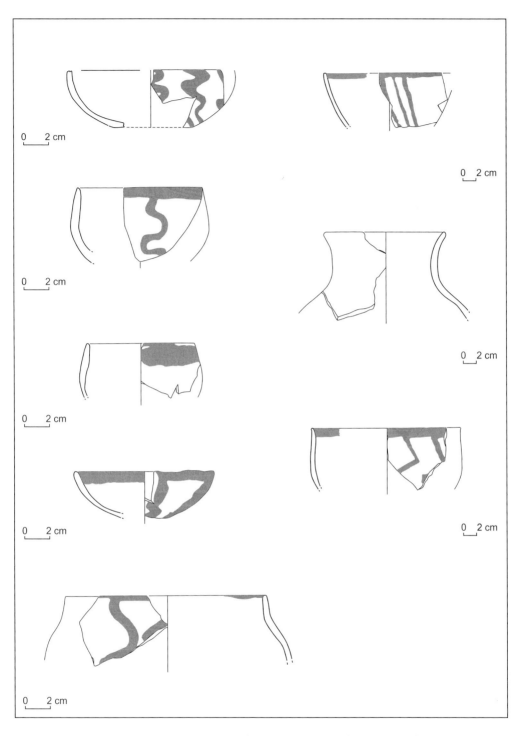

5.8 Early Chalcolithic ceramics from Mersin-Yumuktepe. Reproduced with permission of I. Caneva from Caneva, I. 2004. 'Of terraces, silos and ramparts (6000–5800)'. In *Mersin-Yumuktepe: A Reappraisal*, edited by I. Caneva and V. Sevin, pp. 45–56, fig. 8. Lecce, Italy: Congedo Edditore.

Table 5.2 Periodisation of the Lake District between 6500 and 5500 BC

Pottery	Dates BC	Hacılar	Kuruçay	Höyücek	Bademağacı
Geometric painted	5800–5600	1	7	west trench	LN 1–2 ?
Fantastic style painted	6000–5800	5–2	12–8	SP	–
Monochrome ceramics	6500–6000	9–6	13	ESP/ShP	EN 1–4

radiocarbon sample to about 8000 BC, is probably best rejected.[145] Very few artefacts have been published for these levels, and none would be out of place in the later levels at the site; the same is true for the buildings and features.[146] More importantly, not a single other Aceramic Neolithic site has so far been found in the Lake District.

A new radiocarbon date from Bademağacı, in the Lake District, suggests that this site was occupied from 7000 BC onwards,[147] which makes this the only site in the Lake District with strata dating to the first half of the seventh millennium. Unfortunately, apart from a lime plaster floor that could not be associated with any walls and a few small sherds,[148] nothing has been published for the 'Early Neolithic I' at Bademağacı. It is difficult to judge the reliability of this single radiocarbon date, based on a sample taken from a charred tree. More work is required to determine whether there is good evidence for occupation between 7000 and 6500 BC at Bademağacı.

In a recent article, Schoop has presented a periodisation for the Lake District sites that is more coherent than those previously available.[149] However, Schoop's chronology is unnecessarily complex, and here I will put forward a simpler chronology (Table 5.2). Given that radiocarbon dates are few and difficult to interpret, the chronological ranges provided are tentative.

We can distinguish the following general phases in the Lake District in the late seventh and early sixth millennia BC: first, a predominantly monochrome pottery horizon dating to the second half of the seventh millennium BC; second, an early painted ceramics horizon characterised by the so-called fantastic style, dated to the early sixth millennium; and, third, a later painted ceramic horizon, in which painted motifs are more linear and geometric and carinated shapes become more common, dated to the early sixth millennium.

---

[145] Duru 1989; Thissen 2002; Schoop 2005a: 178–179.
[146] Duru 1989, 2007.
[147] Duru 2004.
[148] Duru 2002, 2004; 2007: 344, 347, 349, figs. 63 and 64.
[149] Schoop 2002.

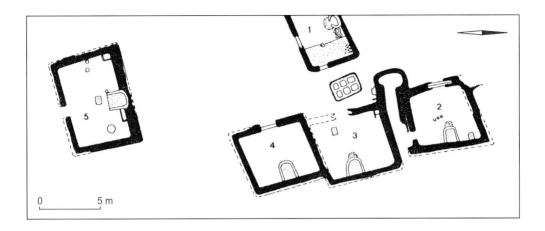

The monochrome pottery horizon of the Lake District has been thoroughly investigated at Hacılar, Bademağacı, and Höyücek, and we can use this combined evidence to build a comprehensive picture of this period.

Buildings from the monochrome phase are rectangular and border on open spaces.[150] In most cases they seem to have been constructed in rows, and within these rows all doors are on the same side. In some cases buildings share a party wall, but free-standings buildings also occur (Fig. 5.9).

Buildings were constructed with various mud techniques. Some walls ere constructed with rectangular bricks (Bademağacı, Höyücek, Hacılar), others with semi-rounded (plano-convex) hand-formed bricks (Bademağacı, Höyücek, Hacılar); a third technique consisted of constructing the walls in horizontal layers, probably between boards (Bademağacı). Walls ranged up to 1 metre in thickness. At Hacılar buildings had stone foundations, but these did not occur at the other sites. Walls and floors were frequently replastered.

The buildings usually measure between 7 and 5 metres in length and between 3.5 and 4.5 metres in width. Most buildings consisted of a single rectangular room, but some buildings at Höyücek and Hacılar had a small side room. The entrances are located in the centre of one of the long walls. In many cases, there are beam slots on both sides of the entrance that probably held a door frame. Opposite the entrance an oven of substantial size was normally attached to the wall, with a semi-oval plan and a flat roof, in some cases with ash pits nearby. A second conspicuous feature present in most buildings is a rectangular raised hearth, up to 1 metre in width, located between the entrance and the oven. Two post supports are located equidistant in the centre of the room.

5.9 Buildings of the monochrome phase at Bademağacı (layer EN II/3). Reproduced with permission of G. Duru G. Umurtak from Umurtak, G. 2000. 'A building type of the Burdur region from the Neolithic period'. *Belleten* LXIV: 683–716, fig. 1.

[150] Umurtak 2000.

Many of the buildings were burned and contained rich inventories of objects and features.[151] These include a range of objects, such as ceramic vessels, figurines, grinding equipment, and spindle whorls. Little is known about the spatial distribution of such objects, apart from the variation in figurine numbers, ranging between 5 and 33 for the Hacılar buildings.

More is known about the distribution of features such as clay silos, post stands, wall niches, and screen walls. To the left of the entrance, part of the room was often separated by a screen wall, and it is behind these screen walls that most grinding equipment and other objects were found. To the right of the entrance large storage silos were often found, many of which contained charred crops. Other features, such as smaller silos and niches in the walls, have less fixed locations. Finally, at Bademağacı, fragments of a so far unique wall painting with a configuration of red triangles were found.[152]

Many additional features were found outside buildings. At Hacılar these include screen walls next to the entrance sheltering silos and ovens, which have been interpreted as outdoor kitchens. Further, complete house interiors with wattle-and-daub exterior walls have been found, using the more solid walls of neighbouring structures for roof support.[153] This suggests that within spatially defined house clusters, mutual accommodation was the norm. It is likely that these house clusters were occupied by kin groups.

A feature found in Hacılar level 6, and without parallels at other sites in Neolithic Asia Minor, is a stone-lined well. A further example has been found in level 2 at Hacılar. Good examples of wells have been found at Cyprus dating to the later ninth millennium BC,[154] and in this context the existence of similar features in the Lake District is not surprising.

To return to the burned houses, Mellaart has argued that fires were common because of inflammable upper storeys. The evidence for upper storeys consists of, first, collapsed roofs with objects and features such as hearths on top; and, second, remains of stairs attached to building exteriors.[155] However, these elements could also be construed as evidence that roofs were in use for domestic activities, a practice well documented in archaeology and ethnography.[156] The buildings at Hacılar are amongst the largest documented in Neolithic Asia Minor: With a main room measuring 45 square

---

[151] Indeed, the publications are skewed towards these burned buildings. For example, very little is known about levels 9–7 and 5–3 at Hacılar as opposed to the burnt level 6 (Mellaart 1970); likewise, little is know about the 'early settlement phase' and the 'sanctuaries phase' at Höyücek, as opposed to the burned 'shrine phase' (Duru 1995).

[152] Duru 2007.

[153] Mellaart 1970: 19.

[154] Peltenburg, ed., 2003.

[155] Mellaart 1970: 17.

[156] Peters 1982: 223; Friedl and Loeffler 1994: 33; Matthews 2005: 373.

metres and containing a range of domestic features, and one wonders exactly what purpose an upper storey would have served.

Various scholars have argued that mud buildings do not combust accidentally, and that such buildings have to be set on fire intentionally by bringing combustible material into the structures.[157] If this was indeed the case, it alters the interpretation of several bodies found within some of these buildings. Two adults and seven children were found in building 8 at Bademağacı,[158] and at Hacılar level 6, one person was found in building Q6 and two more in building Q2.[159] Further, the intentional fire interpretation has an influence on how the rich assemblages within burned buildings are understood. These inventories, like the human bodies, are often interpreted as snapshots in the use life of a building, and some buildings have been interpreted as shrines because their inventories were exceptional. By contrast, if these buildings were intentionally burned, their inventories might inform us about closing rituals rather than normal uses of buildings. Until burned buildings from sites in the Lake District are investigated with arson techniques in order to determine whether they were set on fire or burned by accident, which of these scenarios is accurate must remain an open issue. It is prudent, however, not to accept interpretations of buildings as shrines, proposed for example for buildings 3 and 4 in the 'temple phase' at Höyücek,[160] on the basis of concentrations of figurines or other odd finds.

The subsistence economy in the monochrome phase in the Lake District relies heavily on plant cultivation. No fewer than 10 antler curved sickle handles were found in a handful of level 6 buildings at Hacılar, in one case complete with the inset flint knives.[161] Further, large storage silos were found at all sites, in some cases containing the remains of crops.[162] Finally, various crops, including einkorn, rye, bread wheat, emmer, lentils, bitter vetch, and chickpea, have been documented. Some of the cultivated crops are biologically wild, most notably the einkorn and rye, and these may have been weeds rather than cultivated crops.[163]

A range of gathered tree foods, including hackberry, almond, apple, and pistachio, have also been found,[164] which are also prominent in the Epipalaeolithic/Mesolithic cave sites of the Antalya Region.[165] The faunal

---

[157] Stevanovic 1997; Verhoeven 2000 (AD); Cessford and Near 2006; Özdoğan 2007a. Twiss et al. (2008), however, argue that mud buildings can burn by accident, provided that enough inflammable material is present.
[158] Duru 2004: 548.
[159] Mellaart 1970: 88.
[160] Duru 1994: 728–729.
[161] Mellaart 1970: 161.
[162] Martinoli and Nesbitt 2003.
[163] Martinoli and Nesbitt 2003: 26.
[164] Helbaek 1970: 228–229.
[165] Martinoli 2004; Martinoli and Jacomet 2004.

remains from the monochrome ceramic Neolithic Lake District sites are best documented for Höyücek.[166] Here the remains of aurochs, equids, hare, wild boar, and three deer species point towards hunting, but the same interpretation may be less appropriate for explaining the presence of fox and bear. Domestic animals include dog, pig, sheep, goat, and cattle. The sheep may have been kept in part for products other than meat. At Hacılar a large number of spindle whorls have been recovered from level 6,[167] pointing to textile production.

A large number of figurines were found in the monochrome Neolithic sites of the Lake District (Fig. 5.10). Many of these were found in burned contexts in buildings, predominantly renderings of women. These clay figurines range up to 25 centimetres in height and portray woman ranging from skinny to voluptuous. In most cases they are holding their breasts, and are either completely naked or wear briefs. In all cases the heads are stylised, with large oval eyes and a straight nose, but lacking a mouth. The hair, when depicted, is either fixed on top of the head or hung in a braid. Figurines are standing, seated, or reclining. Mellaart interpreted these representations as focusing on birth and fertility, but it is also possible to interpret some of them as erotic objects, especially given that some figurines appear to depict two actors having sexual intercourse.[168]

In the chipped stone assemblages of the Lake District Neolithic sites, obsidian constitutes about 40 per cent of the assemblage.[169] At contemporary sites in Central Anatolia such as Çatalhöyük, obsidian is much more common. The distance from the Lake District to the Cappadocian obsidian sources is about 400 kilometres as the crow flies. Thus, the 'supply zone' idea – that about 350 kilometres from the sources the amount of obsidian decreases rapidly (§4.3.1)[170] – seems to be borne out in this case. In terms of technology, there seems to be little in common with industries known from Central Anatolia or earlier Mesolithic traditions in the Antalya Region. Chipped stone artefacts are dominated by irregular, non-standardised blades struck from unipolar cores, often reworked into end-scrapers. Very little has been published on lithic industries, however, and our understanding of them is far from satisfactory.

A substantial number of stone vessels were found at the site of Hacılar. These vessels closely resemble the ceramic repertoire in their shapes, with tubular lugs on many of them. Some also have legs, a rare feature in pottery

---

[166] De Cupere and Duru 2003; see also Westley 1970.
[167] Mellaart 1970: 20.
[168] Mellaart 1970, vol. 2: 210–212.
[169] Mortensen 1970: 153; Baykal-Seeher 1994.
[170] Renfrew et al. 1968; Wright 1969; Cauvin 1998.

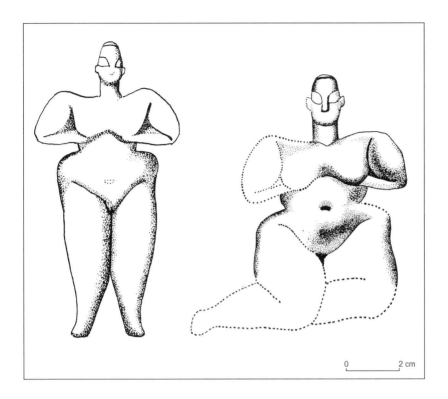

0 ⎯⎯⎯⎯ 2 cm

and difficult to produce in stone. In light of such features, Mellaart is probably correct in interpreting these vessels as prestige goods.[171]

The ceramics of the monochrome Neolithic of the Lake District actually include some painted vessels, all of which consist of simple stripe patterns, in most cases vertical or diagonal; some crosshatching also occurs. These painted vessels start to occur towards the end of the monochrome horizon and are rare. The pottery of this period is grit-tempered and generally well fired, burnished, and in some cases slipped. Colours are usually buff to brown, but there is considerable variety. Forms are simple, including raised bowls with everted rims, holemouth vessels, and S-shaped jars (Fig. 5.11). Carinations and developed feet and rims are rare. Many of the jars have three or four tubular lugs, which probably served to close vessels with ropes and a leather cover. Lugs are not common in Central Anatolia, but are found in Neolithic sites across Western Anatolia and in the Marmara Region. There is a limited amount of pottery with relief-decorated imagery, such as small animal heads applied to the shoulder of a vessel, and there are a few vessels in animal shapes. The vessels on which these elements occur differ in form and fabric from those found at Köşk Höyük and Tepecik (§5.3.6).

5.10 Two female figurines of the monochrome phase from Hacılar. Produced by Joanne Porck after plates 483 and 493 in Mellaart, J. 1970. *Excavations at Hacılar*. Edinburgh, Scotland: Edinburgh University Press.

[171] Mellaart 1970: 149.

Hacılar I

Kuruçay

Hacılar V-II

not to scale

5.11 Pottery from fantastic and geometric phases in the Lake District. Reproduced with permission of U.-D. Schoop from Schoop, U.-D. 2002. 'Frühneolithikum im südwestanatolischen Seengebiet? Eine kritische Betrachtung'. In *Mauerschau: Festschrift für Manfred Korfmann*, edited by R. Aslan, S. Blum, G. Kastl, F. Schweizer, and D. Thumm, pp. 421–436, fig. 3. Remshalden-Grunbach, Germany: Bernhard Albert Greiner.

Layer 2A

Layer 2B

0   5 m

5.12 Level 2A and 2B plans of Hacılar. Produced by the author and Joanne Porck after plans of levels 2A and 2B in Mellaart, J. 1970. *Excavations at Hacılar*. Edinburgh, Scotland: Edinburgh University Press.

Following the monochrome ceramic Neolithic of the Lake District is a painted pottery horizon that has become known as the 'fantastic style'. The proportion of painted pottery increases to about half, and much of the plain pottery is produced with less effort and is coarser than previously. Tubular lugs gradually become less common and are replaced by handles, some of which take the form of animal heads. Some vessels now have feet, but rounded bases remain by far the most common. A massive number of bowls with concave sides were found, along with necked jars and S-shaped vessels. The painted vessels are variations of red on cream. In most cases the base of the vessels was block painted, whereas the upper part was decorated in the fantastic style. Decorations include figurative motifs, on the one hand, such as hands, horned cattle heads, crosses, eyes, and stepped meanders, and geometric patterns on the other, such as triangles, and chevrons, often arranged in two rows of vertical rectangles.

While each vessel is unique, both the individual elements of decoration and their spatial ordering on the vessel seem to adhere to very specific principles. The fantastic style painted pottery is without parallels outside the Lake District Neolithic and thus, like the relief-decorated pottery at Köşk Höyük and Tepecik, represents a regional phenomenon.

The best settlement evidence for the fantastic style horizon derives from level 2 at Hacılar, and this can be augmented with Kuruçay levels 12–8. The level 2 plan at Hacılar is not unproblematic (Fig. 5.12), however. Mellaart distinguished two subphases in level 2: an earlier 2A and a later 2B in which the eastern part of the settlement was abandoned.

Two problems are manifest in the level 2A plan. First, there is no evidence that the eastern part of 2A was contemporary with the western part, much less that it was surrounded by the same perimeter wall. Second, the buildings in the east are entirely different from those in the west in terms of layout, proportions, and inventory. To my mind, level 2B constitutes a plausible phase plan of Hacılar, whereas 2A probably represents two distinct occupation phases, of which the eastern is the older.

The buildings in the east of level 2A are very similar to those found in earlier Hacılar 6. They consist of broad room structures with an entrance in the middle of the long wall, with an oven set opposite the entrance and a hearth in between. As in earlier level 6, there is evidence of two posts placed equidistant, and there is evidence of wattle-and-daub structures as well as more substantial buildings. Although the buildings found in the east of level 2A resemble those of earlier level 6 at Hacılar, the ceramics found within them is akin to those found elsewhere in the 2A/2B settlement, implying that if the eastern section of 2A indeed precedes the rest, the building traditions and ceramics do not change in synchrony.

The buildings in the western part of level 2 at Hacılar are very different from those in the east. A complex of structures built around a central court was found. This complex is surrounded by a perimeter wall up to 3 metres wide and has a narrow entrance to the north. This wall constitutes the back wall of the level 2 structures, which typically have a back room separated by two buttresses from a smaller front room. In some cases the back rooms contain an oven and a hearth, but this is not the norm. More common are storage features, such as silos and bins. One room contained large quantities of grain in bins, suggesting communal storage. The rooms concerned are often relatively small, when compared to the main rooms of level 6 and those in the east of level 2A, measuring about 3 by 4 metres. Given these characteristics, it is plausible that living quarters were upstairs at Hacılar.[172] Indeed, Mellaart notes that in many spaces two superimposed assemblages of artefacts were found, both covered by building debris, and suggested that the upper assemblages derived from a collapsed upper storey.[173]

The level 2A/B remains have been interpreted by Mellaart as representing the complete Hacılar settlement. However, it equally possible that there were multiple contemporary walled compounds, and the level 2B plan represents two such compounds: one in the west and one in the east. If this interpretation holds water, each compound would have housed a group of families pooling their resources, and would thus represent a transformation of the earlier house clusters of the monochrome horizon in the Lake District.

At Kuruçay, building remains of levels 12–8 include stone foundations of rectangular buildings normally measuring about 8 by 6 metres. Due to poor preservation, nothing is known about the interior arrangements. As in older levels at Hacılar and Höyücek, it is common to find buildings that share walls or were constructed in rows.

In level 11 at Kuruçay, a feature was found that was interpreted as a city wall with towers. This interpretation is problematic, however, given that the towers have an entrance on both their exterior and interior, which would make them ill suited for defensive purposes. Further, a very similar 'tower' structure was found in level 12 at Kuruçay adjacent to a building and contained a hearth and numerous grinding stones, suggesting a domestic use of this structure. Given these considerations, it is possible to consider the 'fortification wall' instead as one encircling a compound and the 'towers' as entrance and work areas rather than defensive structures.

Finally, a geometric painted ceramic horizon can be distinguished in the Lake District sites. This phase differs from the previous fantastic-style

[172] Cutting 2003.
[173] Mellaart 1970: 28–29.

horizon both in its buildings and in its ceramics. This phase is best documented at Hacılar level 1; additional evidence is available from level 7 at Kuruçay, in 'Late Neolithic' levels 1 and 2 at Bademağacı, and in the western trench at Höyücek.

At Hacılar two massive room complexes were found, which were built on an area levelled for the purpose and on top of a layer of stone rubble. The complexes had formidable walls, averaging about 2 metres in thickness but ranging up to 4. Apart from a number of narrow spaces, the rooms in the complexes are mostly square and measure about 6 by 6 metres. They generally have several buttresses, and most buildings lack entrances. Although some of the rooms contain hearths, they do not normally include domestic features. Instead, it is more plausible that domestic activities took place in a second storey, while the spaces excavated constitute basements mainly used either for storage or as workshops. Many of the walls were baked red by a fire, which could suggest that combustible goods were stored in some of these spaces. The remains of a collapsed upper storey were found in the form of burned deposits containing pottery and other objects, charred wood, and even skeletons of children.[174]

On the whole, the buildings of level 1 at Hacılar show many similarities to those documented at Canhasan 1 in levels 2B/2A (§5.3.5). They might differ from the Canhasan 2B/2A buildings in their spatial organisation, however. Whereas Canhasan seems to be a clustered neighbourhood settlement, at Hacılar there might have been relatively small building clusters, with between five and eight large basement rooms. It is possible that these clusters represent further transformations of the house clusters documented for earlier periods in the Lake District.

Mellaart reconstructed a series of settlement blocks in a defensive perimeter arrangement. This reconstruction is highly conjectural, given that it is based on very little evidence.[175] The underlying assumption seems to be that the massive building effort at Hacılar 1 must have served a defensive purpose. However, the comparison with Canhasan 2A/2B makes it clear that this need not have been the case. At Canhasan 1, centrally located buildings were constructed in a similar manner. Further, in level 7 at Kuruçay, square buildings measuring about 6 by 6 metres were documented with internal buttresses, very similar in appearance to the rooms at Hacılar, but built adjacent to one another in a haphazard fashion and not in a defensive pattern.[176]

---

[174] Mellaart 1970: 76.
[175] Mellaart 1970: 82.
[176] At Bademağacı, a rectangular building and a series of parallel stone walls were assigned to this period, but their stratigraphic positions remain problematic, and these remains will not be considered here (Duru 2004: 543).

It has been postulated that the pottery from the geometric painted horizon represents a break with previous ceramic traditions, leading Mellaart to postulate the arrival of a new population while simultaneously arguing that there were some continuities in the ceramic traditions.[177] There are marked differences between the level 2 and 1 assemblages at Hacılar, but these could also reflect a gap in the sequence. The excavations at Kuruçay have shown a gradual transition between the fantastic and geometric painted styles.[178] Further, it is probably more appropriate to view ceramic changes as fashion shifts within specific groups rather than as population movements.

Novel forms occur in the ceramic assemblage of Hacılar 1, including large ovoid-necked jars, bowls with flat bases, and cups and vases with vertical sides. Lugs disappear almost entirely from the corpus, but large handles become increasingly common. However, not all shapes from previous periods go out of use; in particular, bowls with round bases and convex sides, now often with knobs at the carination, and S-shaped jars are still fairly common, if often proportioned and painted differently. The division of the vessel into horizontal bands of decoration is abandoned, and the ways in which vessels are painted are more varied. Further, in open vessels the interior is often painted, with motifs that differ from those on the exterior. Popular for the interiors are elaborated crosses, star shapes, and chevrons. The exterior decoration is dominated by chevrons, lozenges, and triangles in various combinations and orientations. Some vessels are more or less completely painted, whereas on others much has been left blank. It is possible to find isolated parallels of these ceramics in the likewise geometric red-on-cream painted wares of Çatalhöyük West and Canhasan 2B/2A, but on the whole, the vessel forms and decorations of the Lake District sites have few similarities with those from the central plateau.[179]

If one takes a comprehensive view of the Lake District Neolithic, the following issues stand out. On the one hand, there is at present surprisingly little evidence of links with earlier Epipalaeolithic/Mesolithic groups that have been investigated in the nearby Antalya Region (§3.2.1). According to the publications, microliths do not appear to be part of the toolkit. The resources of the local environment appear to have been fully exploited, including the collection of a range of gathered tree foods, such as hackberry, almond, apple, and pistachio, and the hunting of aurochs, equids, hare, and wild boar. This 'broad-spectrum' subsistence economy is reminiscent of that found in the Antalya cave sites. Further, the presence of sea shells at Höyücek also fits with what we know from the Antalya Mesolithic, where these were prominent in sites. It is to be hoped that future research

---

[177] Mellaart 1970: 145, 75.
[178] Schoop 2002: 429.
[179] Mellaart 1965: 156; Schoop 2005a: 193–195.

and publications at the promising site of Bademağacı will elucidate links between hunter-gatherer groups and farmers and clarify to what degree they shared cultural practices.

On the other hand, even if local antecedents of the Lake District Neolithic are not clearly demonstrated at present, it is obvious that this cultural horizon cannot be regarded as an offshoot of that of Central Anatolia, from which it differs in almost every respect: Clustered neighbourhoods are absent; domestic buildings in the monochrome ceramic phase take on a form that is standardised but different from that of contemporary buildings in Central Anatolia; sub-floor burials are almost completely absent in the Lake District Neolithic; the ceramics traditions of the Lake District are distinct from those of Central Anatolia; and the chipped stone industries have little in common with those documented farther east. More convincing similarities between the Lake District sites and Central Anatolia emerge only in the Early Chalcolithic, with the heavy-set buttressed basement architecture, but even in this period there are clear differences in the ceramic repertoires.

5.6.1 The Neolithic of Aegean Anatolia

Only a decade ago, virtually nothing was known about the Neolithic of Aegean Anatolia beyond a few ceramic assemblages from surveys tentatively dated to the period. This absence of evidence was all the more conspicuous given the scholarly debates on the possible role of Anatolia in the neolithisation of Greece and, in particular, its early agricultural heartland of Thessaly.[180] Prior to the recent investigations, it was occasionally suggested that the Neolithic of Aegean Anatolia was poorly known because the marked alluviation that has taken place in the river valleys of the region would have buried Neolithic sites: an argument that has proven to be valid only in part.

Research into the Neolithic of Aegean Anatolia took off in earnest with the ongoing excavations at the site of Ulucak, which began in 1995 and the first results of which have been expediently published.[181] To the Ulucak evidence we can now add data from three other excavations – Ege Gübre; Yeşilova Höyük; and, Dedecik-Heybelitepe[182] – as well as survey assemblages known from Köprüova, Coskuntepe, and Kaynarca.[183] Although located outside Asia Minor, the site of Hoca Çeşme, in Turkish Thrace,

[180] Thissen 2000; Perlès 2001, 2005; Reingruber 2005.
[181] Çilingiroğlu et al. 2004; Çilingiroğlu and Çilingiroğlu 2007.
[182] Derin 2007; Lichter and Meriç 2007; Sağlamtimur 2007.
[183] Seeher 1990; Günel 2006a; Özbek 2008.

also provides important evidence.[184] The combined evidence from these sites means that it is now possible to obtain an overview of the Neolithic in this part of Asia Minor, even if many aspects remains elusive.

Most of the sites in this region are relatively small: about 3–4 hectares. Investigated sites are located predominantly on natural hills because their counterparts at lower altitudes are hidden in alluvial deposits. For example, Ege Gübre, near modern Izmir, is 2 metres below the surface and was during construction work.

Aegean Anatolia has a relatively mild Mediterranean climate (§1.2.1). It provided a wealth of natural resources to prehistoric people, such as fish and molluscs along the coast, tree foods on the wooded slopes, timber for buildings, and a wealth of animals to hunt. The river plains, intensively cultivated today, provided excellent farmland. However, there is at present little evidence of Epipalaeolithic or Mesolithic groups in Aegean Anatolia. Given the presence of Epipalaeolithic and Mesolithic groups in the similar environments of Antalya (§3.2.1), in Greece,[185] and in the more temperate Marmara Region (§3.3.1), similar groups probably remain to be discovered in Aegean Anatolia.

In the Latmos Mountains, near Kuşadası, a series of rock paintings have been documented and were dated to the Neolithic on stylistic grounds,[186] but these could also be of Epipalaeolithic/Mesolithic date. Rock paintings of this period have been found in the Antalya Region (§3.2.2). Stylistic dating of rock paintings is always problematic. The Latmos paintings, mostly executed in red paint and consisting of geometric motifs and stylised humans, often with 't-shaped' heads, do not clearly resemble those found elsewhere.

The Neolithic of Aegean Anatolia began around 6500 BC, or possibly a few centuries earlier at Ulucak, and has been documented at several sites (Table 5.3). At Ulucak level 5 the remains of wattle-and-daub structures were uncovered, the most complete of which seems to have been more or less square, measuring about 4.5 by 4.5 metres. Several other buildings appear to abut this structure. The complete building had a large oven against the wall opposite the entrance and contained a large range of *in situ* features and objects, including a multitude of slingshots, silos, ceramic vessels, and grinding equipment.[187]

There is good evidence of plant cultivation in level 5 at Ulucak, including wheat and barley. Among the hunted animals, wild boar and red deer are the most common. Three-quarters of the faunal remains are from domestic animals such as sheep, goats, cattle, and pigs. A fragment of woven fabric

---

[184] Özdoğan 1997b, 1998b, 2007a.
[185] Runnels et al. 2005; Van Andel 2005.
[186] Peschlow-Bindokat 1996a, 1996b.
[187] Çilingiroğlu and Çilingiroğlu 2007: 366–367.

Table 5.3 Schematic chronology of sites in Aegean Anatolian

Period	Ulucak	Ege Gübre	Yeşilova	Hoca Çeşme
6000–5500 BC	4	'1'	–	3 and 2
6500–6000 BC	5	'1'	3	4

was found, and there are a considerable number of loomweights and spindle worlds at Ulucak, pointing towards the importance of wool processing. At the sites of Yeşilova and Ege Gübre, both of which are located closer to the sea than Ulucak, marine resources were important, as indicated by the large amounts of shells.[188]

Level 4 at Ulucak, dated to the Early Chalcolithic, has been uncovered over a large area, and no fewer than 19 buildings were excavated. These are rectangular structures measuring about 6 by 6 metres. They are mostly built on stone foundations, and the walls were constructed either in wattle and daub, in pise, or with mud bricks. All buildings have a main room, but some also have a narrow side room, often containing storage bins, and a veranda in front. Ovens and hearths were found in the main rooms and on the verandas. There seems to be no standardisation in the spatial arrangements of the interiors. One building had both an oven and a hearth on the wall opposite the entrance. Walls and floors were frequently replastered and in some cases painted.

The buildings were organised in rows, but each structure had its own set of outer walls.[189] In some aspects, these buildings and their spatial configuration are reminiscent of the monochrome ceramic Neolithic phase in the Lake District. At present, it is not possible to evaluate how valid such a comparison is, however, because the Ulucak data are ambiguous and lack detail.

The settlement at Ege Gübre, dating to about 6200–5900 BC, differs substantially from that at Ulucak. Around a courtyard a number of stone foundations for rectangular buildings were found, measuring approximately 7 by 6 metres, and some buildings probably had a narrow room on the side. Further, a number of round structures were found, with diameters of about 3 metres, all of which are located near the corners of the rectangular buildings. These round buildings probably served some specific purpose, such as storage or as workshops, in contrast with the more general domestic functions of the rectangular buildings, in which features such as hearths and

---

[188] Derin 2007: 381; Sağlamtimur 2007: 376.
[189] Çilingiroğlu et al. 2004; Derin 2005; Çilingiroğlu and Çilingiroğlu 2007.

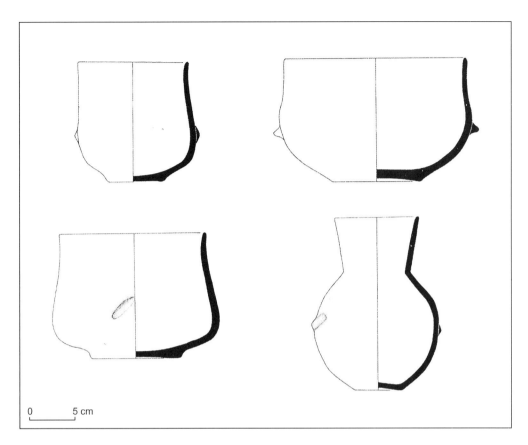

0   5 cm

5.13 Pottery from Ulucak level 4. Reproduced with permission of A. Çilingiroğlu from Çilingiroğlu, A., and Çilingiroğlu, C. 2007. 'Ulucak'. In *Anadolu'da Uygarlığın doğuşu Avrupaya yayılımı Türkiye'de Neolitik dönem, Yeni kazılar, yeni bulgular*, edited by M. Özdoğan and N. Başgelen, pp. 361–372, fig. 9. Istanbul, Turkey: Arkeoloji ve Sanat Yayınları.

ovens were found. Additional fire installations were found in the central courtyard.[190]

It is possible to interpret the Ege Gübre buildings as representing a group of linked households sharing a central courtyard. To the east of the buildings a massive stone wall was found, which has been interpreted both as a protective measure against floods and as a perimeter wall, but too little of the wall has been exposed to evaluate these interpretations.

At Hoca Çeşme, in Turkish Thrace, the level 4 settlement also dates to the second half of the seventh millennium BC. Here three circular hut structures were constructed on the bedrock, and along the perimeter of the huts post holes were found. The huts measure about 5 metres in diameter

---

[190] Sağlamtimur 2007: 374.

and have carefully produced mud floors. A massive stone wall was found that has been interpreted as a defensive perimeter wall.[191] The wall is only about 1 metre high, however, and in many parts it has a smooth surface on top, suggesting that this was the intended upper surface; and it could be traced only over a restricted distance. While the wall could have demarcated a boundary, a defensive function cannot be established. This wall seems to have continued in the subsequent levels 3 and 2 at Hoca Çeşme. In these later levels, rectangular buildings appear at the site along with white-on-red painted ceramics, features better known from early Neolithic sites in Bulgaria.[192]

Reviewing the building remains from Ulucak, Ege Gübre, and Hoca Çeşme dating to between 6500 and 5500 BC, it is clear that there is lot of variability in building forms and in the spatial organisation of buildings. While this may not be surprising for Hoca Çeşme, which is located a long distance from the other sites, Ulucak and Ege Gübre are only about 50 kilometres apart.

The diversity in building forms is especially interesting because, in terms of lithic and ceramic assemblages, there is considerable uniformity between 6500 and 5500 BC in Aegean Anatolia.

Lithics are produced both from local stone varieties and from Central Anatolian obsidian. At Ulucak 40 per cent of the blades are from obsidian, but at nearby Ege Gübre obsidian is absent. The tools published are large, irregular blades with little standardisation, many of which were truncated or retouched on one lateral surface. No microliths or arrowheads have been published, and the latter seem to have been replaced by slingshots.[193]

The specialists who have worked on the ceramics all argue that these constitute a coherent group across Aegean Anatolia, which moreover is distinct from contemporary ceramic traditions in the Lake District and in the Marmara Region (Fig. 5.13).[194] The Aegean ceramics are generally red-slipped and burnished. Shapes are simple, consisting of holemouth and S-shaped vessels and necked jars. Bases are flat or have a ring foot. Vertical tubular lugs are very common, as are knobs at the widest point of the vessel and handles near the rim. Some vessels are decorated with impressed patterns of nails or shells, but painted ceramics are rare, one exception being an anthropomorphic vessel of a person holding the arms in front of the chest. Some relief decoration is also found. The Hoca Çeşme ceramics

[191] Özdoğan 1998b; Karul and Bertram 2005; Özdoğan 2007a.
[192] Karul and Betram 2005: 125; Özdoğan 2007a: 416.
[193] Özdoğan 2002.
[194] Karul and Betram 2005: 127; Lichter 2005: 63–64; Özdoğan 2007a: 414.

are similar in many respects to those from Aegean Anatolia, but nonetheless differ in shapes and other elements.[195]

In general terms, the picture that starts to emerge for Aegean Anatolia in the period between 6500 and 5500 BC is not unlike that for the Lake District. The earliest good evidence for the adoption of a Neolithic way of life dates to the second half of the seventh millennium BC. The regional Neolithic takes on a very distinct form from the start and cannot be regarded simply as an offshoot of the Neolithic elsewhere. For example, some traits of the ceramics are similar to those of early ceramics in the Lake District, but others are not, and painted ceramics do not become popular in Aegean Anatolia. At the same time, there is no evidence at present, either in the lithic industries or in other elements, of cultural continuity with earlier Epipalaeolithic or Mesolithic groups, a situation similar to that encountered in the Lake District.

Where Aegean Anatolia is different from the Lake District, however, is in the much greater degree of variability among sites. The settlements at Ulucak and Ege Gübre are 50 kilometres apart but have completely different settlement forms. At Ulucak 40 per cent of the blades are made from obsidian, but at Ege Gübre this material is absent. At both Ege Gübre and Yeşilova the marine component of subsistence is significant, but this is not the case at the inland site of Ulucak. Such diversity is difficult to evaluate at present, but a similar distinction between inland sites and coastal sites can be drawn in the Marmara Region, to which we now turn.

5.7.1 The Marmara Region Neolithic

The Prehistory of the Marmara Region has been systematically investigated. Long-lasting surveys were undertaken along with a number of long-term excavation projects. While much of this work remains to be adequately published, a series of reports are available that allow for the detailed investigation of the period between 6500 and 5500 BC. Uniquely in Asia Minor, we have good evidence in the Marmara Region of the interaction and co-existence of farmers, on the one hand, and hunter-gatherer groups practicing animal husbandry, on the other.

There is good evidence of Epipalaeolithic/Mesolithic hunter-gatherer groups in the Marmara Region (§3.3.1). In particular, the 'Ağaçlı' has been dated to this period. These sites are located on spots adjacent to a sea or a lake, hinting at the importance of marine resources. The chipped stone assemblages found at the Ağaçlı sites include a microlithic component,

---

[195] Lichter 2005: 63.

predominantly backed bladelets, and circular endscrapers are also ubiquitous. The chipped stone industries have been linked with those from coastal
sites in Bulgaria, Romania, and Ukraine.[196]

The Epipalaeolithic/Mesolithic Ağaçlı assemblages are almost identical
to those found in sites of the 'Fikirtepe' group, a series of sites dated to the
Neolithic. Like Ağaçlı sites, Fikirtepe sites are located almost exclusively
near the shore of a sea or a lake, suggesting a similar focus on marine
resources. Fikirtepe is known mainly through investigations at the sites of
Fikirtepe, Pendik, Yarımburgaz, and Yenikapı, all of which are located near
modern Istanbul.

The site of Fikirtepe was investigated between 1952 and 1954, subsequently in 1960, and has now disappeared into the urban texture of the
Istanbul metropolis.[197] Likewise, Pendik was excavated in 1960, subsequently in 1981 and 1992, and has now largely been destroyed by urban
development.[198] The site of Yarımburgaz was investigated between 1959
and 1965, in 1986, and in three further seasons between 1988 and 1990.[199]
Finally, Yenikapı was recently discovered during the construction of a metro
station. All these sites were investigated in rescue projects, and only preliminary reports have been published. Therefore, our understanding of the
Fikirtepe horizon remains tentative and incomplete.

The evidence from Yarımburgaz seems to consist mainly of redeposited
material, and nothing is known about the nature of the settlement at this
cave site. Much better understood are the open-air sites of Fikirtepe and
Pendik. Fikirtepe was located on a hill overlooking the Marmara Sea near
a spring and is estimated to have measured about 140 by 70 metres, while
Pendik is estimated to have been somewhat larger. At both sites the archaeological deposits were shallow, measuring no more than 1 metre at most,
and were preserved mainly in large pit features rather than in a continuous layer. Thus, these are flat sites rather than mounds, and one can only
wonder whether they would have been found and investigated had they not
been in the Istanbul area.

At both Fikirtepe and Pendik the main features encountered are irregular
ovoid pit features measuring between 3 and 6 metres in diameter, which
are the remains of sunken hut structures. These huts were constructed
with wattle and daub, remains of which were found within the pits, and
post holes were documented along the edge of the ovoids.[200] In some of

[196] Gatsov and Özdoğan 1994: 109–110; Özdoğan 2007b: 662.
[197] Bittel 1960; Kansu 1963; Bittel 1969; Boessneck and Von Den Driesch 1979.
[198] Kansu 1963; Harmankaya 1983; Özdoğan 1983; Pasinli et al. 1994.
[199] Özdoğan et al. 1991; Özbaşaran 1995.
[200] These could not be located at Fikirtepe (Bittel 1969: 6), but they have been reported for
     Pendik (Harmankaya 1983: 27).

these structures hearth features were preserved, and in one case up to six
refloorings were documented, indicating that these structures were in use
over extended periods of time.

Beneath some of the hut features at Fikirtepe and Pendik burials were
found, although these also occur in open areas where evidence of huts is
lacking. These burials include adults, children, and infants, all of which
were primary complete interments, usually in flexed positions on the side.
Some of these burials have grave goods such as necklaces or ceramic
vessels.[201]

The subsistence economy of the Fikirtepe sites is only partially understood. The large amounts of shells and fish bones found point to the importance of marine resources for subsistence, especially given that the deposits
were not sieved and that fish bones are almost certainly underrepresented.
No fewer than 13 fish species were found at Fikirtepe, including 7 sea
species and 6 freshwater species. Many of these fish were very large and
would have weighed up to 100–150 kilograms.

A second important source of subsistence was provided by domestic animals such as cattle, sheep, goats, and pigs; cattle were most important for
subsistence, and sheep may have been kept also for wool. By contrast to
these domestic animals, wild hunted land animals, such as deer and wild
boar, constitute a relatively insignificant proportion of the animal bones
(less than 8 per cent).[202] Thus, the faunal remains from Fikirtepe include a
very interesting mix of fishing and animal husbandry.

Unfortunately, nothing is known about the botanical evidence of these
sites: whether cultivated crops were important to Fikirtepe people and to
what degree the gathering of wild resources was practiced. The evidence is
limited to a few possible sickle blades and grinding tools, which are open
to multiple interpretations.[203]

The ceramics found at the Fikirtepe sites are grey to brown in colour,
predominantly grit- or sand-tempered, and evenly burnished (Fig. 5.14).
The most common shapes are open bowls and S-shaped jars. Many vessels
have tubular lugs on the shoulder, but there are also triangular flat grips
with vertical perforations, also placed on the shoulder. Feet and carinations
are absent, with the exception of the box forms. These are rectangular or
triangular box shapes, often with rectangular handles and with three or four
separate legs. These boxes are generally decorated with geometric incised
motifs, such as checkerboard patterns, triangles, and meanders. A minority
of the other pottery is also decorated with similar geometric incised, or in
some cases impressed, motifs.

[201] Pasinli et al. 1994: 151.
[202] Boessneck and Von Den Driesch 1979.
[203] Özdoğan 1983: 409.

The chronological range of the Fikirtepe assemblages has long been problematic. While it was evident from the start that they were probably older than the Troy sequence, in the absence of radiocarbon scholars differed considerably in their dating of these assemblages. Bittel placed Fikirtepe in the fourth millennium BC, whereas both Mellaart and French placed this horizon in the Ceramic Neolithic.[204] Yakar, on the other hand, dated the Fikirtepe tradition to the Early Bronze Age.[205]

The stratified deposits of the Yarımburgaz cave provided a number of unreliable radiocarbon dates in the range of 6200–5500 BC,[206] but the site has also been dated on the basis of its ceramics. On the basis of rather subtle changes in the ceramics, Özdoğan distinguished, first, archaic Fikirtepe: second, classical Fikirtepe; and, third, developed Fikirtepe.[207] The archaic phase is characterised by simple holemouth forms, sometimes with flat grips or lugs on the shoulder, and with little decoration. Classical Fikirtepe is characterised by the appearance of S-shaped forms, a greater amount of incised geometric decoration, although not exceeding about 10 per cent of the assemblage, and the appearance of decorated boxes on legs. Both phases are supposed to be present at Fikirtepe and Pendik, although there are little stratigraphic data to substantiate a distinction at present, and in terms of ceramics the distinction is also difficult to draw.[208] Finally, the developed Fikirtepe horizon is present at Yarımburgaz level 4, characterised by the appearance of necked jars and impressed decoration in patterns of meanders and lozenges that have been compared to textile motifs.

Ceramics similar to those known from Fikirtepe, Pendik, and Yarımburgaz have been found in a region much wider than the immediate surroundings of Istanbul. To the north of the Marmara Sea, Fikirtepe material seems to be present in a rather limited area: It is absent from the Neolithic sequences of Hoca Çeşme, near the border with Greece, and from Aşağı Pınar, in the north of Turkish Thrace.[209] By contrast, in Asia Minor, it is found as far inland as Demircihüyük, near modern Eskişehir, and along the southern reaches of the Marmara Sea up to the straits of Gelibolu.[210]

At Demircihüyük, Neolithic and Chalcolithic assemblages were found in a re-deposited context. They appear to have been inclusions within soil

[204] French 1967b; Mellaart 1975.
[205] Yakar 1975: 133–134.
[206] Özdoğan 1997b: 21; 1999a: 213.
[207] Özdoğan 1997b, 1999a, 2007a.
[208] Bittel 1969: 10; Schoop 2005a: 215.
[209] Özdoğan 2007a.
[210] Mellaart 1955; French 1967b; Efe 2001: 50–54; Efe 2005: 108–109; Özdoğan 2007a: 413–414.

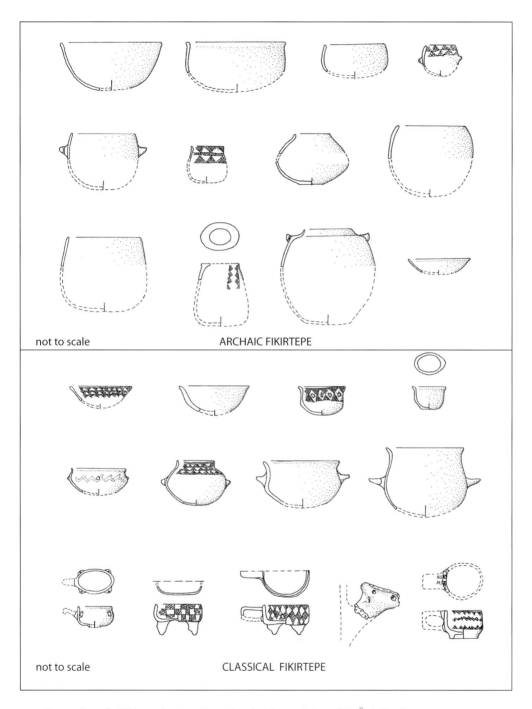

5.14 Pottery from the Fikirtepe horizon. Reproduced with permission of M. Özdoğan from Özdoğan, M., 2007. 'Mamara Bölgesi Neolitik çağ kültürleri'. In *Anadolu'da Uygarlığın doğuşuAvrupaya yayılımı Türkiye'de Neolitik dönem, Yeni kazılar, yeni bulgular*, edited by M. Özdoğan and N. Başgelen, pp. 401–426, fig. 3. Istanbul, Turkey: Arkeoloji ve Sanat Yayıları.

that was used for later construction activities.[211] On the basis of a techno-typological analysis of these ceramics, Seeher distinguished wares A–F, one of which (ware C, consisting of 416 sherds in total) he identified as belonging to the Fikirtepe tradition.

The best evidence of the inland Neolithic in the Marmara Region comes from the excavations at the site of Ilıpınar Höyük, the sequence of which can now be augmented with evidence from the sites of Menteşe Höyük, Barcın Höyük, and Aktopraklık. The earliest inland Neolithic in the area has been found at Menteşe, Barcın, and Aktopraklık, where levels dating to the second half of the seventh millennium BC have been investigated. The Ilıpınar level 10 to 5A sequence can be dated between 6000 and 5500 BC.

The sites of Menteşe and Barcın are both located in the Yenişehir plain. Along the northern edge of the plain, three relatively small Neolithic sites about 10 kilometres apart were found.[212] The sites each measure about 100 metres across and are about 4 metres high. These three sites probably represent a much larger network of similar small settlements, and can be compared to other settlement systems of this period such as those in the Beyşehir-Suğla Region (§5.3.3) or in Thessaly.[213]

At Menteşe and Barcın, Neolithic sites have been reached in limited exposures only, but both sites have good radiocarbon dates to substantiate occupation in the period between 6500 and 6000 BC.[214] At Barcın, excavations started only in 2005. A number of hearths and crouched burials were found in a courtyard area. The remains of a poorly understood building or platform with three infants and one child burial associated with it were found.[215]

A clearer picture was obtained at Menteşe level 3. Here various rectangular buildings were found, measuring up to 6 metres in width. The walls of the best-understood building were built with mud slabs about 30 centimetres wide, with a row of stakes set in the middle. The slabs seem to have been placed in a wet condition and generally consist of unprepared, relatively clean mud. Wooden stakes were subsequently driven through these slabs. It is plausible that at a higher level these walls were constructed of wattle and daub rather than with mud slabs. If this is accurate, the mud slabs, often preserved up to 40 centimetres high, provided the 'frame' for the wattle-and-daub structure above.

---

[211] Seeher 1987a: 13–17.
[212] French 1967b.
[213] Perlès 2001.
[214] Alpaslan-Roodenberg and Maat 1999; Roodenberg 1999; Alpaslan-Roodenberg 2001; Roodenberg et al. 2003, 2008; Roodenberg and Alpaslan 2007.
[215] These remarks are based on my participation in this project and are preliminary assessments open to reinterpretation.

Relatively little is known about the interior arrangements of features at Menteşe, but ovens and ceramic vessels were found outside buildings. In one case, there was a concentration of silos built against the exterior of a building. There is some evidence of the reconstruction of buildings in exactly the same spot, with three successive structures vertically superimposed, something for which there is even more pronounced evidence at later Ilıpınar.

A total of 20 burials were found at Menteşe, almost all of which were single primary burials in flexed positions, the one exception being a double burial containing a woman and an infant. This double burial was located beneath a building, and it was probably dug during the use life of that structure. The remainder of the burials appear to have been in open spaces. Some contained ceramic vessels or necklaces, but most burials were without objects.

Nothing has been published so far on the botanical assemblages of either Menteşe or Barcın, but we do have some data on the faunal remains of Menteşe.[216] At this site hunting wild animals was of secondary importance; the faunal assemblage is dominated by domestic animals, with cattle being the most common, followed by sheep. Domestic goats and pigs are present but are relatively rare, while shells are relatively common. However, molluscs were not important for subsistence. It has been argued on the basis of cull patterns that both sheep and cattle were kept in part for the production of dairy produce. This suggestion has been borne out by recent lipid analysis of sites in the Marmara Region, which shows that dairy product consumption was an important part of subsistence.[217] Further, two cattle bones show deformations that could indicate their use for traction. Given the limited number of bones with these traces and the fact that there is no evidence for the use of ploughs or carts at this time, however, this idea should be treated with caution.

The chipped stone assemblages from basal Menteşe and the earliest levels 10–9 at Ilıpınar are considered to be very similar to those from Fikirtepe and Pendik.[218] At all of these sites we see, on the one hand, irregular flakes struck from irregular cores and reworked mainly into rounded endscrapers with steep retouche, and, on the other hand, bullet cores used to produce narrow, regular blades that were often snapped and retouched into various microliths. Very typical are blades reworked into long perforators by means of steep retouche.

The ceramic vessels found at Menteşe and Barcın are identical to those found at Fikirtepe and Pendik, and seem to correspond with the so-called

[216] Gourichon and Helmer 2008.
[217] Evershed et al. 2008.
[218] Gatsov 2003a:287; 2003b: 156–157; 2008: 242.

archaic Fikirtepe horizon, with predominantly holemouth shapes, simple open and closed forms, few decorated sherds, and some box shapes. Again, the assemblage of Ilıpınar level 10 is very similar, and it is thought that the transition to classical Fikirtepe occurs in level 9 at that site.

The site of Ilıpınar is located near the western shore of the Iznik Lake, measures about 2 hectares, and rises 5 metres above the surrounding plain. The Neolithic occupation spans levels 10 to 5A and can be subdivided into levels 10–7, between approximately 6000 and 5700 BC, and levels 6 to 5A, between approximately 5700 and 5500 BC.[219] Whereas levels 10 to 7 buildings and assemblages are comparable to those at Menteşe, levels 6 and 5A constitute a distinct cultural horizon.

Levels 10–7 at Ilıpınar are documented in the so-called big square, which was dug down to virgin soil. A bewildering mass of post holes was found and some better-preserved structures.[220] The post holes relate mainly to a large number of square and rectangular buildings, typically measuring 6 by 6 metres, which were repeatedly rebuilt in more or less the same spot, although slightly shifted in order to avoid the remains of earlier structures. The associated floors of these buildings were in most cases not preserved, and the sequence of buildings was determined mainly by comparing the depths of the post holes of various structures.

The best-preserved building of these levels is the so-called burnt house of level 10, remains of which stood to a height of 60 centimetres (Fig. 5.15).[221] As at Menteşe, wall bases were constructed with slabs of clean and untreated mud, through which a series of stakes approximately 8 to 10 centimetres in diameter had been driven at distances of about 5 to 10 centimetres. These stakes continued up to 120 centimetres below the slabs. It is plausible that the post structures most commonly found at Ilıpınar are those for which the associated floors and slabs have not been preserved.

Both at Menteşe and at Ilıpınar there are also structures with walls of mud slabs without stakes.[222] These buildings are identical in all other respects to those with stakes, and it is conceivable that the stakes were set in a wooden frame at a higher level in these structures.

In the burnt house, the remains of the wattle-and-daub walls were found in the form of standing mud fragments with rope impressions at intervals of about 15 centimetres. These were probably used to tie horizontal lathes to the stakes, to which mud plaster was then applied. It is clear that these wattle-and-daub walls would have been of little use in supporting the roof, whatever its shape, which would have been supported mainly by posts.

[219] Roodenberg 1995a, 2008a; Roodenberg and Schier 2001.
[220] Roodenberg 1995b, 2008b.
[221] Coockson 2008: 150–153; Roodenberg 2008b: 5–7.
[222] Roodenberg 1999: 196.

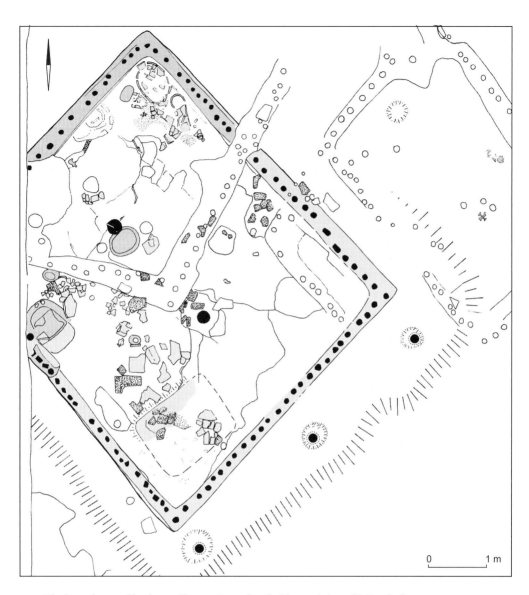

5.15 The burnt house of level 10 at Ilıpınar. Reproduced with permission of J. Roodenberg and B. C. Coockson from Coockson, B. C. 2008. 'The houses from Ilıpınar X and VI compared'. In *Life and Death in a Prehistoric Settlement in Northwest Anatolia: The Ilıpınar Excavations III*, edited by J. Roodenberg and S. Alpaslan-Roodenberg, pp. 149–204, fig. 1. Leiden: Nederlands Instituut voor het Nabije Oosten.

Two main central posts were present in the burnt house. Around the base of these posts, raised plastered features were found that probably served to protect the bases from moisture and animal burrowing. The posts supported the probably gabled roof, given that no further substantial posts were present. A gabled roof would have been both lighter and better suited to the heavy downpours that frequently occur in this region.

Wattle-and-daub buildings with gabled roofs are common in prehistoric sites in the Balkans and have sometimes been contrasted with the mud buildings of Central Anatolia. This contrast has been interpreted as a cultural affiliation,[223] but it is more convincing to argue that climatic differences and the easier access to timber were responsible for the similarities in buildings in the Marmara Region and the Balkans.[224] Here it is of interest to note that both the chipped stone industries and the ceramics of sites in Thrace differ markedly from those documented at Menteşe and at Ilıpınar,[225] and given such differences, it is clear that we are not dealing with widely shared cultural traditions in the two regions.

In a number of buildings at Ilıpınar floors made from wooden boards were found. These raised floors rested on crossbeams set in the outer walls and were covered by plaster. These floors were probably designed to counter the moist conditions of the plain. Raised wooden floors were not a feature found in all buildings, however. For example, the burnt building had a mud floor only. However, this particular building was constructed on a specially created platform up to 1 metre thick.

In the burnt building a variety of features and objects were found. In one corner was a large oval bin containing charred barley; surrounding the bin were a number of pots, a grinding stone, and an axe with an antler socket. In the opposite corner was a platform on which an oven or hearth had been placed. A third large feature consisted of a grinding installation; adjacent to one of the long walls was a raised grinding platform with a cavity in front, in which to place the knees.

The Ilıpınar settlement consisted of a number of more or less square wooden buildings. The buildings were generally rebuilt on the same spot, with similar dimensions and a similar orientation, although they were shifted horizontally over a short distance in order to avoid the remains of earlier posts. Up to seven buildings in sequence were documented.[226] This has been explained by the idea that we are dealing with privately owned family plots.[227]

[223] Roodenberg 1995a: 170.
[224] Rosenstock 2005.
[225] Gatsov 2001; Özdoğan 2005: 22–23.
[226] Roodenberg 1995a: 38.
[227] Roodenberg and Alpaslan 2007: 393.

This interpretation is not convincing, however. In ethnographic studies, households are very dynamic units, expanding and shrinking in size and adapting their houses accordingly.[228] In most societies the household is a key social institution, and houses are transferred from one generation to the next, but rather than resulting in building continuity, this leads to the constant modification of buildings and settlement space. It follows that the building continuity at Ilıpınar is not sufficiently explained as the transference of house sites within a family. Instead, it is plausible that house continuity was a resource drawn upon in the constitution and reproduction of social groups at Ilıpınar.[229]

A total of 48 burials were found in the big square at Ilıpınar, including infants, juveniles, and adults of both sexes.[230] All burials are single and primary inhumations. In some cases a pot or a pierced shell was found in these burials, but on the whole, grave goods are rare. In many cases, remains of wooden boards or basketry were found below the skeleton. Some of the female skeletons have grooves on their incisors indicating the use of their teeth for some undetermined purpose, possibly related to flax preparation. Given that in most cases the floors of buildings were not preserved, it was not possible to determine the links between buildings and burials, but it appears to be the case that burials were interred predominantly in open spaces rather than beneath buildings.[231]

In terms of subsistence, a large range of cultivated crops have been documented at Ilıpınar, including a variety of cereals (barley, einkorn, emmer); pulses (lentil, bitter vetch, grass pea, pea, chickpea, and faba bean); and flax (probably for its fibres), as well as gathered food plants (fig, bramble, grape, apple/pear, hazel nuts, and pistachio).[232] Throughout the Ilıpınar sequence cultivation seems to have been the main source of subsistence, with some shifts in the relative importance of crops over time, and gathered food plants were extra.

As at Menteşe, the faunal remains are predominantly those of domestic animals, which included sheep, goats, pigs, and cattle.[233] There are some shifts in the relative predominance of these species, with sheep and goats most common in the earliest levels 10 and 9, cattle the predominant species in level 5B, and pigs most common in levels 9 to 5A. The initial predominance of sheep/goats was interpreted by Buitenhuis at one point as evidence of colonisation from Central Anatolia, because these animals were argued

[228] Peters 1982; Goodman 1999.
[229] Düring 2009.
[230] Alpaslan-Roodenberg 2008.
[231] Roodenberg 2008a: 72–73.
[232] Cappers 2008.
[233] Buitenhuis 1995, 2008.

to be better suited to the steppe,[234] but the older faunal evidence from
Menteşe, in which cattle play a prominent role, has made this argument
untenable.[235] About 20 per cent of the faunal remains in the oldest level
are from wild animals, mostly deer and wild boar; thereafter, their frequency decreases sharply. It is difficult to imagine that game became rare in
the wooded landscapes of the Iznik Region, and it is also conspicuous that
the large fishes available in the Iznik Lake are not present in the Ilıpınar
assemblage. Both factors probably hint at cultural preferences rather than
ecological factors.

The level 6 and 5A buildings at Ilıpınar are very different from those
of the older levels 10 to 7. Walls are constructed with mould-shaped mud
bricks with the header and stretcher technique. The specific shape that
buildings take differs for levels 6 and 5A and will be discussed separately.

Level 6 appears to have a circular organisation of space. There is a relatively insubstantial circular embankment, which would have stood about 1
metre above its surroundings.[236] This embankment seems to have constituted the outer boundary of the settlement, beyond which the mound sloped
down steeply. On the embankment a series of small rectangular buildings
were constructed in rows, with some alleys between buildings providing
access to the settlement. This configuration of structures went through
a series of reconstruction phases in which both the embankment and the
buildings constructed on them were rebuilt, testifying to a preference for
this settlement form over an extended period.

On the outer side of the embankment there seem to have been blank
walls, with building entrances facing the interior of the settlement. It has
been argued that the central space in the settlement was used in part for
keeping livestock,[237] and some of the plans published suggest a largely
open space (Fig. 5.16). However, buildings of level 6 were in fact found
in this area, and the Ilıpınar spring is currently located near the centre
of the level 6 settlement and was probably in the same spot during the
Neolithic.[238]

Whatever the nature of the settlement's centre, it is clear that the
embankment of Ilıpınar 6 with its buildings on top did not serve a military purpose. Writing about the feature, Roodenberg argues that it was

> a symbolic and physical demarcation between the community and the outer
> world. As a barrier erected against aggressors it would have been far from
> effective, but its significance as a fence for sheltering the life stock [sic] was

[234] Buitenhuis 1995: 153.
[235] Gourichon and Helmer 2008.
[236] Gérard 2001; Coockson 2008; Roodenberg 2008a.
[237] Gérard 2001.
[238] Kayan 1995: 28.

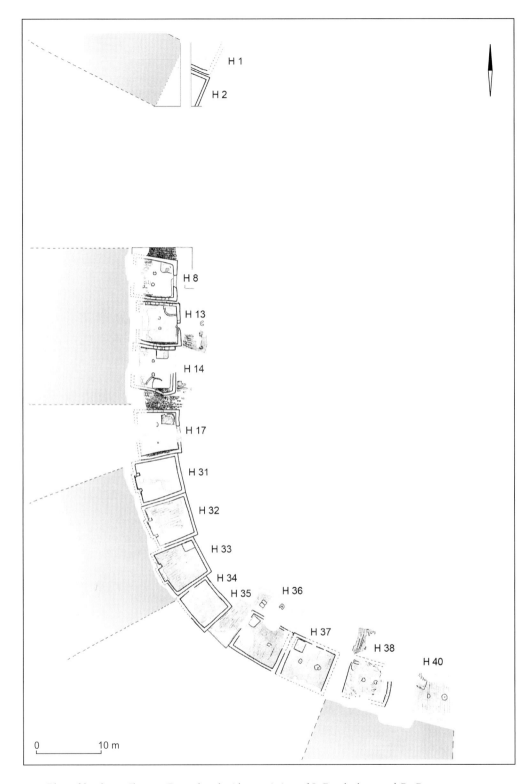

5.16 Plan of level 6 at Ilıpınar. Reproduced with permission of J. Roodenberg and B. C. Coockson from Coockson, B. C. 2008. 'The inhabitants'. In *Life and Death in a Prehistoric Settlement in Northwest Anatolia: The Ilıpınar Excavations III*, edited by J. Roodenberg and S. Alpaslan-Roodenberg, pp. 69–90, fig. 1. Leiden: Nederlands Instituut voor het Nabije Oosten.

demonstrated by a zone of thick deposits of greenish organic origin behind the alignment of buildings.[239]

The embankment at Ilıpınar is paralleled at a number of other Neolithic sites in the region. Similar features that are better understood have been documented at the site of Aktopraklık.[240] In all cases these embankments are relatively shallow, do not appear to have a defensive purpose, and seem to have demarcated the boundary of the settlement.

The level 6 buildings at Ilıpınar are approximately square and measure between 3.8 and 4.5 metres in each dimension. Each was built with separate walls despite the fact that buildings often abut one another. Some buildings have a niche on the embankment side in a location opposite the entrance. The buildings all appear to have had raised floors made of wooden boards subsequently covered with mud plaster. The 14 buildings on the embankment appear to have had a standardised interior organisation of space. There were two posts in the rooms, with small raised plaster platforms at their base. The central area was normally free of features and objects. To the right of the entrance there was often a large flat-topped oven in the corner. In most buildings there was a large storage bin in the left 'wing' of the room. Much of the remaining space on the left and right was taken up by pottery vessels and plastered baskets, and in some instances, grinding platforms. Further, in several instances, there was also evidence of a sort of veranda in front of the building, probably also on a raised floor, where a horseshoe-shaped hearth and grinding installations were often found.

In several of the level 6 houses at Ilıpınar, evidence of collapsed upper storeys was found, overlain in turn by the remnants of wall debris and roof remains from the upper storey.[241] The reconstruction of these buildings consists of two-storey structures with a gabled roof. In these reconstructions, the upper storey had a spatial configuration of features similar to that of the ground floor. If this is accurate, each building would have had two large ovens and two large silos.[242] While the overall reconstruction of the buildings proposed seems plausible, the suggested duplication of the ground floor on the upper storey is more difficult to accept. First, there is the issue of why the inhabitants of these buildings would have needed two large ovens and bins, as well as additional storage facilities. Second, given that an enormous amount of space is taken up by all these features and objects, one wonders where people would have rested and performed their domestic activities.

[239] Roodenberg 2008a: 76–77.
[240] Karul 2006, 2007.
[241] Gérard 2001; Coockson 2008.
[242] Roodenberg 2008a: 84, table 1.

Buildings in level 5A at Ilıpınar again differed in type from those of level 6.[243] Three buildings of level 5A have been documented; they are large rectangular structures measuring some 7.0 by 5.5 metres, with an interior floor surface of about 38 square metres. This size is similar to that of the buildings of levels 10–7 but double that of the ground floors of level 6. However, the 5A buildings are reconstructed as single-storey structures with a gabled roof. The buildings are further characterised by four internal buttresses, two alongside the entrance and two in the centre of side walls. It is presumably over the latter that the main beam was placed given that a post was positioned between them. To the right of the building entrances was a cubicle that contained ovens, grinding stones, and basins. The cubicle to the left of the entrance appears to have been used mainly for storage. Thus, the arrangement of features and objects recalls that of level 6. In front of the buildings were verandas on which large numbers of plastered basket remains were found, as well as a horseshoe-shaped hearth.

Buildings similar to those of Ilıpınar 5A have also been found in contemporary Aktopraklık in the so-called upper mound.[244] Buildings at this site measure about 35 square metres. The walls and some of the floors are covered with lime plaster and there are a number of interior buttresses in these buildings, ranging from three to six, often with rounded ends. These buttresses undoubtedly played a role in supporting the roof, but they also effectively divided the room into sub-spaces. One of the cubicles between a corner and two buttresses contained a round oven. Little has been published on the assemblages associated with these buildings.

The settlement at Aktopraklık seems to have been surrounded by a dry ditch with an embankment next to it, both of which were plastered with lime at least three times. This earthwork is known both from excavations and through geomagnetic prospection and has a diameter of about 100–130 metres. Some 40 metres south of the earthwork more buildings were found. It has been argued that these buildings represent an older building level and are associated with an earlier ditch feature.[245]

The ceramic assemblages of levels 6 and 5A form a development continuous from the older levels at Ilıpınar.[246] Fikirtepe boxes are no longer found in these levels, and impressed decoration also disappears. Instead, carinated bowls and square pots are now found, and knobs at the rim are common. Overall, there seems to be much continuity in Ilıpınar 6 with earlier ceramic shapes and wares, and more pronounced changes appear to occur in level 5A, when lugs are moved from the body to the rim, curvilinear grooved

[243] Gérard 2001: 196–197; Roodenberg 2008a: 77–78.
[244] Karul 2007.
[245] Karul 2007: 390.
[246] Thissen 2001.

decoration occurs, and large handles appear in pairs on the shoulder of vessels. By contrast to the ceramics, the chipped stone assemblages stay more or less the same throughout the Ilıpınar 10 to 5A sequence.[247]

Summarising the evidence from the Marmara Region in the period between 6500 and 5500 BC, two main features stand out. First, there are clearly two different types of sites in the region. On the one hand, there are coastal Fikirtepe sites with huts and evidence of intensive fishing, animal husbandry, and dairy consumption, while little is known about the plant foods consumed. On the other hand, there are inland sites with large rectangular buildings and a subsistence economy characterised by heavy reliance on cultivated crops, animal husbandry, and dairy consumption. The contrasts between the coastal and inland sites are all the more interesting because they share ceramic and lithic traditions. It would be of great interest to know how people in both groups of sites interacted: Are we dealing with seasonal special-purpose sites on the coast, or were both types of sites more or less sedentary interlinked communities that varied in their food production and in the way they constructed their houses?

This question could in theory be addressed by the study of the resources exploited at Fikirtepe and by isotope analyses of human bones at both groups of sites, which could tell us what people were eating and whether they were moving between the coast and the inland area.[248] The evidence from the Marmara Region has a lot of potential to answer such questions.

Another interesting issue in the Marmara Neolithic is its genesis and the role played by the Epipalaeolithic/Mesolithic Ağaçlı groups. Chipped stone assemblages from Fikirtepe sites are nearly identical to those from Ağaçlı sites, and the locations of Ağaçlı sites are also similar to those of Fikirtepe sites. All of this could mean that local hunter-gatherer groups played an important role in the adoption of farming in the Marmara Region. This does not exclude the possibility that people from Central Anatolia also partook in this development. Ideally, more work on both Fikirtepe and Ağaçlı sites could further clarify this issue.

On the other hand, there are clear signs of contact between Central Anatolia and the Marmara Region in the form of domestic crops and animals deriving from the interior and in the form of obsidian. The presence of obsidian from both Cappadocia and Galatia at the sites of Ilıpınar (levels 10 and 9), Pendik, and Fikirtepe[249] hints at frequent, probably mediated, exchange between these regions in the period from about 6500 to 5800 BC. After level 9 at Ilıpınar, both the amount and the percentage of obsidian in

---

[247] Gatsov 2008: 241.
[248] See Tchernov 1991 and Bentley et al. 2002 for examples of such studies.
[249] Bigazzi et al. 1995, Bigazzi et al. 1998: 80–86.

the chipped stone assemblage decrease sharply;[250] the reasons for this are probably primarily socio-ideological.

The location of the Marmara Region has led scholars to assume that the region was the stepping stone by which farming came to Europe, and the Marmara Neolithic has been studied primarily with this transmission in mind. Key questions were from where and when the area was colonised and how the Neolithic expanded to Europe from there. Both questions have proven to be problematic. First, it is clear that local groups played an important role in the adoption of a Neolithic way of life in the Marmara Region. Second, the earliest Neolithic of Thrace is clearly distinct from that of the Marmara Region, and many now favour an Aegean route for the spread of the Neolithic to Europe.[251] Apart from the fact that such debates are problematic, resting on the questionable assumption that similarities in assemblages are a measure of cultural contact and a proxy for the transmission of farming and/or population movement, the focus on the transmission of the Neolithic way of life has detracted from the more interesting and tangible issue of how and why people became sedentary farmers in the Marmara Region.

5.8.1 Dispersing Diversity

Asia Minor has often been conceptualised as a land bridge connecting the Near East and Europe, and it is this perspective that has dominated perceptions of the Neolithic in Anatolia until recently.[252] This view has had a series of implications: First, Anatolia was considered to be a region that transmitted the Neolithic way of life from the Near East to Europe, not a region with its own distinctive Neolithic cultures. Second, the Neolithic of Asia Minor was perceived as a homogeneous entity, with little regard for differences among sites. Third, the study of the Neolithic of Asia Minor has been neglected in comparison to surrounding regions, such as the Levant and the Balkans.[253] Finally, the spread of the Neolithic way of life has often been regarded as a self-evident feature, rather than a development that has to be explained as a result of either interaction between local and non-local groups or colonisation.[254]

The Neolithic of Asia Minor does not fit this picture. After 8500 BC, when farming and sedentary life are first documented on the southern

[250] Gatsov 2001, 281; 2008.
[251] Lichter, ed., 2005; Özdoğan 2007a.
[252] Özdoğan 1995; 1997a: 2–5.
[253] Özdoğan 1995.
[254] Sherratt 2004.

plateau of Asia Minor, it is only at about 6500 BC that farming spreads towards other regions of Asia Minor, such as the Lake District, Aegean Anatolia, and the Marmara Region. This development has been dubbed the 'second Neolithic revolution' in this book. Here I want to pursue two aspects of this phase of Neolithic expansion: first, to what degree changes in farming practices and ecology contributed to this development; and, second, how we can conceptualise the spread of farming across Asia Minor from a social perspective.

The question of why the expansion occurred around 6500 BC remains a challenge. As indicated earlier (§5.1.1), factors that could have played a role are climatic change, agricultural innovations, social changes, and demographics. Of these factors, climate change and demography can best be considered as contributing to the Neolithic expansion: The so-called 8.2 KA climatic event postdates this expansion, and demographics do little to explain why people started moving at around 6500 BC.

It has been argued that an integrated set of crops, as well as optimal farming strategies in which these crops were interlinked, first emerged in the seventh millennium BC.[255] Bogaard argues that optimum yields were achieved through intensive and increasingly artificial farming practices, taking the form of 'intensive mixed farming' in which small garden plots were cultivated intensively, with a mix of crops grown and the use of the manure from husbanded flocks to replenish soil nutrients.[256]

What evidence do we have for such a system of cultivation as the basis of the 6500 BC Neolithic expansion in Asia Minor? This question is presently difficult to answer. The available evidence is generally limited to lists of botanical and faunal species present, and for a substantial number of sites even this basic information is not available. Further, recent comparative studies on crop species in early Neolithic sites of the Near East and Europe almost completely ignore sites from the Lake District, Aegean Anatolia, and the Marmara Region.[257] In any case, to determine cultivation practices, a study of arable weeds is generally more informative than that of the crops themselves,[258] and further work is required to address early Neolithic cultivation systems in Asia Minor.

The most conspicuous changes in agriculture in the period between 6500 and 5500 BC appear to occur in animal husbandry practices, although the picture is far from clear at present (see Table 5.4). Domestic cattle appear in many sites in Asia Minor during this period. It has been posited that cattle were first domesticated in the Middle PPN-B, between about 8500

[255] Kislev 1999; Perrot 2001; Bogaard 2005.
[256] Bogaard 2004, 2005.
[257] Colledge et al. 2004, 2005; Coward et al. 2008.
[258] Bogaard 2004.

Table 5.4 Overview of the earliest domestic cattle in the Neolithic of Asia Minor and possible evidence of dairy products and wool industries

Region	Site	Period BC	Dom. Cattle	Dairy	Wool
Marmara	Ilıpınar	6000–5500	6000 →	n.a.	n.a.
	Menteşe	6500–6000	6500 →	Possibly	n.a.
	Fikirtepe	6500–5500	6500 →	n.a.	Possibly
Aegean	Ulucak	6500–5500	6500 →	n.a.	6000 →
Lake District	Hacılar/Kuruçay/ Höyücek/Bademağacı	6500–5500	6500 →	n.a.	6500 →
Central	Köşk/Tepecik	6000–5500	Possibly	Possibly	n.a.
	Canhasan 1	6200–5500	Possibly	n.a.	Possibly
	Çatalhöyük West	6000–5500	Possibly	n.a.	n.a.
	Çatalhöyük East	7000–6000	No	n.a.	n.a.
Cilicia	Yumuktepe	7000–5500	7000 →	n.a.	6000 →

and 7500 BC, in the Middle Euphrates.[259] From about 7000 BC onwards they are found at Yumuktepe in Cilicia,[260] but at Çatalhöyük East they are not present, and the first tentative evidence comes from the Çatalhöyük West mound, dating to after 6000 BC.[261] Likewise, at contemporary Köşk Höyük, domestic cattle are found. While domestic cattle predating 6000 BC are so far not documented in Central Anatolia, all the sites in the Lake District, Aegean Anatolia, and the Marmara Region have domestic cattle from about 6500 BC onwards, and the case for the transfer of domestic cattle from the plateau to the west and north is problematic.

A second set of questions regarding animal husbandry practices is when and where they started being kept for secondary products, such as wool and milk. It has recently been demonstrated that dairy consumption can be found across the Fertile Crescent and Asia Minor from the seventh millennium BC onwards, but dairy products seem to have been a relatively insignificant component of the diet and were derived at least in part from sheep and goats. An increase in dairy product consumption, probably related to the milking of cows, is documented in the Marmara Neolithic.[262] This corresponds well with a slightly later image at Köşk Höyük, where there is one scene on a pot possibly showing a cow being milked;[263] evidence of dairy consumption from Neolithic sites in the Balkans dating to between 5900 and 5500 BC;[264] and possible evidence of cattle dairy consumption in Menteşe, where it has been argued that cull patterns point in this direction.

[259] Peters et al. 1999: 40.
[260] Buitenhuis 2004.
[261] Russell et al. 2005.
[262] Evershed et al. 2008.
[263] Öztan 2007: 29, fig. 16.
[264] Craig et al. 2005.

Information on wool consumption is potentially available in the form of spindle whorls. These are present in Early Chalcolithic levels at Yumuktepe, from about 6500 BC onwards at Hacılar, and from at least 6000 BC at Ulucak. At many other sites, whorls are either not present or have not been published, making a general assessment of when wool became important across Asia Minor problematic. At some sites, such as Çatalhöyük East and Ilıpınar, there is evidence of flax cultivation, which could have been an alternative fibre for textile production.

In summary, there is little evidence of a well-integrated consolidated farming package with a set of crops and domestic animals that were part of an intensive mixed farming region. Nor is there any good evidence of a 'secondary products revolution' in which dairy and wool consumption quickly spread across large regions and transformed village economies. Instead, it appears more likely at present that farming between 6500 and 5500 BC was quite diverse, with different practices, crops, and animals in the various regions. Such a perspective fits more comfortably with the differential introduction of domestic cattle and with the fact that wool may have been important at some sites and flax at others.

How can we envision the spread of farming and sedentary life from a social perspective? In theory, the spread could have been facilitated by, first, a colonisation movement of people from Central Anatolia; second, a process in which hunter-gatherer groups acquired farming techniques, crops and animals, and a sedentary way of life from neighbouring groups; and, third, a combination of both of these processes.[265] Most debates about neolithisation have been based on the often implicit assumptions that, in the first scenario, we might expect that cultural traits other than farming might also have been transferred from the core region to the newly settled one; that in the second scenario, we would expect continuities with pre-existing Epipalaeolithic/Mesolithic in the earliest Neolithic assemblages; and, in the third scenario, we could expect a bit of both.

In Asia Minor there is only one region, apart from Central Anatolia, where we have good evidence of cultural continuities from the Epipalaeolithic/Mesolithic to the subsequent Neolithic: the Marmara Region with its Ağaçlı–Fikirtepe sequence. It is possible that similar continuity with the Epipalaeolithic/Mesolithic remains to be discovered in Aegean Anatolia and the Lake District.

Further, large, homogeneous early Neolithic horizons, such as the European 'Linear Band Keramik' and 'Cardial',[266] which quickly spread across regions hundreds of kilometres across, are not in evidence in Asia Minor.

---

[265] Zvelebil 2001; Sherratt 2004.
[266] Barnett 2000; Zvelebil 2001.

Instead, the Neolithic expansion in Asia Minor between 6500 and 5500 BC is marked above all by an extraordinary diversity of cultural traditions, in which different regions developed with their own distinct character.

How can we understand this diversity? Here I would like to suggest that a 'founder effect' mechanism could help us understand how such differences arose. The groups triggering the initial neolithisation of much of Asia Minor might have been relatively small and isolated from those of other areas. These groups could have included both enterprising migrant farmers and local hunter-gatherers. In such a situation, new cultural traditions could easily crystallise into a regional cultural horizon, with the subsequent population expansion and consolidation of culture that are more typical of developed cultural systems. Such mechanisms, in which small populations can change rapidly, are well known for biology but can apply equally to cultural changes.[267] It is my contention that such a model adequately explains the fragmentation of the Neolithic of Asia Minor. If it is valid, this would also imply that a factor such as climate change could have been a contributing factor to the Neolithic expansion, but it cannot be considered the driving element behind this development.

A model in which relatively small groups of people moved out of Central Anatolia is also one that fits the evidence from that region, where we can document a shift from large collective settlements in which households were embedded in clustered neighbourhoods and the larger local communities to smaller-scale settlements consisting of a more autonomous group of households. Within the more dispersed social system developing around 6500 BC, perhaps best exemplified by the numerous small settlements in the Suğla/Beyşehir Region, migrating towards new regions would have been more acceptable to society.

In conclusion, reviewing the remarkable expansion of the Neolithic way of life that occurred in Asia Minor around 6500 BC, there is very little evidence of push factors in the form of demographic or ecological stress; nor is there evidence of a consolidated Neolithic package of crops, animals, and cultivation techniques. Instead, a model in which small groups of entrepreneurial farmers moved into new regions, where in some cases they may have chosen to adopt local hunter-gatherer practices as much as hunter-gatherers did the reverse, created a kaleidoscope of unique cultural traditions.

[267] Anthony 1990; Andelson 2002.

CHAPTER SIX

MILLENNIA IN THE MIDDLE (5500–3000 BC)

The time span between 5500 and 3000 BC in Asia Minor is one about which we know so little that it could be called a 'Dark Age' with some justification. This hiatus in our knowledge is a consequence of archaeological research agendas, on the one hand, and is determined by the nature of archaeological remains that have been dated to this period, on the other.

One of the central concerns of archaeological research from its origins to the present is the question of how past societies evolved towards those of modern times. This idea of social evolution has been conceptualised in archaeology mainly along the lines set out by Gordon Childe, who distinguished the following major transitions in Prehistory: first, the emergence of farming and sedentary life in the Neolithic; and, second, the development of urban communities, which started in the Early Bronze Age in Asia Minor.[1]

This 'threshold view of the past' has condensed continuous historical developments into a few key events that occurred relatively rapidly and had widespread consequences. The most explicit and systematic example of an evolutionary perspective in Near Eastern Prehistory is that put forward by Redman in his *The Rise of Civilization*.[2] Although explicitly evolutionary approaches fell out of fashion in archaeology from the 1980s onwards,[3] it is arguably the case that most scholars working on the Prehistory of Asia Minor, and for that matter in archaeology in general, have implicitly adopted a Childean view of the past,[4] and this frame of reference has resulted in a very uneven investigation of the Prehistory of Asia Minor.

Within a Childean view of the past, the Chalcolithic is a period during which nothing of interest happened. This problem is mitigated for the Early

[1] Childe 1928, 1936.
[2] Redman 1978.
[3] Hodder 1982; Trigger 1998.
[4] Flannery 1994; Trigger 1994.

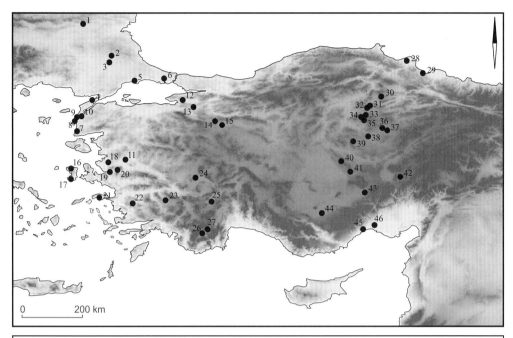

1 Karanovo; 2 Aşağı Pınar; 3 Tilkiburnu; 4 Kilia; 5 Toptepe; 6 Yarımburgaz; 7 Gülpınar; 8 Beşik-Sivritepe; 9 Kumtepe;
10 Alacalıgöl; 11 Kulaksızlar; 12 Ilıpınar; 13 Barcın Höyük; 14 Demircihüyük; 15 Orman Fidanlığı; 16 Ayio Gala; 17 Emporio;
18 Araptepe; 19 Yassıtepe; 20 Ulucak; 21 Tigani; 22 Çine-Tepecik; 23 Aphrodisias-Pekmez; 24 Beycesultan; 25 Kuruçay;
26 Bağbaşı; 27 Kizilbel; 28 İkiztepe; 29 Dundartepe; 30 Kuşsaray; 31 Büyük Göllücek; 32 Alaca Höyük; 33 Büyükkaya;
34 Yarıkkaya; 35 Camlibel Tarlası; 36 Çadır Höyük; 37 Alişar Höyük; 38 Çengeltepe; 39 Hashöyük; 40 Kabakulak;
41 Güvercinkayası; 42 Fıraktın; 43 Köşk Höyük; 44 Canhasan 1; 45 Mersin-Yumuktepe; 46 Tarsus-Gözlükule.

Chalcolithic, which is often considered as part of the Neolithic, and the Late Chalcolithic, which is commonly perceived as the initial stage of the subsequent Early Bronze Age,[5] while the Middle Chalcolithic in particular has been caught in the middle as an eventless span of time.

6.1 Middle and Late Chalcolithic sites of Asia Minor, 5500–4000 BC. Produced by Joanne Porck and the author.

Previously, it was shown for the Neolithic that the focus on the initial processes of domestication and sedentarisation in the Early Neolithic detracted from the study of social and economic transformations in the Late Neolithic that were in fact of key importance in the development and spread of sedentary farming lifeways. Reducing archaeological analysis to a few key events or sites fundamentally distorts our understanding of the past. If the Chalcolithic is seen as a span of time during which nothing of significance happened, this tells us more about our own interpretive frameworks than about the Chalcolithic.

The view of the Chalcolithic as an eventless and unimportant period has had clear repercussions on research agendas; this is reflected in the focus of

[5] For example, Mellaart 1966b: 110.

both excavation projects and publications. In particular, few projects have explicitly aimed to investigate the Middle Chalcolithic: In most cases the aim was to investigate other periods, such as the Neolithic, and Chalcolithic strata were investigated by default. In some cases, excavators have gone so far as to present Chalcolithic strata as dating to the Neolithic, for example at Köşk Höyük (§5.3.6). Clear exceptions to this general avoidance of the Middle Chalcolithic are the excavations at Güvercinkayası and Orman Fidanlığı (Fig. 6.1).

Many synthetic books dealing with the Neolithic and Early Chalcolithic of Asia Minor have been published,[6] and the same is also true for the Late Chalcolithic and the Early Bronze Age.[7] A good example is the work of Yakar, who first published a synthesis of the Late Chalcolithic and Early Bronze Age of Anatolia, and subsequently a monograph on the Neolithic and Early Chalcolithic, leaving the Middle Chalcolithic to one side.[8]

In his recent book *Das anatolische Chalkolithicum*, Schoop[9] provides an overview of the most important Chalcolithic sequences dating to between 6000 and 3000 BC in Asia Minor, with a focus on the ceramic assemblages, in an effort to construct a comparative dating for a number of elusive assemblages in North-Central Anatolia. Schoop's book is an important research resource, bringing together a vast amount of data in a single volume. However, there are some problems with his synthesis. First, his discussion is almost entirely concerned with ceramic chronology and typology, and reduces the study of the Chalcolithic to the comparative analysis of ceramic assemblages. Second, the 3,000-year period he deals with is not subdivided anywhere, and developments within the Chalcolithic are not considered. In effect, the question of what happened in Asia Minor during the Middle Chalcolithic, between 5500 and 4000 BC, is avoided, and the discussion focuses mainly on the Early Chalcolithic and the Late Chalcolithic, periods that are better known. For example, while Schoop discusses the Neolithic and Early Chalcolithic sites of Menteşe and Ilıpınar at length, the Middle Chalcolithic sites of Toptepe, Yarımburgaz (levels 3–0), and Aşağı Pınar are not discussed at all. Finally, in recent years, new data on the Chalcolithic have emerged through excavations at the sites of Güvercinkayası, Köşk Höyük, and Çadır Höyük, which can now be used to augment Schoop's work.

The far from satisfactory understanding of the Chalcolithic of Asia Minor can be contrasted with the much better researched contemporary horizons

---

[6] Yakar 1991, 1994; Özdoğan and Başgelen, eds., 1999, 2007; Gérard and Thissen 2002; Lichter ed. 2005.

[7] Orthmann 1963; Yakar 1985; Yener 2000; Wagner et al., eds., 2003; Korfmann, ed., 2006.

[8] Yakar 1985, 1991, 1994.

[9] Schoop 2005a.

in the Fertile Crescent and Mesopotamia, where the period between 5400 and 3000 BC is taken up by the Ubaid–Uruk sequence, which has been the subject of many systematic investigations.[10] The fact that the period between 5400 and 3000 BC is better investigated in Mesopotamia and the upper Fertile Crescent than it is in Asia Minor is explained largely by the emergence of increasingly complex societies in the Ubaid and Uruk periods, culminating in urbanisation, writing, states, and the emergence of long-distance trade networks.

By contrast, the evidence from Asia Minor dating to between 5500 and 3000 BC is indicative of smaller, less complex societies, fitting the idea of an eventless and unimportant period to some extent; this is probably one of the main reasons why the Chalcolithic has been poorly investigated in Asia Minor. In some respects, we are dealing with a classic feedback loop here: Lack of knowledge about the Chalcolithic has created a situation in which few scholars are interested in investigating this period, given that it is difficult to formulate specific research questions about it and that funding bodies are generally not interested in funding projects aimed at investigating a hiatus in culture-historical knowledge.

A similar situation prevailed until a few decades ago for the Halaf in the upper Fertile Crescent, a period that was considered to be of little culture-historical interest, much like the Anatolian Middle Chalcolithic. It was only in the wake of new and systematic investigations at sites like Tell Sabi Abyad and Domuztepe that the Halaf became a renewed focus for investigations.[11] The point that emerges from this comparison is that once a certain amount of knowledge is available about a period, researchers tend to be more interested in investigating further aspects of the horizon; this point has not been reached so far for the Middle Chalcolithic of Anatolia.

6.1.1 Widening Horizons: Asia Minor and the Balkans

Notwithstanding the fact that Chalcolithic Asia Minor has been poorly investigated and that we know very little about this period, the literature abounds with bold claims about the cultural interactions occurring between Asia Minor and adjacent regions. On the one hand, it is clear that the cultural horizons of Halaf, Ubaid, and Uruk of the Fertile Crescent and Mesopotamia affected developments in Asia Minor only marginally, in contrast with East Anatolia, where sites such as Arslantepe, Değirmentepe,

---

[10] Yasin 1985; Henrickson and Thuessen, eds., 1989; Algaze 1993; Stein, ed., 2005.
[11] Akkermans and Verhoeven 1995; Cambell et al. 1999; Verhoeven 1999; Nieuwenhuyse 2007.

Korucutepe, Norsuntepe, Tepecik, and Tülintepe have clear affinities with the Ubaid and Uruk horizons in Syro-Mesopotamia.[12] In this period, as in the preceding Neolithic, the eastern boundary of Asia Minor is a cultural watershed.[13]

On the other hand, clear similarities have been noted between assemblages of Asia Minor, the Balkans, and the Aegean. Cultural connections with the Balkans especially have been the topic of a series of studies.[14] For example, Özdoğan considers Asia Minor and the Balkans as a single cultural formative zone from the Late Neolithic up to the start of the Early Bronze Age, and he states:

> [W]e imply neither that identical cultural assemblages existed throughout this region or that a cultural homogeneity was due to the impetus of diffusion. The model we are suggesting manifests a large cultural formation zone, developing together with the same trend, but also displaying a considerable diversity in the composition of cultural and artefactual assemblages.[15]

The problem with this model is that it has little explanatory content and cannot be developed further with more research. The cultural formation zone proposed is not defined in any meaningful way, and both similarities and differences between regions are subsumed within its terms. Where similarities exist, they are seen as a self-evident manifestation of the cultural formation zone, which does not provide explanations for how such similarities arose in the first place, and where there are differences between assemblages, they likewise confirm the model.

A model that posits Asia Minor and the Balkans as a single archaeological complex between 5500 and 3000 BC is problematic, however. There are clear distinctions between assemblages in Asia Minor and those in the Balkans. For example, Schwarzberg has studied the distribution of polypod vessels in Asia Minor and the Balkans.[16] These are triangular or rectangular box-shaped ceramic vessels on legs, which are mostly decorated with geometric impressed or incised motifs such as checkerboards or composites of triangles. The earliest of these vessels, often labeled 'cult tables', are found at Fikirtepe sites in the Marmara Region, and some isolated examples have also been found in Central Anatolia and the Lake District. After 5500 BC polypod vessels become very common in the Balkans, where they persist until 4000 BC, but they are no longer in evidence in Asia Minor. Limited as

---

[12] Brandt 1978; Gülçür 2000; Frangipane 2001a.
[13] Özdoğan 1993.
[14] Efe 1990, 2001; Esin 1993a; Makkay 1993; Özdoğan 1993, 2007b; Thissen 1993; Steadman 1995.
[15] Özdoğan 1993: 177.
[16] Schwarzberg 2005.

this example may be, it shows that we are not dealing with a single archaeological complex stretching from Asia Minor across the Balkans between 5500 and 3000 BC.

Further, it is fairly common to encounter comparisons in the literature between black pattern–burnished and rippled ceramics found in Asia Minor and Vinča assemblages of the central Balkans.[17] This comparison suffers from various problems, however. First, the similarities between assemblages from Asia Minor and those from Vinča are often very general. If assemblages are compared more substantially, it often emerges that there are more differences than similarities between them. For example, most of the Vinča vessel shapes and decoration styles[18] do not have counterparts in Asia Minor, and similarities are restricted to general features such as pattern burnishing. Second, Vinča as conceived by Balkan archaeologists does not occupy an area bordering Asia Minor. Instead, there are other assemblages, such as those known from Karanovo, separating Vinča from Asia Minor.[19] This circumstance, of course, makes comparisons between Vinča and Asia Minor more problematic. Third, there are a series of correlations with Vinča that proved to be unreliable as research progressed. For example, for a long time Vinča was equated with Troy I, a correlation that was only grudgingly abandoned with the advent of radiocarbon dating, and we know today that the two assemblages are separated by three millennia.[20]

Another case of cross-dating ceramics from Asia Minor with Vinča/ Gumelnitsa assemblages consists of the Gelveri ware found in Central Anatolia (§5.3.6). On the basis of a comparison with faraway Balkan assemblages, this material was dated to the fifth and fourth millennia BC.[21] It has even been linked with the arrival of people speaking Indo-European languages because the time frame fitted with ideas about when that language family would have spread,[22] whereas in fact this material has now been found in levels 4–2 at Köşk Höyük, levels that date to the Early Chalcolithic (§5.3.6). The point that emerges from such cases is that comparing far-removed ceramic assemblages is problematic, especially if there are no other ways of dating these assemblages, and such comparisons should be treated with caution.

I do not argue that interactions between Asia Minor and the Balkans in the period between 5500 and 3000 BC did not exist. However, discussions of interregional contacts on the basis of similarities in artifacts – and not all

---

[17] Efe 1990, 2001; Özdoğan 1993; Nikolov 1998; Gabriel 2006; Takaoğlu 2006.
[18] Chapman 1981.
[19] Chapman 1981; Bailey 2000; Parzinger 2005.
[20] Mellaart 1960; Özdoğan 1982: 2.
[21] Esin 1993b; Makkay 1993; Özdoğan 1996.
[22] Makkay 1993.

contacts result in the convergence or exchange of material culture styles – should preferentially focus on assemblages securely dated through other means and on assemblages from neighbouring regions.

For example, in recent years, fifth millennium sites in the Troad, such as Kumtepe A and Gülpınar, have been linked with sites in the Aegean, such as Emporio and Tigani. In combination with radiocarbon dating, such comparisons are much stronger than earlier postulated links with Vinča.[23]

Linked to these Aegean assemblages, various researchers have argued for a ceramic horizon, characterised by horned handles, carinated bowls, and incised and grooved decoration, stretching from North-Central Anatolia (Büyük Güllücek) and the Black Sea (Dündartepe and İkiztepe) to the Aegean, between approximately 5000 and 4500 BC.[24] However, ceramics are not interchangeable across this large area. Rather, there are some comparable traits in the assemblages that may hint at contacts between these regions.[25]

The 'Balkan–Anatolian' complex posited by various authors[26] is not one that stands up to scrutiny. However, the fact that, from about 5000 BC onwards, parallels in material culture across large areas can be investigated is remarkable when compared to the regional fragmentation that characterised the preceding period. Slowly, during the course of the Chalcolithic and the ensuing Early Bronze Age, we can see an increasing widening of horizons, culminating in the creation of large cultural horizons in the Early Bronze Age, when artefact types became similar across Asia Minor and beyond. In the Middle and Late Chalcolithic periods discussed in this chapter, regional differences continue to dominate the assemblages, but there is sufficient evidence of regular contacts between regions and the exchange of material culture.

6.2.1 The Chalcolithic of the Greater Marmara Region

The Marmara Region, broadly defined, is one of the best-investigated areas for the Chalcolithic in Asia Minor. The main reasons are the temporal proximity with the Neolithic in this region and the fact that many sites investigated primarily for their Neolithic deposits also contained substantial Chalcolithic strata.

Although located outside of Asia Minor, the sequence from Aşağı Pınar, augmented with data from Toptepe, is without doubt of key importance

---

[23] Gabriel 2006; Takaoğlu 2006.
[24] Thissen 1993; Steadman 1995; Schoop 2005a: 326–327.
[25] Steadman 1995: 23; Schoop 2005a: 326–327.
[26] Efe 1990; Özdoğan 1993; Todorova 1998: 31; Garasanin 2000.

6.2 Plan of Aşağı Pınar level 5. Reproduced with permission of N. Karul from Karul, N. 2003. 'Die Architektur von Aşağı Pınar'. In *Aşağı Pınar I, Einführung, Forschungsgeschichte, Stratigraphie und Architektur*, edited by N. Karul, Z. Eres, M. Özdoğan, and H. Parzinger, pp. 42–125, fig. 10. Mainz am Rhein, Germany: Philipp von Zabern.

for any understanding of the Chalcolithic in the Marmara Region. Seven main levels have been distinguished at Aşağı Pınar, of which levels 7 and 6 date between 5700 and 5500 BC and levels 5–1 to 5500–5000 BC.[27]

A total of 32 buildings were found at Aşağı Pınar. These consist of rectangular wattle-and-daub freestanding structures often built in linear alignments.[28] The buildings vary considerably in proportions and dimensions throughout the sequence. The best-understood building phase is that of level 5 (Fig. 6.2), in which seven buildings were found. These buildings are all similar, measuring about 6.5 by 5.0 metres, with an entrance in one

[27] Özdoğan et al. 2003: 37–38; Görsdorf 2005.
[28] Eres 2003; Karul 2003.

of the long walls and an oven situated on the wall opposite. Floors were constructed of gravel and yellowish sandy clay.

Buildings of later levels differ from those of level 5. In level 4, houses with two rooms have been found, and some of these buildings are up to 80 square metres in size. In one of these buildings ('4–5') no fewer than eight floors were found, as well as remnants of platforms and *in situ* vessels and silos. In most cases one of the rooms was larger than the other, but a differentiation of functions cannot be established. In levels 3 and 2 buildings become even larger, reaching up to 120 square metres in size, but most are smaller and have two rooms, one of which contains an oven.

Extended linear ditches and wall-like features were found in levels 6, 5, and 3 of Aşağı Pınar, and it is possible that they demarcated the settlement in some way. Given that similar features existed at sites such as Ilıpınar, Aktopraklık, and Hoca Çeşme (§5.7.1), this seems plausible, although the evidence from Aşağı Pınar is limited to short trajectories. These boundary markers need not have been defensive in purpose.

In terms of material culture, Aşağı Pınar can best be compared with nearby Balkan assemblages, such as those at Drama-Gerana and Karanovo, often labelled collectively as 'Karanovo'. Although numerous parallels have been noted between Aşağı Pınar and Balkan sites, differences are also apparent within these largely comparable assemblages.[29] The ceramics consist mostly of dark-burnished vessels, with small grit inclusions in the fabric. Shapes include open and carinated bowls, in some cases with a distinct rim, holemouth vessels, and funnel-necked jars. Raised feet and handles on the shoulders of vessels, the latter in some cases with a raised knob on the elbow, are common. From 30 to 40 per cent of the ceramics are decorated, either with rippled decoration ('Kannelur'), incised dot and line patterns, or impressed patterns. The incised and impressed patterns were sometimes filled with a white paste. A conspicuous category of ceramics consists of the polypod vessels. The decorated box-shaped vessels on legs found at Aşağı Pınar have parallels in the Balkans rather than in Asia Minor, where they are not known from this period.[30]

Toptepe is a small site on the European coast of the Sea of Marmara (see Fig. 6.1) with large deposits of shells hinting at intensive exploitation of marine resources. The site was excavated in a rescue project in 1989, and the excavated material is in many respects similar to what has been found in the upper levels at Aşağı Pınar.[31] This assessment is borne out by radiocarbon dates from the site, which suggests a span of 5300–5000 BC

[29] Parzinger 2005: 43–64.
[30] Schwarzberg 2005.
[31] Özdoğan et al. 1991.

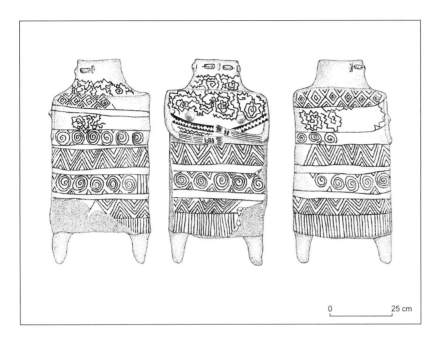

6.3 Anthropomorphic vessel from Toptepe. Reproduced with permission of M. Özdoğan from Özdoğan, M., and Dede, Y. 1998. 'An anthropomorphic vessel from Toptepe, eastern Thrace'. In *James Harvey Gaul – In Memorium*, edited by M. Stefanovich, H. Todorova, and H. Hauptmann, pp. 143–152, fig. 1. Sofia, Turkey: James Harvey Gaul Foundation.

for levels 5 to 3.[32] The ceramics found at the site are very similar to those of levels 2 and 3 of Aşağı Pınar.[33]

Among the ceramics are two anthropomorphic vessels, the better preserved of which is an unbaked rectangular vessel 85 centimetres high on four legs with a round neck on which a face has been painted in red on cream (Fig. 6.3). The vessel is decorated with two arms in front of the 'chest' and geometric motifs below that could represent a garment. Both the shape of the vessel and the fact that charred grain was found nearby suggest that it might have served as a storage silo. Although parallels are often drawn with anthropomorphic vessels from the Balkans, in particular Tisza sites,[34] similar vessels have also been found in Early Chalcolithic levels at Ulucak and Köşk Höyük.[35] Both sets of parallels are superficial in that they highlight only one particular find category instead of comparing entire complexes.

The anthropomorphic vessel at Toptepe was found in a partly burned building with a collapsed roof, which also contained a large domed oven, a

[32] Özdoğan and Dede 1998: 150; Erdoğu et al. 2003b.
[33] Parzinger 2005: 46–47.
[34] Özdoğan and Dede 1998; Parzinger 2005.
[35] Çilingiroğlu and Çilingiroğlu 2007: fig. 8; Öztan 2007: fig. 13.

platform, fragments of wall plaster with geometric painting, and a number of bone tools. The plan of the building is similar to that found in levels 2 and 3 at Aşağı Pınar.

On the basis of similarities in the buildings and ceramics at Aşağı Pınar and Toptepe, located at opposite ends of what is today Turkish Thrace, it is clear that we are dealing with a shared cultural horizon. This is not surprising given that the sites are not very far from each other.

By contrast, across the Sea of Marmara, at Ilıpınar 5B, to be dated between about 5500 and 5400 BC, we are dealing with distinct cultural traditions. Here a series of sunken hut structures measuring about 2 by 3 metres were uncovered. They were dug about 40 centimetres into the mound and covered with plaster. In some cases, post holes were found along the perimeters of the huts, hinting at a superstructure that probably consisted of a wattle-and-daub roof. A number of the huts had a raised bench along one side. The centre of these huts usually included a range of features: oval domed ovens, grinding installations, plastered baskets, and a multitude of ceramic vessels.[36] On the exterior of one of the huts a series of loom weights were found.[37] These features and objects were very well preserved because some structures were burnt, resulting in, first, the preservation of plaster basket coatings, a textile fragment, and charred foodstuffs; and, second, a large number of objects and features in these spaces. For example, hut 5 contained 17 pots, and hut 3 contained 11 pots and 2 plastered baskets. In both cases, the total capacity of these containers was about 50 litres. This density of features and objects begs the question of where people were living in these structures. The excavators interpret the hut structures as seasonally occupied, suggesting that the objects found represent a storage situation, with a staple supply of crops such as emmer, barley, lentil, and chickpea that was kept for sowing purposes later in the year.

On the basis of the Ilıpınar 5B ceramics, which includes dark-patterned burnished and rippled ceramics, it was originally argued that new groups of people had arrived at the site from the Balkans.[38] However, a recent study of this assemblage has demonstrated significant continuities with older periods at Ilıpınar and argues that only some elements of the Ilıpınar 5B ceramics can be linked with Balkan (specifically, Karanovo 2 and 3) assemblages.[39] Further, there are very few parallels, either in pottery shape or in decoration techniques and motifs, between Ilıpınar 5B, on the one hand, and Aşağı Pınar and Toptepe, on the other. Thus, as in the preceding Neolithic, when Fikirtepe assemblages are absent in Thrace (§5.7.1), the Sea of Marmara

[36] Roodenberg 2001: 231–235; Roodenberg 2008a: 78–80; Cappers 2008.
[37] The excavator prefers an interpretation as 'net weights' (Roodenberg 2008a: 79).
[38] Roodenberg 1999: 200; Roodenberg 2001.
[39] Thissen 2008: 100.

seems to have separated regional cultures rather than acting as a nexus for cultural exchange.

In contrast to the relatively well-documented second half of the sixth millennium BC in Turkish Thrace, relatively little is known about the following fifth millennium in the region. It is plausible that Yarımburgaz levels 3, 2, and 0 date to this millennium, but the evidence from Yarımburgaz is problematic.[40] In effect, the Yarımburgaz evidence is limited to the published, predominantly dark-burnished ceramics, consisting mainly of simple shapes, such as bowls, S-shaped pots, and necked jars. New are large strap handles, along with less broad horned handles. Some vessels have simple geometric decorations below the rim, such as chevrons, often executed in stab-and-drag techniques, or wavy patterns. This material has tentatively been linked with ceramics from Büyük Güllücek in Central Anatolia and Vinča B/Vesselinovo in the Balkans,[41] although given the small corpus of material and its mixed character, such equations should be treated with caution.

On the Asian side of the Sea of Marmara, better information is available for the fifth millennium BC, from sites such as Orman Fidanlığı, Aktopraklık, Kumtepe, Beşik-Sivritepe, and Gülpınar.

The site of Orman Fidanlığı is the most systematically investigated and published of all these fifth millennium sites. Its discovery was a lucky coincidence. Site deposits do not exceed 150 centimetres, were covered with 2 to 10 metres of eroded material, and were uncovered during road construction works.[42] The added circumstance that a group of archaeologists was performing a surface survey nearby led to the investigation of the site, which was excavated between 1992 and 1994.

Hardly any clear features were found in the Orman Fidanlığı excavations, two exceptions being an apsidal structure with stone walls measuring about 2 by 3 metres in the interior and a fragmentary oven associated with a surface. Otherwise, features consisted of poorly constructed stone walls, most of which probably served to shore up terraces. Given the lack of clear features and the fact that the excavated strata are on a rocky slope, it is likely that the main Orman Fidanlığı settlement was located elsewhere.[43]

Among the excavated assemblages, a distinction has been noted between the older levels 1–5, on the one hand, and levels 6 and 7, on the other. These assemblages can be distinguished on the basis of, first, lithic industries: the upper levels have macroblades of good-quality flint, whereas the lower levels have unstandardised flake tools of poor-quality flint; second, faunal

[40] Özdoğan et al. 1991.
[41] Özdoğan 1985: 180; Özdoğan et al. 1991: 84.
[42] Efe 1990: 67–69; 2001: xvi, 1.
[43] Efe 2001: 21.

remains: the lower levels are dominated by domestic sheep, the upper ones by wild horses; third, figurines: these were found only in the early levels; and, finally, the ceramics.

The ceramics from the early levels 1–5 consist of dark-faced burnished wares, red-slipped and red-painted wares, and white-slipped wares occasionally painted in red. Forms include open bowls and plates, globular pots and holemouth vessels, and S-shaped jars. Carinations and feet are rare or absent; there are a few strap handles, along with some string-hole lugs. There is a wide repertoire of decoration, including pattern burnishing, incision, impressed decoration, grooving, rippling, fluting (often with white inlay), and painting. Most decorations can be seen on the shoulder of jars, and consist of various geometric motifs such as triangles, parallel vertical lines, half-circles, and waves.

The later level 6 and 7 ceramics at Orman Fidanlığı differ in a number of respects. Carinated bowls make their appearance. True handles appear, some with a protrusion on the elbow and often designated 'horned handles'. The ornamentation seen in levels 1–5 is absent, but there are some sherds with geometric patterns in white paint. Further, a pin with spirals and an awl, both produced from hammered copper, were found in level 7.

No radiocarbon samples have been taken at Orman Fidanlığı. As a result, it is difficult to date the assemblages. Both the level 1–5 and 6/7 assemblages have been dated by comparison to assemblages in surrounding regions. There are some parallels between the level 1–5 ceramics and figurines at Orman Fidanlığı and the levels 5A/5B ceramics at Ilıpınar; however, on the other hand, the decorative techniques and motifs of Orman Fidanlığı differ from those found at Ilıpınar and other Fikirtepe sites. This suggests that Orman Fidanlığı postdates Ilıpınar.[44] Both Efe and Schoop have argued for parallels between early Orman Fidanlığı and Hacılar 1,[45] but points of comparison are few and not particularly convincing. It is possible to date Orman Fidanlığı 1–5 to either the late sixth or the early fifth millennium BC. The level 6/7 assemblages at Orman Fidanlığı are normally dated to the end of the Middle Chalcolithic, approximately 4500–4000 BC, on the basis of parallels with Yarımburgaz 2, Yazır Höyük, and İkiztepe.[46] None of these sites are securely dated, however, and this date too must be regarded as tentative.

In the Troy Region, a number of fifth millennium sites have been investigated. These include Kumtepe layer 1A, Beşik-Sivritepe, Gülpınar, and

[44] Contra Efe 2001: 50–52; Schoop 2005a: 302.
[45] Efe 2001: 58–59; Schoop 2005a: 297–298.
[46] Efe 2001: 50–68; Schoop 2005a: 300.

Alacalıgöl.[47] Kumtepe 1A has been radiocarbon dated to about 5000–4700 BC and Beşik-Sivritepe to 4700–4500 BC.[48] On stylistic grounds it has been posited that Alacalıgöl postdates Beşik-Sivritepe,[49] so possibly dated to the third quarter of the fifth millennium BC.

Like Orman Fidanlığı, all these sites in the Troad are relatively shallow, generally not more than 70 centimetres deep. The limited depth of these sites has been linked with wattle-and-daub building technologies, a way of constructing that would have resulted in less building debris and therefore less substantial deposits. The insubstantial nature of these sites, many of which were discovered more or less by accident, explains in part why the fifth millennium is so poorly known.

Further, in most cases, fifth millennium layers were not systematically excavated. At Beşik-Sivritepe we are dealing predominantly with redeposited material disturbed by a later tumulus; Alacalıgöl is known only from a surface investigation; and at Gülpınar and Kumtepe, small exposures were dug and no clear features could be distinguished. As a result, we know next to nothing about the nature of the settlements of this period, and the evidence consists mostly of ceramic assemblages (Fig. 6.4). These include elaborate handles, some with horns, others with diagonal rippling, and some pattern-burnished vessels ('politur muster'). Typical are coarse sherds with perforations and rims or ridges with pinch impressions. Vessel shapes include bowls with and without a foot – sometimes perforated with a series of vertical slots – plates with inward-turning rims, and necked jars with handles.

The fifth millennium ceramics from the Troad have little in common with the Orman Fidanlığı assemblages, apart from the horned handles that occur in levels 6 and 7. Likewise, there appear to be only a few isolated parallels with Thracian sites such as Toptepe, levels 2 and 3 at Yarımburgaz, and Aşağı Pınar. By contrast, frequent and convincing comparisons are drawn with sites such as Tigani, Aghio Gala, and Emporio, all of which are located on Aegean islands just off the coast of Asia Minor. Given the fact that these sites are no closer to the Troad than, for instance, Toptepe or Ilıpınar, it has been argued that the Troadic sites are part of a wider (eastern) Aegean cultural horizon.[50]

At Emporio, stone walls surrounding a well, a small D-shaped room measuring about 2 by 4 metres with an associated hearth and floor, and

---

[47] Sperling 1976; Seeher 1985, 1987b; Gabriel 2000, 2006; Gabriel et al. 2004; Takaoğlu 2006.

[48] Gabriel 2000.

[49] Gabriel et al. 2004.

[50] Takaoğlu 2006.

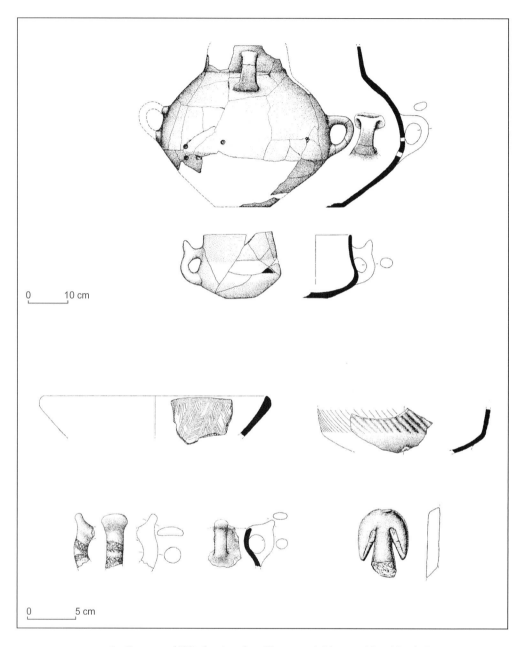

6.4 Pottery and Kilia figurines from Kumtepe 1A (above scale) and Beşik-Sivritepe. Reassembled with permission of U. Gabriel from Gabriel, U. 2006. 'Ein Blick zurück – Das funfte Jahrtausend vor Christus in der Troas'. In *Troia: Archäologie eines Siedlungshügels und seiner Landschaft*, edited by M. O. Korfmann, pp. 355–360, figs. 1 and 2. Main am Rhein, Germany: Philipp von Zabern.

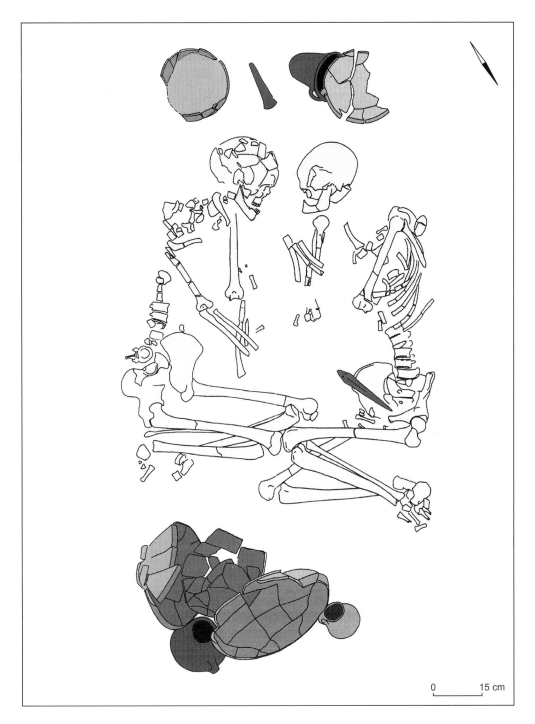

6.5 Double burial from Ilıpınar level 4. Reproduced with permission of J. Roodenberg and B. C. Coockson from Roodenberg, J. 2008. 'The Late Chalcolithic cemetery'. In *Life and Death in a Prehistoric Settlement in Northwest Anatolia: The Ilıpınar Excavations III*, edited by J. Roodenberg and S. Alpaslan-Roodenberg, pp. 315–334, fig. 5. Leiden: Nederlands Instituut voor het Nabije Oosten.

some burial remains were found.[51] In spite of these features, relatively little is known about the scale and nature of this and other settlements in the Aegean. However, it has been argued that marine resources were of great importance in these fifth millennium sites,[52] a suggestion that fits well with the coastal location of a number of sites and the sharing of cultural traditions in this part of the Aegean.

At present, it is uncertain whether the Troadic sites were occupied in the second half of the fifth millennium BC, and more investigations are required to settle the issue. Todorova has argued for a hiatus between 4500 and 4000 BC in the Balkans and Anatolia that was caused by climatic deterioration.[53] In view of the limited amount of research to the present and the absence of radiocarbon dates for many sites, such interpretations should be treated with caution. Even if we were to accept the argument for climatic change, the question would be how this affected people in Anatolia and the Balkans; it is unlikely that these lands were simply abandoned.

For the next half-millennium, between about 4000 and 3500 BC, our database for the greater Marmara Region remains scant. Some evidence dating to this period has been obtained at the sites of Ilıpınar (level 4), Tilkiburnu, and Barcın Höyük.

Tilkiburnu, located in the centre of Turkish Thrace, was investigated through the inspection of a section left standing following soil extraction. This section contained a number of large silo pits as well as remnants of mud brick buildings. From the silos a number of complete vessels were extracted. The ceramics consisted of dark-coloured wares, either fine and burnished or coarse and unburnished. Shapes include deep bowls with in-turned rims, necked jars, and holemouth pots. There is some impressed and grooved decoration, but this is quite rare. Horned handles and standing feet seem to be absent. Of special interest is a funnel-shaped beaker with a small handle attached to the rim that has been found at Tilkiburnu.

This funnel-shaped beaker has direct parallels with those found in level 4 at Ilıpınar. Level 4 at this site consists of a cemetery containing the remains of at least 40 people.[54] No associated settlement has been identified. The burials include both single and double primary inhumations, mostly of adults and adolescents. Bodies were generally placed on their right side and were mostly slightly flexed (Fig. 6.5). Many of these burials contained burials goods, located both near the feet and near the skulls. These include ceramic vessels, metal objects, bone tools, beads, and whetstones.

---

[51] Hood 1981: 96–104.
[52] Gabriel 2000: 234.
[53] Todorova 1998.
[54] Roodenberg et al. 1990; Roodenberg 2001, 2008c.

The pottery consists of dark-burnished vessels that include jars with one or two handles connecting the rim with the shoulder, shallow bowls with carinations on the shoulder, holemouth pots with a small handle on the rim, and funnel-shaped beakers, which are the most common type. The funnel-shaped beakers have either one or two strap handles along the rim. They occur both decorated and plain. The decoration consists of horizontal bands or chevrons with dots or triangles within.

The metal objects include flat axes with fan-shaped cutting edges, knives, a dagger, and pins. Analysis of these objects has shown that they were made of arsenical copper. Along with similar artefacts made of arsenical copper from the site of İkiztepe, the Ilıpınar 4 artefacts are currently amongst the earliest arsenical copper objects in Anatolia and the Balkans.[55] The debate about whether arsenic was intentionally added or was present in the ores used is ongoing. Whatever the case, the presence of arsenic significantly enhanced the mechanical properties of copper and facilitated its use for new purposes, a development that is at the root of the rising importance of metals in subsequent periods.

At the site of Barcın Höyük, Late Chalcolithic assemblages have been found that are similar in some respects to those found at Ilıpınar 4, including a flat fan-shaped ax. There are some similarities in the shallow carinated bowls and amongst the jars. The funnel-shaped beaker is absent, however, and it may be that this type is associated with burials.[56] Alternatively, the Barcın Late Chalcolithic, radiocarbon dated to 3900–3700 BC, predates that of Ilıpınar 4, radiocarbon dated to approximately 3800–3600 BC.

At Demircihüyük, near Eskişehir, Late Chalcolithic ceramics were found in redeposited contexts, which were designated complexes 'F' and 'G'. The Late Chalcolithic ceramics of Demircihüyük include fine burnished ceramics tempered with dung and coarse unburnished material with chaff temper. The exterior is normally dark in tone, and the core of the sherds is usually lighter. Typical shapes include carinated bowls (*Knickrandschalen*), some with an everted rim (*Kehlrandschalen*), as well as broad-necked jars with a handle connecting the rim and the shoulder and S-shaped pots. Parallels with Ilıpınar 4, Barcın Höyük, and Beycesultan Late Chalcolithic 3 and 4[57] can be drawn, and a date of about 3600–3400 BC can be suggested.

Finally, the 1B/B layer at Kumtepe in the Troad can be dated to the final centuries of the Late Chalcolithic, between about 3300 and 3000 BC. Excavations were first executed here in the 1930s and mainly provided a pottery

[55] Begeman et al. 1994; Özbal et al. 2002.
[56] Roodenberg 2008c: 319.
[57] Seeher 1987a: 58; Efe 1990; 2001: 57; Schoop 2005a: 303.

assemblage.[58] Rescue excavations undertaken in 1993 have clarified the site stratigraphy considerably.[59] A number of well-built stone walls were found belonging to two buildings that were frequently altered and renovated. The incompletely exposed buildings included various small rooms, which might have served as a sub-structure of the actual building. One somewhat larger room, measuring about 2.5 by 1.5 metres, had a stone pavement, however. It is unfortunate that a larger exposure of the buildings could not be obtained.

The ceramics of Kumtepe 1B/B consist of both fine mineral-tempered, dark-burnished slipped ware and coarse ware. Rolled-rim bowls with an inward-curving rim are typical of the assemblage, as are horizontal tubular lug handles on the rim and shoulder of the bowls. Some inward-carinated bowls have also been found, in some cases with knobs on the carination. Feet are either rounded, flat, or raised. Decoration is rare and mostly takes the form of incised lines on the rim. Finally, some holemouth pots and simple jars have been found.

It has often been observed that the Kumtepe 1B/B ceramics have many similarities with those of Troy 1, the earliest Bronze Age site in the Troad. At the same time, it has not been possible to link the Kumtepe 1B/B assemblages with the Late Chalcolithic assemblages elsewhere, such as those at Beycesultan or Kuruçay.[60] Given that there must be at least some temporal overlap between these sites, it is most likely that Kumtepe 1B/B was a regional ceramic tradition only.

Summarising this discussion of the greater Marmara Region between 5500 and 3000 BC, a number of points have emerged. First, this period of two and a half millennia is very poorly investigated. For many periods, all we have are ceramic assemblages that have been assigned to them on the basis of circumstantial evidence. Nonetheless, a culture-historical sequence is slowly emerging for the Middle and Late Chalcolithic, even if it is patchy and problematic. Second, the discussion of the period between 5500 and 3000 BC in this area is by necessity almost exclusively about artefact types and chronology: There is simply not enough settlement and burial evidence to attempt a more social reconstruction. Third, the idea that there was a form of cultural homogeneity across Asia Minor and the Balkans in the Middle and Late Chalcolithic has been shown to be highly problematic. Many assemblages have a regional distribution only, and attempts to link these assemblages with those farther afield often fail because of a lack of common elements. Larger material culture horizons seem to occur in the fifth millennium – for example, with reference to horned handles – but even in this period the differences far outweigh the similarities. Thus, the

[58] Sperling 1976.
[59] Korfmann et al. 1995.
[60] Sperling 1976; Korfmann et al. 1995: 260; Schoop 2005a: 270.

Balkan–Anatolian complex often discussed in the literature seems to have little basis in the evidence at present.

6.2.2 The Chalcolithic of the Lake District and the Southern Aegean

In the research history of the Anatolian Chalcolithic, the Lake District and the southern Aegean have been significant, because various Chalcolithic sequences were obtained in this part of Asia Minor relatively early in the nineteenth century. These sequences, however, are not unproblematic, and polemic discussions about the relative ordering of various sequences have complicated studies of the Chalcolithic across Asia Minor considerably.

For the Early Chalcolithic, between 6000 and 5500 BC, a considerable amount of detailed information is available about ceramic styles and settlement forms (§5.5.1 and §5.6.1). This abundance of data stands in stark contrast with the subsequent period, the Middle Chalcolithic, between 5500 and 4000 BC, about which we are poorly informed.

Excavations in the 1950s at the site of Beycesultan have provided a Late Chalcolithic sequence. Mellaart argued that the Beycesultan sequence directly followed that of Hacılar, and that together they represented the complete Chalcolithic sequence in this part of Asia Minor.[61] This view has found some support among archaeologists.[62]

From the outset it was clear, however, that the proposed late Hacılar–early Beycesultan sequence was problematic. One problem is that the assemblages of late Hacılar and early Beycesultan are completely dissimilar. These differences were explained by postulating the influx of a new population bringing their own distinct material culture.[63] While such explanations have since fallen out of fashion, radiocarbon data have been instrumental in demonstrating that the two sequences are separated by a temporal gap of about 1,500 years.[64]

For the Middle Chalcolithic in western Asia Minor evidence is scarce. In the Elmalı plain in Lycia, some material at the sites of Bağbaşı and Kızılbel may date to this period.[65] At the site of Bağbaşı, ceramics were found beneath strata containing Late Chalcolithic ceramics, which were similar to sherds found in a redeposited context at Kızılbel. These ceramics are predominantly unpainted but have some features absent in earlier sites

---

[61] Lloyd and Mellaart 1962: 106, 112; Mellaart 1966b: 109–110; Mellaart 1975: 15.
[62] Duru 1996: 143; Seeher 1987b; 1990; Duru 2008: 8–9.
[63] Lloyd and Mellaart 1962: 106; Duru 1996: 111.
[64] Schoop 2005a: 185–189.
[65] Eslick 1980; 1992.

in the region, such as rounded and strap handles and knobs, hence their assignation to the Middle Chalcolithic. The ceramics are coarse, poorly fired, and burnished. Forms include simple holemouths, some of which have perforations below the rim, and open bowls, some of which have handles attached to the rim. At both sites the sample of sherds is small, and nothing is known about the strata from which they derive.

Another site that has been dated to the Middle Chalcolithic in south-western Asia Minor is Kulaksizlar.[66] A regional survey in the Akhısar region recognised 5 Neolithic/Early Chalcolithic sites and no fewer than 13 Late Chalcolithic sites. By contrast, Kulaksızlar is the only Middle Chalcolithic site that was found. In the surface survey a total of 220 sherds were collected, but importantly, many of them were similar to those found in Troadic sites such as Kumtepe layer 1A, Beşik-Sivritepe, and Gülpınar and were radiocarbon dated to about 5000–4500 BC (§6.2.1). The fabric of this pottery is described as unevenly fired, coarse, and lightly burnished. Among the characteristic features that link these ceramics to the Troadic sites and those on the Aegean islands (Emporio and Tigani) are handles with diagonal ridges (false twists), handles attached to bowl rims that in some cases have knobs, and crescent-shaped lugs. The most convincing similarities to these ceramics are found at the site of Gülpınar.[67]

Some pottery resembling that of Kulaksızlar has also been published for the Izmir Region, at Yassıtepe, and, more tentatively, at Araptepe.[68] Finally, at the site of Çine-Tepecik in the Aydın Region, ceramics have been excavated that in some elements resemble those of the fifth millennium sites from the Troad. Similarities include twisted handles, rippled decoration, and horned handles. Not paralleled in the Troad or elsewhere are fine black-painted lattices on the interior of bowls and broad vertical stripes.[69] The Chalcolithic strata from Çine-Tepecik will undoubtedly become important in our future understanding of the Middle Chalcolithic in western Asia Minor.

The site of Kulaksızlar is of special interest because there is evidence of the production of stone vessels and figurines. These were produced from marble. A large number of blanks, waste by-products, manufactured rejects, and stone working tools were found at this site. These constitute about 90 per cent of the surface assemblage at Kulaksızlar, with the remainder consisting of more ordinary domestic artefacts.[70]

---

[66] Takaoğlu 2002, 2004, 2005.
[67] Takaoğlu 2006: 296.
[68] Caymaz 2006: 9; Derin 2006: 12.
[69] Günel 2006b, 2007, 2008.
[70] Takaoğlu 2002: 72.

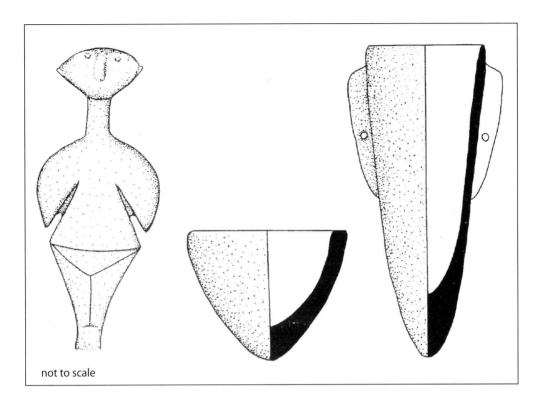

not to scale

The marble raw material for these stone vessels and other rocks used in the manufacturing process, such as gabbro, basalt, and sandstone, were located within walking distance of Kulaksızlar. The stone vessels and figurines were produced with a combination of hammering, drilling, and grinding techniques. The figurines were much more difficult to produce than the stone vessels and took longer to make. The most common artefacts produced at Kulaksızlar are pointed beakers and 'Kilia figurines'.

The latter are named after the site of Kilia in the Gallipoli Peninsula, where the first example was found. These figurines depict a stylized humanoid, most likely female, with a long neck, round sloping shoulders, arms folded upwards in front of the chest, and a lozenge-shaped lower body and legs, with incisions to indicate the legs and the pubic triangle.[71] Whereas the bodies are flat, the necks are cylindrical and the heads are much broader than the body and have raised facial features (Fig. 6.6). The beakers are conical and have two vertical lugs with piercings near the rim. Pointed bowls are also found.

Both the pointed marble beakers and the Kilia figurines have been found over large areas. While there may have been other production centres

6.6 Kilia figurine, pointed bowl, and pointed beaker from Kulaksızlar. Reproduced with permission of T. Takaoğlu from Takaoğlu, T. 2002. 'Chalcolithic marble working at Kulaksizlar in Western Anatolia'. *TUBA-AR* 5: 71–93, fig. 2.

[71] Seeher 1992.

besides Kulaksızlar, the distribution of such artefacts does tell us something about prehistoric exchange patterns and cultural preferences. Pointed marble beakers similar to those produced at Kulaksızlar have also been found at Tigani on Samos; on the islands of Keos and Naxos; at Kumtepe and Beşik-Sivritepe in the Troad; at Demircihüyük in the Eşkişehir Region; and at Varna in western Bulgaria.[72] Kilia figurines were found across Western Anatolia but not, it seems, in the Aegean: at sites such as Beşik-Yassıtepe, Hanaytepe and Troy in the Troad; and Yortan, Alaağaç, Selendi, Gavurtepe, and Aphrodisias in Western Anatolia.

The pointed beakers and the Kilia figurines appear to have different distributions in time and space. Whereas pointed marble beakers are found at sites dating to the early and middle fifth millennium BC, such as Kumtepe, Gülpınar, and Beşik-Sivritepe, Kilia figurines are found at sites dating from the late fifth millennium BC to the Early Bronze Age, such as Aphrodisias-Pekmez and Troy. While it is possible that Kilia figurines found in Early Bronze Age levels were ancient heirlooms,[73] it is plausible that these artefacts were produced into the Late Chalcolithic.

At Aphrodisias two Kilia figurines were found in level 8A of trench 2, in a layer that could date to about 4300–4000 BC. The associated ceramics, which include sherds with white-painted decoration, are similar to those found in early fourth millennium Late Chalcolithic sites such as Beycesultan. Future research will have to establish whether Aphrodisias-Pekmez starts in the late fifth millennium, as argued by Joukowsky,[74] or not. However one interprets levels 8B and 8A at Aphrodisias-Pekmez, it is clear that Kilia-type figurines are found well into the Late Chalcolithic at other sites.

The simplest interpretation of the Kulaksızlar site is that it was used roughly between 4500 and 4000 BC.[75] In that case, the earliest ceramics and the pointed beakers relate to the fifth millennium Troadic and Aegean sites, and the Kilia figurines are part of a West Anatolian cultural phenomenon starting in the final quarter of the fifth millennium BC and continuing into the subsequent fourth millennium BC. Alternatively, an occupation gap of unknown duration could be postulated between the Kilia figurine production and that of the pointed beakers.

In any case, the importance of evidence at Kulaksızlar is clear. Here we find evidence of specialised production geared towards exchange. The goods were consumed in settlements about which we know very little, and the site of Kulaksızlar must be considered atypical. Second, we see a shift from an early fifth millennium West Anatolian–Aegean interaction sphere

[72] Takaoğlu 2002: 78–79; 2004: 3.
[73] Seeher 1992: 163; Takaoğlu 2002: 80.
[74] Joukowsky 1986: 161.
[75] Takaoğlu 2005: 20.

to one focussed on West Anatolia only later in that millennium. It is clear that only the surface of the fifth millennium exchange patterns in West Anatolia has been scratched, but here we might witness the first steps in the rise of complex long-distance trade networks.

Finally, at the site of Ulucak, Middle Chalcolithic deposits have been excavated in level 3. Two L-shaped stone foundation walls were found associated with a small amount of pottery.[76] Some of this pottery was pattern-burnished and resembles the ceramics of the Troadic sites, such as Kumtepe 1A and Beşik-Sivritepe, suggesting that this level at Ulucak may date to the early fifth millennium BC.

If this discussion of the Middle Chalcolithic in West Anatolia is considered meagre, it should be remembered that the period is not discussed at all in the synthetic books of Yakar and Schoop.[77] Evidence from Kulaksızlar, Çine-Tepecik, and Ulucak has only recently become available, and investigations have been very limited. However, at least the Middle Chalcolithic is now slowly being put on the archaeological map.

In contrast to the paucity of knowledge on the Middle Chalcolithic in western Asia Minor, the Late Chalcolithic, to be dated between about 4000 and 3000 BC, is relatively well known from excavations such as those at Beycesultan, Aphrodisias-Pekmez, Kuruçay, and Bağbaşı.

In their publication report of Beycesultan, the first site in this part of Asia Minor where Late Chalcolithic strata were systematically excavated, Lloyd and Mellaart distinguished four sub-phases in the Late Chalcolithic: 1 to 4 (LC1 to LC4, early to late) in their sequence.[78] Although the authors stress that the distinctions between these sub-periods are fluid, such terminological schemes inevitably take on a life of their own. Thus, when Joukowsky processed the Late Chalcolithic ceramics from the site of Aphrodisias-Pekmez, she ordered them into the same four sub-periods.[79] Recently, it has been argued, on the basis of radiocarbon dates and ceramic typology, that LC1 at Aphrodisias actually precedes LC1 at Beycesultan and that LC2 at Aphrodisias should be dated to a period between LC2 and LC3 at Beycesultan.[80] Given these complications, the fourfold subdivision of the Late Chalcolithic will be avoided here.

At Beycesultan in deep sounding 'SX' a long Late Chalcolithic sequence was excavated, consisting of no fewer than 11 metres of deposits and subdivided into levels 40 to 20. Apart from the final layers, 23 to 20, all these levels contained architectural remains, suggesting that occupation in this

[76] Çilingiroğlu et al. 2004: 18–20.
[77] Yakar 1985: 108; Schoop 2005a: 172–196.
[78] Mellaart 1962b: 73–77.
[79] Joukowsky 1986: 161.
[80] Schoop 2005a: 182–191.

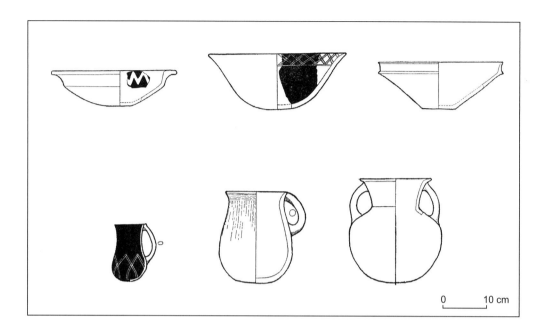

0   10 cm

6.7 Late Chal-
colithic pottery
from Beycesul-
tan. Produced
by Joanne Porck
after sheets 1 and
2 in Mellaart,
J. 1962. 'The
Late Chalcol-
ithic pottery'.
In *Beycesultan I:
The Chalcolithic
and Early Bronze
Age Levels*, edited
by S. Lloyd and
J. Mellaart, pp.
71–115. Lon-
don, England:
British Institute
of Archaeology at
Ankara.

part of the mound was dense and more or less continuous. In levels 34 to 24, a series of rooms built of mud bricks were excavated that measured about 3 by 4 metres. In most levels a hearth was present, located either in the centre or against one of the long walls. In some levels bins, grinding stones, and *in situ* pottery were also encountered. There are also two examples of infant burials below the floor.[81] Unfortunately, very few details have been provided about these buildings, but it seems likely that we are dealing with living rooms of domestic structures, which, given their size of about 15 square metres, probably served a nuclear rather than an extended household.

The Beycesultan pottery was sub-divided into four phases. However, most of the shapes and fabrics are present throughout the sequence, and the distinctions can only be made on the basis of the excavated stratigraphy.[82] The most common fabric at the site is dark-burnished, grey at the core and dark grey to brown on the surface, often with a slip on the surface. There are also coarse wares, which are not burnished and have larger inclusions.

Decoration is rare, consisting of geometric painted patterns executed in thin white lines. It is found predominantly on the everted or flaring rims of bowls and on the lower exterior of jugs (Fig. 6.7). This type of decoration is especially common in the early part of the Beycesultan sequence and becomes rare towards the end of the Late Chalcolithic.

[81] Lloyd 1962a.
[82] Mellaart 1962b: 73.

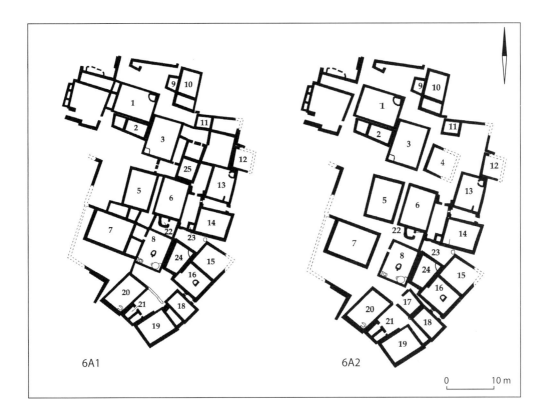

6A1   6A2

0   10 m

The shape repertoire of Beycesultan is limited[83] and consists in the main of, first, shallow open bowls with everted or flaring rims; second, flat dishes with outcurving rims; third, jugs of varying proportions and sizes with a handle running between the rim and the shoulder, some of which have knobs applied to the top of the handle or the lower part of the vessel; fourth, globular pots with handles rising above the rim; and, fifth, carinated bowls with concave rims, in some cases with a handle attached to the rim, a form found only towards the end of the Beycesultan sequence.

Two radiocarbon dates are available for the Beycesultan Late Chalcolithic sequence, one from level 37 and the other from level 28. Taken together, they suggest that the Beycesultan Late Chalcolithic dates to 3900–3400 BC.[84]

The Late Chalcolithic ceramics from Beycesultan have good parallels at Aphrodisias-Pekmez, located about 100 kilometres to the southwest.

6.8 Plans of levels 6A1 and 6A2 at Kuruçay. Reproduced with permission of R. Duru and G. Umurtak from Duru, R. 2008. *From 8000 BC to 2000 BC: Six Thousand Years of the Burdur–Antalya Region.* Istanbul, Turkey: Suna-Inan Kirac Akdeniz Medeniyetleri Arastirma Enstitusa, figs. 231 and 232.

---

[83] According to Mellaart (1962b: 71): "At Beycesultan the Late Chalcolithic potters reveal themselves as endowed with the most pronounced lack of imagination in West Anatolian Prehistory."

[84] Schoop 2005a: 188–191.

Two trenches in the Pekmez mound contained Late Chalcolithic remains.[85] These trenches were poorly dug, and the evidence is therefore restricted to the assemblages. It is possible that the oldest Aphrodisias material predates the Beycesultan sequence, given that vessel forms occur that are absent at Beycesultan and that two radiocarbon dates fall into the late fifth and early fourth millennia BC.[86]

Bağbaşı in the Elmalı plain in Lycia also has Late Chalcolithic remains. The building remains were poorly preserved, and here too the only information available is artefactual. The predominantly coarse ceramics have a number of characteristics comparable to those of the latest pottery from Late Chalcolithic Beycesultan, thus probably dating to the mid-fourth millennium BC.[87] A substantial number of very large storage vessels with vertical walls and flat bases were recovered at the site,[88] suggesting that storage was more important than at other sites, perhaps pointing to seasonal use of the site.

In contrast to all other Late Chalcolithic sites in western Asia Minor, at Kuruçay we have good settlement data. Here levels 6 to 3 (early to late) date to the Late Chalcolithic. Although Duru has suggested that these levels predate the Beycesultan sequence, both the radiocarbon dates and the ceramic assemblages suggest a date at the tail end of the Beycesultan sequence, between approximately 3600 and 3200 BC.[89] Six radiocarbon dates from level 6 cluster in the range of 3600–3400 BC, while levels 5–3 have not been radiocarbon dated.

The ceramic assemblages of Kuruçay 6–3 have clear affinities with those of Beycesultan. The white-painted bowls and jugs typical of early Beycesultan are absent, but vessels comparable to those of later Beycesultan are ubiquitous. These include jug shapes, deep conical bowls, and simple cups with flat bases with or without handles. Some features that occur at Kuruçay are not found at Beycesultan, such as rim protrusions and vertical handles on the shoulders of jars.[90] Given such elements, it seems plausible that the Kuruçay Late Chalcolithic largely postdates that of Beycesultan.[91]

While only limited architectural evidence is available for levels 5 to 3, a substantial part of the settlement of level 6 has been excavated at Kuruçay. It is the only Late Chalcolithic settlement of western Asia Minor investigated on this scale (Fig. 6.8). Approximately 23 buildings of the Kuruçay

[85] Joukowsky 1986: 175.
[86] Schoop 2005a: 182–184, 191.
[87] Schoop 2005a: 185.
[88] Eslick 1992: 46.
[89] Duru 1996: 143–144; Schoop 2005a: 191
[90] Similar pottery in an undefined context has also been found at the site of Bademağacı (Umurtak 2005).
[91] Schoop 2005a: 184–185.

6 settlement, dated to about 3500 BC, were excavated. These consisted mostly of single-room rectangular buildings, usually measuring about 4 by 7 metres. In some cases, buildings had two rooms or a small room was added to the exterior of the rectangular structure.[92]

The buildings had stone foundations upon which mud walls with a width of about 30 centimetres were raised. The remains of a collapsed roof point to single-storey structures with a flat roof. In many buildings post holes were found in the central axis of the room; these posts would have held up the roof.

Most Kuruçay buildings were found in a degraded condition, with only the stone foundations preserved and without evidence of their interior arrangements. A number of level 6 buildings were better preserved, however, in exceptional cases with walls standing up to 1.5 metres. In one instance, a door complete with the lintel and a section of the wall above were preserved.

In such buildings, a variety of features were present that shed light on the use of space. Few details have been published, but the living rooms normally seem to have included the following elements: Doors occur on various sides of buildings, and these locations were probably determined mainly by the way buildings could be accessed most easily from open spaces. In one instance, impressions of the timber frame in which the wooden door hinged were still clearly visible. Second, the buildings usually contained a large domed oval oven that was normally located in one of the corners farthest removed from the entrance. Third, a central hearth was also common in these buildings. These features were ovoid in shape and usually had a small upstanding pillar on their rear side. This is interpreted as a religious feature by the excavator,[93] but it would also have served to protect the post positioned behind the hearth from catching fire. Fourth, additional features and objects, such as grinding installations, stone grinding vessels, looms, and storage pots, were found in the back of some rooms. Finally, the well-preserved building 8 was interpreted as a 'shrine' by Duru.[94] However, except for its excellent preservation, this building and its contents are similar to those of other structures at the site.

In general, Duru's interpretation of Kuruçay 6 as a kind of small urban centre is problematic.[95] In his view, there were a number of central buildings in the settlement, which included the shrine but also houses for postulated dignitaries, which were surrounded by a series of domestic buildings whose rear walls would have constituted a 'saw-toothed' defense wall, with various small alleys acting as 'gates'. In truth, this interpretation is a very particular

[92] Duru 1996, 2008.
[93] Duru 1996: 19.
[94] Duru 1996: 12.
[95] See also Schoop 2005a: 165–166.

and unconvincing reading of the evidence and requires some manipulation of the data. Much of the 'defense wall' consists of domestic buildings walls of various phases presented as one feature. Even if the defense wall is accepted, many 'ungated' entrances to the settlement remain, such as that between buildings 15 and 14.

One matter that complicates assessment of the Kuruçay 6 plan is that no fewer than seven stratigraphic phases were distinguished at the site (old to young: 6A2-early, 6A2-late, 6A1-early, 6A1-late, 6c, 6b, and 6a), during which a number of minor changes occurred in the overall settlement. The general picture that emerges from this stratigraphy is one in which the level 6 settlement initially contained houses that were mostly freestanding and were accessed from the surrounding small courts and alleys. Later these open spaces were largely built up, due to the construction of small structures and walls between existing buildings, effectively closing off much of the open spaces of the settlement. It is not entirely clear to what degree this development outlined is an artifact of the premise that level 6 at Kuruçay was initially a planned settlement, with a defensive wall.

A close reading of the published plans suggests that in all phases of the level 6 settlement there are clusters of spatially associated buildings. Such a reading of the plans would imply that Kuruçay was not inhabited by autonomous households, each occupying a discrete freestanding building, but that we may be dealing with household clusters of about three to five closely associated households, presumably organised along the lines of kinship.

No fewer than 50 child burials in ceramic vessels were found in Kuruçay 6, and almost all buildings must have contained 1 or 2.[96] Normally, these bodies were buried beneath room corners, probably during the occupation of the houses. Nearly half of these children were neonates, and the remainder were less than four years of age. Grave goods were absent. Only four adult burials were recovered; these were placed outside houses, and one was accompanied by two ceramic vessels. It is likely that adults were normally buried elsewhere, but no Late Chalcolithic cemetery has so far been excavated in western Asia Minor.

Summarising this overview of western Asia Minor between 5500 and 3000 BC, it is clear that we know very little, especially about the Middle Chalcolithic. There are a number of ceramic assemblages that can be slotted into this period, such as those from Bağbaşı, Kızılbel, Ulucak, Kulaksızlar, and Çine-Tepecik, but very little substantive work has been done at these sites. The evidence for specialised production geared towards exchange in the

---

[96] Duru 1996: 24.

Kulaksızlar stone workshop provides a fascinating window into this unexplored period. In the following Late Chalcolithic, stratigraphic sequences at Beycesultan and Aphrodisias-Pekmez provide us with dated ceramic assemblages, but these are of little use for the reconstruction of past societies. By contrast, at Kuruçay 6 a sizable village was excavated. There burial data and the spatial association of domestic buildings provide us with important clues about how people interacted in this horizon.

6.2.3 The Chalcolithic in Northern Asia Minor

The Prehistory of northern Asia Minor, here defined as including both the Pontus and the interior plateau north of the Tüz Gölü, is among the most problematic in the land. Notwithstanding the fact that some of the earliest archaeological investigations in Asia Minor took place in this region, such as at Alişar Höyük and Alaca Höyük (§2.1.4), large parts of the prehistoric sequence remain obscure across northern Asia Minor.

The preceding period between 10,000 and 6000 BC in northern Asia Minor is effectively *terra incognita*. Although various claims have been put forward for sites that could potentially date to the Early Holocene in this region, none can be confidently dated to this period.[97] Thus, we do not know what sorts of societies were present in northern Asia Minor in these four millennia, how and when a farming economy was taken up in the region, and in what manner farmers might have co-existed with 'Mesolithic' groups in the area.

The apparent absence of Neolithic settlements in northern Asia Minor contrasts with the well-known early Neolithic in the southern reaches of the Anatolian Plateau, which starts at around 8500 BC (§4.4.1), and also with the evidence from the Marmara Region, starting at around 6500 BC (§5.7.1). The 'absent Neolithic' of northern Asia Minor is therefore an anomaly. It has been argued that the ecology and climate of the region were adverse to early farming economies: for example, that the region was too forested or too cold.[98] However, at least part of the region has a climate very similar to that of the southern plateau.[99]

Given the evidence of Mesolithic communities in sites in the Antalya Region (§3.2.1), on the Konya Plain (§3.4.1), and in the Marmara Region (§3.3.1), it seems unlikely that northern Asia Minor was not occupied in the early Holocene. Further, obsidian found at sites such as Ilıpınar, Fikirtepe, and Pendik, some of which dates back to 6500 BC, derives in part from the

---

[97] Düring 2008: 20–21.
[98] Mellaart 1972, 1975; Todd 1980; Roberts 1982; Matthews 2000; Wilkinson 2003.
[99] Düring 2008: 26–30.

Galatian Mountains, with two known sources in central Çankırı (Sakaeli) and northern Ankara (Yağlar).[100] Given that these sources are difficult to locate within the landscape, it has to be assumed that there were people in the region with an intimate knowledge of its resources.

The fact that no Neolithic sites have been discovered in northern Asia Minor suggests that the conspicuous large settlements found in the southern plateau are probably absent from the region: Sites with dimensions similar to those of Aşıklı Höyük and Çatalhöyük would probably have been found. On the other hand, relatively small sites might have been overlooked, whether linked to a Mesolithic or a Neolithic economy. Much of northern Asia Minor is forested to some degree, and erosion in the river valleys has been substantial.[101] In addition, the availability of timber and heavy rains in much of the Pontic Region means that buildings in parts of the region have traditionally been constructed of wood rather than mud,[102] resulting in less substantial mound formation.[103] In concert, such factors could have resulted in the absence, destruction, or poor visibility of sites that might have been small and inconspicuous to start with.

The surveys that have been undertaken in northern Asia Minor are mostly very extensive, often with densities of about one site per 60 square kilometres. In theory, more intensive surveys targeting landscapes zones in which early sites might be expected to have been preserved, in concert with absolute dating of such sites, should clarify the settlement history of the first four millennia of the Holocene. Here a parallel can be drawn with the Middle Chalcolithic in western Asia Minor, discussed in the previous section, which is now slowly emerging at various sites, or with the recent discovery of an early Aceramic Neolithic on Cyprus.[104]

Turning to the Early Chalcolithic in northern Asia Minor, the situation is not much clearer. Across the region, a number of more or less distinct ceramic assemblages have been found at sites such as Büyükkaya, Büyük Güllücek, Dündartepe, Kuşsaray, and Yarıkkaya that are difficult to order chronologically and cannot be securely connected with excavated sequences in other parts of Asia Minor.

A series of studies have sought to put these ceramic complexes in some chronological order by comparing these ceramics with excavated sequences elsewhere in Asia Minor.[105] The problem is that various scholars have

[100] Bigazzi et al. 1995.
[101] Marsh 1999; Summers 2002.
[102] Tuna 2008.
[103] Rosenstock 2005.
[104] Peltenburg and Wasse, eds., 2004.
[105] Bittel 1934, 1945; von der Osten 1937; Orthmann 1963; Parzinger 1993; Thissen 1993; Schoop 2005a.

arrived at very different chronologies on the basis of the same methodology of morphological and stylistic comparison of ceramic assemblages,
in which the same assemblages are dated up to thousands of years apart
and the relative sequences are also at odds. Many of the ceramic complexes mentioned seem to have only a regional distribution and cannot be
linked with sequences elsewhere. The poor state of our knowledge of the
Middle Chalcolithic in Asia Minor in general also makes such correlations
difficult.

To illustrate this point, the recent thorough study by Schoop can be
mentioned,[106] in which he dates the distinct assemblages of Büyükkaya and
Yarıkkaya to the Early Chalcolithic, between 6000 and 5500 BC. Subsequently, the same researcher excavated a site with ceramics similar to those
at Yarıkkaya at Çamlibel Tarlası and updated his chronological assessment
to the mid-fourth millennium BC,[107] two millennia later than had been
anticipated.

The assignment of the Büyükkaya assemblage to the Early Chalcolithic
may be confirmed in future investigations, but we are dealing with a small,
fragmented ceramic assemblage that was previously dated to the Middle
Chalcolithic.[108] Apart from a single parallel at Canhasan level 2B, the dating
of Büyükkaya is based on a selective comparison with sites in the Lake
District, rather than with those found in geographically intermediate sites
such as Canhasan, Köşk Höyük, or Tepecik-Çiftlik.

A number of sites found in the surveys in central Kastamonu, such
as Sokukayası, Çatalkaya, Pazardoruğu, Kayabaşı, and Tepecik,[109] and in
the Paphlagonia survey, in particular Salur Höyük, Turba Mevkii, and
Maltepe,[110] have also been dated to the Early Chalcolithic. At most of
these sites only a few sherds were found, and these can only be connected
with Early Chalcolithic assemblages elsewhere in a very indirect manner.[111]

In summary, for the Early Chalcolithic in northern Asia Minor, our
knowledge is only marginally better than for the Early Holocene. Instead of
an absence of sites, we have a number of survey sites that could potentially
date to this period but that require further investigation.

The Middle Chalcolithic in northern Asia Minor is somewhat better
known. There are a number of excavated ceramic assemblages that can be
dated to this period, either on the basis of comparison with sites farther west
(Büyük Güllücek and İkiztepe) or on the basis of radiocarbon dates (Çadır

[106] Schoop 2005a.
[107] Schoop 2008.
[108] Parzinger 1993.
[109] Marro et al. 1996, 1998; Kuzucuoğlu et al. 1997.
[110] Matthews 2000.
[111] Marro et al. 1996: 279.

Höyük).[112] However, all these sequences are problematic. Büyük Güllücek was excavated in the 1940s, prior to the advent of modern excavation techniques, and its stratigraphy and building remains are poorly understood. İkiztepe has been excavated from the 1970s onwards, but there are considerable problems with its stratigraphy and chronology.[113] Finally, at the site of Çadır Höyük, where recent well-executed excavations of Middle Chalcolithic excavations have taken place, the sounding in which these layers were investigated is only 2 by 2 metres.

Notwithstanding these problems, our understanding of the Middle Chalcolithic of northern Asia Minor has been significantly enhanced over the last few decades. This is due to various circumstances, including the availability of absolute dates for Çadır Höyük, the re-examination of the İkiztepe sequence by Thissen and Schoop,[114] and the availability of the excavated sequences of Orman Fidanlığı and Güvercinkayası in adjacent regions.

At Büyük Güllücek, where 50 to 95 workers were employed in the excavations, a large excavation area was opened up. Stone foundations of Middle Chalcolithic buildings were found that were assigned to two different stratigraphic phases, but in reality, the stratigraphy must have been more complicated, as various buildings appear to crosscut each other. Not a single comprehensive plan of a building was obtained, but various rectangular rooms measuring about 3 by 4 metres and with preserved floors and ovens were excavated. These rooms were all part of larger buildings, but it is not clear whether all rooms were domestic or whether some served a special purpose. The excavators reconstruct the settlement as a hamlet consisting of four or five houses, but this hypothesis cannot be evaluated.

The Chalcolithic ceramics from Büyük Güllücek include a few painted examples with white or red lattices on the interior of bowls, but most pots were not painted. Instead, many were decorated with scratches, incised decorations, or impressed dots. Decorative patterns were applied mostly in horizontal bands and included diagonal lines, triangles, and checkerboards with impressed dots. Handles were attached to the area between the shoulder of the vessel and the rim, and were often decorated with protrusions of various forms on their upper bend. Further, knob ledges on the shoulder or rim were common, as were horizontal raised ledges with diagonal impressions resembling a rope (Fig. 6.9). In all, about 6 per cent of the sherds were decorated, but we know next to nothing about the undecorated sherds. There are only a few depictions of vessels shapes; these include carinated jars, pedestalled bowls, and raised bowls.

[112] Koşay and Akok 1957; Alkım et al. 1988, 2003; Steadman 1995; Steadman et al. 2008.
[113] Parzinger 1993; Thissen 1993; Schoop 2005a: 307–320.
[114] Thissen 1993: Schoop 2005a.

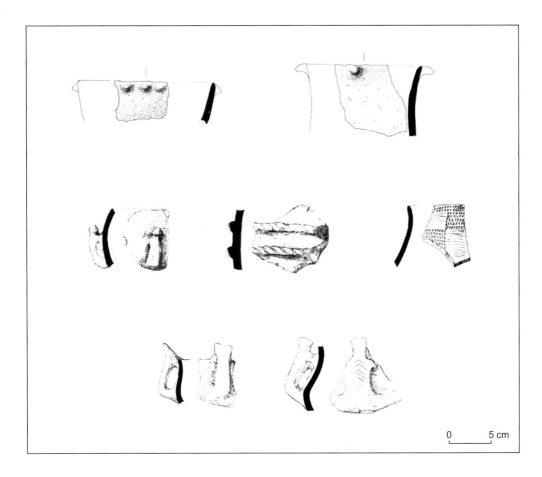

The ceramic assemblage from Büyük Güllücek is very characteristic and has not been found at other sites.[115] Nonetheless, some elements of the decoration and shape repertoire are also documented elsewhere. Some of the impressed decoration below rims, for example, is also encountered in the surface assemblage of Kabakulak, near Niğde.[116] The pedestalled bowls found at Büyük Güllücek have good parallels at Early Chalcolithic level 2 of Tepecik-Çiftlik,[117] while the checkboard impressed decoration has good parallels at Güvercinkayası.[118] Other features of the Büyük Güllücek ceramics do not have clear parallels to the south, however, such as the

6.9 Pottery from Büyük Güllücek. Reassembled with permission of U.-D. Schoop from plates 9–11 in Schoop, U.-D. 2005. *Das anatolische Chalkolithicum.* Remshalden, Germany: Albert Greiner Verlag.

[115] A number of sherds that appear very similar to those from Büyük Güllücek have been found in nearby Alaca Höyük in an assemblage that dates to the end of the Late Chalcolithic (Koşay and Akok 1966; Thissen 1993: 209; Schoop 2005a: 38–43). These sherds are few, small, and most likely in a secondary context, probably deriving from decomposed mud bricks.

[116] Summers 1991

[117] Bıçakçı et al. 2007.

[118] Gülçür 1997, 2004.

horned handles and knobs on the rim. These have better parallels in layers 6 and 7 at Orman Fidanlığı[119] and in the Troadic and Aegean sites farther west.[120]

Whereas the parallels at sites such as Tepecik-Çiftlik and Güvercinkayası hint at a date in the early fifth millennium, those at Orman Fidanlığı suggest a late fifth millennium date for Büyük Güllücek. Only further research can clarify the Büyük Güllücek chronology and whether the site was occupied in one phase or several during the Chalcolithic.

At Çadır Höyük, Middle Chalcolithic levels were excavated in a deep sounding measuring 2 by 2 metres.[121] Nothing is known about the nature of the settlement, and a relatively small sample of ceramics was recovered. These consisted of dark grey sherds, fired in a reducing atmosphere, with little temper. The sherds were mostly from open bowls, the exterior of which was often burnished. The only decoration consists of white paint applied diagonally. At present, it is not possible to link the Çadır ceramics with those from Büyük Güllücek, but this could simply be a matter of sample size. Alternatively, the radiocarbon date obtained at Çadır Höyük, of 5220–4940 BC, could be interpreted as meaning that the Çadır Middle Chalcolithic precedes that of Büyük Güllücek.

The third excavated site with Middle Chalcolithic strata in northern Asia Minor is İkiztepe.[122] This site is located on the Black Sea coast on the Bafra Delta of the Kızılırmak River. Although the site has been excavated from 1974 to the present, considerable confusion exists regarding its stratigraphy and chronology. In the publications, three main periods of occupation are distinguished: Period 1 is dated to the 'Early Hittite Period' (actually to be dated to the Early Bronze Age 3); period 2 is assigned to the Early Bronze Age; and period 3 is dated to the Chalcolithic. The main problems with this stratigraphy are that period 2 includes heterogeneous assemblages and that much of this material is in fact to be dated to the Chalcolithic rather than the Early Bronze Age.[123]

For convenience, I will adhere to a new phasing of the site proposed by Schoop on the basis of ceramic types in conjunction with the site stratigraphy. In trench B, on the mound labelled 'İkiztepe 2' at the site, he distinguished two ceramic complexes, designated 'AA' and 'BB', both of which can be dated to the Middle Chalcolithic on comparative grounds. This can now be augmented with evidence from the second excavation report.[124] Various

---

[119] Efe 2001.
[120] Thissen 1993; Schoop 2005a: 326–328.
[121] Steadman et al. 2008.
[122] Alkım et al. 1988; 2003.
[123] Thissen 1993; Schoop 2005a: 308.
[124] Alkım et al. 2003: pls. 4–14, 25–31, and 44–54 (all from Area B on İkiztepe mound II).

radiocarbon dates are available that seem to place these complexes in the second half of the fifth millennium BC,[125] although the relevant radiocarbon dates have wide error margins and provide imprecise and conflicting dates.

Little is known about the nature of the settlement in this period at İkiztepe, except that multiple buildings co-existed there at any one time in close proximity. Various rectangular floors were encountered, some with pebble paving and with hearths and ovens. These were part of wattle-and-daub structures that appear to have been poorly preserved. Beyond such general characteristics, few details are available on the İkiztepe 2 buildings.

The early ceramics from İkiztepe 2 consist of handmade dark wares, in many cases burnished on the exterior and in some cases decorated with relief, incised or scratched geometric patterns, or impressed dots. The İkiztepe AA ceramics include bowl shapes, large ovoid holemouth vessels with handles on the shoulder, and S-shaped pots. Some bowls have handles running from the rim to the base. Characteristic are handles in which the upper ends are extended into arched eyebrows on the vessel, with raised knobs representing eyes below. Many of these features have good parallels to the south at Güvercinkayası and Köşk Höyük, which would suggest a date in the early fifth millennium BC for İkiztepe AA.[126] The İkiztepe BB ceramics are characterised by horned handles, simple open bowls shapes, some with raised grips on the rim, horizontal bands of geometric incised and scratched decoration, and impressed decoration below the rim. Parallels for these ceramics can be found in Büyük Güllücek, Kabakulak, in Orman Fidanlığı 6 and 7, and in the Aegean sites (§6.2.1).[127]

The Late Chalcolithic in northern Asia Minor is known from a range of excavations, including those at Alaca Höyük, Alişar Höyük, Büyükkaya, Çadır Höyük, Çengeltepe, Dündartepe, İkiztepe, Kuşsaray, and Yarıkkaya. Despite this long list of sites, the state of knowledge for the Late Chalcolithic in northern Asia Minor is far from satisfactory. Many of these sites were excavated in the 1930s and 1940s, prior to the advent of modern excavation techniques, and have been poorly published. By consequence, the reconstruction of Late Chalcolithic northern Asia Minor rests primarily on the evidence from Alişar Höyük, Çadır Höyük, and İkiztepe, augmented with data from other sites.

At Çadır Höyük Late Chalcolithic levels, radiocarbon dated to about 3600–3100 BC have been excavated over a large area.[128] Here a number of substantial stone walls were encountered that were interpreted as constituting a (poorly preserved) defense wall and an entrance gate to the

[125] Alkım et al. 2003: 144; Schoop 2005a: 321.
[126] Gülçür 1997, 2004; Öztan and Faydalı 2003; Schoop 2005a.
[127] Summers 1991; Thissen 1993; Schoop 2005a: 325–328.
[128] Steadman et al. 2007, 2008.

settlement. Next to the entrance, a burnt building with a collapsed roof and an associated courtyard was found. This contained a range of finds, including spindle whorls, loom weights, needles, pottery, charred food remains, metal objects, and chipped stone debris, cores, half-fabricates, and tools. A radiocarbon sample dates this burnt building to 3600–3300 BC. Farther towards the interior of the settlement at Çadır Höyük, another building was found containing large numbers of pottery vessels. This two-room structure contained a raised hearth and a bench set against the wall.

The Late Chalcolithic pottery from Çadır Höyük is similar in fabric to that of the Middle Chalcolithic at the same site: a dark grey to orange fabric that is often burnished. Shapes are predominantly simple and include open bowls and S-shaped jars. Characteristic is a bowl with a dimple at the base known as an 'ompholos bowl'. Many vessels have knobs on the rim or shoulder, and there are also examples of small, round handles attached to the rim. Decoration is rare and includes geometric patterns in white paint and scratched geometric patterns.

Although some elements of the Çadır Höyük assemblage, such as the ompholos bowl, are not found at other sites, other features are also present at other sites. For example, the knobs on the rims and on carinations, on the one hand, and small circular handles on rims, on the other, are also found at sites such as Kuşsaray, at Yarıkkaya (plateau), and at what has been labelled assemblage 'CC' at İkiztepe, the material deriving from the uppermost strata of Area B at İkiztepe 2.[129]

At the sites of Kuşsaray and Yarıkkaya, there are also vessels decorated with elaborate geometric incised patterns covering the whole surface of the vessel (Fig. 6.10). Another pot type has crescent-shaped ledges with a perforation below near the base, a vessel type that has been linked with butter production on the basis of dairy residues.[130] Given the absence of these features at Çadır Höyük, it could be that these two sites predate the excavated Late Chalcolithic levels at Çadır.

Recent excavations at Çamlibel Tarlası, a site with ceramics similar to those found at Yarıkkaya, have recently been dated to 3600–3400 BC.[131] At the site of Yarıkkaya, a series of rectangular to square rooms measuring some 7 by 5 metres were excavated; some were freestanding, whereas others shared party walls with adjacent rooms. Walls were constructed from stones at the base, with stamped mud in the higher reaches. In the centre of some rooms a post was found. The entrances were located in one of the long walls near the corner, and in one of the corners a large rectangular oven was found, in many cases with a base layer of sherds. Finally, some other features,

[129] Schoop 2005a.
[130] Schoop 2008: 154, note 99.
[131] Schoop 2008, 2009.

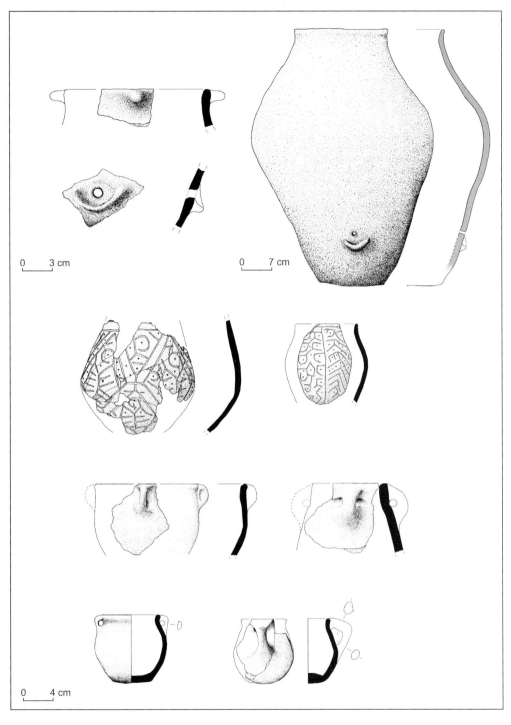

6.10 Pottery from Kuşsaray (two sherds, top left) and Yarıkkaya. Reassembled with permission of U.-D. Schoop from plates 12, 28, and 29 in Schoop, U.-D. 2005. *Das anatolische Chalkolithicum*. Remschalden, Germany: Albert Greiner Verlag.

such as benches and silos, appear to have been found. Unfortunately, we are still awaiting the Yarıkkaya publication more than 40 years after their excavation.

In recent years, another settlement from this period was excavated at the site of Çamlibel Tarlası.[132] This consists of a very small settlement, estimated to have measured about 50 by 50 metres. Notwithstanding the small size of the settlement, excavations revealed a stratigraphy with various building phases. The best preserved of these levels revealed remnants of about three square rooms measuring about 5 by 5 metres that are similar to those found at Yarıkkaya but less well preserved. Three child burials were placed beneath the floors, two of which were placed in a vessel. At Çamlibel Tarlası there was evidence of metal production in the form of simple furnaces, copper slags, and moulds: the earliest metallurgical production site known from the Prehistory of Asia Minor.

Probably postdating the assemblages from Yarıkkaya, Çadır Höyük, and Kuşsaray are assemblages found at the summit of Dündartepe and in excavation areas C and F at İkiztepe (labeled 'DD' and 'EE' by Schoop). The İkiztepe ceramics are discussed jointly with ceramics from other excavation areas that date to later periods in the İkiztepe publications, and they cannot be clearly distinguished as a consequence.[133] Better known are the ceramics from the summit of Dündartepe.[134] Typical are carinated bowls, in some cases with upturned handles on the carination, with incised geometric decoration, mostly chevrons executed in parallel lines. Another common type is a bowl shape with a red interior and a black burnished exterior decorated with parallel lines of white paint. This white-painted decoration also occurs on large jars.

Finally, on the plateau, there is a group of sites with assemblages dating to the end of the Chalcolithic. These include Alişar Höyük, Alaca Höyük, Çadır Höyük (transitional levels), Çengeltepe, and Yarıkkaya (south slope).[135] At all of these sites, more or less similar ceramics have been found. Typical forms include the so-called fruit stands: bowls on an extended foot in the shape of a reversed tulip, vases with a foot and knobs on the shoulder, jars with a carination near the base and a handle connecting the carination with the rim, and carinated bowls. Many of these shapes continue into the subsequent Early Bronze Age, and the distinction between the two periods can be difficult to make. For this reason, these assemblages were designated 'transitional' at the site of Çadır Höyük, where they are dated to between 3100 and 3000 BC. While some of the assemblages at other sites

---

[132] Schoop 2008, 2009.
[133] Schoop 2005a: 314.
[134] Kökten et al. 1945; Thissen 1993.
[135] Von der Osten 1937; Schoop 2005a; Steadman et al. 2008.

might be older, perhaps dating to about 3400 BC, the Alişar-style Chalcolithic assemblages almost certainly date to the final centuries of the fourth millennium.

Some archaeologists have suggested that the earliest levels from Alişar date to the Early Chalcolithic or even to the Neolithic,[136] but there is nothing in the published ceramic assemblages with which such an early date can be substantiated. Instead, the Chalcolithic sequence of Alişar, which encompasses about 11 metres, seems to date entirely to the final centuries of the Late Chalcolithic.[137] One argument used by those claiming older dates for basal Alişar is that the Chalcolithic deposits of the site are too substantial to represent only a short final phase of the Late Chalcolithic. However, here we can refer to the Beycesultan Late Chalcolithic sequence, where deposits that were likewise about 11 metres could be dated to a period of about 500 years (§6.2.2). While the question of what caused the substantial buildup at sites such as Beycesultan and Alişar is of interest, we cannot treat the depth of deposits as a simple proxy for time. Instead, the deposition of archaeological deposits must have been variable, depending on, among other matters, construction methods and intensity of occupation.

Relatively little is known about the settlement remains and burial practices of this final Chalcolithic on the northern plateau of Asia Minor. At Çengeltepe no well-preserved building remains were found,[138] whereas on the south slope of Yarıkkaya a burned building, constructed with mud brick on stone foundations and with *in situ* pottery vessels, was found, but no details, photos, or drawings are provided in the publication.[139] At Çadır Höyük the main feature of this period is a partially exposed irregular building consisting of several small rooms. Elsewhere, a cluster of fruit stands was found, but their context is not entirely clear.[140]

At Alaca Höyük substantial amounts of building remains from the Final Chalcolithic were excavated, as well as a number of burials. These have been published only in drawings and are not discussed in the excavation reports.[141] The burials include crouched skeletons, often with accompanying ceramic vessels. In one case an animal, possibly a dog, seems also to have been placed with the deceased. Various poorly understood large buildings with multiple rooms were found. The best-preserved building at Alaca, at level 12, consisted of a rectangular building constructed on a raised

[136] Parzinger 1993; Özdoğan 1996; Efe 2001: 55.
[137] Schoop 2005a: 331–334.
[138] Ünal 1966.
[139] Hauptmann 1969: 69.
[140] Steadman et al. 2008.
[141] Koşay and Akok 1966: 142–146.

platform. Opposite the reconstructed entrance is a niche in the centre of the back wall.

The best evidence for Final Chalcolithic buildings at Alişar comes from level 13. Here the remains of two buildings were excavated.[142] One of them contained a well-preserved mud floor on top of which nine clay loom weights were found. Another building contained a variety of *in situ* finds and features, such as grinding stones, a mortar, a fireplace, and various objects of stone and bone. Furthermore, a total of six burials were associated with this building: two adults and four children. These were placed in pits, in pots, or in stone or wooden 'boxes', mirroring a practice also documented in this period at Alaca Höyük. Two of the graves at Alişar contained organic remains, textiles and leather, probably the cloths of the deceased. Other grave goods include copper bracelets and pins and a stamp seal.

Summarising this overview of the Chalcolithic of northern Asia Minor, it is clear that our knowledge of these two and a half millennia is far from satisfactory, and the account provided here is no more than a rough sketch. For the Early Chalcolithic, all we have are a few small ceramic collections that could possibly date to this period. The Middle Chalcolithic is represented at three excavated sites: Büyük Güllücek, Çadır Höyük, and İkiztepe II. At two of these sites, Büyük Güllücek and İkiztepe, the excavations and publication records leave much to be desired, and the third has been investigated only in a 2-by-2-metre trench. In consequence, the Middle Chalcolithic is known mainly from poorly dated ceramic assemblages. Finally, for the Late Chalcolithic, our evidence derives from a number of sites. Many of these sites are insufficiently published, however, so our understanding of the settlements and industries of this period remains poor. It could be argued that a differentiation of settlement types occurred – for example, the small villages of Yarıkkaya summit and Çamlibel Tarlası could be contrasted with the seemingly walled settlement at Çadır Höyük – but such interpretations are hazardous given the poor resolution of the available data. Thus, much work remains to be done to clarify further the Chalcolithic in northern Asia Minor.

6.2.4 The Chalcolithic of Southern Central Anatolia

Whereas in the north and west of Asia Minor the Middle Chalcolithic is poorly known and the Late Chalcolithic is better understood, the situation is reversed for southern Central Anatolia. Especially in Cappadocia, the Middle Chalcolithic has been well documented in various recent excavations.

---

[142] Von der Osten 1937: 28–48.

By contrast, the Late Chalcolithic in this part of Asia Minor remains poorly investigated, although ceramic assemblages that can be dated to this period have been found in surveys across the region.

An important recent development in the Prehistory of Asia Minor has been the excavation of substantial exposures at Güvercinkayası and Köşk Höyük with strata that can be dated between 5200 and 4800 BC.

The site of Güvercinkayası, radiocarbon dated to 5210–4810 BC, is located in the western reaches of the volcanic landscape of Cappadocia.[143] The settlement is placed on top of a steep rock formation. It seems to have been occupied only in the earlier part of the Middle Chalcolithic, and in most areas only shallow remains of the settlement were preserved. Nonetheless, the overall plan of the settlement has emerged through a programme of systematic excavations.

The settlement was defined by the limits of the rock outcrop upon it was constructed, which measured approximately 40 by 60 metres. Within these limits the site seems to have been densely occupied for about 400 years, and three main building levels were distinguished in the excavations. During the latest phase of occupation, the settlement consisted of small neighbourhoods separated by streets about 3 metres wide. These neighbourhoods consisted mainly of domestic buildings; in the best-documented case, there seems to have been about 10 of them. Tentatively, on the basis of the available space on the rock outcrop, it can be suggested that no more than 40 of these domestic buildings could have been present at Güvercinkayası. If we assume that they were inhabited by nuclear households of about five people, a hypothesis that can be based on the building sizes and inventories discussed below, then the total population of Güvercinkayası can be estimated at about 200 people, a figure not exceeding that of a face-to-face community (§4.4.7).

The houses at Güvercinkayası were built of stone and appear to share walls with neighbouring units in many cases. Nonetheless, distinguishing domestic buildings is relatively straightforward because these are more or less standardised in their organisation of space and limited in their size range. Buildings are between 20 and 30 square metres in size and consist of a main room with an entrance in the centre of one of the short walls. Along the back wall, a narrow storage room was separated off by means of a wattle-and-daub skin wall. In this back space, pots with conical bases were often found embedded in the floor, and silos were encountered. In the main room, standard features include an oven located in one of the corners next to the entrance and a hearth placed in the centre.

---

[143] Gülçür 1997; Gülçür and Firat 2005.

At Köşk Höyük, about 60 kilometres from Güvercinkayası as the crow flies, a series of buildings were found in level 1 that are nearly identical to those found at Güvercinkayası (Fig. 6.11), with a similar configuration of features.[144] However, at Köşk Höyük the buildings were much better preserved. Buildings were entered by one or two steps from the street, which was located at a higher elevation. In the walls many niches were found, and usually one was located opposite the entrance. In the narrow wall separating off the storage area, there was a central opening in the same axis as the entrance. In one of the back corners of the main room a platform was normally encountered, which might have served as the main resting area. Additional platforms and features, including post supports, were sometimes found in the buildings at Köşk Höyük, but their presence and location were more random.

One building at Köşk Höyük was exceptionally well preserved and appears to have burned twice. In this building an enormous amount of ceramics were found, some of which might have been placed on shelves, as well as grinding stone implements, figurines representing 'big females', and bone tools. Moreover, it was possible, on the basis of preserved building timbers, to estimate that the second building phase occurred 52 years after the first: in absolute terms 4942 ± 120 and 4890 ± 120 cal BC.[145] Such a resolution of evidence is unparalleled in the Prehistory of Asia Minor, and it allows us to estimate the use life of the buildings of level 1 at Köşk Höyük at around 50 years, or approximately two generations.

In association with the platforms of the Köşk Höyük level 1 buildings and beneath the walls, a large number of burials were found. These consisted predominantly of infants and children, although some adults were also found. They were buried in contracted positions either in pits or in pots. Grave goods were common and often included ceramic vessels, necklaces, seals, and lumps of ochre and limonite. Although the meaning of these burials is elusive, it is of interest that the association between the burial of children and domestic buildings is one that is found in other Chalcolithic settlements, such as Alişar 13 and Kuruçay 6.

There are some similarities in the settlement layout of the Köşk Höyük level 1 and Güvercinkayası. At both sites, domestic buildings are built in clusters in which all were accessed from the same direction. However, the overall nature of the two settlements differs in significant ways. Whereas at Güvercinkayası we are dealing with a small settlement on top of a rock outcrop that was densely built up, Köşk Höyük is in a much more accessible location and there is much more open space in the settlement. On the basis

[144] Öztan 2003; Öztan and Faydalı 2003.
[145] Kuniholm and Newton 2002; Öztan and Faydalı 2003: 49

0   10 m

of the evidence from Güvercinkayası, it has been suggested that defence was of key importance in the (Middle) Chalcolithic.[146] However, the Köşk Höyük settlement location is less convincing as a defensive location, and furthermore can be seen as a continuation of an older settlement on the same spot. There is no reason to assume that Güvercinkayası is the more representative site for developments in the period.

An issue that is presently unclear is to what degree nondomestic or elite buildings were present at these sites. At both Köşk Höyük level 1 and Güvercinkayası, buildings have been found that are substantially larger than the normal houses, but that appear similar to the domestic buildings in

6.11 Plan of Köşk Höyük level 1. Reproduced with permission of A. Öztan from plan 1 in Öztan, A. 2003. 'A Neolithic and Chalcolithic settlement in Anatolia: Köşk Höyük'. *Colloquium Anatolicum* 2: 69–86.

[146] Gülçür and Fırat 2005: 41.

most other respects. In theory, these could have served as residences of more powerful people in the community, but other interpretations are also viable. In addition, at Güvercinkayası, a massive double stone wall was found associated with a round tower-like feature. These structures are located in the centre of the settlement, and their functions are poorly understood. Given the small size of the Güvercinkayası settlement and its predominantly domestic nature, a developed social hierarchy does not appear to be the most likely explanation for such features, but it cannot be excluded.

The pottery found at Güvercinkayası and level 1 at Köşk Höyük consists predominantly of black to red highly burnished fabrics.[147] Shapes include simple semi-globular bowls, carinated bowls with concave sides, and jar shapes with handles set above the carination. At Köşk Höyük the handles often occur in pairs, but these pairs are not found at Güvercinkayası. Likewise, bowls with small handles just below the rim are seen at Köşk only. Some knobs occur, but they are not very common. Raised relief decoration is occasionally found, mostly stylised human faces or horns often integrated with handles. There is also some impressed decoration below the rim, as well as dots placed in rectangular panels, techniques similar to the decoration found in the survey assemblage at Kabakulak and in the excavated material from Büyük Güllücek.[148]

At both Güvercinkayası and Köşk Höyük, small amounts of painted ceramics were found that are identical to the material of Canhasan 2B, which can be assigned with some confidence to the Early Chalcolithic on the basis of radiocarbon data. The occurrence of Canhasan 2B ceramics in levels that can be dated to between 5200 and 4800 BC raises the question of how this material got there. There are three possibilities: first, that the Canhasan 2B/2A painted tradition ends later than so far documented; second, that we are dealing with curated objects in circulation long after such vessels stopped being produced; and, third, that these Canhasan 2B ceramics belong to older levels at these sites and that the stratigraphy has been misunderstood. Which of the three applies cannot be determined at present.

Whereas the late fifth millennium and early fourth millennium BC are relatively well known from the excavations at Köşk Höyük and Güvercinkayası, the later part of the Middle Chalcolithic and the Late Chalcolithic, the period between 4800 and 3000 BC, is very poorly known in this part of Asia Minor. While the presence of excavated Chalcolithic sequences to the west, north, and south has facilitated the recognition of Chalcolithic sites in various survey projects, the chronology of these assemblages often

[147] Öztan and Faydalı 2003; Gülçür 2004.
[148] Koşay and Akok 1957; Summers 1991.

remains problematic.[149] In survey reports one often finds sites dated to the 'Chalcolithic' as if this is a precise label for a short period rather than one lasting two and a half millennia and poorly known.[150]

To my knowledge, the only systematic attempt to establish a regional chronology on the basis of ceramic assemblages is one proposed by Mellaart in his report on the surface assemblages he investigated in South-Central Anatolia.[151] Surface assemblages are, of course, very difficult to date in the absence of excavated sequences, and much debate has ensued about issues of chronology and cultural interrelations.[152]

Three Chalcolithic sites postdating 4800 BC have been excavated in South-Central Anatolia. Two of these, Fıraktin and Hashöyük, have been poorly published, and little is known about their nature or date in consequence.[153] At both sites the pottery found has been compared to that of the final Chalcolithic at Alişar Höyük, but such comparisons cannot be evaluated. At Fıraktin, a large building measuring 12 by 9 metres was found that was subdivided in width into three narrow, long rooms. In some of these rooms, domestic features such as hearths, grinding tools, and pottery vessels were found. A staircase was also encountered, and it has been argued that the building had an upper storey.

Without doubt the most systematically excavated and published Chalcolithic site postdating Köşk Höyük and Güvercinkayası on the southern plateau is level 1 at Canhasan 1.[154] In this uppermost level of the site, a series of buildings was found in association with ceramic assemblages that were assigned to the Late Chalcolithic by French on the basis of a comparison with level 12A at Mersin.[155]

By contrast, Thissen has argued that level 1 of Canhasan dates to the final centuries of the sixth millennium BC on the basis of ceramic parallels with İkiztepe and in the Aegean.[156] This would put Canhasan level 1 in the same time period as Köşk Höyük and Güvercinkayası. However, the absence of any resemblance between the assemblages from those sites and those of Canhasan 1 makes this proposed late sixth millennium date implausible and suggests that Canhasan 1 postdates 4800 BC. Schoop, on the other hand, has questioned the equation put forward by French between Canhasan level 1 and Mersin 12A, and opts for a fourth millennium BC date on the basis of

[149] French 1970b: 141.
[150] Bahar and Koçak 2002; Gülçur and Fırat 2005: 49.
[151] Mellaart 1963b.
[152] Thissen 2000: 91–95; Schoop 2005a.
[153] Delaporte 1932; Özgüç 1956.
[154] French 1998, 2005.
[155] French 1966: 121.
[156] Thissen 2000: 91–95.

circumstantial evidence without proposing a more specific time range for this assemblage.[157]

The ceramics are predominantly monochrome burnished wares. Forms are generally simple, including semi-globular bowls, sometimes with small horizontal strap handles set below the rim, holemouth pots, and carinated jars with handles on the shoulder. The best parallels are from survey assemblages in the Konya Plain assigned to the Late Chalcolithic by Mellaart.[158]

The buildings of level 1 at Canhasan are transient in nature. They were poorly constructed and were modified on a more or less constant basis. As a result, no comprehensive plans were obtained in the excavations. The mud walls of these structures were narrow, about 20 centimetres wide, and could not have supported a heavy overburden. On the interior, these walls were plastered with a white material. One large structure with two rooms measured some 14 by 6 metres and contained benches, large bins, a hearth, and a large vessel set in the floor.[159] Other structures also seem to have been large, poorly constructed, and often contained large bins.

Given the characteristics of these buildings, one wonders what purpose they might have served. Whereas their size, about 84 square metres in the best-preserved example, suggests that they might have been used by multiple households, the poor quality of construction and the frequent modification and alteration of buildings could suggest that occupation at the site was episodic rather than permanent. One model that springs to mind is that of pastoral nomads who might have used the site for a short period during seasonal movements.

Ethnographic studies of sub-recent pastoralists in the Near East have demonstrated that nomads often construct buildings, ranging from makeshift structures to complete houses, in locations where they reside regularly for extended periods.[160] In particular, a well-documented feature of pastoral campsites is the construction of moderately high walls of stone or mud bricks, above which a tent or a temporary roof is raised, thus creating a hybrid building.[161] Building remains of campsites from such locations are not unlike those found at Canhasan level 1, and could explain why the walls were poorly built and why structures were often altered.

Furthermore, the large storage bins at the site could also have been used to keep goods in this location while people were absent. While this hypothesis requires further investigation and is very tentative, Canhasan level 1

---

[157] Schoop 2005a: 140–141.
[158] Mellaart 1963b.
[159] French 1998: 52–53.
[160] Cribb 1991; Böhmer 2004.
[161] Cribb 1991: 95–96; Saidel 2008.

could be an example of a pastoral mobile community otherwise poorly documented in the Prehistory of Asia Minor.

Summarising the Chalcolithic of South-Central Anatolia, a rich picture has started to emerge in recent years for the earliest part of the Middle Chalcolithic, between about 5200 and 4800 BC, in Köşk Höyük level 1 and at Güvercinkayası. Much is known about the house types and settlement forms at both sites, and we can tentatively reconstruct the types of households and communities that existed in these places even if many questions remain. The period between 4800 and 3000 BC is more poorly known in this part of Asia Minor, and the only systematically excavated assemblage of the period, level 1 at Canhasan 1, cannot be dated with any certainty. Further excavations are required to clarify the cultural developments in this large region during this period lasting nearly two millennia.

6.2.5 The Chalcolithic of Cilicia

In a previous section (§5.4.1), the geography of Cilicia was described as that of a region intermediate between Central Anatolia and the Fertile Crescent, while separated from both by mountain ranges. This geography has facilitated changing cultural affiliations in Cilicia: During some periods, links with the Levant were strongest; in others, those with central Anatolia predominated; and finally, the region was also culturally autonomous to varying degrees during its development. In the seventh millennium, the ceramics produced in Cilicia were interchangeable with those of northern Syria, whereas in the first half of the sixth millennium a local tradition of pottery prevailed.

During the Middle and Late Chalcolithic the pendulum made another full swing in Cilicia. At Mersin-Yumuktepe, ceramics were excavated that can be linked with the Halaf and Ubaid traditions of Syro-Mesopotamia, although it will be shown that we are not dealing with a Cilician Halaf and/or Ubaid. In the fourth millennium, or the Late Chalcolithic, however, there are no Uruk influences discernible in Cilicia. Instead, a more local pottery tradition prevailed, which is also found in the Amuq to the east and is present throughout most of the fourth millennium, to be replaced by a style of ceramics similar to that of Central Anatolia towards the end of the Chalcolithic.

At Mersin-Yumuktepe the levels dating to the Chalcolithic can be subdivided on the basis of their ceramic assemblages as follows: first, levels 19 to 17; second levels 16 to 12B; and, third, level 12A.

Levels 19 to 17 are those that were linked with the Halaf horizon of northern Syria by Garstang and most likely date to the second half of the sixth millennium BC.[162] The ceramics from these levels are painted with geometric designs, some of which are similar to those known from Halaf sites to the east. Likewise, some of the shapes, such as collared rim bowls and tall necked jars, also have good Halaf parallels. However, not all of these ceramics are true Halaf. Garstang distinguished some imported Halaf ceramics from locally produced imitations of this Halaf style.[163] In a study of Tell Kurdu, located in the Amuq Valley east of Cilicia, which has a Halafian phase in many respects similar to that of Mersin-Yumuktepe, it was emphasised that imported Halaf ware constituted only a minority of the ceramics at the site, with the majority consisting of local painted and unpainted wares.[164]

No building remains of substance were found in levels 19 to 17 at Mersin-Yumuktepe. This may be due in part to the fact that excavation methodologies were in their infancy during the decades when the site was dug, with a bias towards more easily discernible stone structures. Another possibility is that levels 19 to 17 were disturbed in leveling operations prior to the construction of the level 16 buildings.[165] Whatever the case, the absence of building remains in levels 19–17 can be contrasted with six burials attributed to these levels, which included infants and adults, primary and secondary burials, some with traces of burning, and all without grave goods.

The level 16 plan of Mersin-Yumuktepe is well known (Fig. 6.12). Level 16 was interpreted as a fortified settlement surrounded by a massive city wall measuring about 1 metre across, which was offset at regular distances, had slit windows at regular intervals from which enemies could be shot at in safety, and was complete with a 'city gate' flanked by two towers.

To the east of the city gate a series of domestic residences was built up against the city wall, each consisting of a front room and a back room. The latter seems to have been most intensively in use for domestic purposes, as manifested by a wealth of features and finds present in the rooms including bins, grinding equipment, hearths, and ceramic vessels. By contrast, the front rooms were less well built, contained fewer features and finds, and perhaps served as workshops.

The back rooms ranged from 9 to 15 square metres and might have served as the living rooms of nuclear households. Garstang suggests that they were inhabited by soldiers with their families.[166]

To the west of the gate a large building was excavated, the extant remains of which include a large hall, measuring about 10 by 4 metres, and with a

[162] Garstang 1953: 101–124; Schoop 2005a: 146.
[163] Also Breniquet 1995: 14–17.
[164] Özbal et al. 2004.
[165] Breniquet 1995: 15–16.
[166] Garstang 1953: 133.

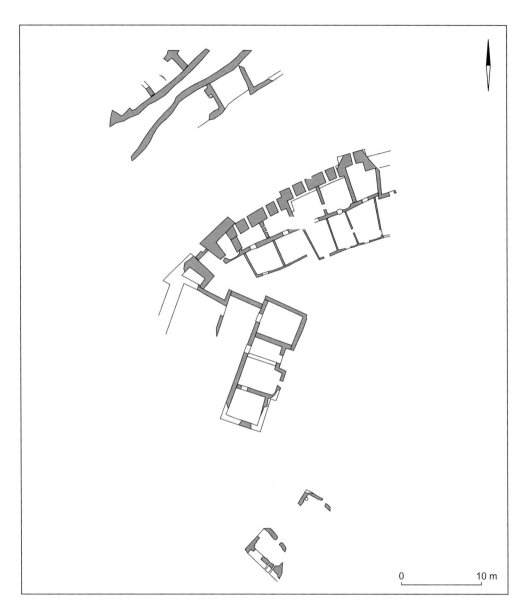

6.12 Plan of Mersin-Yumuktepe level 16. Reassembled with permission of I. Caneva from figs. 2 and 6 in Caneva, I. 2004. 'The citadel tradition (5000–4200 BC)'. In *Mersin-Yumuktepe: A Reappraisal*, edited by I. Caneva and V. Sevin, pp. 57-72. Lecce, Italy: Congedo Editore.

number of rooms of substantial size on its eastern side. The hall contained a large oven, while the side rooms contained considerable quantities of pots and some metal artifacts, as well as one sub-floor burial of a young female. This building was interpreted as an elite residence by Garstang. It is equally possible, of course, that this was a communal building of sorts or had a religious function in part.

Following Garstang's interpretation, level 16 at Mersin-Yumuktepe would be a small fortified community complete with a palace of sorts. This would then constitute the earliest settlement with urban characteristics so far attested in the Prehistory of Asia Minor, with convincing later parallels documented only some two millennia later.

Garstang further suggests that the large 'chiefly' building had a wing west of the central hall similar to that in the east that was lost due to erosion. If this reconstruction is accepted, we would be dealing with a large tripartite building of a type that is well known in Ubaid sites across Syro-Mesopotamia.[167] This would tie in well with Ubaidian features in the pottery.

Recent excavations at Mersin-Yumuktepe have thrown new light on the nature of the level 16 settlement at the site.[168] In 'Area K', at some distance south of the gate, fragmented remains were found of buildings similar to the wall houses east of the gate. They also had a massive stone terrace wall on the slope, with slit windows in the back wall; a back room with domestic equipment, such as a hearth, a basin, and grinding equipment; and a less sturdy front room. This find now makes it possible to estimate the interior of the 'citadel' of Yumuktepe at about 35 by 40 metres, which would mean that we are dealing with a tiny citadel. Even more revealing was the find of a road paved with cobblestones down the slope from the citadel, which was flanked by terrace walls and against which buildings were constructed that are very similar to the wall houses found by Garstang.

This find throws the reconstruction of Mersin-Yumuktepe into new relief. It appears that we are not dealing with a fortified citadel at all, but rather with a series of terraces against which terraced buildings were constructed! At Mersin, as at other settlements discussed in this book, such as Hacılar 1 and 2 and Kuruçay 13 and 6, claims for defence walls in Neolithic and Chalcolithic Asia Minor should thus be treated with caution.

The pottery found in levels 16 to 12B has many parallels with the Ubaid horizon of Syro-Mesopotamia. It has been argued that the spread of the Ubaid horizon to the north came about through the selective appropriation of Ubaid-style artifacts and building types, which were mixed with and embedded in local cultural traditions.[169] The situation at Yumuktepe

[167] Breniquet 1995: 24.
[168] Caneva 2004c.
[169] Stein and Özbal 2007: 334.

appears to fit this model nicely. Thus, we see a Ubaid-style tripartite building on the mound summit in level 16 combined with a local tradition of
two-room terrace houses.[170] Likewise, some of the pottery of levels 16–
12B at the site shows affinities with Ubaid ceramics, whereas other pots
do not.

Typical of the Ubaidian-inspired material are squat jars with two strap
handles on the widest point of the vessel with black painted decoration,
often with festoons attached to a horizontal line, but also geometric patterns executed with parallel lines. Apart from the Ubaid-inspired pottery,
there are also vessels and wares that are more local. These include semi-
globular bowls with raised handles and vessels decorated with white-filled
dots arranged in panels. While some of this material superficially resembles ceramics from Güvercinkayası and Büyük Güllücek, there is no link
between these assemblages and Yumuktepe. Mainly on the basis of the
Ubaid links and a few radiocarbon dates, levels 16 to 12B can be dated to
between about 4900 and 4200 BC.[171]

The final Chalcolithic level at Mersin-Yumuktepe is that of 12A. No
building remains could be assigned to this level, and it was distinguished
mainly on the basis of a distinct assemblage of ceramics. These include
dark-faced burnished wares with white-painted decoration, mostly geometric patterns executed in parallel lines. Shapes include pedestalled bowls
with everted rims and vases with knobs on the shoulder. Although little of
this material has been published, there are clear parallels with the vessel
shapes of the Final Chalcolithic assemblages from Alişar, Çengeltepe, and
the Yarıkkaya south slope in northern Asia Minor (§6.2.3), even if there is
no direct correspondence and white-painted decoration is not documented
in North-Central Anatolia.[172] The fact that no related intermediate assemblages on the southern plateau are known from this period probably tells
us more about the state of research than anything else.

The later part of the sequence of Mersin-Yumuktepe has also been excavated at the site of Tarsus-Gözlükule, where levels with Ubaid-inspired
ceramics and Late Chalcolithic ceramics have been investigated.[173] Unfortunately, these levels were explored only in a narrow deep sounding, which
means that although many floors and features were encountered in the
excavations, no complete building remains were exposed and little is known
about their nature.

---

[170] The building remains from levels 15 to 12B are much less well understood but seem to be
similar in most respects to those from level 16 (Garstang 1953: 155–176; Caneva 2004c)
[171] Caneva and Marcolongo 2004: 29; Schoop 2005a: 148.
[172] Schoop 2005a: 334.
[173] Goldman 1956.

Relatively little is known about the Chalcolithic pottery at Tarsus-Gözlükule, the publication of which consists mainly of photographs of decorated sherds. Among these, there are some that resemble levels 23–20 at Mersin and others that are similar to levels 16–12B at that site and have some affinity with the Ubaid. One period that is better represented at Tarsus-Gözlükule than at Mersin-Yumuktepe, however, is the Late Chalcolithic.[174] An assemblage of chaff-faced, usually buff-coloured wares was found, some of which is slipped and some of which is painted on the exterior with vertically arranged brown-red chevrons or stripes. Shapes are simple and include semi-globular dishes and simple jars, some of which had a handle running from the rim to the shoulder, as well as deep bowls with everted ledge rims.

In two adjacent trenches located at the base of Tarsus-Gözlükule a total of about 13 burials were excavated, which appear to have been placed outside the settlement. Most were jar burials, including primary and secondary burials, multiple and single interments, and both children and adults. In many cases these burials were accompanied by ceramic vessels, which are similar to the Late Chalcolithic ceramics found in the settlement. It appears, then, that we are dealing with a cemetery connected to the nearby settlement. While this in itself is not surprising, it is one of the few instances where there is clear evidence of such a link between settlement and graveyard.

The Late Chalcolithic assemblage at Tarsus-Gözlükule has clear parallels in the Amuq sequence to the east, where it can be linked with phase F, and more recently, additional survey material similar to that for the Tarsus Late Chalcolithic has been published.[175] While these assemblages cannot be dated in absolute terms, on the basis of circumstantial evidence it can be postulated that they must date somewhere in the first three-quarters of the fourth millennium BC.

Summarising the evidence of Chalcolithic Cilicia, our state of knowledge is still determined largely by two older excavation projects of Mersin-Yumuktepe and Tarsus-Gözlükule that have been published in some detail. Relatively speedy excavations have led to long stratigraphic sequences facilitating a diachronic view of developments in this part of Asia Minor. On the downside, for many of these periods, we know little more than what sorts of assemblages belong to them. Building remains often remain poorly understood, and considerable problems exist in the stratigraphies and chronologies of both sites.

Without doubt the best-understood settlement of the Cilician Chalcolithic is that of level 16 at Mersin-Yumuktepe, which has been interpreted as a fortified settlement with a chiefly residence. More recent excavations

---

[174] Goldman 1956: 82–91.
[175] Braidwood and Braidwood 1960: 513–514; Steadman 1994.

at this site have demonstrated that we are probably dealing with terraced houses rather than fortifications, while the large building could have had a communal function instead of being an elite residence. This latter interpretation would fit well with current ideas about Ubaid societies farther east, which are interpreted as grounded in corporate or communal modes of leadership.[176] The example of Mersin-Yumuktepe level 16 clearly shows that further research is required even in cases where older investigations have seemingly provided a comprehensive plan and interpretation of a settlement.

6.3.1 Millennia in the Middle? Reassessing the Chalcolithic

At the start of this chapter, I characterised the Chalcolithic of Asia Minor, and in particular the Middle Chalcolithic period, as a neglected period in the Prehistory of Asia Minor. This is to a large degree the result of the neo-evolutionary paradigms that are shared by Turkish and foreign archaeologists, which condense prehistoric developments into a few threshold events, such as the Neolithic and urban 'revolutions' occurring relatively rapidly and separated by long periods of stagnation during which nothing much of significance is thought to have occurred.

The Chalcolithic in Asia Minor is often thought to have been such an eventless period, and this is one of the main reasons why so few archaeologists have been actively pursuing its study. This situation can be contrasted with that in Syro-Mesopotamia, where the period between 5500 and 3000 BC comprises the sequence of Ubaid and Uruk: periods that have attracted many scholars because they can be related with increasing social complexity and witness the origins of urbanism, stratified societies, organised religion, writing, and states.

The neo-evolutionary view of the past, with its focus on threshold events, to my mind seriously distorts the past. On closer analysis, classical thresholds such as the Neolithic and urban revolutions appear to be long-drawn-out gradual processes rather than sudden events. Moreover, it is a mistake to conceive of a period such as the Chalcolithic of Asia Minor, which lasted no less than two and a half millennia, as an eventless period. The fact that phenomena such as the rise of agriculture and urbanism determine our collective focus on the past to such a degree demonstrates that we tend to reduce Prehistory to no more than a prelude to the glorious present.

So, what happened in the Chalcolithic of Asia Minor? A solid answer to this question is nearly impossible to develop given the paucity of data for

---

[176] Stein and Özbal 2007: 331.

this period in general. Nonetheless, some outlines are starting to emerge through increases in our knowledge over the past decades.

First, the Balkan–Anatolian complex one often encounters in the literature cannot be substantiated by the evidence. In the analysis of Chalcolithic assemblages across Asia Minor presented here, it is above all the regionality of ceramic traditions that can be noted, instead of an overall similarity stretching from Asia Minor across the Balkans. In this respect, the pattern of diversity in material culture witnessed in the period 6500–5500 BC perseveres in the Chalcolithic. Claims for links between Vinča and Asia Minor, or Gelveri and Gumelnitsa, can be discredited upon closer scrutiny, and often revolve around facile comparisons between superficially similar artefacts that are found in sites thousands of kilometres apart and often divided by hundreds, if not thousands, of years. Above all, Chalcolithic Asia Minor was diverse in its material manifestations.

Second, the available settlement evidence is relatively scant, but what there is points to considerable differences among settlements. There are a number of settlements that appear to consist only of a collection of houses, either freestanding or built in clusters. These include Aşağı Pınar, Beycesultan, Kuruçay 6, Yarıkkaya, and possibly Çamlibel Tarlası, İkiztepe, Alişar, and Kumtepe 1B.

Villages that might have been somewhat more complex, with possible public buildings and possible defensive structures besides domestic residences, are those found at Güvercinkayası, Mersin-Yumuktepe 16, and Çadır Höyük, and the argument has also been made for Kuruçay 6. Such settlements have been interpreted as 'proto-urban', but it has been argued in this chapter that such interpretations do not rest on strong arguments, as best exemplified by the recent data on Mersin-Yumuktepe 16.

Finally, there are a large number of settlements that have evidence of brief or seasonal occupation. At Ilıpınar 5B we are dealing with a series of sunken huts that have been interpreted as seasonally occupied structures related to agriculture. At Troadic sites such as Kumtepe, Beşik-Sivritepe, Gülpınar, and Alacalıgöl, to be dated to the fifth millennium BC, settlement remains were shallow and buildings seem to have consisted of wattle-and-daub structures. Here the possibility that sites may have been occupied briefly must be considered. The same is probably true for other sites, such as Toptepe, Bağbaşı, and Canhasan level 1. The ephemeral nature of such settlements may be linked to a mobile way of life, and it possible that sites such as Canhasan level 1 and Bağbaşı were used by pastoral nomads. The insubstantial nature of such sites also explains in part why Chalcolithic sites have been difficult to find in large parts of Asia Minor.

Third, in terms of economy, an argument can be made that the Chalcolithic was a period in which very diverse resources were exploited and during which at least some settlements obtained significant income by specialising in specific activities.

At many sites in the Marmara and Aegaean, such as Toptepe, Kumtepe, and Beşik-Sivritepe, there is an abundance of shellfish remains, a factor pointing to the importance of marine resources. While marine resources had been significant in the subsistence economy in earlier periods in the Marmara Region at Ağaçlı and Fikirtepe sites (§3.3.1, §5.7.1), in the Chalcolithic there is circumstantial evidence that people ventured onto the sea with boats on a regular basis. Perhaps the clearest indication of this consists of the occurrence of similar artefacts in the Troad and at sites on Aegean islands such as Tigani, Emporio, and Aghio Gala. Such similarities suggest that people were frequently in contact, which means, by definition, that seafaring was important in their way of life.

Further, as has already been mentioned, there is some evidence of mobile communities, which may have exploited resources distributed across the landscape in the course of the year. The exchange of goods across large distances in the Chalcolithic could also tie in well with such mobile ways of life.

Finally, we can document the rise of complex exchange systems and export-oriented production of goods. This is manifested, for example, in the exchange of obsidian: A site such as Aphrodisias contains obsidian from Cappadocian sources and the Aegean islands of Melos and Giali,[177] but also in the stone workshop of Kulaksızlar, where pointed beakers and Kilia figurines were produced on a large scale and are found across western Asia Minor and in the Aegean.

In the Late Chalcolithic, we see the emergence of high-quality metal artefacts, in the form of fan-shaped axes and pins of various sorts, at sites such as Ilıpınar 4, Kuruçay 6, Çadır Höyük, Büyük Güllücek, and İkiztepe, and in many cases we are dealing with a deliberate alloy of arsenic and copper to create arsenic-bronze artefacts.[178] While this early metallurgy remains poorly understood in many respects, it is clear that the production of such tools requires considerable expertise and resources, suggesting both that specialisation was an important strategy in Late Chalcolithic economies and that these objects were traded with people elsewhere, much like the stone vessel and figurine production at Middle Chalcolithic Kulaksızlar.

In conclusion, while the database for Middle and Late Chalcolithic Asia Minor remain frustratingly inadequate, the idea that we are dealing with an eventless period in the Prehistory of Asia Minor can be discredited. It is plausible to conclude, on the basis of the data, that people were expanding

---

[177] Blackman 1986.
[178] Begeman et al. 1994; Özbal et al. 2002.

their economies in multiple and often ingenious ways and were increasingly partners in large exchange networks. Apart from farming, it seems that practices such as seafaring, nomadic pastoralism, and export-driven production of labour-intensive goods, such as stone vessels, figurines, and, later, metal artefacts, took off in the Chalcolithic period. Whether or not such developments led to the emergence of complex or stratified societies at some sites remains to be investigated in future research, although at present it seems that during the Chalcolithic, people in Asia Minor largely managed to circumvent such tendencies by living in small communities and possibly by adopting mobile ways of life.

CHAPTER SEVEN

ELITES AND COMMONERS
(3000–2000 BC)

The archaeology of the Early Bronze Age (EBA) in Asia Minor is worlds apart from that of the Chalcolithic, a difference clearly marked by the abundance of data for the EBA, on the one hand, and the research questions dominating EBA investigations, on the other.

In the previous chapter it was argued that a Childean research agenda, in which developments in Prehistory are condensed into a few major threshold events, is dominant in the archaeology of Asia Minor and has led to a very uneven investigation of the past. For example, for the Middle and Late Chalcolithic a total of 68 sites have been excavated in Asia Minor, a figure that can be contrasted with a total of about 163 excavated sites dating to the EBA.[1] The difference between the two periods is even more marked if we take the duration of these periods into account: Per Chalcolithic millennium there are about 27 excavated sites in contrast to the 163 EBA sites.

Apart from the number of excavations of EBA sites, the dominant research questions in this period are also distinct. The EBA is regarded as a dynamic period in Asia Minor in which various developments towards more complex societies occurred. These include the development of urban communities, the emergence of stratified societies, higher population densities than in earlier periods, and the development of metallurgy and long-distance trade networks. This broad range of developments has raised a substantial amount of interest and is reflected in many publications.

To discuss the rich evidence and complex research issues of EBA Asia Minor comprehensively would require a separate monograph. Here the EBA is nonetheless included in this synthesis of the Prehistory of Asia Minor for three main reasons. First, the EBA is part of the Prehistory of Asia Minor. Immediately subsequent to the EBA, we have the earliest

---

[1] www.tayproject.org.

written evidence in Old Assyrian script from Kültepe (Fig. 7.1).[2] While that period, strictly speaking, is protohistorical, autochthonous texts follow a few centuries later. Second, the EBA is often discussed as an isolated period starting from a *tabula rasa*, whereas it is better understood in the context of the long-term Prehistory of Asia Minor. For example, the metallurgy and exchange networks of the EBA have their roots in the preceding Chalcolithic period. Third, although a synthesis of the EBA of Anatolia has recently become available in *Ancient Turkey*,[3] the focus is to a large degree on developments outside Asia Minor, and a number of relevant issues, such as language/migrations, the emergence of long-distance trade and elite culture, the emergence of wine consumption, and how urban EBA Asia Minor really is, are not thoroughly discussed. This chapter on the EBA, however, differs in nature from the other chapters in this book. For the EBA, it is not possible to scrutinise sites and data to the same degree as for the earlier periods simply because of the abundance of available evidence.

The fact that 163 excavated EBA sites exist does not mean that we are well informed about all of them. Many sites were dug only in a small area or were not published in any meaningful manner. Thus, as for most other periods, the study of EBA Asia Minor relies heavily on a few well-excavated and well-published sequences. These include the sites of Alişar Höyük, Beycesultan, Demircihüyük, Tarsus-Gözlükule, and Troy.

Of course, the evidence from these key sites can be augmented by other evidence: first, from sites that were poorly dug and published but that produced significant finds, such as Alaca Höyük, Horoztepe, and Yortan; second, from sites that were poorly dug but adequately published, such as Aphrodisias-Pekmez; and, third, from sites that were well excavated but await meaningful publication, such as Bademağacı, Harmanören, Kanlıgeçit, Küllüoba, Liman Tepe, and Panaz Tepe.

7.1.1 The Chronology of EBA Asia Minor

Surprisingly little up-to-date synthetic and interpretative studies exist dealing with the EBA of Asia Minor. Most synthetic work is several decades old,[4] and much of the literature is narrowly focussed on the chronology of the EBA in Asia Minor: which levels at one site should be equated with those at another, how the EBA should be subdivided, and how subperiods should be dated in calendar years.[5]

---

[2] Larsen 1987; Özgüç 2003.
[3] Sagona and Zimansky 2009.
[4] Mellaart 1966b, 1971; Yakar 1985.
[5] Mellink 1965; Easton 1976; Yakar 1985; Warren and Hankey 1989; Korfmann and Kromer 1993; Manning 1995.

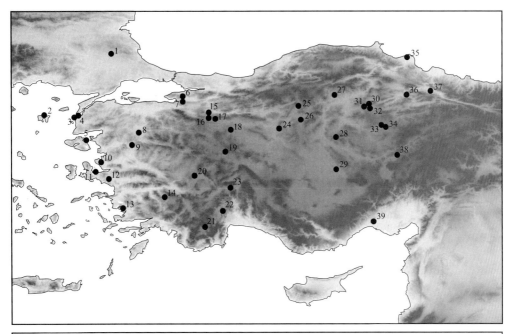

1 Kanlıgeçit; 2 Poliochni; 3 Beşik-Yassıtepe; 4 Troy-Hissarlık; 5 Thermi; 6 Ilıpınar; 7 Hacılartepe; 8 Babaköy; 9 Yortan; 10 Panaztepe; 11 Limantepe; 12 Baklatepe; 13 Iasos; 14 Aphrodisias; 15 Demircihüyük; 16 Demircihüyük-Sarıket; 17 Küllüoba; 18 Küçükhöyük; 19 Kaklık Mevkii; 20 Beycesultan; 21 Karataş; 22 Bademağacı; 23 Harmanören; 24 Polatlı; 25 Salur North; 26 Ahlatlibel; 27 Balıbağı; 28 Kaman-Kalehöyük; 29 Acemhöyük; 30 Kalınkaya; 31 Alaca Höyük; 32 Eskiyapar; 33 Çadır Höyük; 34 Alişar Höyük; 35 İkiztepe; 36 Mahmatlar; 37 Horoztepe; 38 Kültepe; 39 Tarsus-Gözlükule.

7.1 Main EBA sites of Asia Minor, 3000–2000 BC. Produced by Joanne Porck and the author.

In general, the EBA is subdivided into EBA I, II, and III (Table 7.1). However, there is considerable debate among scholars as to how these three periods should be dated and how the stratigraphic sequences of particular sites fit into this scheme. Moreover, some of the subperiods are often further subdivided into shorter periods – for example, into EBA IIIa and EBA IIIb. As is often the case, such chronological schemes quickly take on a life of their own and confuse matters rather than providing clarification. For example, EBA IIIa at Tarsus is held to be contemporary with EBA IIIc/IIIb at Kültepe.[6] In Central Anatolia some sites were dated to the 'Copper Age' in the past,[7] a stage that was held to precede the EBA, but these assemblages are now dated to EBA II.[8] In order to avoid confusion, I will restrict the terminology in this chapter to the tripartite division of the EBA.

An issue that complicates matters considerably is that terms such as 'EBA II' and 'EBA III' are not clearly defined. For example, Efe and Mellink place

[6] Mellink 1965: 126.
[7] Von der Osten 1937.
[8] Yakar 1985: 175.

Table 7.1 The chronology of the EBA

Period	Years BC	Main sites
EBA III	2300–2000	Alaca Höyük, Alişar, Beycesultan, Tarsus, Troy III–IV
EBA II	2600–2300	Alişar, Bademağaci, Beycesultan, Demircihüyük-Sariket, Karataş, Kültepe, Küllüoba, Tarsus, Troy If–II
EBA I	3000–2600	Beycesultan, Beşik-Yassitepe, Demircihüyük, Tarsus, Troy Ia-e

Troy II in the EBA III rather than the EBA II,[9] whereas others put Troy II in the EBA II, and place Troy III-IV in the EBA III. This latter periodisation is backed up by the recent radiocarbon dates from Troy and is therefore used here.[10]

The earliest excavated sequences of EBA Asia Minor were those of Troy, Tarsus-Gözlükule, and Beycesultan. While Tarsus-Gözlükule and Beycesultan were well excavated, the sequence of Troy is problematic because the earliest Schliemann expeditions destroyed much of the evidence, a problem that subsequent projects, directed by Blegen and Korfmann, were able to solve only to a limited degree.[11]

While there are some ceramic parallels between Troy and Tarsus-Gözlükule in the later part of the EBA, there has been considerable debate about the relative ordering of both sequences. For a long time few radiocarbon dates were available to anchor these sequences, and many archaeologists preferred 'historical' dating methods, in which sites such as Tarsus-Gözlükule were dated relative to the sequences of Mesopotamia and Egypt using artefacts deriving from one region and found in the other.[12]

The main problem with the chronology of EBA Asia Minor has always been the Troy sequence, which, for better or worse, has functioned as the yardstick of this period. Much ink has been spilled on the question of how this sequence relates to other sequences in surrounding regions and how it should be dated and subdivided. In 1993 Korfmann and Kromer tabulated no fewer than 14 distinct chronologies for Troy.[13]

Due to new excavations and many new radiocarbon dates from Troy,[14] this chronology is now much better known than previously, and the chronology debate has been largely put to rest. At present, the Trojan

9 Mellink 1986; Efe 2006.
10 Mellaart 1971; Korfmann and Kromer 1993; Şahoğlu 2008a.
11 Easton 1976: 147; Mansfeld 2001.
12 Mellink 1965: 109–117; Yakar 1985: 111–120; Manning 1995: 98–103.
13 Korfmann and Kromer 1993: 138.
14 Korfmann and Kromer 1993; Mansfeld 2001.

sequence remains the most complete and best documented for the EBA of Asia Minor. Other sequences are mainly known from small exposures, as for example at Beycesultan, or represent only part of the EBA sequence, as at Demircihüyük.

7.1.2 Destruction Layers, Migrations, and Paleo-Linguistics

Shortly after the end of the third millennium BC, the first textual evidence in Asia Minor is available at Kültepe. Here a trade factory was established in which one group of traders hailed from the distant city of Assur, located in what today is northern Iraq, who kept records of their transactions and dealings with local authorities.[15] Reflected in this correspondence of the Assyrians are diverse linguistic communities, including Hattian, Hurrian, Luwian, and Hittite.[16]

The linguistic diversity encountered by the Assyrians in central Asia Minor is of interest for various reasons. First, it demonstrates that many groups speaking distinct languages were present in Asia Minor. This constellation is one that could not have been reconstructed or anticipated on the basis of archaeological data. Second, it is clear that some of the languages spoken in Asia Minor at the time when the Asssyrians were trading at Kültepe were not indigenous. In particular, the mechanisms through which Hittite and related Indo-European languages of the 'Anatolian branch', which also include Luwian and Palaic, came to Asia Minor have raised considerable interest given that these are the oldest documented Indo-European languages.

There is a broad consensus amongst paleo-philologists that Indo-European languages were spoken in the north Pontic steppes and that the first split occurred at around 4000 BC.[17] An alternative minority view postulated by some archaeologists is that Asia Minor was in fact the homeland of Indo-European and that the language spread with the farming economy from about 6500 BC,[18] but this position does not stand up to scrutiny (§4.5.1).

If a north Pontic origin for Indo-European and a post-Neolithic date for the spread of Hittite and related languages into Asia Minor are accepted, the question is when and how these languages arrived in the land. To my mind, while this is a valid question, it is not clear whether archaeology can provide the answer.

[15] Larsen 1987; Özgüç 2003; Dercksen 2005.
[16] Özgüç 2003: 62.
[17] Mallory 1997; Anthony 2007.
[18] Renfrew 1987; Bellwood 2005.

Languages can spread either through large-scale migrations of people, as in the colonisation of North America, or through foreign elites inducing language shifts among the populace, as occurred in much of colonial Africa. From a number of historically documented language spreads, such as Arabic and Turkish, we know that relatively few speakers of these languages migrated. Instead, local groups appear to have shifted into these languages because substantial advantages could be obtained by such shifts.[19] While these two particular examples occurred in imperial contexts, similar mechanisms have been noted for language shifts in pre-state contexts, such as the rise of the Luo language in east Africa.[20] Thus, language spreads do not necessarily need to be conceived of as migration waves accompanied by war and destruction. Further, even if one opts for a model in which languages such as Hittite and Luwian spread to Asia Minor primarily through the migration of people speaking these languages, this migration need not have led to conflict and war.[21]

These points are important in the context of the many hypotheses of invading Indo-Europeans that have been put forward in the Prehistory of Asia Minor.[22] In particular, the older studies of the EBA in Asia Minor are replete with violent invasions of populations from Europe and the Caucasus, bringing destruction and depopulation to Asia Minor and resulting in language shifts. For example, in an influential essay, Mellaart postulated one such invasion and destruction phase at the end of Troy I, in which the Luwians were supposed to have arrived; a second such 'event' at the end of Troy IIg, at which point Greeks arrived in the Troad; and, finally, at the end of Troy V, the supposed arrival of the Hittites in similar fashion.[23] Subsequently, this schema was modified somewhat in that the end of Troy V was considered too late for the Hittite wave, and the Hittites were now argued to have entered Asia Minor via the Caucasus.[24] Yakar, by contrast, argued that Indo-Europeans arrived in Asia Minor at the start of the Late Chalcolithic and at the end of Troy IIg.[25] Finally, there have been claims for a link between the elaborate tomb inventories of Alaca Höyük, dating to the late third millennium BC, and those of Maikop in southern Russia, and it has been suggested that these are evidence of the migration of Indo-Europeans to Asia Minor.[26] More recently, Bilgi has claimed that there is evidence of early Indo-Europeans at the site of İkiztepe.[27]

---

[19] Nichols 1998; Campbell 2002.
[20] Anthony 2007: 117–118.
[21] Anthony 1990.
[22] See Pullen (2009: 39–41) for very similar debates about Greek Prehistory.
[23] Mellaart 1958.
[24] Mellaart 1966b: 194–195; 1971: 407–410.
[25] Yakar 1985: 28–33.
[26] Frankfort 1970: 211–214.
[27] Bilgi 2001.

All these claims for Indo-European assemblages and migrations are problematic. For example, it is now clear that Maikop dates to about 3700–3400 BC, about a millennium before the Alaca Höyük graves, and that resemblances between Alaca and Maikop assemblages are few.[28] Likewise, where Mellaart saw cultural breaks between Troy I and II, it now argued that there is considerable overlap between the two phases.[29] While there may be a gap at the Trojan citadel following level IIg, between about 2500 and 2300 BC, it is by no means clear that this can be interpreted as resulting from a migration. One of the arguments for this migration was the appearance of northwest Anatolian pottery types at Tarsus, which was interpreted by Mellaart as evidence of a population on the move. By contrast, the same development is currently interpreted as evidence of the emergence of dense trade relations between both regions in the EBA III.[30]

On balance, there is no convincing archaeological evidence at present for the migration of Indo-European-speaking groups into Asia Minor. A relevant question is whether the resolution of the extant Late Chalcolithic and EBA data for Asia Minor would allow us to identify unequivocally a 'migration age', assuming it did occur. I am sceptical on this issue. A second issue is whether large-scale migration is the most plausible mechanism for the dispersal of Indo-European languages into Asia Minor. Here it is of interest that historically documented migration periods have often not impacted the linguistic landscapes: neither in Lombardy (Lombards) nor in Andulucia (Vandals) is Germanic spoken today.[31] By contrast, in the examples of Arabic, Latin, and Turkish already mentioned, it was political hegemony by a small elite that resulted in language shift. To my mind, the latter is a more likely model for the uptake of Indo-European in Asia Minor, and it is one that would be more difficult to substantiate on the basis of archaeological data.

7.2.1 The EBA I in Asia Minor

It has often been observed that the distinction between the Late Chalcolithic and the subsequent EBA I is an arbitrary one in that many assemblages and cultural practices in both periods are very similar. This perceived cultural continuity is one reason why these periods are often discussed together.[32] Some scholars have argued for a transitional phase because of the difficulty of assigning assemblages to either the Late Chalcolithic

---

[28] Govedarica 2002; Anthony 2007.
[29] Korfmann and Kromer 1993.
[30] Efe and Ay-Efe 2007: 258.
[31] Goffart 2006.
[32] Mellaart 1966b, 1971; Yakar 1985.

or the EBA.[33] Like the preceding Chalcolithic, the EBA I is a period of regional ceramic traditions that are difficult to crossdate. For example, the EBA I at Beycesultan is distinct from that of Troy and that of Tarsus. This is one reason why the chronology of the EBA I in particular raised controversies prior to the systematic application of radiocarbon dating.

The EBA I has been labeled the 'proto-urban' period by Yakar, according to whom we are dealing with villages of various sizes, in some cases surrounded by defensive walls, relying primarily on agriculture for subsistence, but with some evidence of craft specialization and long-distance trade.[34] The metallurgy of the EBA I has been characterised as one of local cottage-scale industries, without large-scale production of copper, and with considerable regional variability in production techniques.[35] Artefacts produced from copper-arsenic alloys were found at various EBA I sites, such as İkiztepe, Beycesultan, and Demirci, a technology also found in Late Chalcolithic Ilıpınar and at İkiztepe.[36] Further, there is considerable circumstantial evidence of an increase in metal artefacts in this period in the form of skeuomorph ceramic vessels. The evidence of the imitation of metal prototypes in pots is clearest at the site of Beycesultan (see the following discussion).

Various regional ceramic traditions have been distinguished for EBA I Asia Minor.[37] The recognition of such regional traditions rests largely on existing research. For example, the EBA I on the plateau has been poorly investigated, and little is known about it.

One EBA I group is found in northwestern Asia Minor, with Troy Ia-e as the typesite, augmented with evidence from Beşik-Yassıtepe and from the Aegean sites of Thermi and Poliochni. This period at Troy, and the subsequent Troy II and III strata, are often labeled the 'maritime culture of Troy'[38] because of cultural links across the Aegean. In this respect, the situation mirrors that discussed earlier for the fifth millennium BC (§6.2.1) in the same region and demonstrates that a boundary between Aegean Asia Minor and the islands is often non existent. At the same time, Troy I ceramics also have a lot in common with assemblages in northwestern Anatolian, such as that found at Hacılartepe near Bursa.[39]

Typical EBA I pottery types (Fig. 7.2) include bowls with inverted rims, sometimes placed on a pedestal, globular jugs with vertical spouts, cooking

---

[33] Efe et al. 1995; Efe and Ay-Efe 2007: 252; Steadman et al. 2008.
[34] Yakar 1985: 3–4.
[35] Özbal et al. 2002: 40.
[36] Bachmann et al. 1987; Begeman et al. 1994; Özbal et al. 2002.
[37] Mellaart 1971; Yakar 1985; Efe 2006.
[38] Sazci 2005; Şahoğlu 2008a: 155.
[39] Eimermann 2008.

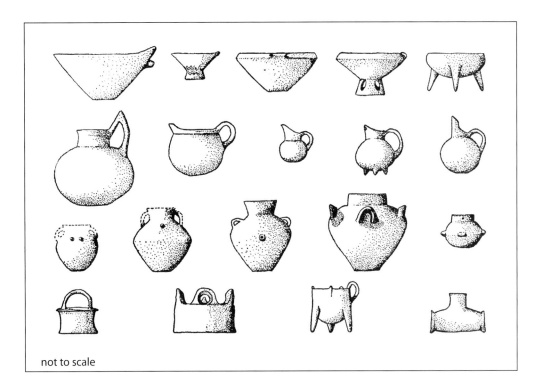

not to scale

pots with a round base and three legs, and large jars with handles on the shoulder or the neck and straight or funnel-shaped necks.[40]

The second regional EBA I tradition often distinguished in Asia Minor is that of southwestern Asia Minor, with Beycesultan as the typesite, which can be augmented with data from Liman Tepe.[41] Here the pedestalled bowls and spouted jugs found at Troy are absent. Bowls with inverted rims are present, however, as are vessels with three legs. Globular jars with everted rims and handles running from the rim to the shoulder are prominent in the Beycesultan EBA I assemblage, and many of them are decorated with either horizontal fluting or vertical barbotine relief below the collar. This later technique of decoration is especially reminiscent of metal vessels, which are often fashioned in similar ways, as is the fact that much of the pottery is thin-walled and highly burnished. This can be taken as indirect evidence that metal prototypes existed and that these prototypes were valued.

A third ceramic tradition has been documented at the site of Demir-cihüyük.[42] At this site, elements such as inverted-rim bowls, pedestal bases,

7.2 Pottery from Troy I. Reproduced with permission of the Department of Classics, University of Cincinnati, from Blegen, C. W. 1963. *Troy and the Trojans*. London, England: Thames and Hudson, fig. 11.

[40] Blegen et al. 1950.
[41] Mellaart 1962c; Şahoğlu 2008b.
[42] Efe 1987; Seeher 1987a.

horizontal fluting, and vertical barbotine decoration are absent. Characteristic are globular bowls with a round handle rising above and applied to
the rim, jars with tilted collars, and some spouted jars in later vases. There
are also globular jars with everted rims with small handles on the shoulder.
Decoration occurs through incision, often in diagonal geometric bands on
jars, and on handles, which are often twisted. Finally, a considerable number of large storage jars, usually with handles applied on the shoulder, were
found at Demircihüyük.

In Central Anatolia the EBA I is very poorly known at present, although
some evidence is now available for the site of Çadır Höyük.[43] The ceramics
of the EBA I at this site are similar in many respects to those of the preceding
Late Chalcolithic, and the lack of distinct EBA I ceramics may be one reason
why the EBA I is poorly known in the area.

At Tarsus, relatively little has been published on the EBA I ceramics, and
few vessel shapes have been reconstructed.[44] Among the shapes typical of
the period are spouted jars with a leaf-shaped orifice, inverted-rim bowls,
simple globular bowls, some with a round handle applied to the rim, jars
with a handle running from the rim to the shoulder, and cups with a flat
base and flaring sides with a handle attached to the rim. As at other sites,
the Tarsus ceramics are best understood as a regional tradition, and few
comparanda exist with other sites in Asia Minor.

İkiztepe has radiocarbon dates suggesting that the site has levels dating
to the EBA I and II periods.[45] The ceramics from this site do not include
any of the types that become widespread elsewhere in Asia Minor from the
Late EBA II onwards. It is possible that the EBA occupation of İkiztepe
precedes this Late EBA II spread; alternatively, the site may have differed
from other regions in Asia Minor in the Late EBA II. The ceramics bear
little or no resemblance to EBA I and Early EBA II assemblages elsewhere
in Asia Minor.

The best-documented settlement of the EBA I in Asia Minor is that
of Demircihüyük (Fig. 7.3).[46] Here large-scale excavations have exposed
a small, well-preserved burnt village in level H. The buildings were constructed adjacent to one another, each with its entrance at the same end.
The buildings have a trapezoidal shape, widening towards the back, and in
this way a radial arrangement of the settlement was obtained.

The whole settlement was surrounded by a stone wall, which sloped
backwards. This was interpreted as a defensive wall by the excavators but it
looks more like a terrace wall (one sloping wall face), a view supported by the

[43] Steadman et al. 2008.
[44] Goldman 1956: 92–103.
[45] Alkım et al. 2003; Schoop 2005a: 321–322.
[46] Korfmann, ed., 1983.

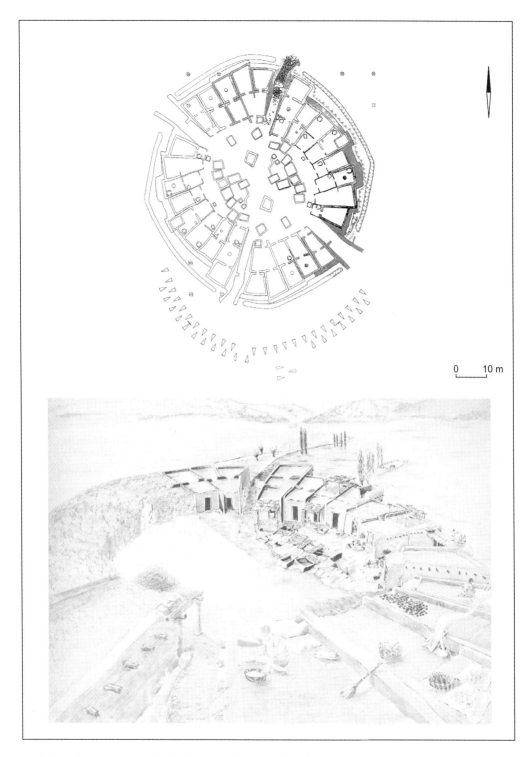

7.3 Plan and reconstruction of level H at Demircihüyük. Produced by Joanne Porck after figs. 343 and 345 in Korfmann, M. ed. 1983. *Demircihüyük, Die Ergebnisse der Ausgrabungen 1975–1978, Band I: Archiktektur, Stratigraphie und Befunde.* Mainz am Rhein, Germany: Philipp von Zabern.

fact that the surroundings of the site were swampy during the excavations and might have been flooded regularly.[47]

The settlement as reconstructed has no fewer than four entrances and is best understood as a small agricultural village; there seems little reason to interpret Demircihüyük H as a fortified settlement. Rather, the settlement seems comparable to earlier communities, such as Ilıpınar 6 and 5A (§5.7.1), which were also radial settlements oriented towards a central open area, but without a defensive purpose.

Given the radial arrangement of the settlement and the fact that half of the area was excavated, the village can be estimated to have encompassed about 26 buildings, of which 15 have been excavated. If the figure of 5 people per house put forward by the excavators is accepted, the total settlement would have encompassed about 130 people.[48] Even if the household sizes were doubled, we would still be dealing with a very small community.

The houses at Demircihüyük H are on average about 50 square metres in size. They normally consist of a front and a back room, each with its entrance in the short wall. In many cases, each room in a building had its own walls. The composite plan of Demircihüyük represents a snapshot moment, caught in a fire, in what appears to have been a dynamically evolving rather than a planned settlement. For example, in some buildings a third room was added at the back of the building, and in others the front room was constructed of wattle and daub rather than brick.

The rooms at Demircihüyük often contained an oven in the back corner to the left of the entrance, and many also contained a central round hearth. Surprisingly, these features occur regularly in both the front and back rooms. This configuration casts some doubt on the view that the buildings were inhabited by nuclear families consisting of about five people. It is conceivable that each room was inhabited by a separate household, presumable linked to each other by kinship.

Other features in the Demircihüyük houses were less regularly distributed; they included bins and platforms of about 4.0 by 1.5 metres, which have been interpreted as beds for about two adults and three children.[49] Another feature associated with the houses is storage bins placed in front of the entrances on the common courtyard. Each house had about 5 square metres of storage capacity: a capacity that is more than sufficient for farmers in ethnographic studies of the pre-modern Near East.

The fact that these storage bins were placed on the central courtyard reinforces the idea that we are dealing with a society in which the communal component was at least as important as the household. Evidently, there was no need to place storage inside the house to protect it from neighbours.

---

[47] Korfmann, ed., 1983: 216.
[48] Korfmann, ed., 1983: 218.
[49] Korfmann, ed., 1983: 216.

Further, the orientation of all buildings towards a common courtyard suggests that interaction was socially appreciated in this community.

Korfmann has argued that the spatial arrangement of Demircihüyük is representative of a deep-rooted settlement form in Anatolian Prehistory that he has labeled 'das anatolische Siedlungsschema'.[50] Casting his net wide, he included cases from Neolithic Asia Minor to the EBA in the Balkans as examples of settlements in which buildings were arranged around a central court.

However, many of the cases provided by Korfmann are unconvincing as central court settlements, such as Hacılar I, Mersin 16, Ahlatlibel, Karataş, and Ali̇şar in Asia Minor. Moreover, Korfmann selected a number of settlements that seemed to fit his thesis, many of which are widely separated in geography and time and have no genealogical relation, while ignoring other settlements that differ from his model and were also known at that time, such as Çatalhöyük, Canhasan 1, Erbaba, and Poliochni.

However, in the context of the EBA in Asia Minor and adjacent regions, some remarkable parallels to the Demircihüyük settlements can be found. These include the settlement of Pulur-Sakyol in East Anatolia, which is dated to the EBA I/II, and that of Bademağacı Höyük in the Lake District, which is dated to the EBA II.[51] Whereas the settlement of Pulur-Sakyol seems to have been very similar in scale to that of Demircihüyük, the settlement of Bademağacı Höyük was substantially larger and perhaps more complex (§7.3.1).

Much less is known about EBA I settlements elsewhere in Asia Minor. At Beycesultan, a single building of the hall and porch type was found in level 17 and was interpreted as a temple by analogy with later EBA II buildings constructed on the same spot.[52] However, there is little to substantiate this interpretation, and the building is probably a domestic structure.

At Troy the settlement dating to level Ia-e is poorly understood. Blegen and his team found a poorly preserved building with an apse on one side, which was overlain by a substantial hall and porch building dated to level Ib.[53] This building '102' had impressive proportions, measuring about 19 by 7 metres, with outer walls about 80 centimetres wide. In the centre of the large main room, measuring about 14 by 5 metres, a hearth was found. This building was called a 'megaron', a term that links EBA Troy to a building type from Greece in the Late Bronze Age and is perhaps better avoided because it remains to be demonstrated that there is a genealogical link between this building and those of Mycenaean Greece (§2.1.2).

---

[50] Korfmann, ed., 1983: 222–241.
[51] Koşay 1976; Duru 2008: 145–177.
[52] Lloyd 1962b.
[53] Blegen et al. 1950.

At first, it may be tempting to ascribe to building 102 some sort of communal purpose, given the monumental size of the hall and porch building. However, when placed in the context of EBA I settlements of this region, building 102 is not that exceptional. At Troy, to the south of building 102, a row of further buildings were excavated[54] along more or less the same alignment. These consisted of rectangular rooms measuring 10 to 14 metres in length and 3.0 to 5.5 metres in width. The buildings share walls between units as well as those in the back and front; thus, it is likely that they were built as a single complex of terraced houses. Further, at contemporary sites such as Thermi and Beşik-Yassıtepe, similar large buildings were the norm.[55] Building 102 at Troy might have been somewhat larger and more monumental than most buildings, but it did not differ in kind from other structures. Most buildings were substantial in size and it can be posited, although not proven, that they were occupied by extended households, in which case the household associated with building 102 might have been more affluent than others at Troy.

It is not clear, on the basis of the limited exposure at Troy, whether we are dealing with a settlement that was spatially similar to that of Demircihüyük, that is, a group of buildings oriented towards a central open area with the back walls forming a continuous façade,[56] or with a settlement where buildings were placed along streets, as at the nearby and contemporary sites of Beşik-Yassıtepe and Thermi or at Tarsus in Cilicia.[57] Further, the idea that the early Troy I settlement was surrounded by a city wall, as suggested by Mellaart, has been disproven.[58]

7.3.1 The EBA II in Asia Minor

The EBA II in Asia Minor, to be dated between about 2600 and 2300 BC, is in many ways a transformative period in the Prehistory of Asia Minor. Among the developments that occur in these centuries are the rise of more industrial and complex metallurgical industries, the emergence of long-distance exchange networks, the formation of a prestige segment in material culture, the development of fortified settlements and monumental architecture, and the emergence of a set of novel burial traditions.

In terms of material culture, there is no clear distinction between the assemblages of the preceding EBA I and those of the EBA II. It has recently

[54] Mellaart 1959; Schirmer 1971; Ünlüsoy 2006.
[55] Lamb 1936; Korfmann 1988.
[56] This has been argued by Ünlüsoy (2006).
[57] Lamb 1936; Goldman 1956: 9–12; Korfmann 1988: 392.
[58] Mellaart 1959; Schirmer 1971; Ünlüsoy 2006.

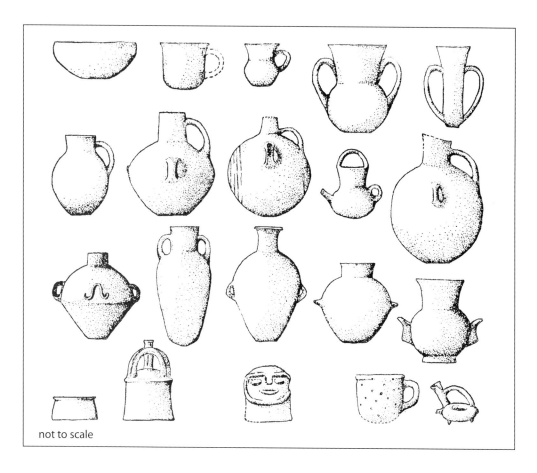

not to scale

become clear that the later stages of Troy If-j are in fact contemporary with Troy II, which was earlier thought to mark the start of the EBA II.[59] Given these circumstances, Troy II–type ceramics can be used to argue for an EBA II date, but Troy I ceramics can be assigned either to the EBA I or the EBA II. To complicate matters further, there are marked developments within the EBA II: In the later stages of this period wheel-made pottery is found, and an increasing convergence of pottery types and wares can be documented across much of Asia Minor and in the Aegean.[60] By contrast, in the early EBA II, regional traditions and handmade ceramics are the norm.

Whereas the early EBA II ceramics at Troy are similar to those from the preceding period, in the late EBA II a range of new shapes are documented (Fig. 7.4). These include forms such as the 'tankard', a pot with a globular

7.4 Pottery from Troy II. Reproduced with permission of the Department of Classics, University of Cincinnati, from Blegen, C. W. *Troy and the Trojans*. London, England: Thames and Hudson, fig. 19.

[59] Korfman and Kromer 1993.
[60] Podzuweit 1979; Efe 2006: 24; Şahoğlu 2008a: 156; Broodbank 2009; Pullen 2009.

base surmounted by a funnel-shaped neck with two large handles attached; flaring bowls and shallow dishes; ovoid two-handled jars and jugs; and a slender two-handled goblet, which was labeled the *depas amphikypellon* by Schliemann, who originally equated Troy II with the period in which the story of the *Iliad* was supposed to have unfolded and in which a vessel with this name occurs. In Troy II an orange to red slip is common, which is often burnished.[61]

At Küllüoba, a site in the Eskişehir Region, an assemblage has been excavated that bears a close resemblance to the Late EBA II ceramics from Troy, including forms such as tankards and the depas, also with a red slip.[62]

By contrast, at EBA II Beycesultan these vessels are completely absent; this probably means that the later part of the EBA II was not present in the excavated area of the site. The Beycesultan Early EBA II ceramics include jars with horizontal fluting on the lower body, jugs on three legs, bowls with inverted rims, some with knobs or elaborate lug handles, and pedestalled bowls with inverted rims and elaborate handles applied to the rim. Some of the Beycesultan features can also be seen in the Bademağacı and Karataş EBA layers.[63] Towards the end of the EBA II, depas and tankards are also found in southwestern Asia Minor at sites such as Karataş, Bakla Tepe, and Liman Tepe.[64] In this period some ceramic types, such as sauceboats and depas, also make their appearance in the Cyclades and Greece in the so-called Kastri and Lefkandi I assemblages.[65]

Similar developments, in which local EBA II assemblages show increasing convergence with a broader ceramic style towards the end of the EBA II, are evident at other sites. At Alişar Höyük the 'Copper Age', or levels 11–7, which can now be equated with the EBA II,[66] is characterised by handmade pottery that has little in common with assemblages in western Asia Minor.[67] Characteristic shapes are globular pots with everted rims, simple round bowls, and cups with an ear from the rim to the middle of the vessel. At Alişar Höyük pots painted with geometric designs were found, a feature not known from the west. However, some two-handled goblets and spouted jars have also been documented in the later stages of the Copper Age that are identical to those found elsewhere in Asia Minor. These ceramics were found in what appears to have been a rather large and

---

[61] Blegen et al. 1950.

[62] Efe and Ay-Efe 2001; Efe 2006. Note that Efe has a periodisation of the EBA that is not shared by other researchers, in which Troy IIb and later levels are assigned to the EBA III.

[63] Duru 2008: 164–167.

[64] Şahoğlu 2008a: 156.

[65] Broodbank 2009: 61; Pullen 2009: 35–36.

[66] It is possible, however, that Alişar Höyük 11 and 10 date to the EBA I (Steadman et al. 2008).

[67] Von der Osten 1937.

possibly walled settlement. Numerous buildings remains of this settlement have been found, but no comprehensive understanding of these buildings and their spatial arrangement can be obtained at present.

At Tarsus similar developments do not seem to occur. Shapes such as the tankard and the two-handled goblet do not surface in the repertoire at Tarsus, which has a range of shapes and features that are not found elsewhere in Asia Minor.[68] These include a jar with a flat everted rim often decorated with geometric motifs in horizontal bands, and black burnished ware with incised decoration with a white fill. Also typical are globular bowls with a round vertical handle on the side and globular pots with an everted rim and a perforated raised lip on one side. Some of these shapes and decoration techniques appear to have parallels in Syria and Cyprus rather than Asia Minor. It is possible, however, that the absence of late EBA II wares similar to those elsewhere in Asia Minor could represent a gap in the sequence of Tarsus rather than a cultural difference. This issue can only be resolved through further research and radiocarbon dating.

The convergence of ceramic repertoires across Asia Minor in the later EBA II might point to the emergence of shared cultural practices in the region. For example, it has been argued that the two-handled goblets, which cannot stand for lack of a base but can be passed easily from one person to another, served as a prehistoric 'joint' and were linked with the consumption of alcohol, in particular wine.[69]

The earliest wine, rather than grape consumption and cultivation, has been found at sixth millennium BC Haji Firuz in northwestern Iran, and it has been argued that the Caucasus and Eastern Anatolia were a centre for early wine production.[70] In the Aegean and Asia Minor, however, the earliest convincing evidence of wine dates to the third millennium BC,[71] and this would fit the interpretation of two-handled goblets and other vessels as wine-drinking sets.

It has been argued, on the basis of Mesopotamian parallels, that wine was an expensive commodity that was drunk mainly by elite groups.[72] However, in Asia Minor, wine could have been produced locally, and the relative ubiquity of two-handled goblets in EBA II Asia Minor, which are found in village-type settlement contexts as well as in more monumentalised settings, might suggest that in Asia Minor wine was not as expensive as in other places and that most people could afford it.

---

[68] Goldman 1956: 104–130.
[69] Gorny 1996; Çalış-Sazcı 2006: 205; Broodbank 2009: 61.
[70] McGovern 2003.
[71] Gorny 1996; J. M. Renfrew 1996.
[72] Powell 1996; Çalış-Sazcı 2006: 205.

Other types of evidence, often consisting of valuable goods and materials, point to the growing importance of long-distance relations in the EBA II period. A range of items and materials can be traced over long distances and suggest that supra-regional trade took off in earnest during the EBA II.

At Troy, items and goods that fit into this picture are jade from the northern Black Sea; amber from the Baltic; lapis lazuli, tin, and jade from Afghanistan; and faience from Egypt.[73] Other items pointing to long-distance exchange are beads found at Aigina, Greece, hailing from the Indus Valley; Mesopotamian cylinder seals found at Poliochni, Kültepe, and Alişar Höyük; mace heads occurring from the Caucasus into Asia Minor; Syrian bottles and metallic ware occurring in Asia Minor; and Anatolian two-handled goblets occurring in Syria.[74]

While the precise origins of many goods and artefacts can be debated – for example, whether jade came from Afghanistan or from the northern Black Sea – the aggregate picture, that EBA II Asia Minor was linked with distant regions by a flow of goods and materials, is beyond doubt.

Of course, the mechanisms operating behind this flow of goods and materials remain enigmatic. While we have evidence of organised long-distance trade with donkey caravans at Middle Bronze Age Kültepe, this type of trade cannot be simply extrapolated to EBA II Asia Minor. In general, whereas archaeology is very good at identifying durable goods and materials of exotic origin, it is only through chance discoveries such as the Kültepe archives or the Late Bronze Age shipwrecks of Uluburun and Gelidonya with their trade cargoes[75] that we can hope to learn about the mechanisms operating behind the flow of goods and materials. Such contexts are so far lacking for EBA Asia Minor; consequently, we know little about how trade was organised in this period.

Most of the exotic materials and items imported into Asia Minor can be classified in one way or another as items of value that were probably used by local elites to create and reproduce social distinctions between themselves and commoners. Such mechanisms, in which items of value, preferably made from conspicuous and rare materials obtained from distant locations, were used in the articulation of elites, are, of course, well documented in ethnographic and historical accounts of societies.[76]

It is in this context of the articulation of elites that the transformation of metallurgical industries can best be understood. The EBA II period is the first period in which artefacts produced from bronze, in the specific sense of an alloy of tin and copper, have been found in Asia Minor. Tin has been

[73] Çalış-Sazcı 2006.
[74] Von der Osten 1937: 184; Mellink 1986, 1998; Özgüç 1986; Aruz 2006; Zimmerman 2006a.
[75] Bachhuber 2006.
[76] Malinowsky 1922; Kristiansen and Larson 2005; Wengrow 2006: 72–98.

found in northwestern Asia Minor and the Aegean, for example at Troy II, Poliochni and Thermi III–V, Ahlatlibel, Alişar, Polatlı, Kültepe, Alaca Höyük, Horoztepe, and Tarsus.[77]

The appearance of bronze marks a significant departure from earlier metalworking practices in Asia Minor. Although previously the production of metal artefacts was a labour-intensive process requiring significant knowledge and skill, it could nonetheless be organised regionally. Asia Minor is rich in metal ores of various kinds, and in each region there would have been small mining operations and local procedures and techniques for the production of metals, which have been described as cottage industries.[78] With the use of alloys containing tin, the production methods departed sharply from those of this pre-existing regional tradition. Tin is a mineral that occurs in relatively few places in ore variants that could have been worked in Prehistory. Known sources are few and far between. Possible sources that most researchers believe might have been exploited in Prehistory are located in Afghanistan, Uzbekistan, and Tajikistan.[79] This means that tin was transported over long distances and that artefacts produced with tin alloys would have been much more expensive than artefacts produced from local ores.

The advent of bronze is all the more remarkable given that this alloy seems to have no mechanical advantages over an alloy of arsenic and copper, which could be produced from local ores. For this reason, it has been argued that bronze was used for prestige goods and that the adoption of bronze cannot be explained from a functional point of view. Instead, bronze might have been valued for its colour, resembling gold.[80] Further, it has been argued that the absence of tin at some sites, such as İkiztepe, can best be explained as an absence of elite groups who could afford this substance.[81]

Given the considerable distances from which tin allegedly needed to be brought to Asia Minor, there has been considerable debate about how the tin trade was organised and where this material came from. In this debate, scholars have been greatly influenced by textual evidence from the early second millennium BC. It is generally accepted that the Assyrian merchants at Kültepe imported large quantities of tin to Asia Minor: Conservative estimates are in the range of 80,000 kilograms. It is plausible that this tin

[77] Begemann et al. 1992; Yener et al. 1994: 379; Stech 1999: 64; Özbal et al. 2002. I have dated Thermi to the start of the EBA II here, but it is also possible that it dates to the late EBA I (see also Lambrianides 1995).

[78] Özbal et al. 2002.

[79] Weisgerber and Cierny 2002; Gale 2008. There are also tin sources in western Serbia, but these remain to be investigated (McGeehan-Liritzis and Taylor 1987; Harding 2000: 201).

[80] Moorey 1994: 301; Pernicka 1998: 136–137; 2006: 350; Zimmermann 2007: 71; Broodbank 2009: 61.

[81] Özbal et al. 2002: 47.

hailed from the east; otherwise, the Assyrians would not have been able to set themselves up as middlemen.[82]

For the EBA, a popular idea has been that tin was transported by ship over the Black Sea to Troy and the Aegean, and was traded along with prized goods such as gold and lapis lazuli, all deriving from Afghanistan.[83] However, at İkiztepe, the only excavated EBA site along the Black Sea coast, bronze is absent, and there is no evidence of maritime trade along the Black Sea in this period. The alternative sea route via the Mediterranean is also problematic because bronze appears on Cyprus only towards the end of the EBA.[84]

An argument has been put forward that there was a tin mine at Göltepe-Kestel, about 30 kilometres southeast of Niğde, in the EBA II/III. This interpretation rests on circumstantial evidence.[85] According to the investigators of this site, all substantial tin deposits were retrieved from the mine in the EBA, which was then abandoned. For this reason, substantial tin ores can no longer be found at this locality.

There has been a lot of academic controversy about this interpretation, which has been critiqued in a number of papers,[86] to which many replies were formulated.[87] Although the debate is very technical in nature, it appears that the better arguments are on the side of the excavators, who have a coherent argument supported by independent experts, whereas their detractors have generally used any argument they could find and have been less consistent. On the whole, the possible presence of low-grade tin mineralisation in Central Anatolia that was systematically exploited in the EBA is not unlikely, and one wonders why the idea has met with such strong resistance. If the Göltepe-Kestel mine was in use for tin extraction during the EBA, it might have been in use alongside other sources.[88]

Another aspect of EBA II metallurgy that represents a significant new development is the appearance of rich sets of jewelry and prestige goods. These are known in the main from a series of hoards found in the burned remains of Troy IIg.[89]

The most famous of the hoard finds of Troy is the so-called treasure of Priam (Fig. 7.5), presently identified as 'treasure A', which comprised a large group of objects, including 5 gold vessels, 9 silver vessels, 1 electrum vessel, 5 bronze or copper vessels, 6 silver ingots, 8 bronze spearheads,

[82] Larsen 1987; Dercksen 2005.
[83] Muhly 1985; Stech 1999: 67.
[84] Özbal et al. 2002; 40–41.
[85] Yener and Özbal 1987; Yener 2000.
[86] Hall and Steadman 1991; Pernicka et al. 1992; Muhly 1993.
[87] Willies 1992; Yener and Goodway 1992; Yener and Vandiver 1993a, 1993b; Kaptan 1995.
[88] Weisgerber and Cierny 2002: 180.
[89] Schmidt 1902; Easton 1984; Sazcı and Treister 2006.

7.5 Sophie Schliemann wearing jewelry from treasure A from Troy. After fig. 53 in Siebler, M. 1994. 'Sie Schliemann-Sammlung und der Schatz des Priamus'. *Antike Welt* 25: 40–54.

14 bronze flat axes, 3 bronze chisels, 1 bronze saw, 6 gold bracelets, 3 gold headdresses, 4 gold earrings, some 50 gold rings, and 8,700 beads![90]

This hoard is the most impressive one found at the site, but in total no fewer than 20 hoards have been found at Troy, which include a large variety of metal artefacts, such as jewelry, metal vessels, ingots, axes, daggers, and spearheads, as well as crystal mace heads.

The treasures of Troy have often been presented in the context of the evidence of the destruction and conflagration of the Troy IIg settlement as treasures hidden before a conflict but not retrieved after those who buried them had died.[91] Recently, this view has been challenged, with one of the treasures deriving from a grave, while others may have been placed in pits that were dug from Troy III levels into the burnt Troy IIg deposits.[92] If these cases are accepted, it follows that not all of the Trojan treasures can be understood as resulting from circumstances surrounding a hostile destruction of the town, and it appears that in some instances deposition was intentional. Indeed, this argument, that the hoards were intentionally

[90] Easton 1984: 151–156.
[91] Blegen 1963: 73–74; Joukowsky 1996: 152.
[92] Sazcı and Treister 2006: 210.

deposited during feasts by elites bent on increasing their prestige through such dramatic gestures, has recently been put forward.[93] Practices in which precious metal artefacts were deposited in hoards have been widely documented in the Prehistory of Europe,[94] and these are often interpreted as a mechanism through which valuable goods were kept rare. Another means of disposing of valuable goods is by placing them in burials. This is a practice witnessed in North Anatolia in the period immediately following the EBA II at sites like Alaca Höyük and Horoztepe.

There is one strong parallel for the Trojan hoards at the site of Eskiyapar, which is located in North-Central Anatolia.[95] Here two hoards were found, both beneath the floor of a single building; one of them contained only a few items, but the other contained a large number of objects. These objects were made of gold, silver, electrum, and carnelian and included items of jewelry, metal vessels, and axes. Many of the Eskiyapar objects have direct parallels at Troy. These parallels between the Troy and Eskiyapar hoards make it plausible that more hoards of similar nature await discovery.

The artefacts found in the spectacular Trojan and Eskiyapar hoards might be less exceptional than they appear to be from the archaeological record. Many of the metal vessels have their counterparts in EBA II ceramic vessels, which appear to imitate metal prototypes. This suggests that these metal vessels might have been widespread. Other items found in the hoards, such as gold diadems and earrings, have good parallels in the Aegean and Asia Minor. Axes, daggers, and chisels can be compared to others found in Asia Minor.[96]

The EBA II in Asia Minor is marked by the appearance of numerous cemeteries, although some may have started in the late EBA I. Cemeteries of the EBA II have been found at, among other places, Babaköy, Bakla Tepe, Demircihüyük-Sarıket, Harmanören-Göndürle Höyük, Iasos, Ilıpınar, Kaklık-Mevkii, Karataş-Semayük, Küçükhüyük, and Yortan.[97] In some places, such as Karataş-Semayük and perhaps Ilıpınar/Hacılartepe, the cemetery could be linked with a nearby settlement of the same period.

The distribution of the EBA II cemeteries is mainly confined to western and northern Asia Minor (see Fig. 7.1), although similar burials within settlements are known from the Aegean islands, for example at Kephala on Kea and at Aghioi Anagyroi on Naxos.[98] In recent years, cemeteries

---

[93] Bachhuber 2009.
[94] Fontijn 2002.
[95] Özgüç and Temizer 1993.
[96] Easton 1984: 157–161; Mellink 1986: 142.
[97] Wheeler 1974; Kamil 1982; Pecorella 1984; Gürkan and Seeher 1991; Seeher 2000; Özsait 2003; Şahoğlu 2008b.
[98] Wheeler 1974: 422–423.

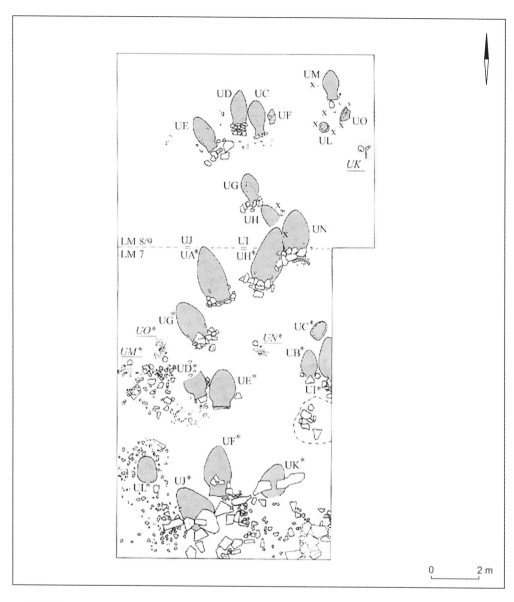

7.6 EBA II cemetery at Ilıpınar. Reproduced with permission of J. Roodenberg and B. C. Coockson from Roodenberg, J. 2008. 'The Early Bronze Age cemetery'. In *Life and Death in a Prehistoric Settlement in Northwest Anatolia: The Ilıpınar Excavations III*, edited by J. Roodenberg and S. Alpaslan-Roodenberg, pp. 335–346, fig. 1. Leiden: Nederlands Instituut voor het Nabije Oosten.

have been found in North-Central Anatolia, at Balıbağı and Salur-North, and similar burials have also been documented at Alişar Höyük.[99] As in the preceding EBA I, cultural relations in the EBA II between western Asia Minor and the Aegean seem to have been strong, whereas there appears to be a disjunction with South-Central Anatolia and Cilicia.[100]

The EBA II cemeteries of western Asia Minor consist of hundreds of burials. For example, the cemetery at Demircihüyük-Sarıket, the most systematically investigated and best-published graveyard, contained about 500 preserved EBA II burials.[101] These were arranged in neat rows with a similar orientation: with heads predominantly towards the southeast. Disturbance by later burials appears to be rare (Fig. 7.6). The regular nature of these cemeteries suggests that graves were marked on the surface. Indeed, at the site of Karataş-Semayük, grave markers have been found that consist of stone circles. The graves are of various types: Some burials were placed in pits, others in stone-lined graves (*Steinkistengrab*), but by far the largest number were placed in ceramic containers. Normally, these are very large vessels ranging up to 2 metres in size ('pithos'), and usually the opening of these vessels was blocked with stones. Alternatively, one finds two smaller vessels facing each other.

It is plausible that many of the burial vessels were produced for this purpose even if similar vessels were also known from settlement contexts. The sheer number of these vessels and the fact that most of them seem to have been whole and complete makes reuse of these vessels for burial unlikely. At Demircihüyük-Sarıket, it is not uncommon to find multiple individuals in these burial vessels, with the last body fully articulated and earlier skeletal remains pushed to the side.[102] Such burial practices are probably to be understood as a collective tomb of relatives used periodically.

At Demircihüyük-Sarıket a variety of burial goods were found in the graves, including pots, most commonly spouted jugs and bowls; toggle pins; spindle whorls; and stone objects such as axes. Rarer are metal objects such as jewels, bronze daggers and spear points, and bottles produced from lead. No fewer than 32 of these lead vessels were found in the Demircihüyük-Sarıket cemetery.

Included in the Demircihüyük-Sarıket graves were people from all age categories and both sexes. There is no correlation between age or gender, on the one hand, and grave types and categories of grave goods, on the other. Elaborate burials, for example constructed with stone slabs, do not contain more grave goods than others. Overall, the impression is that if variability in

[99] Von der Osten 1937; Süel 1989; Matthews 2004.
[100] Mellaart 1971: 370–371; Sazcı 2005; Şahoğlu 2008a.
[101] Seeher 2000: 17.
[102] Wheeler 1974: 417.

social status is expressed in these burials, it is relatively slight. According to Seeher, grave goods were often gifts from the mourners, rather than objects closely associated with the deceased or grave goods linked with perceptions of gender or status, so it is hazardous to reconstruct social identities on the basis of these objects.[103]

The excavated settlements of the EBA II in Asia Minor are much more diverse than those known from the preceding EBA I period. Whereas the EBA I settlements thus far known all seem to consist of small villages, the investigated EBA II settlements include both villages and settlements with urban features.

What 'urban' means varies from one scholar to next, but two main schools of thought can be distinguished. Some argue that settlements of a significant size with evidence of communal structures should be understood as socially complex and can be interpreted as towns or cities.[104] Others hold that urban settlements are those that are central places in a differentiated settlement system, in which hamlets and villages rely on towns or cities in various ways. Further, a substantial part of urban populations should consist of specialists of various kinds, such as craftsmen, religious personnel, the military, and managers, who subsist on food produced by others.[105]

Here I will adhere to the second perspective on urbanism. Thus, I do not agree with the argument sometimes put forward that because settlements in EBA Asia Minor are relatively small when compared with contemporary settlements in Syro-Mesopotamia, they cannot be urban.[106]

A village-type settlement dating to the EBA II is that of Bademağacı.[107] Here a settlement was found that is in many respects very similar to that found at Demircihüyük H. Rectangular buildings with a front and a back room were built side by side, with their rear walls arranged as a continuous façade and their entrances oriented towards a central court. Little is known about the interior furnishings in these buildings, which, like those at Demircihüyük, measured about 50 square metres.

Surrounding the settlements, starting from the rear of the houses, was a shallow slope clad in stones, which was 4 to 7 metres wide and had an angle of about 10 to 15 degrees. Probably this was not a defensive feature but a measure against floods.[108] Again, the parallel with Demircihüyük is clear, and it is likely that the two settlements are part of a broader settlement tradition spanning the EBA I and II periods.

[103] Seeher 2000: 29.
[104] Kenyon 1956; Bintliff 1999; Rollefson 2004: 147–148.
[105] Hole 2000; Emberling 2003: 255; Trigger 2003: 120.
[106] Özdoğan 2006; Çevik 2007.
[107] Duru 2008: 145–161.
[108] Duru 2008: 154.

According to the excavator, the EBA settlement at Bademağacı had a 'palace' at the centre. While this claim is not completely implausible for the EBA II, as will become clear from other settlements discussed later, there are some problems with this interpretation for Bademağacı. First, there are no data to support a palace interpretation: No extraordinary buildings were found or inventories that cannot be explained as domestic. Second, the central buildings in question probably predate the central court settlement, as they were found at a much deeper level in the centre of the mound.

What is clear, however, is that the EBA central court settlement at Bademağacı is substantially larger than that known from Demircihüyük. Whereas the latter can be estimated at about 26 houses, at Bademağacı a figure in the range of 60 to 100 houses is plausible given the contours of the mound, about half of which has been excavated. This means that the population of Bademağacı was two to four times larger than that of Demircihüyük and can be estimated at 300 to 500 people (assuming 5 inhabitants for each house). Bademağacı, then, was a village of a significant size.

At Küllüoba a series of hall and porch terraced buildings were found, which are similar in scale and interior arrangements to those at Demircihüyük and Bademağacı and are oriented towards a common courtyard.[109] However, at Küllüoba there also appear to have been groups of buildings in the centre of the settlement, so that the settlement is no longer organised around a central court and instead has a plan with streets.

In the initial publications of Küllüoba, a centrally located group of buildings was interpreted as a palace complex surrounded by a fortified upper city, which in turn was surrounded by a lower city. This interpretation, like that of the Bademağacı settlement, is problematic. The settlement plan changes considerably in the course of the site publications. The palace in the upper city interpretation is now less convincing, given that a second centrally located cluster of buildings has since been uncovered, and the fortifications initially reconstructed now appear to be local terraces rather than continuous features. Here, as in some sites discussed earlier, such as Kuruçay 6 and Mersin 16, the tendency of scholars to attribute urban characteristics to a settlement should be treated with caution.

Similarly, the interpretation of EBA II buildings at Beycesultan as 'twin shrines'[110] is not unproblematic. These level 16–14 buildings contained large amounts of pottery and other objects on their floors. They had elaborate hearth structures that were associated with something labeled as 'horns' by the excavators, which could also be seen more prosaically as andirons. Positioned behind them are post stands that were plastered at the front

[109] Efe and Ay-Efe 2001, 2007; Efe 2003, 2006.
[110] Lloyd 1962c.

to protect them from fire, which are reminiscent of those found at Late Chalcolithic Kuruçay 6.[111]

The arrangement of hearths, andiron, and post stands found at EBA II Beycesultan has close parallels at Karataş and at Tarsus.[112] Apart from the elaborate hearths and the *in situ* finds at Beycesultan, the twin shrine buildings do not differ significantly from EBA II domestic buildings elsewhere in western Asia Minor, which they resemble in proportions, organization of space, and interior arrangements. While the elaborate hearths and *in situ* artefacts at Beycesultan could have been symbolically important, these buildings appear to be first and foremost domestic in nature.

An EBA II settlement that has been exposed on a large scale is that of Poliochni in phase 'yellow' on the island of Lemnos. This settlement had a spatial layout very different from that of Bademağacı and Demircihüyük but might resemble that of Küllüoba.[113] Houses were clustered in small neighbourhood blocks, of no more than a dozen houses each, which were separated from each other by streets, alleys, and small squares.

The village was well built and included paved streets and stone-lined wells in the squares. There are a number of rectangular hall and porch buildings similar in dimensions to those known from Bademağacı, Küllüoba, and EBA I Troy. However, there are also other structures with similar proportions that were subdivided into a larger number of rooms, and smaller buildings more irregular in shape or interior subdivision.

It appears that each neighbourhood had one regular hall and porch building, suggesting that they were inhabited by associated groups of households and that the hall and porch buildings served as the central building of these clusters. Household clusters have been postulated earlier for the Lake District Neolithic (§5.5.1) and Late Chalcolthic Kuruçay (§6.2.2). In those cases the houses were all more or less similar, however. By contrast, at Poliochni yellow, one house probably dominated the other structures. Similar clusters in other cultural horizons have been interpreted as the residence of a patriarch plus associated households,[114] but at Poliochni we can only suggest that some houses served as a nexus for a group of associated households.

The Tarsus settlements remains resemble those from Poliochni in some respects.[115] In the early EBA II, a series of rectangular buildings were constructed along a street. These buildings are similar in size to those known elsewhere in EBA II Asia Minor but were not of the hall and porch type.

[111] Duru 2008: 127.
[112] Goldman 1956: plates 62–67; Warner 1994: 185–186, plate 145.
[113] Bernabo-Brea 1964; 1976.
[114] Schloen 2001.
[115] Goldman 1956: 12–32.

They had several rooms, and the division of space was not standardised. As in other EBA II buildings, each unit had one main room with a hearth.

Halfway through the EBA II sequence at Tarsus, a row of houses was abandoned and a large defense wall with indentations was built in their place. This development suggests a rather sudden need for defensive measures at this site, especially given that the nature of the buildings inside the fortified area does not seem to change.

Even more impressive are the fortifications of Troy in the EBA II (Fig. 7.7). A series of stone city walls dating to the EBA II have been excavated. Over time, the fortified area was expanded southwards and the fortifications became more and more impressive, with imposing towers and gates and well-built walls.[116] Inside the fortifications, a number of monumental hall and porch–type buildings have been found in levels IIa, IIc, and IIg, which measure about 30 by 10 metres and which are reconstructed with a large central hearth in the main room.

Given the substantial proportions of these buildings and their location within a heavily fortified complex, the often postulated idea that these buildings expressed and mediated the activities of powerful elites seems plausible. However, it is perhaps too simple to label these structures palaces, that is, the residences of rulers. In Troy IIc not one but two large hall and porch buildings were found, and it seems implausible that there were two rulers at the same time. Instead, these buildings might have served multiple purposes, one of which probably would have been the reception and entertainment of guests.

One of the remarkable aspects of Troy II is the enormous amount of energy expended on the fortifications and the buildings within when juxtaposed to the size of this fortified area. At maximum the Troy II fortifications spanned an area only about 125 metres across. By contrast, the contemporary village of Poliochni, which has been only partially exposed, measures at least 250 metres from one end to the other, yet lacks the kinds of monumental buildings documented at Troy, although it might have been fortified.[117] In light of these characteristics, it is plausible that the Troy II fortified area was in fact a citadel surrounded by a lower town. Although the size and density of occupation of this lower town cannot be established, buildings located outside the fortifications have in fact been excavated in recent years.[118]

Conceptualising the fortified area of Troy II as a citadel may also help explain what happened towards the later part of the Troy II sequence.[119] At

[116] Mellaart 1959; Schirmer 1971; Ünlüsoy 2006.
[117] Mellaart 1971: 387; Doumas 2008.
[118] Sazcı 2005: 47–52.
[119] Ünlüsoy 2006.

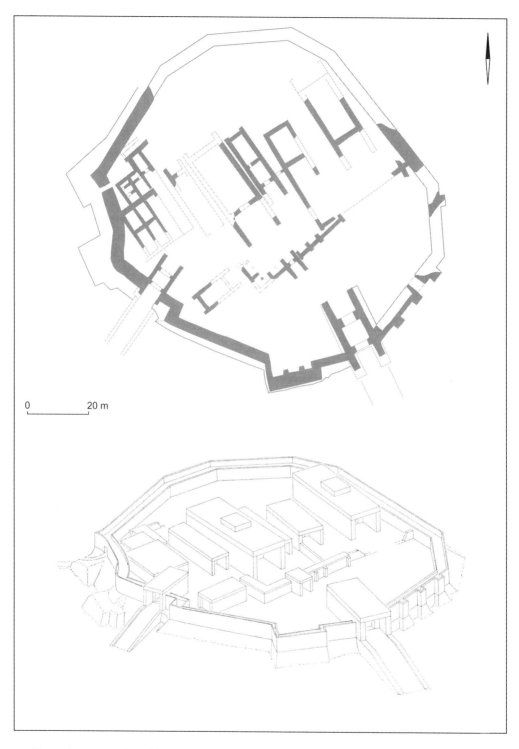

7.7 Plan and reconstruction of Troy II fortifications. Reproduced with permission of W. Schirmer from Schirmer, W. 1971. 'Überlegungen zu einige Baufragen de Schichten I und II in Troja'. *Istanbuler Mitteilungen* 21: 1–43, figs. 10 and 12.

the end of Troy IId, the settlement seems to have been destroyed and burned on a massive scale. In the subsequent period, the citadel was no longer occupied exclusively by large, monumental buildings and open courts. While one large hall and porch building remained in use, the rest of the citadel was now densely built up with buildings consisting of small rooms.

While it has been suggested that the inhabitants of the lower town moved into the citadel at this stage,[120] this interpretation is unconvincing for two reasons. First, the buildings on the citadel of Troy IIg do not resemble the hall and porch houses documented across western Asia Minor. Instead, we can identify a number of large complexes that might have been used for storage and as workshops. Second, if a substantial lower city is postulated, then the Troy IIg citadel would have been too small to accommodate all the people who would have lived there previously.

The Troy II citadel and the associated lower town are not unique in the Prehistory of Asia Minor. Parallels can be drawn with settlements of Karataş-Semayük and Liman Tepe in southwestern Asia Minor and Kanlıgeçit in Thrace.[121] The Kanlıgeçit fortifications are almost a carbon copy of those at Troy on a smaller scale. The settlement has a citadel about 50 metres across and contains a number of hall and porch buildings. The citadel appears to have been surrounded by a lower town.

Likewise very small was the citadel of Karataş, where good evidence of a lower city has been found. The citadel at this site consisted of a single rectangular building measuring about 11 by 7 metres and was surrounded by fortification walls. In the surrounding area, many rectangular freestanding buildings from the same period (level 5) were found.[122]

The Karataş buildings were mainly of the hall and porch type and typically measured about 4 by 10 metres, in line with buildings elsewhere in EBA Asia Minor. These buildings do not appear to have been oriented towards streets or courts, and house clusters are not apparent. No fewer than 128 houses are reconstructed for this settlement, a figure that seems plausible given the size of contemporary Bademağacı. Karataş would have had a substantial population, which has been estimated at about 740 people.[123]

If we assume that the citadel size was a function of the size of the overall settlement, we can use the Karataş evidence to assess the Troy evidence. On the basis of the Karataş parallel, it is possible to suggest that the lower city of Troy II included thousands of people. The Liman Tepe settlement, where the citadel is reconstructed to have been 300 metres across, would have been even more substantial than Troy.

---

[120] Blegen 1963: 69; Ünlüsoy 2006: 142.
[121] Warner 1994; Özdoğan and Parzinger 2000; Erkanal 2008.
[122] Warner 1994.
[123] Warner 1994: 177.

Summarising the developments in the EBA II in Asia Minor, the following trends have become apparent. Whereas the ceramics of the early EBA II are difficult to distinguish from those of the EBA I, in the later part of the EBA II the emergence of a shared pottery horizon across Asia Minor can be documented that includes typical vessels such as spouted jars, tankards, and two-handled goblets. There are good indications that some of these vessels might have been used for the consumption of wine in company.

Apart from the emergence of a cultural horizon spanning Asia Minor in the later EBA II, there is evidence of the participation of Asia Minor in long-distance exchange networks, as manifested in a range of exotic materials and goods found in the region. The point of many of these goods and materials seems to have been that they came from afar, were precious, and thus were useful in the articulation and reproduction of elite groups at this time. It is even possible that these elites at times purposely deposited some of these valuables in order to keep them rare.

In contrast, the large cemeteries that date to the EBA II in Asia Minor have relatively moderate grave goods, typically some ceramic vessels or a bronze pin. These cemeteries are associated with village-type settlements, where a link can be made. It could be argued that the people buried in the cemeteries were 'common'.

Finally, in the settlements of Asia Minor a range can be documented, from large villages, which were well built and included hundreds of inhabitants, up to urban settlements with a fortified citadel containing public buildings and a lower town that in some cases probably included thousands of people. While there is little evidence to assess the question of whether these urban settlements were surrounded by a hinterland of villages, this seems very plausible.

7.4.1 The EBA III in Asia Minor

The EBA III is here dated between about 2300 and 2000 BC. At some sites, such as Troy, Beycesultan, Alişar, and Tarsus, there seems to be an occupation gap between the EBA II and III, which might have lasted as long as two centuries.[124] This hiatus in these sequences, together with evidence of destruction, fire, and the interment of metal hoards that were not retrieved, has been interpreted by some as evidence of an Indo-European migration into Asia Minor from the Balkans (§7.1.2).

However, the postulated hiatus between the EBA II and III may not be real. At Troy, recent investigations have shown that whereas there might

---

[124] Korfmann and Kromer 1993: 168–169; Joukowsky 1996: 145.

have been a temporal abandonment of the citadel, the lower town was probably occupied more or less continuously.[125] Further, there is much continuity between the late EBA II and the early EBA III at Troy in the ceramic assemblages, and in a number of cemeteries that continue into the EBA III,[126] such as those at Bakla Tepe and Kaklık Mevkii,[127] which makes a lengthy hiatus implausible.

Generally speaking, there are relatively few sequences that can be firmly dated to the EBA III and for which detailed publications are available. The main sequences that are available are those of Troy, Beycesultan, and Tarsus.

At Troy, levels III and IV can be dated to the EBA III, whereas level V seems to date mainly to the second millennium BC. The EBA III levels of Troy were labeled 'miserable villages' by Dörpfeld, but it appears that the absence of comprehensive building remains may be due in part to their removal in early excavation seasons. In the subsequent projects at Troy, these phases were investigated in a small area within the citadel left unexcavated by the earliest expeditions; various monumental structures located outside the citadel and dating to these levels have also been excavated.[128]

In recent years, a distinction has been made by the Troy project between level III, which is grouped with Troy I and II into the 'Maritime Troy Culture', and levels IV and V, which are assigned to the 'Anatolian Troy Culture'. Troy III is thus perceived as a continuation of the preceding Troy II period. For example: "Considered as a whole, the pottery of Troy III is practically indistinguishable from that of Troy II."[129] One of the few new features in the ceramic assemblage in Troy III consists of ceramic lids with human faces modeled on them.

As for Troy III, few building remains are known from Troy IV. What we have consists mainly of domestic architecture, which is restricted in extent and is similar to buildings in earlier levels. The ceramics of Troy IV developed out of the earlier tradition but have some new characteristics. Most of the pottery is now wheel made, and larger vessels are chaff tempered. Some new forms appear, such as jars with vertically placed triangular grips, red cross bowls, two-handled goblets with a base, and cloverleaf-shaped jars.[130]

At Beycesultan EBA III, buildings were excavated in a relatively small area.[131] In levels 10–8 the remains of three hall and porch buildings were excavated, which are similar in scale and furnishings to domestic buildings

---

[125] Korfmann and Kromer 1993: 168–169.
[126] Blegen 1963; Sazcı 2005; Ünlüsoy 2006;
[127] Topbaş et al. 1998; Şahoğlu 2008b.
[128] Blegen 1963: 91–105; Sazcı 2005; Ünlüsoy 2006.
[129] Blegen 1963: 96.
[130] Sazcı 2005.
[131] Lloyd 1962d.

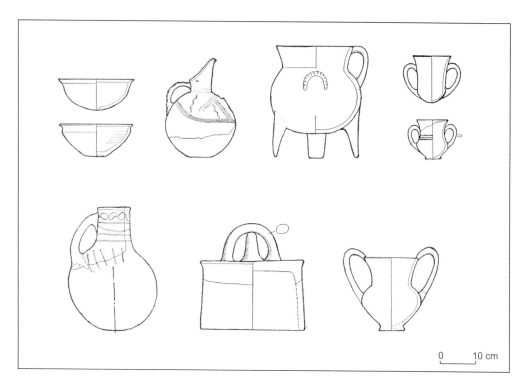

7.8 EBA III pottery from Beycesultan. Produced by Joanne Porck after sheets 6 and 7 in Mellaart, J. 1962. 'Pottery of the Early Bronze 3 period'. In *Beycesultan I: The Chalcolithic and Early Bronze Age Levels*, edited by S. Lloyd and J. Mellaart, pp. 199–264. London, England: British Institute of Archaeology at Ankara.

of the EBA elsewhere in Asia Minor. They contained a large hearth in the centre of the main room and a platform in the right-hand corner adjacent to the entrance of the room. Subsequently, in levels 7 and 6, smaller multiroom rectangular structures were found. These buildings diverge in many respects from those that had been the norm in Asia Minor during the EBA. The abandonment of the large hall and porch buildings may be significant as an index of changes in the fabric of households and society, but the exposure at Beycesultan is too small to base anything on.

The ceramics found at Beycesultan are in many ways similar to those of Troy (Fig. 7.8). Typical are tankards with raised loop handles extending above the rim, spouted jars with knobs, cloverleaf-shaped jars, two-handled goblets with a base, and red cross bowls. As at Troy, these ceramics develop gradually into those that are typical of the subsequent Middle Bronze Age, and the distinction between the two periods is arbitrary.

The EBA III ceramics from Tarsus show strong parallels with those found elsewhere in Asia Minor during this period, including, for example, flaring dishes, tankards, and two-handled goblets with a base.[132] Another shape that is common at Tarsus, as well as in Central Anatolia, is the Syrian flask, an elongated bottle with a pointed base, a straight neck, and an everted rim.

[132] Goldman 1956: 131–163.

On the basis of what was perceived as a sudden appearance of 'western' wares at Tarsus, it has been suggested that there was a migration of people from western Asia Minor to Cilicia in this period, which was linked with the arrival of Luwian-speaking groups.[133] However, it is also possible to explain the Tarsus sequence in other ways; for example, there may be a gap in this sequence, and the introduction of western wares into Cilicia could have been more gradual. Further, there are also Syrian influences at Tarsus, which have not been linked with migrations, and the earlier Tarsus EBA II cloverleaf-shaped jugs are also found at Troy in the EBA III, indicating that there might also have been ceramic types that moved west rather than east.

The Tarsus EBA III settlement appears to have been densely built up, with rectangular buildings of about 4 by 10 metres. Some of these are of the hall and porch type, while others have an alternative subdivision of space. There are some streets, and buildings appear to have been constantly modified. Given its dense occupation and street network, it is possible that Tarsus was an urban settlement, but more research is required to evaluate this.

The region of Central Anatolia seems to have developed in a trajectory that differed considerably from that of the west during the EBA III. Unfortunately, our knowledge of this period in Central Anatolia is far from sufficient. The relevant sequences were either obtained before the Second World War, with methods that have yielded confusing results, or were obtained more recently but have been inadequately published.

The most spectacular finds of the EBA III in Central Anatolia are the burials found at sites such as Alaca Höyük, Horoztepe, Kalınkaya, and Mahmatlar.[134] At these sites a number of elaborate burials with rich inventories were discovered, of which those from Alaca Höyük are the best known.[135] At this site, a total of 13 elaborate burials were found that were labeled 'royal graves' on account of their contents.

It is unfortunate that the Alaca Höyük graves were excavated prior to the advent of modern excavation methodologies and dating methods. In consequence, many studies have been devoted to the question of how the graves should be dated, mostly on the basis of comparative methods. In a recent paper, Gerber lists five earlier studies that dealt with this problem without reaching a consensus.[136] However, most researchers argue that these graves date either to the Late EBA II or the early EBA III.

---

[133] Mellaart 1971.
[134] Arık 1937; Koşay and Akok 1944; Koşay 1951; Yakar 1985: 200–203; Zimmermann 2006b.
[135] Tschora 2004.
[136] Gerber 2006: 379.

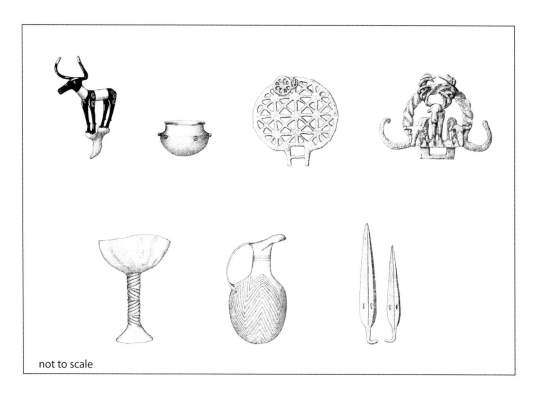

not to scale

Here, following Gürsan-Salzmann, they are provisionally dated to the early EBA III.[137]

The Alaca Höyük burials were placed in shafts. The lower part of these shafts consisted of rectangular stone-lined pits in which a single person was normally buried. This pit was covered with wooden beams that were sealed with mud. On top of this pit a variety of animal remains were found: in some cases the entire skeleton of a goat, sheep, or pig, but more commonly assorted cattle skulls and hind legs. Subsequently, the shafts were refilled.

Within the Alaca Höyük graves, rich inventories of burials goods were found (Fig. 7.9) that included jewelry items such as diadems, bracelets, pins, earrings, and beads; ceremonial weapons such as mace heads, daggers, axes, and swords; standards and figurines; and metal vessels.[138] These objects were produced from materials such as gold, silver, electrum, copper, iron, crystal, and jade. The most conspicuous of the Alaca Höyük objects are the so-called standards, which are metal objects with a tang at the base and usually in the shape of a disk or lozenge. These standards occur as plates with a hole at the centre; as a composite of geometric motifs, for example swastikas or simple crosshatching; and with animal figures, usually bulls

7.9 Grave goods from Alaca Höyük burials. Reproduced with permission of H. Müller-Karpe from Müller-Karpe, H. 1974. *Handbuch der Vorgeschichte III: Kupferzeit.* München, Germany: C. H. Beck, plates 310/311.

---

[137] Gürsan-Salzmann 1992; also Sagona 2004.
[138] Akurgal 1962: 15–29.

or deer, at the centre surrounded by a garland. Similar in many respects are single animal figurines with a tang at the base, again mostly deer and bulls. Other objects for which the Alaca Höyük graves are famous include human figurines, metal vessels of various sorts, and an iron dagger, produced more than two millennia before iron casting became common in the Near East.[139]

It has been argued that the Alaca Höyük standards were attached either to a baldaquin or to a wagon.[140] The latter interpretation in particular has some circumstantial evidence to support it. First, the standards and tanged figurines often occur in pairs or quartets, which suggests that they might have been part of a larger structure such as a wagon. Second, some of the standards have loose parts that would have rattled in movement, like a sistrum. Third, it is of interest to note that the cattle skulls and legs found on the wooden cover of the burials always occur in multiples of two; it has been argued that these might have been animals that pulled the wagon on which the deceased was transported to the grave, after which they might have been slaughtered and consumed in the course of the funeral ceremonies.

A possible parallel has been documented at the earlier cemetery of Demircihüyük-Sarıket. Here seven double and complete cattle burials were found, both facing in the same direction. These may be associated with a nearby human burial. This could suggest that these were indeed animals used for traction and for the transport of the deceased.[141]

Four-wheeled wagons are known since the late fourth millennium BC in southern Mesopotamia. Clay wagon models found in Upper Mesopotamia date to the third millennium BC. In Asia Minor, a variety of wagon types are documented in early second millennium texts from Kültepe. Thus, wagons were probably well known around 2300 BC in Asia Minor.[142]

How are we to interpret the occurrence of the richly furnished burials at Alaca Höyük? From the start, these burials have been given the label 'royal', and it was originally argued that they were associated with a palace. However, this palace was not found, nor can the Alaca graves be linked with any substantial settlement.[143] Further, there is no evidence that there were states in this part of Asia Minor in the EBA III. Thus, the Alaca burials are better described as 'elite'. There are good examples from adjacent areas – such in the Balkans: at Varna, in Transcaucasia: at Maikop and in the Martkopi, Bedeni, and Trialeti horizons, and in East Anatolia: at Arslantepe – of richly furnished burials that were produced by societies without states or urban

---

[139] Pernicka 2006.
[140] Mellaart 1966b: 153; Orthmann 1967.
[141] Seeher 2000: 30–32.
[142] Littauer and Crouwel 1979; Özgen 1986; Gökçek 2006.
[143] Yakar 1985: 200.

settlements.[144] For such cases, it has been argued that "there emerged a new ideology, in which hierarchy was legitimated through the consumption of prestige items by individuals."[145] This model appears to fit the evidence at Alaca Höyük better than that of a political dynasty.

The Alaca Höyük graves are often discussed in an inter-regional context. On the one hand, the Alaca grave inventories are often compared to the hoards from Troy, the 'royal cemetery' from Ur, and the Kinneret plaque from the Levant. The argument is often put forward that the later third millennium BC witnessed the rise of elite cultures across the Near East, resulting in the emergence of long-distance exchange of valuable materials, the emergence of complex metallurgies, and the appearance of objects of value with which the elites set themselves apart from the rest of society.[146] On the other hand, one often encounters a comparison between the Alaca Höyük graves and burials from southern Russia and the Caucasus, an argument that is often linked with the arrival of Indo-European-speaking groups in Asia Minor ancestral to the later Hittites and Luwians.[147]

Both views of the Alaca Höyük burials are unsatisfactory. The parallels between Alaca Höyük and other sites in the Near East often focus on a few specific elements, such as earrings and how they resemble those at other sites. However, if one takes the complete corpus of grave goods at Alaca Höyük into account, it is clear that most objects do not have parallels elsewhere. In this respect the Alaca Höyük burial inventories differ from the hoards of nearby Eskiyapar, which do have clear parallels at Troy and beyond.[148]

Likewise, the resemblances between Alaca Höyük and Transcaucasian sites and horizons, such as Maikop, Bedeni, Martkopi, and Trialeti, is often restricted to single objects rather than complete assemblages, and in many cases the assemblages compared are not from the same time period. For example, the tomb inventory of Maikop, which has often been compared with that of Alaca, contains only object that bears a superficial resemblance to one object from Alaca in a much larger assemblage of goods. Further, Maikop is now dated to about 3700–3400 BC: more than 1,000 years earlier than Alaca Höyük.[149]

In contrast to the preceding conclusion, I would argue that the Alaca Höyük burials are best understood as part of a regional phenomenon, given

---

[144] Renfrew 1986; Frangipane 2001b; Sagona 2004.
[145] Renfrew 1986: 154.
[146] Mellaart 1971: 392–395; Mellink 1986: 142; Amiran 1993; Sazcı and Treister 2006: 213–215.
[147] Mellink 1956: 54–56; Frankfort 1970: 211–214; Sagona 2004; Tschora 2004.
[148] Özgüç and Temizer 1993.
[149] Govedarica 2002; Anthony 2007: 287–293.

that many of the key components, such as the standards, are without convincing parallels in the adjacent regions. In the region of north-central
Asia Minor, some comparanda do exist, however. At Horoztepe, located
about 150 kilometres to the northeast of Alaca, a burial has been excavated
that has an inventory very similar to those at Alaca.[150] Objects that bear a
resemblance to those from Alaca Höyük, but without a clear context, have
also been retrieved from two other sites in north-central Asia Minor: Mahmatlar, where metal vessels were found, and Hassanoğlan, where a human
figurine was discovered.[151]

Finally, at the site of Kalınkaya, only 3 kilometres from Alaca, a cemetery
of EBA III date was found with three types of burials: pit burials, pithos
burials, and cist burials.[152] Some of these burials contained grave goods,
such as bronze pins and daggers. Interestingly, a number of objects resembling those from Alaca Höyük were also found, including two bull figurines
and two ceremonial standards. However, these objects were produced from
less precious materials, such as bronze, and were crude in their manufacture
and appearance. Most likely, these objects, which were found in relatively
simple graves, were an effort to emulate high-status objects such as those
at Alaca Höyük by people who evidently were not part of the elite.

On the basis of these parallels for the Alaca Höyük burial inventories,
it can be concluded, first, that we are dealing with a regional tradition;
and, second, that the mechanism of using valuable metal artefacts in the
articulation of an elite was successful at least in part, a point borne out by
the unsuccessful effort at emulation documented at the site of Kalınkaya.

Very little is known about the settlements of North-Central Anatolia in
Asia Minor during the EBA III. At Alişar little was found dating to this
period apart from a monumental city wall.[153] Other sites, such as Ahlatlı-
bel, Alaca Höyük, Eskiyapar, and Karaoğlan, remain poorly published and
poorly understood.[154] Many of these sites were excavated long ago, and
only short notes are available.

At the site of Ahlatlibel, a large complex of stone rooms, measuring some
40 metres in diameter, was excavated,[155] which also is poorly understood.
It has been suggested that the plan consists mainly of the basements of a
castle of sorts, but no outer fortifications have been excavated and some
of the rooms contain hearths. Nonetheless, it is clear that this settlement
differs substantially from other known settlements in EBA Asia Minor.

---

[150] Özgüç and Akok 1958; Özgüç 1964.
[151] Koşay and Akok 1950; Akurgal 1962.
[152] Zimmermann 2006b.
[153] Von der Osten 1937: 208–223.
[154] Harmankaya and Erdoğu 2002.
[155] Koşay 1934; Bittel 1936.

The ceramics found at Ahlatlibel have characteristics typical of Central Anatolia, including shapes that are similar to those of metal vessels from Alaca Höyük, and a squat spouted jar with a second spout lower on the body: a form also found at EBA II Alişar and EBA III Tarsus.[156] These types, and the absence of some other pot shapes and decoration styles, in particular Cappadocian painted ware (see the following discussion), suggest that Ahlatlibel dates to the end of the EBA II or the beginning of the EBA III.

The settlements of South-Central Anatolia are also poorly known in the EBA III period. Various long-lasting excavation projects in this region, such as those of Acemhöyük, Kaman Kalehöyük, and Kültepe, have uncovered EBA III strata, but the main focus of these projects and their publications has been on the second millennium BC. This is especially unfortunate because only a few centuries later, in the early second millennium BC, a system of relatively large, prosperous urban communities, which were part of regional states vying for supremacy and which were involved in long-distance trade, has been documented both in texts and in excavations.[157] At present, we know very little about the rise of these cities and how far back the processes of urbanization in Central Anatolia reach into the EBA.

There is a famous text from later periods in which the Akkadian King Sargon, who should be dated to the EBA III of Asia Minor, is beseeched by traders operating in Central Anatolia to take measures against King Nur-Dagan of the city of Puruskhanda.[158] According to the text, Sargon does undertake an expedition to subdue this king after some deliberation, and has little trouble imposing his supremacy.

While the city of Puruskhanda is known from early second millennium BC texts to be one of the main cities of the central plateau and would most likely have already existed in the late third millennium BC, there is little reason to see the Sargon text as anything other than a myth created in later centuries. There is no evidence at all that an Akkadian army crossed into Asia Minor, and perhaps most telling is the fact that the king of Puruskhanda in the narrative has a Semitic name: Nur-Dagan, which means 'light of (the god) Dagan'.

At Kültepe a number of monumental buildings dating to the EBA III levels 13–11 were excavated. One of these, dating to level 12, might have been a monumental hall and porch building such as those known from Troy II, with a large central round hearth and an anteroom, but it is flanked by smaller side rooms, which can be accessed from the main

---

[156] Von der Osten 1937: fig. 169; Goldman 1956.
[157] Özgüç 2003; Dercksen 2005.
[158] Güterbock 1969.

hall.[159] Another building, from level 11B, likewise had a large hall, measuring 10 by 17 metres, a large round hearth, and a number of side rooms.[160] The building is impressive in its size and construction, and it is clear that the large hall served in part to receive substantial groups of people, but beyond that, little can be said about the functions of this structure.

The objects found at Kültepe in the EBA III levels hint at a prosperous settlement involved in long-distance trade. Amongst the most attractive finds are vessels belonging to what has been labeled 'Cappadocian painted ware', also well attested at Alişar: buff pottery decorated with reddish brown painted geometric designs (Fig. 7.10). This decoration is applied to what are mostly typical EBA III ceramic shapes, such as spouted jars, large jars with handles on the shoulder, and tankards with a single handle rising above the rim.[161] Typical also of Central Anatolia are composite vessels, consisting of two or three small cups combined into one object, and stylized alabaster figurines, often with two or three faces, which are paralleled in gold at Alaca Höyük. There are also a substantial number of imported items in the EBA III layers at Kültepe, including Syrian flasks, Syrian metallic ware, a Mesopotamian cylinder seal, and many jewelry items that may have been imported.[162]

Summarising the evidence for the EBA III discussed in this section, the following issues have become clear. First, the hiatus between EBA II and III that one often encounters in the literature, and that has been linked with a migration wave and the coming of Indo-Europeans, can be discounted. There is both continuity of occupation and continuity of cultural traditions across this chronological boundary.

Due to various factors, but mostly relating to archaeological research and publication practices, we are relatively uninformed about the nature of settlements in western Asia Minor. However, there is some evidence that this was not a period of regression in the west, as was postulated in the past.

By contrast, Central Anatolia comes into sharper relief during the EBA III, mainly due to the spectacular inventories of the Alaca Höyük burials. These burials were probably created by relatively simple societies without states and cities. It is in South-Central Anatolia that the EBA III period probably saw the rise of large urban settlements, and possibly regional polities, the precursors of those that are well known from texts and archaeology in the early second millennium BC.

---

[159] Baydir 1970.
[160] Özgüç 1986.
[161] Von der Osten 1937; Baydir 1970.
[162] Özgüç 1986.

7.5.1 The Rise of Hierarchical Societies

In comparison to the adjacent region of Syro-Mesopotamia, societies in Asia Minor became urban and created hierarchical societies relatively late. This is remarkable given that the pattern was very different in earlier Prehistory: The Neolithic of Asia Minor developed relatively rapidly after sedentary village life took off in earnest in the Fertile Crescent. By contrast, the urban transition in Asia Minor occurred about a millennium later than in Syro-Mesopotamia.

This delayed urbanization is often perceived by Near Eastern archaeologists as a negative phenomenon. The idea is that progress was made in Mesopotamia and that, by contrast, Asia Minor was a cultural backwater. Moreover, when this region finally started to become more complex, it is often argued that this happened under the influence of Syro-Mesopotamia – for example, as a result of trade relations with that region.[163]

7.10 EBA III Cappadocian painted ware from Kültepe. Reproduced with permission of H. Müller-Karpe from Müller-Karpe, H. 1974. *Handbuch der Vorgeschichte III: Kupferzeit.* München, Germany: C. H. Beck, plate 295.

[163] Yakar 1985: 40; Efe 2003.

Here I argue that such a perspective on the emergence of urbanism and non-egalitarian societies in Asia Minor is inadequate for two reasons. First, it does little to help us understand why urbanism and social stratification developed in Asia Minor. These are surely processes that are to be understood as local phenomena developing out of local conditions. Contact with more complex societies does not automatically result in their emulation. Second, the normative idea that urban life and social hierarchy are great achievements, and that people not living in this manner are culturally backward, is a modern teleological way of perceiving human societies.

The pertinent question is not why Asia Minor became urban and socially stratified later than Mesopotamia, but what induced people to give up a life of relative autonomy in favour of a way of life in which only a few people would have been able to join the elite class and the rest would have had to settle for the status of commoner. One possible mechanism that might explain this development is that everybody benefited from the process in that the standard of life was raised even for commoners.

On current evidence, the EBA I and the earlier part of the EBA II did not differ substantially from the preceding Chalcolithic horizons in Asia Minor. In the ceramic assemblages a large number of regional traditions can be distinguished. The degree to which these regional traditions gradually merged into one another or were discrete is an issue that future research will have to determine, but the former seems more plausible. In contrast to the ceramics, the buildings of the EBA I are more or less comparable across Asia Minor: Large hall and porch buildings of about 50 square metres are found across the land and continue to dominate throughout the third millennium BC. Given the large size of these structures, it is possible to interpret them tentatively as buildings inhabited by extended households. During the EBA I, villages seem to have remained the norm in Asia Minor.

In the later EBA II a number of decisive changes took place in Asia Minor. First, there was an increasing convergence of pottery repertoires across the land. Some of the ceramic types that are typical of this period have been argued to be related to the communal consumption of wine, an argument that can be supported by circumstantial evidence. This consumption of wine might have been fairly common, as vessels linked to it are found in small village settlements as well as in more monumental settings. Second, there is the emergence of fortified upper towns, or citadels, with impressive fortifications and monumental buildings within them. Although the evidence is tenuous, it seems that some of the late EBA II settlements had substantial lower towns that would have included thousands of people. Third, in the late EBA II, there is evidence of the emergence of an elite culture expressed in the production, consumption, and deposition of valuable goods. The hoards found in Troy IIg and III, which contained large quantities of jewels, ceremonial weapons, and precious vessels produced from conspicuous materials such as gold, and with a preference for materials obtained through long-distance exchange networks, clearly attest to the rise of an elite in EBA II Asia Minor.

Finally, in the EBA III, we can dimly grasp a continuation of the processes set in motion in the late EBA II. Especially in South-Central Anatolia settlements seem to have become increasingly large, and we can posit the emergence of states that are documented a few centuries later in the early second millennium BC. In the north of Asia Minor it appears that social hierarchies and urbanisation were not yet equally well established, and in this context it is probable that the regional tradition of conspicuous burial best known from Alaca Höyük developed.

CONCLUSIONS

What are the main conclusions that can be drawn form the contents of this book? First, Asia Minor cannot be reduced to a periphery of the Fertile Crescent or Mesopotamia, on the one hand, and the Aegean, on the other. Nor is Asia Minor a clearly bounded entity either geographically or culturally. Any division of the globe is arbitrary, and especially in the Aegean and the Marmara Region, the distinction between Asia Minor and adjacent areas is often arbitrary. Nonetheless, clear cultural differences between Asia Minor and regions to the east can be documented from the Early Neolithic to the EBA. In the west, the Sea of Marmara was a cultural watershed in the Neolithic and the subsequent Chalcolithic, but this was no longer the case in the Late Chalcolithic and the EBA. In the Aegean, cultural connections between mainland Asia Minor and the islands appear to have been especially strong in the Middle Chalcolithic and the EBA II and III periods.

Second, fault lines of cultural difference occur as much within Asia Minor as at its borders. Above all, this overview demonstrates the remarkable diversity of cultural horizons in prehistoric Asia Minor. While the Early Neolithic in southern Central Anatolia has some coherence, in that settlement types and chipped stone industries can often be compared amongst sites, from the Late Neolithic onwards we can document a large number of regional cultural horizons in the archaeological evidence. This fragmentation disappears only in the latter part of the EBA II , when pottery styles and building types across Asia Minor become largely interchangeable.

Third, evidence of Epipalaeolithic and Mesolithic societies is emerging across Asia Minor. These periods are at present poorly known, mainly because Turkey has been extensively investigated. It seems increasingly clear that Mesolithic groups played a significant role in the processes of neolithisation both in Central Anatolia and in the Marmara Region. Future research will hopefully clarify whether or not these groups were important in the shift to sedentary farming life in the Lake District and Aegean Anatolia.

Fourth, from the incredibly rich evidence at sites such as Aşıklı Höyük and Çatalhöyük, it is clear that the Central Anatolian Neolithic was culturally distinct from that of the Fertile Crescent from the very start, and that many of the characteristic institutions of this Neolithic persisted over more than a millennium. Amongst these institutions are the clustered neighbourhoods, building continuity as an integral component of social identities, and sub-floor burials.

Fifth, the earliest horizon of sedentary farmers beyond Central Anatolia can be dated to about 6500 BC, or nearly two millennia after the Neolithic arrived in Central Anatolia, and culturally is remarkably diverse. This cultural diversity suggests that, rather than colonisation from Central Anatolia, local hunter-gatherer groups might have played an important role in this spread of farming, which was possibly triggered by new agricultural technologies and climatic fluctuations.

Sixth, in contrast to the Neolithic, we are very poorly informed about the Middle and Late Chalcolithic in Asia Minor. Nonetheless, the idea that we are dealing with an eventless period dominated by small autarkic communities can be discounted. Instead, people were expanding their economies in multiple and ingenious ways and were increasingly becoming partners in larger exchange networks. It appears that practices such as seafaring, nomadic pastoralism, and export-driven production of labour-intensive goods, such as stone figurines and metal artefacts, first took off in the Chalcolithic.

Seventh, from the late EBA II onwards, we witness the emergence of stratified urban societies in Asia Minor. In this period fortified sites and monumental buildings appear, as do prestige goods used by the elites to set themselves apart from commoners. These elite goods were usually produced from exotic and expensive materials that were beyond the reach of most people. In order to maintain scarcity or to increase the prestige of elite members, many of these objects were intentionally deposited in hoards or burials. Ironically, many of these strategies used by elites to assert their superior status seem to signal the fact that the social distinctions they sought to create were not self-evident and were challenged. Nonetheless, it is clear that towards the end of the EBA, stratified urban societies had become entrenched in society and constituted the bases for the polities documented in the second millennium BC in Asia Minor.

The conclusions outlined here fit the core business of archaeology, conceived of as our purpose for society at large rather than for the community of peers and students in which we are most comfortable. This purpose is to create grand narratives concerning what happened in the past. On the whole, we have been remarkably successful in this endeavour, in that we have reconstructed in considerable detail the processes surrounding the transition to farming and sedentary life and the rise of urbanism and hierarchical societies. Any archaeological study with a significant time depth, including this book, will document these developments.

What we have been much less good at is the study of the past in total, rather than simply those periods that best fit the grand narratives, and the incorporation of the complex and locally specific trajectories of past societies. In the archaeology of Asia Minor this threshold view of the past, in which the Neolithic and urban revolutions are mainly studied and in which these processes are perceived as occurring relatively rapidly, has led to the neglect of, among others, complex hunter-gatherer communities of the Early Holocene that co-existed with farming communities and the Middle and Late Chalcolithic, which lasted no less than 2.5 millennia.

The uneven investigation of the Prehistory of Asia Minor has affected the contents of this study considerably. Whereas for some periods it is possible to reconstruct what sorts of lives prehistoric people had in considerable detail, especially for the Neolithic and the EBA, even if many questions and problems remain to be investigated, for other periods, such as much of the Chalcolithic, one is reduced to a discussion of ceramic assemblages and how they link up with sequences elsewhere, and little is known about how people lived, how they were treated after death, and what sort of economy they relied upon.

It is clear, then, that although an enormous amount of information has been gained on the Prehistory of Asia Minor since the 1870s, when Schliemann first started to excavate at Troy, the archaeology of Asia Minor is still far from maturity, defined as a state in which all periods of the past have been documented and researched in some detail. At present, significant geographical and temporal gaps continue to exist in our understanding of the Prehistory of Asia Minor.

Nonetheless, both the quantity and the quality of the data on the Prehistory of Asia Minor have increased considerably over the last few decades, and a much fuller reconstruction of the prehistoric past is now possible. I hope this book has managed to capture the potential of these rich datasets. We know much more today about the kinds of settlements and communities people lived in, how they buried their dead, what their economy looked like, and how much they interacted with people in other regions.

Further, the gaps in our knowledge are slowly being filled in. A promising model for how fast this can happen is the unveiling of the Neolithic of Aegean Anatolia, which was due mainly to the Ulucak excavations and has led to a spinoff of research at other Neolithic sites in the region. Within a decade or so, an enormous amount of knowledge has been gained. Although, the Chalcolithic in particular remains very poorly known, at least a sketchy outline of the developments in this period is now emerging, and this can be used to direct the quest for further knowledge about this period. Likewise, the Mesolithic of Asia Minor seems to be slowly taking shape (although here too, our overall knowledge remains extremely scant), but at least it is becoming clear how the knowledge of this period can be expanded.

Given that much remains to be learned about the Prehistory of Asia Minor and that fieldwork can and does change our understanding of developments in prehistoric Asia Minor on a more or less constant basis, it is possible that the arguments presented in this book will be superseded in a decade or so. Especially for the less well known periods such as the Mesolithic and Chalcolithic, the picture may change dramatically in the coming years.

The possibility that this book may become obsolete within 10 years or so does not worry me. Progress in our knowledge of the past is not only driven by new data. Like any scientific publication, this book is primarily a contribution to a much broader effort towards a better understanding of our subject, in this case the Prehistory of Asia Minor. Synthetic studies, presenting new questions and new ideas, are as much the source for the generation of new knowledge as fieldwork. I hope this book will inspire new research into the prehistoric past of Asia Minor and contribute to our understanding of this horizon.

BIBLIOGRAPHY

Abbes, F., Balkan-Atlı, N., Binder, D., and Cauvin, M.-C. 1999. 'Etude téchno-logique préliminaire de l'industrie lithique d'Aşıklı Höyük'. *Türkiye Bilimler Akademisi – Arkeoloji Dergisi (TUBA-AR)* **2**:117–138.

Abu-Lughod, J. L. 1987. 'The Islamic city – Historic myth, Islamic essence, and contemporary relevance'. *International Journal of Middle East Studies* **19**:155–176.

Adams, J. W., and Kasakoff, A. B. 1976. 'Factors underlying endogamous group size'. In C. A. Smith, ed. *Regional Analysis, Volume II: Social Systems.* New York: Academic Press, pp. 149–173.

Adams, R. L. 2005. 'Ethnoarchaeology in Indonesia illuminating the ancient past at Çatalhöyük?' *American Antiquity* **70**:181–188.

Akkermans, P. M. M. G. 2004. *Het Einde van de Oude Wereld en het Begin van de Nieuwe Tijd, Verandering in Syrië en de Levant in het Late Neolithicum.* Leiden, the Netherlands: Inaugural thesis.

Akkermans, P. M. M. G., and Schwartz, G. M. 2003. *The Archaeology of Syria: From Complex Hunter-Gatherers to Early Urban Societies.* Cambridge, England: Cambridge University Press.

Akkermans, P. M. M. G., and Verhoeven, M. 1995. 'An image of complexity: The burnt village at Late Neolithic Sabi Abyad, Syria'. *American Journal of Archaeology* **99**:5–32.

Aksu, A. E., Hiscott, R. N., and Yaşar, D. 1999. 'Oscillating quaternary water levels of the Marmara Sea and vigorous outflow into the Aegean Sea from the Marmara Sea–Black Sea drainage corridor.' *Marine Geology* **153**:275–302.

Akurgal, E. 1962. *The Art of the Hittites.* London: Thames and Hudson.

Albrecht, G. 1988. 'Preliminary results of the excavations in the Karain B cave near Antalya, Turkey: The Upper Palaeolithic assemblages and the Upper Pleistocene climatic development'. *Paleorient* **14**:211–222.

Albrecht, G., Albrecht, B., Berke, H., Burger, D., Moser, J., Rähle, W., Schoch, W., Storch, G., Uerpmann, H. P., and Urban, B. 1992. Late Pleistocene and Early Holocene finds from Öküzini: A contribution to the settlement history of the Bay of Antalya, Turkey'. *Paleorient* **18**:123–141.

Alex, M. 1985. *Klimadaten ausgewählter Stationen des Vorderen Orients.* Wiesbaden, Germany: Dr. Ludwig Reichert Verlag.

Algaze, G. 1993. *The Uruk World System: The Dynamics of Early Mesopotamian Civilization*. Chicago: University of Chicago Press.

Alkım, U. B., Alkım, H., and Bilgi, Ö. 1988. *İkiztepe I, Birinçi ve Ikinçi dönem kazıları (1974–1975)*. Ankara: Türk Tarih Kurumu Basımevi.

2003. *İkiztepe II, Üçüncü, dördüncü, besçinci, altıncı, yedinci dönem kazıları (1976–1980)*. Ankara: Türk Tarih Kurumu Basımevi.

Allen, S. H. 1999. *Finding the Walls of Troy: Frank Calvert and Heinrich Schliemann at Hısarlik*. Berkeley: University of California Press.

Alpaslan-Roodenberg, S. 2001. 'Newly found human remains from Menteşe in the Yenişehir Plain: The season of 2000'. *Anatolica* 27:1–21.

2008. 'The Neolithic cemetery: The anthropological view'. In J. Roodenberg and S. Alpaslan-Roodenberg, eds., *Life and Death in a Prehistoric Settlement in Northwest Anatolia: The Ilıpınar Excavations III, With Contributions on Hacılartepe and Menteşe*. Leiden: Nederlands Instituut voor het Nabije Oosten, pp. 35–68.

Alpaslan-Roodenberg, S., and Maat, G. J. R. 1999. 'Human skeletons from Menteşe Höyük near Yenışehır'. *Anatolica* 25:37–51.

Amiran, R. 1993. 'The Kinneret gold plaque and the Alaca Royal Tombs again'. In M. Mellink, E. Porada, and T. Özgüç, eds., *Aspects of Art and Iconography: Anatolia and Its Neighbors: Studies in Honor of Nimet Özguç*. Ankara: Türk Tarih Kurumu Basımevi, pp. 23–24.

Anati, E. 1968. 'Anatolia's earliest art'. *Archaeology* 21/1:22–35.

1972. *Arte Preistorica in Anatolia*. Brescia, Italy: Studi Camuni.

Andelson, J. G. 2002. 'Coming together and breaking apart: Sociogenesis and schismogenesis in intentional communities'. In S. L. Brown, ed., *Intentional Communities: An Anthroplogical Perspective*. New York: State University of New York Press, pp. 131–151.

Anderson, S., and Ertug-Yaras, F. 1998. 'Fuel fodder and faeces: An ethnographic and botanical study of dung fuel use in Central Anatolia'. *Environmental Archaeology* 1:99–104.

Andrews, P., Molleson, T., and Boz, B. 2005. 'The human burials at Çatalhöyük'. In I. Hodder, ed., *Inhabiting Çatalhöyük: Reports from the 1995–1999 Seasons*. Cambridge, England: MacDonald Institute, pp. 261–278.

Angel, L. 1971. 'Early Neolithic skeletons from Çatal Hüyük: Demography and pathology'. *Anatolian Studies* 21:77–98.

Anthony, D. W. 1990. 'Migration in archeology: The baby and the bathwater'. *American Anthropologist* 92:895–914.

2007. *The Horse, the Wheel, and Language: How Bronze-Age Riders from the Eurasian Steppes Shaped the Modern World*. Princeton, NJ: Princeton University Press.

Antoun, R. T. 1972. *Arab Village: A Social Structural Study of a Trans-Jordanian Peasant Community*. Bloomington: Indiana University Press.

Arbuckle, B. S., and Özkaya, V. 2008. 'Revisiting Neolithic caprine exploitation at Suberde, Turkey'. *Journal of Field Archaeology* 33:219–236.

Arık, R. O. 1937. *Les fouilles d'Alaca Höyük: Entreprises par la Société d'histoire turque: Rapport préliminaire sur les travaux en 1935*. Ankara: Türk Tarih Kurumu Basımevi.

1950. *Les fouilles archeologiques en Turquie*. Ankara, Turkey: Milli Eğitim Basımevi.

Arsebük, G., Mellink, M. J., and Schirmer, W., eds. 1998. *Light on Top of the Black Hill: Studies Presented to Halet Çambel*. Istanbul, Turkey: Ege Yayınları.

Aruz, J. 2006. 'Central Anatolia and the Aegean (2650–1700 B.C.): Beads, seals, and ivories: Enhancing the case for interaction'. In A. Erkanal-Öktü, E. Özgen, S. Günel, A. Tuba Ökse, H. Hüryılmaz, H. Tekin, N. Çınardalı-Karaaslan, B. Uysal, F. A. Karaduman, A. Engin, R. Spieß, A. Aykurt, R. Tuncel, U. Deniz, and A. Rennie, eds. *Studies in Honor of Hayat Erkanal: Cultural Reflections.* Istanbul, Turkey: Homer, pp. 48–58.

Asouti, E. 2005. 'Woodland vegetation and the exploitation of fuel and timber at Neolithic Çatalhöyük: Report on the wood charcoal macro-remains'. In I. Hodder, ed., *Inhabiting Çatalhöyük: Reports from the 1995–1999 Seasons.* Cambridge, England: MacDonald Institute, pp. 213–258.

Asouti, E., and Fairbairn, A. 2002. 'Subsistence economy in Central Anatolia during the Neolithic: The archaeobotanical evidence'. In F. Gerard and L. Thissen, eds., *The Neolithic of Central Anatolia: Internal Developments and External Relations during the 9th–6th Millennia cal. BC.* Istanbul, Turkey: Ege Yayınları, pp. 181–192.

Asouti, E., and Hather, J. 2001. 'Charcoal analysis and the reconstruction of ancient woodland vegetation in the Konya Basin, south-central Anatolia, Turkey: Results from the Neolithic site of Çatalhöyük East'. *Vegetation History and Archaeobotany* **10**:23–32.

Atakuman, Ç. 2008. 'Cradle or crucible: Anatolia and archaeology in the early years of the Turkish Republic (1923–1938)'. *Journal of Social Archaeology* **8**/2:214–235.

Atalay, S. 2005. 'Domesticating clay: The role of clay balls, mini balls and geometric objects in daily life at Çatalhöyük.' In I. Hodder, ed., *Changing Materialities at Çatalhöyük: Reports from the 1995–1999 Seasons.* Cambridge, England: MacDonald Institute, pp. 139–168.

Ataman, K. 1988. 'The chipped stone assemblage from Canhasan III: A study in typology, technology, and function'. London: Unpublished PhD thesis, University College London, England.

Atici, A. L., and Stutz, A. J. 2002. 'Mortality profile analysis of the ungulate fauna from Öküzini: A preliminary reconstruction of site use, seasonality and mobility patterns'. In I. Yalçınkaya, M. Otte, J. Kozlowski, and O. Bar-Yosef, eds., *La grotte d'Öküzini: Evolution du Paleolithique Final du sud-ouest de l'Anatolie.* Liege, France: Universite de Liege, pp. 101–108.

Aurenche, O. 1981. *La maison orientale, L'architecture du proche orient ancien: Des origines au milieu du quatrième millénaire.* Paris, France: Paul Geuthner.

Aurenche, O., Bazin, M., and Sadler, S. 1997. *Villages engloutis: Enquête ethnoarchéologique à Cafer Höyük (vallée de l'Euphrate).* Paris, France: Maison de l'Orient Méditteranéen.

Aurenche, O., and Kozlowski, S. K. 1999. *La naissance du Néolithique au Proche Orient.* Paris, France: Editions Errance.

Bachhuber, C. 2006. 'Aegean interest on the Uluburun ship'. *American Journal of Archaeology* **110**:345–363.

2009. 'The treasure deposit of Troy: Rethinking crisis and agency on the Early Bronze Age citade'. *Anatolian Studies* **59**:1–18.

2011. *Material and Landscape in Early Bronze Age Anatolia.* London, England: Equinox.

Bachmann, H.-G., Otto, H., and Prunnbauer, F. 1987. 'Analyse von Metallfunden'. In M. Korfmann, ed., *Demircihöyük: Die Ergebnisse der Ausgrabungen*

1975–1978, Band II: Naturwissenschaftliche Untersuchungen. Mainz am Rhein, Germany: Phillip von Zabern, pp. 21–24.

Bahar, H., and Koçak, Ö. 2002. Erken dönemlerde Konya-Karaman bölgesi yerleşmeleri I (Ilgın, Kadınhanı, Doğanhisar ve Sarayönü kesimi). *Anadolu Araştırmaları* **16**:35–53.

Bailey, D. W. 2000. *Balkan Prehistory: Exclusion, Incorporation and Identity*. London, England: Routledge.

Baird, D. 2002. 'Early Holocene settlement in Central Anatolia: Problems and prospects as seen from the Konya Plain'. In F. Gérard and L. Thissen, eds., *The Neolithic of Central Anatolia*. Istanbul, Turkey: Ege Yayınları, pp. 139–159.

2003. 'Pınarbaşı'. *Anatolian Archaeology* **9**:2–4.

2004. 'Pınarbaşı'. *Anatolian Archaeology* **10**:2–3.

2006a. 'The history of settlement and social landscapes in the Early Holocene in the Çatalhöyük area'. In I. Hodder, ed., *Çatalhöyük Perspectives: Themes from the 1995–1999 Seasons*. Cambridge, England: MacDonald Institute, pp. 55–74.

2006b. 'The Boncuklu project: The origins of sedentism, cultivation and herding in central Anatolia'. *Anatolian Archaeology* **12**:13–16.

2007. 'The Boncuklu project: The origins of sedentism, cultivation and herding in central Anatolia'. *Anatolian Archaeology* **13**:14–17.

2008. 'The Boncuklu project: The origins of sedentism, cultivation and herding in central Anatolia'. *Anatolian Archaeology* **14**:11–12.

2009. 'The Boncuklu project: Investigating the beginnings of agriculture, sedentism and herding in central Anatolia'. *Anatolian Archaeology* **15**:9–10.

Balkan-Atlı, N. 1994a. 'The typological characteristics of the Aşıklı Höyük chipped stone industry'. In H. G. Gebel and S. K. Kozlowski, eds., *Neolithic Chipped Stone Industries of the Fertile Crescent*. Berlin, Germany: Ex Oriente, pp. 209–221.

1994b. *La Neolithisation de l'Anatolie*. Istanbul: Institut Français d'Etudes Anatoliennes.

1998. 'The Aceramic Neolithic of Central Anatolia: Recent finds in the chipped stone industry'. In G. Arsebük, M. J. Mellink, and W. Schirmer, eds., *Light on Top of the Black Hill: Studies Presented to Halet Çambel*. Istanbul, Turkey: Ege Yayınları, pp. 81–94.

Balkan-Atlı, N., and Binder, D. 2000. 'L'atelier Néolithique de Kömürcü-Kaletepe: Fouilles de 1999'. *Anatolia Antiqua* **8**:199–214.

2001. 'Les ateliers de taille d'obsidienne fouilles de Kömürcü – Kaletepe 2000'. *Anatolia Antiqua* **9**:193–205.

Balkan-Atlı, N., Binder, D., and Cauvin, M.-C. 1999a. 'Obsidian: Sources, workshops and trade in Central Anatolia'. In M. Özdoğan and N. Başgelen, eds., *Neolithic in Turkey*. Istanbul, Turkey: Arkeoloji ve Sanat Yayınları, pp. 133–145.

Balkan-Atlı, N., Binder, D., and Kuzucuoğlu, C. 1999b. 'L'atelier Néolithique de Kömürcü-Kaletepe: Fouilles de 1998'. *Anatolia Antiqua* **7**:231–243.

Balkan-Atlı, N., and Der Aprahamian, G. 1998. 'Les nucleus de Kaletepe et deux ateliers de taille en Cappadoce'. In M. C. Cauvin, A. Gourgaud, B. Gratuze, N. Arnaud, G. Poupeau, J.-L. Poidevin, and C. Chataigner, eds., *L'Obsidienne au Proche et Moyen Orient: Du Volcan a l'Outil*. Oxford, England: British Archaeological Reports International Series, pp. 241–257.

Ballard, R. D., Hiebert, F. T., Coleman, D. F., Ward, C., Smith, J. S., Willis, K., Foley, B., Croff, K., Major, C., and Torbe, F. 2001. 'Deepwater archaeology of the Black Sea: The 2000 season at Sinop, Turkey'. *American Journal of Archaeology* **105**:607–623.

Balossi Restelli, F. 2001. *Formation Processes of the First Developed Neolithic Societies in the Zagros and the Northern Mesopotamian Plain*. Rome, Italy: Universita di Roma 'La Sapienza'.

2004. 'New data for the definition of the DFBW horizon and its internal developments: The earliest phases of the Amuq sequence revisited'. *Anatolica* **30**:109–149.

2006. *The Development of 'Cultural Regions' in the Neolithic of the Near East: The Dark Faced Burnished Ware Horizon*. Oxford, England: British Archaeological Reports International Series.

Barker, G. 2006. *The Agricultural Revolution in Prehistory*. Oxford, England: Oxford University Press.

Barnett, W. K. 2000. 'Cardial pottery and the agricultural transition in Europe'. In T. D. Price, ed., *Europe's First Farmers*. Cambridge, England: Cambridge University Press, pp. 93–116.

Bar-Yosef, O. 1998. 'Öküzini: Comparisons with the Levant'. In M. Otte, ed., *Préhistoire d'Anatolie: Genèse des Deux Mondes*. Liège, France: Université de Liège, pp. 501–507.

2001. 'From sedentary foragers to village hierarchies: The emergence of social institutions'. In W. G. Runciman, ed., *The Origins of Human Social Institutions*. Oxford, England: British Academy, pp. 1–38.

Bar-Yosef, O. 2007. 'The emergence of social complexity in the Neolithic of the Near East'. *Bulletin of the American Society of Oriental Research* **60/61**:19–40.

Bar-Yosef, O., and Meadow, R. H. 1995. 'The origins of agriculture in the Near East'. In T. D. Price and A. B. Gebauer, eds., *Last Hunters, First Farmers: New Perspectives on the Prehistoric Transition to Agriculture*. Santa Fe, NM: School of American Research, pp. 39–94.

Bar-Yosef, O., and Belfer-Cohen, A. 2002. 'Facing environmental crisis: Societal and cultural changes at the transition from the Younger Dryas to the Holocene in the Levant'. In R. T. J. Cappers and S. Bottema, eds., *The Dawn of Farming in the Near East*. Berlin, Germany: Ex Oriente, pp. 55–66.

Bar-Yosef, O., and Valla, F. R., eds. 1991. *The Natufian Culture in the Levant*. Ann Arbor: University of Michigan Press.

Baydir, N. 1970. *Kültepe (Kanes) ve Kayseri Tarihi üzerine Araştırmalar*. Istanbul, Turkey: Istanbul Üniversitesi Edibiyat Fakültesi.

Baykal-Seeher, A. 1994. 'Silex und obsidiaanindustrien'. In R. Duru, ed., *Kuruçay Höyük I: Results of the Excavations 1978–1988: The Neolithic and Early Chalcolithic Periods*. Ankara: Türk Tarihi Kürümü Basımevi, pp. 106–109.

Baysal, A., and Wright, K. I. 2005. 'Cooking, crafts and curation: Ground stone artefacts from Çatalhöyük (1995–1999 excavations)'. In I. Hodder, ed., *Changing Materialities at Çatalhöyük: Reports from the 1995–1999 Seasons*. Cambridge, England: MacDonald Institute, pp. 307–324.

Begemann, F., Schmitt-Stecker, S., and Pernicka, E. 1992. 'The metal finds from Thermi III–V: A chemical and lead-isotope study'. *Studia Troica* **2**:219–239.

Begeman, F., Pernicka, E., and Schmitt-Strecker, S. 1994. 'Metal finds from Ilıpınar and the advent of arsenic copper'. *Anatolica* **20**:15–36.

Beile-Bohn, M., Gerber, C., Morsch, M., and Schmidt, K. 1998. 'Neolithische Forschungen in Obermesopotamien, Gürcütepe und Göbekli Tepe'. *Istanbuler Mitteilungen* **48**:5–78.

Bellwood, P. 2001. 'Early agricultural population diasporas? Farming, language and genes'. *Annual Review of Anthropology* **30**:181–207.

2005. *First Farmers: The Origins of Agricultural Societies.* Oxford, England: Blackwell.

Bentley, R. A., Price, T. D., Lüning, J., Gronenborn, D., Wahl, J., and Fullagar, P. D. 2002. 'Prehistoric migration in Europe: Strontium isotope analysis of Early Neolithic skeletons'. *Current Anthropology* **43**:799–804.

Bernabo-Brea, L. 1964. *Poliochni I: Citta Preistorica nell'Isola di Lemnos.* Roma, Italy: l'Erma di Bretschneider.

1976. *Poliochni II: Citta Preistorica nell'Isola di Lemnos.* Roma: l'Erma di Bretschneider.

Bernbeck, R. 1994. *Die Auflösung der häuslichen Produktionsweise: Das Beispiel Mesopotamiens.* Berlin, Germany: Dietrich Reimer Verlag.

Bıçakçı, E., Altınbilek-Algül, C., Balcı, S., and Godon, M. 2007. 'Tepecik-Çiftlik'. In M. Özdoğan and N. Başgelen, eds., *Anadolu'da Uygarlığın Doğuşu Avrupaya Yayılımı Türkiye'de Neolitik Dönem, Yeni Kazılar, Yeni Bulgular.* Istanbul, Turkey: Arkeoloji ve Sanat Yayınları, pp. 237–254.

Biehl, P. F., Erdoğu, B., and Rosenstock, E. 2006. 'West Mound'. *Çatalhöyük Archive Reports* 122–130. Available at http://www.catalhoyuk.com/archive_reports/.

Biehl, P. F., and Rosenstock, E. 2007. 'West Mound excavations, trenches 5 and 7'. *Çatalhöyük Archive Reports* 124–132.

Bienert, H.-D. 1991. 'Skull cult in the prehistoric Near East'. *Journal of Prehistoric Religion* **5**:9–23.

Bigazzi, G., Oddone, M., and Yeğengil, Z. 1995. 'A provenance study of obsidian artifacts from Ilıpınar'. In J. Roodenberg, ed., *The Ilıpınar Excavations I.* Istanbul, Turkey: Nederlands Historisch Archaeologisch Istituut te Istanbul, pp. 143–150.

Bigazzi, G., Poupeau, G., Yeğengil, Z., and Bellot-Gurlet, L. 1998. 'Provenance studies of obsidian artefacts in Anatolia using the fission-track dating method: An overview'. In M. C. Cauvin, A. Gourgaud, B. Gratuze, N. Arnaud, G. Poupeau, J. L. Poidevin, and C. Chataigner, eds., *L'obsidienne au Proche et Moyen Orient: Du Volcan `a l'Outil.* Oxford, England: British Archaeological Reports Internationa Series, pp. 69–89.

Bilgi, Ö. 2001. *Metallurgists of the Central Black Sea Region: A New Perspective on the Question of the Indo-Europeans' Original Homeland.* Istanbul, Turkey: Tarih Arkeoloji Sanat ve Kültür Mirasını Koruma Vakfı.

Binder, D. 2002. 'Stones making sense: What obsidian could tell about origins'. In F. Gérard and L. Thissen, eds., *The Neolithic of Central Anatolia: Internal Developments and External Relations during the 9th–6th Millennia cal. BC.* Istanbul, Turkey: Ege Yayınları, pp. 79–90.

Binder, D., and Balkan-Atlı, N. 2001. 'Obsidian exploitation and blade technology at Kömürcü-Kaletepe, Cappadocia, Turkey'. In I. Caneva, C. Lemorini, D. Zampetti, and P. Biagi, eds., *Beyond Tools: Redefining the PPN Lithic Assemblages of the Levant.* Berlin, Germany: Ex Oriente, pp. 1–16.

Bintliff, J. L. 1999. 'Settlement and territory'. In G. Barker, ed., *Companion Encyclopedia of Archaeology.* London, England: Routledge, pp. 505–545.

Birdsell, J. B. 1973. 'A basic demographic unit'. *Current Anthropology* **14**:337–356.

Bittel, K. 1934. *Prähistorische Forschung in Kleinasien*. Istanbul, Turkey: Universum.

1936. 'Beiträge für kleinasiatische Archäologie: Die prähistorische Siedlung bei Ahlatlibel'. *Archif für Orientforschung* **10**:38–48.

1945. *Grundzüge der Vor – und Frühgeschichte Kleinasiens*. Tübingen, Germany: Ernst Wasmuth.

1960. 'Fikirtepe Kazısı'. *Türk Tarih Kongresi* **5**:29–36.

1969. 'Bemerkungen über die prähistorische Ansiedlung auf dem Fikirtepe bei Kadıköy (Istanbul)'. *Istanbuler Mitteilungen* **19**:1–19.

Blackman, M. J. 1986. 'The provenience of obsidian artifacts from Late Chalcolithic levels at Aphrodisias'. In M. S. Joukowsky, ed., *Prehistoric Aphrodisias I: An Account of the Excavation and Artefact Studies*. Providence, RI: Brown University Press, pp. 279–285.

Blegen, C. W. 1963. *Troy and the Trojans*. London, England: Thames and Hudson.

Blegen, C. W., Caskey, J. L., Rawson, M., and Sperling, J. 1950. *Troy: The First and the Second Settlements*. Princeton, NJ: Princeton University Press.

Bloch, M. E. F. 1998. 'Time, narratives, and the multiplicity of representations of the past'. In M. E. F. Bloch, ed., *How We Think They Think: Anthropological Approaches to Cognition, Memory, and Literacy*. Boulder, CO: Westview Press, pp. 100–113.

Blumler, M. A. 1996. 'Ecology, evolutionary theory and agricultural origins'. In D. R. Harris, ed., *The Origins and Spread of Agriculture and Pastoralism in Eurasia*. London, England: University College London Press, pp. 25–45.

Bocquet-Appel, J.-P., and Demars, P.-Y. 2000. 'Population kinetics in the Upper Palaeolithic in Western Europe'. *Journal of Archaeological Science* **27**:551–570.

Boessneck, J., and von den Driesch, A. 1979. *Die Tierknochenfunde aus der neolithische Siedlung auf dem Fikirtepe bei Kadiköy am Marmarameer*. München, Germany: Universität München.

Bogaard, A. 2004. *Neolithic Farming in Central Europe: An Archaeobotanical Study of Crop Husbandry Practices*. London, England: Routledge.

2005. '"Garden agriculture" and the nature of early farming in Europe and the Near East'. *World Archaeology* **37**:177–196.

Böhmer, H. 2004. *Nomaden in Anatolien: Begegnungen mit einer ausklingenden Kultur*. Ganderkesee, Germany: Remhöb Verlag.

Boivin, N. 2000. 'Life rhythms and floor sequences; excavating time in rural Rajasthan and Neolithic Çatalhöyük'. *World Archaeology* **31**:367–388.

Bordaz, J. 1965. 'Suberde excavations 1964'. *Anatolian Studies* **15**:30–32.

1966. 'Suberde excavations 1965'. *Anatolian Studies* **16**:32–33.

1968. 'The Suberde excavations, southwestern Turkey, an interim report'. *Türk Arkeoloji Dergisi* **17**:43–71.

1969. 'A preliminairy report of the 1969 excavations at Erbaba, a Neolithic site near Beyşehir, Turkey'. *Türk Arkeoloji Dergisi* **18**:59–64.

1973. 'Current research in the Neolithic of south central Turkey, Suberde, Erbaba and their chronological implications'. *American Journal of Archaeology* **77**:282–288.

Bordaz, J., and Alpers-Bordaz, L. L. 1976. 'Erbaba excavations, 1974'. *Türk Arkeoloji Dergisi* **23**:39–43.

1977a. 'Beyşehir-Suğla basin project'. *American Journal of Archaeology* **81**:291.

1977b. 'Erbaba excavations 1976'. *Anatolian Studies* **27**:32–33.

1978a. 'Beyşehir-Erbaba'. *American Journal of Archaeology* **82**:316.

1978b. 'Erbaba excavations 1977'. *Anatolian Studies* **28**:20–21.

1982. 'Erbaba: The 1977 and 1978 seasons in perspective'. *Türk Arkeoloji Dergisi* **26**:85–92.

Bostancı, E. 1962. 'A new Upper Palaeolithic and Mesolithic facies at Belbaşı Rock Shelter on the Mediterranean coast of Anatolia'. *Belleten* **26**:252–292.

1967. 'Beldibi ve Mağracıkta Yapılan 1967 Yaz Mevsimi Kazıları ve Yeni Buluntular'. *Türk Arkeoloji Dergisi* **16**:51–60.

Bottema, S. 1995. 'The Younger Dryas in the eastern Mediterranean'. *Quarternary Science Reviews* **14**:883–891.

2002. 'The use of palynology in tracing early agriculture'. In R. T. J. Cappers and S. Bottema, eds., *The Dawn of Farming in the Near East*. Berlin, Germany: Ex Oriente, pp. 27–38.

Bottema, S., and Woldring, H. 1990. 'Anthropogenic indicators in the pollen record of the eastern Mediterranean'. In S. Bottema, G. Entjes-Nieborg, and W. Van Zeist, eds., *Man's Role in the Shaping of the Eastern Mediteranean Landscape*. Rotterdam, the Netherlands: A. A. Balkema, pp. 231–264.

Bottema, S., Woldring, H., and Aytuğ, B. 1993/1994. 'Late quarternary vegetation history of northern Turkey'. *Palaeohistoria* **35/36**:13–73.

Bottema, S., Woldring, H., and Kayan, I. 2001. 'The late quaternary vegetation history of western Turkey'. In J. J. Roodenberg and L. C. Thissen, eds., *The Ilıpınar Excavations II*. Istanbul, Turkey: Nederlands Historisch Archaeologisch Istituut te Istanbul, pp. 327–354.

Boyer, P., Roberts, N., and Baird, D. 2006. 'Holocene environment and settlement on the Çarsamba alluvial fan, south-central Turkey: Integrating geoarchaeology and archaeological field survey'. *Geoarchaeology* **21**:675–698.

Braidwood, R. J., and Braidwood, L. S. 1960. *Excavations in the Plain of Antioch I.* Chicago: University of Chicago Press.

Brandt, R. W. 1978. 'The Chalcolithic pottery'. In M. N. Van Loon, ed., *Korucutepe* 2. Amsterdam, the Netherlands: North-Holland, pp. 57–60.

Breniquet, C. 1995. 'La stratigraphie des niveaux prehistoriques de Mersin et l'evolution culturelle en Cilicie'. *Anatolia Antiqua* **3**:1–31.

Brinkmann, R. 1976. *Geology of Turkey*. Stuttgart, Germany: Ferdinand Enke Verlag.

Broodbank, C. 2006. 'The origins and early development of Mediterranean maritime activity'. *Journal of Mediterranean Archaeology* **19**:199–230.

2009. 'The Early Bronze Age in the Cyclades'. In C. W. Shelmerdine, ed., *The Cambridge Companion to the Aegean Bronze Age*. Cambridge, England: Cambridge University Press, pp. 47–76.

Brückner, H. 2003. 'Delta evolution and culture: Aspects of geoarchaeological research in Miletos and Prienne'. In G. A. Wagner, E. Pernicka, and H.-P. Uerpmann, eds., *Troia and the Troad: Scientific Approaches*. Berlin, Germany: Springer, pp. 121–142.

Bryce, T. 2005. *The Kingdom of the Hittites*. Oxford, England: Oxford University Press.

Bryson, R. A., and Bryson, R. U. 1999. 'Holocene climates as simulated with archaeoclimatic models'. *Türkiye Bilimler Akademisi – Arkeoloji Dergisi (TUBA-AR)* **2**:1–14.

Budja, M. 2007. 'The 8200 cal BP "climate event" and the process of neolithisation in south-eastern Europe'. *Documenta Praehistorica* **34**:191–201.

Buitenhuis, H. 1995. 'The faunal remains'. In J. Roodenberg, ed., *The Ilıpınar Excavations I*. Leiden: Nederlands Instituut voor het Nabije Oosten, pp. 151–157.

1997. 'Aşıklı Höyük, A "protodomestic" site'. *Anthropozoologica* **25**:655–662.

2004. 'The importance of Yumuktepe in the origin and spread of animal domestication'. In I. Caneva and V. Sevin, eds., *Mersin-Yumuktepe: A Reppraisal*. Lecce, Italy: Congedo Editore, 163–168.

2008. 'Faunal remains from the Late Neolithic and Early Chalcolithic levels'. In J. Roodenberg and S. Alpaslan-Roodenberg, eds., *Life and Death in a Prehistoric Settlement in Northwest Anatolia: The Ilıpınar Excavations III, with Contributions on Hacılartepe and Menteşe*. Leiden: Nederlands Instituut voor het Nabije Oosten, pp. 205–226.

Bull, I. D., Elhmmali, M. M., Perret, V., Matthews, W., Roberts, D. J., and Evershed, R. P. 2005. 'Biomarker evidence of faecal deposition in archaeological sediments at Çatalhöyük'. In I. Hodder, ed., *Inhabiting Çatalhöyük: Reports from the 1995–1999 Seasons*. Cambridge, England: MacDonald Institute, pp. 415–420.

Burnham, H. B. 1965. 'Çatal Hüyük: The textiles and the twined fabrics'. *Anatolian Studies* **15**:169–174.

Byrd, B. F. 2000. 'Households in transition: Neolithic social organization within Southwest Asia'. In I. Kuijt, ed., *Life in Neolithic Farming Communities: Social Organization, Identity, and Differentiation*. New York: Kluwer Academic Press, pp. 63–98.

Çalış-Sazcı, D. 2006. 'Die Troianer und das Meer, Keramik und Handelsbeziehungen der sog. "Maritime Troia-Kultur"'. In M. O. Korfmann, ed., *Troia: Archäologie eines Siedlungshügels und seiner Landschaft*. Main am Rhein, Germany: Philipp von Zabern, pp. 201–208.

Çambel, H., ed. 1995. *Readings in Prehistory: Studies Presented to Halet Çambel*. Istanbul, Germany: Graphics Yayınları.

Cambell, S., Carter, E., Healey, E., Anderson, S., Kennedy, A., and Whitcher, S. 1999. 'Emerging complexity on the Kahramanmaras Plain, Turkey: The Domuztepe Project, 1995–1997'. *American Journal of Archaeology* **103**:395–418.

Campbell, L. 2002. 'What drives linguistic diversification and language spread?' In P. Bellwood and C. Renfrew, eds., *Examining the Farming/Language Dispersal Hypothesis*. Cambridge, England: MacDonald Institute, 49–63.

Caneva, I. 2004a. 'The early human occupation (7000–6000 BC)'. In I. Caneva and V. Sevin, eds., *Mersin-Yumuktepe: A Reppraisal*. Lecce, Italy: Congedo Editores, pp. 33–44.

2004b. 'Of terraces, silos and ramparts (6000–5800)'. In I. Caneva and V. Sevin, eds., *Mersin-Yumuktepe: A Reppraisal*. Lecce, Italy: Congedo Editore, pp. 45–56.

2004c. 'The citadel tradition (5000–4200 BC)'. In I. Caneva and V. Sevin, eds., *Mersin-Yumuktepe: A Reppraisal*. Lecce, Italy: Congedo Editore, pp. 57–72.

2007. 'Mersin-Yumuktepe, Son veriler ışığnda MÖ binyila yeni bir bakış'. In M. Özdoğan and N. Başgelen, eds., *Anadolu'da Uygarlığın Doğuşu Avrupaya Yayılımı Türkiye'de Neolitik Dönem, Yeni Kazılar, Yeni Bulgular*. Istanbul, Turkey: Arkeoloji ve Sanat Yayınları, pp. 203–216.

Caneva, I., and Marcolongo, B. 2004. 'The history of the mound'. In I. Caneva and V. Sevin, eds., *Mersin-Yumuktepe: A Reppraisal*. Lecce, Italy: Congedo Editore, pp. 23–32.

Caneva, I., and Sevin, V., eds. 2004. *Mersin-Yumuktepe: A Reappraisal*. Lecce, Italy: Congedo Editore.

Cappers, R. 2008. 'Plant remains'. In J. Roodenberg and S. Alpaslan-Roodenberg, eds., *Life and Death in a Prehistoric Settlement in Northwest Anatolia: The Ilıpınar Excavations III, with Contributions on Hacılartepe and Menteşe*. Leiden: Nederlands Instituut voor het Nabije Oosten, pp. 117–148.

Carsten, J., and Hugh-Jones, S. 1995. 'Introduction'. In J. Carsten and S. Hugh-Jones, eds., *About the House: Lévi Strauss and Beyond*. Cambridge, England: Cambridge University Press, pp. 1–47.

Carter, T., Conolly, J., and Spasojevíc, A. 2005a. 'The chipped stone'. In I. Hodder, ed., *Changing Materialities at Çatalhöyük: Reports from the 1995–1999 Seasons*. Cambridge, England: MacDonald Institute, pp. 221–283.

Carter, T., Poupeau, G., Bressy, C., and Pearce, N. J. G. 2005b. 'From chemistry to consumption: Towards a history of obsidian use at Çatalhöyük through a programme of inter-laboratory trace-element characterization'. In I. Hodder, ed., *Changing Materialities at Çatalhöyük: Reports from the 1995–1999 Seasons*. Cambridge, England: MacDonald Institute, pp. 285–306.

Carter, T., and Shackley, M. S. 2007. 'Sourcing obsidian from Neolithic Çatalhöyük (Turkey) using energy dispersive x-ray fluorescence'. *Archaeometry* **49**:437–454.

Casselberry, S. E. 1974. 'Further refinement of formulae for determining population from floor area'. *World Archaeology* **6**:116–122.

Cauvin, J. 1989. 'La neolithisation au Levant et sa premiere diffusion'. In O. Aurenche and J. Cauvin, eds., *Neolithisations: Proche et Moyen Orient, Mediterranee Orientale, Chine, Afrique du Sud*. Oxford, England: British Archaeological Reports International Series, pp. 3–36.

1997. *Naissance des Divinites: Naissance de l'Agriculture*. Paris, France: Flammarion.

Cauvin, M.-C. 1996. 'L'Obsidienne dans le Proche-Orient Préhistorique: État de recherches en 1996'. *Anatolica* **22**:1–31.

1998. 'L'obsidienne: Donnees recentes provenant de sites-habitats Neolithiques'. In M.-C. Cauvin, A. Gourgaud, B. Gratuze, N. Arnaud, G. Poupeau, J.-L. Poidevin and C. Chataigner, eds., *L'Obsidienne au Proche et Moyen Orient: Du Volcan a l'Outil*. Oxford, England: British Archaeological Reports International Series, pp. 259–271.

Cauvin, M.-C., and Balkan-Atlı, N. 1996. 'Rapport sur les recherches sur l'obsidienne en Cappadoce, 1993–1995'. *Anatolia Antiqua* **4**:249–271.

Cauvin, M.-C., and Chataigner, C. 1998. 'Distribution de l'obsidienne dans les sites archeologiques du Proche et du Moyen Orient (par phase chronologique)'. In M.-C. Cauvin, A. Gourgaud, B. Gratuze, N. Arnaud, G. Poupeau, J.-L. Poidevin, and C. Chataigner, eds., *L'Obsidienne au Proche et Moyen Orient: Du Volcan a l'Outil*. Oxford, England: British Archaeological Reports International Series, pp. 325–350.

Caymaz, T. 2006. 'Aliağa-Helvacıköy bölgesinde bir Neolitik yerleşim: Arap Tepe'. *Ege Üniversitesi Arkeoloji Dergisi* **2006**/2:1–12.

Cessford, C. 2001. 'A new dating for Çatalhöyük'. *Antiquity* **75**:717–725.

2005a. 'Absolute dating at Çatalhöyük'. In I. Hodder, ed., *Changing Materialities at Çatalhöyük: Reports from the 1995–1999 Seasons*. Cambridge, England: MacDonald Institute, pp. 65–100.

2005b. 'Estimating the Neolithic population of Çatalhöyük'. In I. Hodder, ed., *Inhabiting Çatalhöyük: Reports from the 1995–1999 Seasons*. Cambridge, England: MacDonald Institute, pp. 323–326.

2007a. 'Level Pre-XII.E–A and levels XII and XI, spaces 181, 199 and 198'. In I. Hodder, ed., *Excavating Çatalhöyük, South, North and KOPAL Area: Reports from the 1995–1999 Seasons.* Cambridge, England: MacDonald Institute, pp. 59–102.

2007b. 'Building 1'. In I. Hodder, ed., *Excavating Çatalhöyük, South, North and KOPAL Area: Reports from the 1995–1999 Seasons.* Cambridge, England: MacDonald Institute, pp. 405–530.

Cessford, C., and Carter, T. 2005. 'Quantifying the consumption of obsidian at Neolithic Çatalhöyük, Turkey'. *Journal of Field Archaeology* **30**:305–315.

Cessford, C., and Near, J. 2006. 'Fire, burning and pyrotechnology at Çatalhöyük'. In I. Hodder, ed., *Çatalhöyük Perspectives: Themes from the 1995–1999 Seasons.* Cambridge, England: MacDonald Institute, pp. 171–182.

Çevik, O. 2007. 'The emergence of different social systems in Early Bronze Age Anatolia: Urbanisation versus centralisation'. *Anatolian Studies* **57**:131–140.

Chapman, J. 1981. *The Vinča Culture of South-East Europe: Studies in Chronology, Economy and Society.* Oxford, England: British Archaeological Reports.

Chataigner, C. 1998. 'Sources des artefacts du Proche Orient d'apres leur characterisation geochemique'. In M-C. Cauvin, A. Gourgaud, B. Gratuze, N. Arnaud, G. Poupeau, J.-L. Poidevin, and C. Chataigner, eds., *L'Obsidienne au Proche et Moyen Orient: Du Volcan a l'Outil.* Oxford, England: British Archaeological Reports International Series, pp. 273–350.

Chesson, M. S. 2001. 'Embodied memories of place and people: Death and society in an early urban community'. In M. S. Chesson, ed., *Social Memory, Identity, and Death: Anthropological Perspectives on Mortuary Rituals.* Arlington, VA: American Anthropological Association, pp. 100–113.

Childe, V. G. 1928. *The Most Ancient East.* London: Routledge and Kegan Paul. 1936. *Man Makes Himself.* London, England: Routledge.

Christensen, N. 1967. 'Haustupen und Gehöftbildung in Westpersie'. *Anthropos* **62**:89–138.

Çilingiroğlu, A., and Çilingiroğlu, C. 2007. 'Ulucak'. In M. Özdoğan and N. Başgelen, eds., *Anadolu'da Uygarlığın Doğuşu Avrupaya Yayılımı Türkiye'de Neolitik Dönem, Yeni Kazılar, Yeni Bulgular.* Istanbul, Turkey: Arkeoloji ve Sanat Yayınları, pp. 361–372.

Çilingiroğlu, A., Derin, Z., Abay, E., Sağlamtimur, H., and Kayan, I. 2004. *Ulucak Höyük: Excavations Conducted Between 1995 and 2002.* Louvain, Belgium: Peeters.

Clamagirand, A.-C. 2004. 'L'Apparition du phénomène religieux dans l'Anatolie Néolithique'. In O. Pelon, ed., *Studia Aegeo-Anatolica.* Lyon, France: Maison de L'Orient, pp. 119–148.

Cline, E. H. 1996. 'Assuwa and the Achaeans: The "Mycanean" sword at Hattusas and its possible implications'. *Annual of the British School at Athens* **91**:137–151.

Cohen, H. R. 1970. 'The palaeoecology of South Central Anatolia at the end of the Pleistocene and the beginning of the Holocene'. *Anatolian Studies* **20**:119–137.

Colledge, S. 2001. *Plant Exploitation on Epipalaeolithic and Early Neolithic Sites in the Levant.* Oxford, England: British Archaeological Reports International Series.

Colledge, S., and Conolly, J., eds., 2007. *The Origins and Spread of Domestic Plants in Southwest Asia and Europe.* Walnut Creek, CA: Left Coast Press.

Colledge, S., Conolly, J., and Shennan, S. 2004. 'Archaeobotanical evidence for the spread of farming in the Eastern Mediterranean'. *Current Anthropology* **45**(supplement): 35–58.

2005. 'The evolution of Neolithic farming from SW Asia origins to NW European limits'. *European Journal of Archaeology* **8**:137–156.

Conolly, J. 1996. 'The knapped stone'. In I. Hodder, ed., *On the Surface: Çatalhöyük 1993–95*. Cambridge, England: MacDonald Institute, pp. 173–198.

1999a. *The Çatalhöyük Flint and Obsidian Industry: Technology and Typology in Context*. Oxford, England: British Archaeological Reports International Series.

1999b. 'Technical strategies and technical change at Neolithic Çatalhöyük, Turkey'. *Antiquity* **73**:791–800.

2003. 'The Çatalhöyük obsidian hoards: A contextual analysis of technology'. In N. Moloney and M. J. Shott, eds., *Lithic Analysis at the Millennium*. London, England: Institute of Archaeology, pp. 55–78.

Coockson, B. C. 2008. 'The houses from Ilıpınar X and VI compared'. In J. Roodenberg and S. Alpaslan-Roodenberg, eds., *Life and Death in a Prehistoric Settlement in Northwest Anatolia: The Ilıpınar Excavations III, with Contributions on Hacılartepe and Menteşe*. Leiden: Nederlands Instituut voor het Nabije Oosten, pp. 149–204.

Cook, S. F., and Heizer, R. F. 1968. 'Relationship among houses, settlement areas, and population in Aboriginal California'. In K. C. Chang, ed., *Settlement Archaeology*. Palo Alto, CA: National Press Books, pp. 79–116.

Coqueugniot, E. 1998. 'L'Obsidienne en Méditerranée Orientale aux Époques posy-Néolithiques'. In M.-C. Cauvin, A. Gourgaud, B. Gratuze, N. Arnaud, G. Poupeau, J.-L. Poidevin, and C. Chataigner, eds., *L'Obsidienne au Proche et Moyen Orient: Du Volcan a l'Outil*. Oxford, England: British Archaeological Reports International Series, pp. 351–362.

Corbey, R., Layton, R., and Tanner, J. 2004. 'Archaeology and art'. In J. L. Bintliff ed., *Companion to Archaeology*. Oxford, England: Blackwell, pp. 357–379.

Coward, F., Shennan, S., Colledge, S., Conolly, J., and Collard, M. 2008. 'The spread of Neolithic plant economies from the Near East to northwest Europe: A phylogenetic approach'. *Journal of Archaeological Science* **35**:42–56.

Craig, O. E., Chapman, J., Heron, C., Willis, L. H., Bartosiewicz, L., Taylor, G., Whittle, A., and Collins, M. 2005. 'Did the first farmers of central and eastern Europe produce dairy foods?' *Antiquity* **79**:882–894.

Cribb, R. 1991. *Nomads in Archaeology*. Cambridge, England: Cambridge University Press.

Cutting, M. 2003. 'The use of spatial analysis to study Prehistoric settlement architecture'. *Oxford Journal of Archaeology* **22**:1–21.

2006. 'The architecture of Çatalhöyük: Continuity, households and the lost upper levels'. In I. Hodder, ed., *Çatalhöyük Perspectives: Themes from the 1995–1999 Seasons*. Cambridge, England: MacDonald Institute, pp. 151–170.

Czerniak, L., and Marciniak, A. 2003. 'The excavations of the TP (Team Poznan) Area in the 2003 season'. *Çatalhöyük Archive Reports*. Available at http://www.catalhoyuk.com/archive_reports/.

Davis, J. L. 2003. 'A foreign school of archaeology and the politics of archaeological practice: Anatolia, 1922'. *Journal of Mediterranean Archaeology* **16**/2:145–172.

Davis, P. H. 1965–1988. *Flora of Turkey and the East Aegean Islands: Volumes 1–10*. Edinburgh, Scotland: Edinburgh University Press.

De Cupere, B., and Duru, R. 2003. 'Faunal remains from Neolithic Höyücek (SW-Turkey) and the presence of early domestic cattle in Anatolia'. *Paleorient* **29**:107–120.

De Jesus, P. S. 1980. *The Development of Prehistoric Mining and Metallurgy in Anatolia.* Oxford, England: British Archaeology Reports.

    1985. 'Notes on the symbolism in the Çatal Hüyük wall paintings'. In J. L. Huot, M. Yon, and Y. Calvet, eds., *De l'Indus aux Balkans: Recueil a la mémoire de Jean Deshayes.* Paris, France: Centre National du Recherche Scientifique, pp. 127–145.

Delaporte, L. 1932. 'Grabung am Hashhüyük 1931'. *Archäologischer Anzeiger* **47**:230–233.

Dercksen, J. G. 2005. 'Metals according to documents from Kültepe-Kanish dating to the Old Assyrian colony period'. In Ü. Yalçın, ed., *Anatolian Metal III.* Bochum: Deutschen Bergbau-Museum, pp. 17–34.

Derin, Z. 2005. 'The neolithic architecture of Ulucak Höyük'. In, C. Lichter, ed., *How Did Farming Reach Europe? Anatolian–European Relations from the Second Half of the 7th through the First Half of the 6th Millennium BC.* Istanbul, Turkey: Ege Yayınları, pp. 85–94.

    2006. 'İzmir'den iki yeni prehistorik yerleşim yeri: Yassıtepe Höyüğü, Çakallar Tepesi Höyüğü'. *Ege Üniversitesi Arkeoloji Dergisi* **2006**/1:1–15.

    2007. 'Yeşilova Höyüğü'. In M. Özdoğan and N. Başgelen, eds., *Anadolu'da Uygarlığın Doğuşu Avrupaya Yayılımı Türkiye'de Neolitik Dönem, Yeni Kazılar, Yeni Bulgular.* Istanbul, Turkey: Arkeoloji ve Sanat Yayınları, pp. 377–384.

Dewdney, J. C. 1971. *Turkey.* London, England: Chatto and Windus.

Dickinson, O. T. P. K. 1994. *The Aegean Bronze Age.* Cambridge, England: Cambridge University Press.

Dietrich, B. C. 1967. 'Some light from the east on Cretan cult practice'. *Historia* **16**:385–413.

Doonan, O. 2004. *Sinop Landscapes: Exploring Connectivities in a Black Sea Hinterland.* Phildelphia: University of Pennsylvania Museum.

Doumas, C. 2008. 'The Aegean islands and their role in the development of civilisation'. In H. Erkanal, H. Hauptmann, V. Şahoğlu, and R. Tuncel, eds., *The Aegean in the Neolithic, Chalcolithic and Early Bronze Age.* Ankara, Turkey: Ankara Üniversitesi Basımevi, pp. 131–140.

Downs, E. F. 1995. 'Identification of archaeological blood proteins: A cautionary note'. *Journal of Archaeological Science* **22**:11–16.

Ducos, P. 1988. *Archaeozoologie quantitative: Les valeurs immediates à Çatal Hüyük.* Paris, France: Centre National du Recherche Scientifique.

Dunbar, R. 1992. 'Neocortex size as a constraint on group size in primates'. *Journal of Human Evolution* **22**:469–493.

Düring, B. S. 2001. 'Social dimensions in the architecture of Neolithic Çatalhöyük'. *Anatolian Studies* **51**:1–18.

    2002. 'Cultural dynamics of the Central Anatolian Neolithic: The Early Ceramic Neolithic – Late Ceramic Neolithic transition'. In F. Gérard and L. Thissen, eds., *The Neolithic of Central Anatolia: Internal Developments and External Relations during the 9th–6th Millennia cal. BC.* Istanbul, Turkey: Ege Yayınları, pp. 219–236.

    2003. 'Burials in context: The 1960s inhumations of Çatalhöyük East'. *Anatolian Studies* **53**:1–15.

    2005. 'Building continuity in the Central Anatolian Neolithic: Exploring the meaning of buildings at Aşıklı Höyük and Çatalhöyük'. *Journal of Mediterranean Archaeology* **18**:3–29.

2006. *Constructing Communities: Clustered Neighbourhood Settlements of the Central Anatolian Neolithic, ca. 8500–5500 Cal. BC*. Leiden: Nederlands Instituut voor het Nabije Oosten.

2007. 'Reconsidering the Çatalhöyük community: From households to settlement systems'. *Journal of Mediterranean Archaeology* **20**:155–182.

2008. 'The Early Holocene occupation of North-Central Anatolia between 10,000 and 6000 BC cal: Investigating an archaeological terra incognita'. *Anatolian Studies* **58**:15–46.

2009. 'Exploring building continuity in the Anatolian Neolithic: Functional and symbolic aspects'. In M. Bachmann, ed., *Bautechnik im antiken und vorantiken Kleinasien*. Istanbul, Turkey: Ege Yayınları, pp. 23–37.

Düring, B. S., and Marciniak, A. 2005. 'Households and communities in the central Anatolian Neolithic'. *Archaeological Dialogues* **12**:165–187.

Duru, G., and Özbaşaran, M. 2005. 'A "non-domestic" site in Central Anatolia'. *Anatolia Antiqua* **13**:15–28.

Duru, R. 1989. 'Were the earliest cultures at Hacılar really aceramic?' In K. Emre, M. Mellink, B. Hrouda, and N. Özgüç, eds., *Anatolia and the Ancient Near East: Studies in Honor of Tahsın Özgüç*. Ankara: Türk Tarih Kurumu Basımevi, pp. 99–106.

1994. *Kuruçay Höyük I: Results of the Excavations 1978–1988: The Neolithic and Early Chalcolithic Periods*. Ankara: Türk Tarih Kürümü Basımevi.

1995. 'Höyüçek kazıları 1991/1992'. *Belleten* **59**:447–476.

1996. *Kuruçay Höyük II: Results of the Excavations 1978–1988: The Late Chalcolithic and Early Bronze Age Settlements*. Ankara: Türk Tarih Kürümü Basımevi.

1999. 'The Neolithic of the Lake District'. In M. Özdoğan and N. Başgelen, eds., *The Neolithic of Turkey*. Istanbul, Turkey: Arkeoloji ve Sanat Yayınları, pp. 147–156.

2002. 'Bademağacı kazıları 2000 ve 2001 yılları çalısma raporu'. *Belleten* **66**:549–594.

2004. 'Excavations at Bademağacı: Preliminary report, 2002 and 2003'. *Belleten* **68**:540–560.

2007. 'Göller Bölgesi Neolitiği: Hacılar – Kuruçay Höyüğü – Höyücek – Bademağacı Höyüğü'. In M. Özdoğan and N. Başgelen, eds., *Anadolu'da Uygarlığın Doğuşu Avrupaya Yayılımı Türkiye'de Neolitik Dönem, Yeni Kazılar, Yeni Bulgular*. Istanbul, Turkey: Arkeoloji ve Sanat Yayınları, pp. 331–360.

2008. *From 8000 BC to 2000 BC: Six Thousand Years of the Burdur–Antalya Region*. Istanbul, Turkey: Suna-Inan Kirac Akdeniz Medeniyetleri Arastirma Enstitusu.

Easton, D. F. 1976. 'Towards a chronology for the Anatolian Early Bronze Age'. *Anatolian Studies* **26**:145–173.

1984. 'Priam's treasure'. *Anatolian Studies* **34**:141–169.

1992. 'Schliemanns Ausgrabungen in Troja'. In J. Cobet and B. Patzek, eds., *Archäologie und historische Erinnerung: Nach 100 Jahren Heinrich Schliemann*. Koblenz, Germany: Klartext, pp. 51–72.

Eastwood, W. J., Roberts, N., Lamb, H. F., and Tibby, J. C. 1999. 'Holocene environmental change in southwest Turkey: A palaeoecological record of lake and catchment-related changes'. *Quarternary Science Reviews* **18**:671–695.

Efe, T. 1987. *Demircihüyük: die Ergebnisse der Ausgrabungen, 1975–1978: Die frühbronzezeitliche Keramik der jüngeren Phasen (ab Phase H)*. Mainz am Rhein, Germany: Philipp von Zabern.

1990. 'An inland Anatolian site with pre-Vinča elements, Orman Fıdanlığı, Eskişehir: A re-examination of Balkan–Anatolian connections in the fifth millennium B.C'. *Germania* **68**:67–113.

2001. *The Salvage Excavations at Orman Fıdanlığı: A Chalcolithic Site in Inland Northwestern Anatolia*. Istanbul, Turkey: TASK.

2003. 'Küllüoba and the initial stages of urbanism in Western Anatolia'. In M. Özdoğan, H. Hauptmann, and N. Başgelen, eds., *Köyden Kente, Yakıdoğu'da ilk Yerleşimler – Ufuk Esin'e Armağan*. Istanbul, Turkey: Arkeoloji ve Sanat Yayınları, pp. 265–282.

2005. 'The neolithisation in inland nortwestern Anatolia'. In C. Lichter, ed., *How Did Farming Reach Europe? Anatolian–European Relations from the Second Half of the 7th through the First Half of the 6th Millennium BC*. Istanbul, Turkey: Ege Yayınları, pp. 107–115.

2006. 'Anatolische Wurzeln – Troia und die frühe Bronzezeit im Westen Kleinasiens'. In M. O. Korfmann, ed., *Troia: Archäologie eines Siedlungshügels und seiner Landschaft*. Main am Rhein, Germany: Philipp von Zabern, pp. 15–28.

Efe, T., and Ay-Efe, D. S. M.. 2001. 'Küllüoba: İç kuzeybatı Anadolu'da bir Ilk Tunç Çağı Kenti, 1996–2000 yılları arasında yapılan kazı çalışmalarının genel değerlendirmesi'. *Türkiye Bilimler Akademisi – Arkeoloji Degisi (TUBA-AR)* **4**:43–78.

2007. 'The Küllüoba excavations and the cultural/political development of western Anatolia before the second millennium BC'. In M. Alparslan, M. Doğan-Alparslan, and H. Peker, eds., *Bekis Dinçol ve Ali Dinçol'a Armağan*. Istanbul, Turkey: Ege Yayınları, pp. 251–267.

Efe, T., Ilaslı, A., and Topbaş, A. 1995. 'Salvage excavations of the Afyon Archaeological Museum, Part I: Kaklik Mevkii: A site transitional to the Early Bronze Age'. *Studia Troica* **5**:357–399.

Efstratiou, N., Karetsou, A., Banou, E. S., and Margomenou, D. 2004. 'The Neolithic settlement of Knossos: New light on an old picture'. In G. Cadogan, E. Hatzaki, and A. Vasilakis, eds., *Knossos: Palace, City, State*. Athens, Greece: British School at Athens, pp. 39–49.

Eiland, M. L. 1993. 'The past re-made: The case of oriental carpets'. *Antiquity* **67**:859–863.

Eimermann, E. 2008. 'Soundings at Early Bronze Age Hacılartepe: Stratigraphy, pottery tradition and chronology'. In J. Roodenberg and S. Alpaslan Roodenberg, eds., *Life and Death in a Prehistoric Settlement in Northwest Anatolia: The Ilıpınar Excavations III*. Leiden: Nederlands Instituut voor het Nabije Oosten, pp. 361–417.

Ellen, R. 1986. 'Microcosm, macrocosm and the Nuaulu house: Concerning the reductionist fallacy as applied to methaporical levels'. *Bijdragen tot de Taal – Land – en Volkenkunde* **142**:1–30.

Emberling, G. 2003. 'Urban social transformations and the problem of the "first city": New research from Mesopotamia'. In M. L. Smith, ed., *The Social Construction of Ancient Cities*. Washington, DC, and London, England: Smithsonian Books, pp. 254–268.

Ercan, T., Şaroğlu, F., and Kuşçu, I. 1994. 'Features of obsidian beds formed by volcanic activity in Anatolia since 25 million years BP'. In S. Demirçi, A. M. Özer, and G. D. Summers, eds., *Archaeometry 94: The Proceedings of the 29th*

International Symposium on Archaeometry. Ankara, Turkey: Tübitak, pp. 505–513.

Ercan, T., Yegingil, Z., Bigazzi, G., Öddöne, M., and Özdoğan, M. 1990. 'Kuzeybatı Anadolu obsidiyen buluntularını kaynak belirme çalışmaları'. *Jeoloji Mühendisliği* **36**:19–32.

Erciyas, D. B. 2005. 'Ethnic identity and archaeology in the Black Sea region of Turkey'. *Antiquity* **79**:179–190.

Erdoğu, B. 2007. 'West Mound: Trench 8'. *Çatalhöyük Archive Reports* 132–142. Available at http://www.catalhoyuk.com/archive_reports/.

Erdoğu, B., and Fazlıoğlu, I. 2006. 'The Central Anatolian salt project: A preliminary report on the 2004 and 2005 surveys'. *Anatolia Antiqua* **14**:189–203.

Erdoğu, B., and Kayacan, N. 2004. 'Drive into the White Lake: 2003 field survey in the Tuz Gölü region of Central Anatolia'. *Anatolia Antiqua* **12**:217–226.

Erdoğu, B., Özbaşaran, M., Erdoğu, R., and Chapman, J. 2003a. 'Prehistoric salt exploitation in Tuz Gölü, Central Anatolia: Preliminary investigations'. *Anatolia Antiqua* **9**:11–20.

Erdoğu, B., Tanindi, O., and Uygun, D. 2003b. *The 14C Database of Archaeological Settlements in Turkey*. Istanbul, Turkey: Ege Yayınları.

Eres, Z. 2003. 'Die Hüttenlehmreste von Aşağı Pınar'. In N. Karul, Z. Eres, M. Özdoğan, and H. Parzinger, eds., *Aşağı Pınar I: Einführung, Forschungsgeschichte, Stratigraphie und Archiktektur*. Mainz am Rhein, Germany: Philipp von Zabern, pp. 126–142.

Erkanal, H. 2008. 'Liman Tepe: A new light on Prehistoric Aegean cultures'. In H. Erkanal, H. Hauptmann, V. Şahoğlu, and R. Tuncel, eds., *The Aegean in the Neolithic, Chalcolithic and Early Bronze Age*. Ankara, Turkey: Ankara Üniversitesi Basımevi, pp. 179–190.

Erol, O. 1983. *Die naturräumliche Gliederung der Türkei*. Wiesbaden, Germany: Dr. Ludwig Reichert Verlag.

Esin, U. 1993a. '19. Yüzyıl Sonlarında Heinrich Schliemann'ın Troja Kazıları'. In Z. Rona, ed., *Osman Hamdi Bey ve Dönemi*. Istanbul, Turkey: Tarih Vakfı Yurt Yayınları, pp. 179–191.

1993b. 'Gelveri – Ein Beispiel für die kulturellen Beziehungen zwischen Zentralanatolien und Südosteuropa während des Chalkolithikums'. *Anatolica* **19**:47–56.

1995. 'Early copper metallurgy at the Pre-Pottery site of Aşıklı'. In H. Çambel, ed., *Readings in Prehistory: Studies Presented to Halet Çambel*. Istanbul, Turkey: Graphics Yayınları, pp. 61–77.

1998. 'The Aceramic site of Aşıklı and its ecological conditions based on its floral and faunal remains'. *Türkiye Bilimler Akademisi – Arkeoloji Dergisi (TUBA-AR)* **1**:63–94.

1999. 'Introduction: The Neolithic in Turkey: A general review'. In M. Özdoğan and N. Başgelen, eds., *The Neolithic of Turkey*. Istanbul, Turkey: Arkeoloji ve Sanat Yayınları, pp. 13–23.

Esin, U., and Benedict, P. 1963. 'Recent developments in the prehistory of Anatolia'. *Current Anthropology* **4**:339–346.

Esin, U., Bıçakçı, E., Özbaşaran, M., Balkan-Atlı, N., Berker, D., Yağmur, I., and Korkut-Ali, A. 1991. 'Salvage excavations at the Pre-Pottery Neolithic site of Aşıklı Höyük in Central Anatolia'. *Anatolica* **17**:123–174.

Esin, U., and Harmankaya, S. 1999. 'Aşıklı'. In M. Özdoğan and N. Başgelen, eds., *The Neolithic of Turkey*. Istanbul, Turkey: Arkeoloji ve Sanat Yayınları, pp. 115–132.

  2007. 'Aşıklı Höyük'. In M. Özdoğan and N. Başgelen, eds., *Anadolu'da Uygarlığın Doğuşu Avrupaya Yayılımı Türkiye'de Neolitik Dönem, Yeni Kazılar, Yeni Bulgular*. Istanbul, Turkey: Arkeoloji ve Sanat Yayınları, pp. 255–272.

Eslick, C. 1980. 'Middle Chalcolithic pottery from southwestern Anatolia'. *American Journal of Archaeology* **84**:5–14.

  1992. *Elmalı – Karataş I: The Neolithic and Chalcolithic Periods, Bağbaşı and Other Sites*. Bryn Mawr, PA: Bryn Mawr Archaeological Monographs.

Evans, J. D. 1964. 'Excavations in the Neolithic settlement of Knossos, 1957–1960'. *Annual of the British School at Athens* **59**:233–245.

Evershed, R. P., Payne, S., Sherratt, A. G., Copley, M. S., Coolidge, J., Urem-Kotsu, D., Kotsakis, K., Özdoğan, M., Özdoğan, A., Nieuwenhuyse, O., Akkermans, P. M. M. G., Bailey, D., Andeescu, R. R., Campbell, S., Farid, S., Hodder, I., Yalman, N., Özbasaran, M., Bıçakcı, E., Garfinkel, Y., Levy, T., and Burton, M. M. 2008. 'Earliest date for milk use in the Near East and southeastern Europe linked to cattle herding'. *Nature* **07180**:1–4.

Facey, W. 1997. *Back to Earth: Adobe Building in Saudi Arabia*. London, England: Al-Turath.

Fairbarn, A., Asouti, E., Near, J., and Martinoli, D. 2002. 'Macro-botanical evidence for plant use at Neolithic Çatalhöyük, south-central Anatolia, Turkey'. *Vegetation History and Archaeobotany* **11**:41–54.

Fairbarn, A., Near, J., and Martinoli, D. 2005. 'Macrobotanical investigations of the North, South and KOPAL Area excavations at Çatalhöyük East'. In I. Hodder, ed., *Inhabiting Çatalhöyük: Reports from the 1995–1999 Seasons*. Cambridge, England: MacDonald Institute, pp. 137–201.

Farid, S. 2007a. 'Introduction to the South Area excavations'. In I. Hodder, ed., *Excavating Çatalhöyük, South, North and KOPAL Area: Reports from the 1995–1999 Seasons*. Cambridge, England: MacDonald Institute, pp. 41–58.

  2007b. 'Level IX relative heights, Building 2, Buildings 22 and 16 and Building 17'. In I. Hodder, ed., *Excavating Çatalhöyük, South, North and KOPAL Area: Reports from the 1995–1999 Seasons*. Cambridge, England: MacDonald Institute, pp. 139–226.

Feblot-Augustins, J. 1993. 'Mobility strategies in the Late Middle Palaeolithic of Central and Western Europe: Elements of stability and variation'. *Journal of Anthropological Archaeology* **12**:211–265.

Fiorentino, G. 2004. 'The botanical view of food and landscape at Yumuktepe'. In I. Caneva and V. Sevin, eds., *Mersin-Yumuktepe: A Reppraisal*. Lecce, Italy: Congedo Editore, pp. 159–161.

Flannery, K. V. 1994. 'Childe the evolutionist: A perspective from nuclear America'. In D. R. Harris, ed., *The Archaeology of V. Gordon Childe*. Chicago: University of Chicago Press, pp. 101–120.

Flemming, N. C. 1978. 'Holocene eustatic changes and coastal tectonics in the northeast Mediterranean: Implications for models of crustal consumption'. *Philosophical Transactions of the Royal Society of London. Series A, Mathematical and Physical Sciences* **289**:405–458.

Fontijn, D. 2002. *Sacrificial Landscapes: Cultural Biographies of Persons, Objects and 'Natural' Places in the Bronze Age of the Southern Netherlands, c. 2300–600 BC.* Leiden, the Netherlands: Leiden University.

Forest, J. D. 1993. 'Çatal Hüyük et son décor: Pour le dechiffrement d'une code symbolique'. *Anatolia Antiqua* 2:1–42.

Forge, A. 1972. 'Normative factors in the settlement size of Neolithic cultivators (New Guinea)'. In P. J. Ucko, R. Tringham, and G. W. Dimbledy, eds., *Man, Settlement and Urbanism*. London, England: Duckworth, pp. 363–376.

Frame, S. 2001. 'West Mound: 2001 animal bone report'. *Çatalhöyük Archive Reports.* Available at http://www.catalhoyuk.com/archive_reports/.

Frangipane, M. 2001a. 'Centralization processes in greater Mesopotamia: Uruk "expansion" as the climax of systemic interactions among areas of the greater Mesopotamian region'. In M. S. Rothman, ed., *Uruk Mesopotamia and Its Neighbours: Cross-Cultural Interactions in the Era of State Formation.* Santa Fe, NM: School of American Research Press, pp. 307–348.

2001b. 'The transition between the two opposing forms of power at Arslantepe (Malatya) at the beginning of the 3rd millennium BC'. *Türkiye Bilimler Akademisi – Arkeoloji Dergisi (TUBA-AR)* 4:1–24.

Frankfort, H. 1970 [1954]. *The Art and Architecture of the Ancient Orient.* Harmondsworth, England: Penguin Books.

Franz, I. 2007. 'Pottery [West Mound]'. *Çatalhöyük Archive Reports* 129–131. Available at http://www.catalhoyuk.com/archive_reports/.

French, D. 1962. 'Excavations at Can Hasan: First preliminary report, 1961'. *Anatolian Studies* 12:27–40.

1966. 'Excavations at Can Hasan: Fifth preliminary report, 1965'. *Anatolian Studies* 16:113–123.

1967a. 'Excavations at Can Hasan: Sixth preliminary report, 1966'. *Anatolian Studies* 17:165–178.

1967b. 'Prehistoric sites in northwestern Anatolia, I: The Iznik area'. *Anatolian Studies* 17:49–100.

1968. 'Excavations at Can Hasan: Seventh preliminary report, 1967'. *Anatolian Studies* 18:45–54.

1970a. 'Can Hasan'. *Türk Arkeoloji Dergisi* 19:39–44.

1970b. 'Notes on the sites distribution in the Çumra area'. *Anatolian Studies* 20:139–148.

1998. *Canhasan Sites 1: Stratigraphy and Structures.* London, England: British Institute at Ankara.

2005. *Canhasan Sites 2, Canhasan I: The Pottery.* London, England: British Institute at Ankara.

French, D., Hillman, G. C., Payne, S., and Payne, R. J. 1972. 'Excavations at Can Hasan III, 1969–1970'. In E. S. Higgs, ed., *Papers in Economic Prehistory.* Cambridge, England: Cambridge University Press, pp. 181–190.

Friedl, E., and Loeffler, A. G. 1994. 'The ups and downs of dwellings in a village in west Iran: The history of two compounds'. *Archiv für Völkerkünde* 48:1–44.

Gabriel, U. 2000. 'Mitteilungen zum Stand der Neolithikumsforschung in der Umgebung von Troia'. *Studia Troica* 10:233–238.

2006. 'Ein Blick zurück – Das funfte Jahrtausend vor Christus in der Troas'. In M. O. Korfmann, ed., *Troia: Archäologie eines Siedlungshügels und seiner Landschaft.* Mainz am Rhein, Germany: Philipp von Zabern, pp. 355–360.

Gabriel, U., Aslan, R., and Blum, S. W. E. 2004. 'Alacaligöl: Eine neuentdeckte Siedlung des 5. Jahrtausend v. Chr. in der Troas'. *Studia Troica* **14**:121–133.

Gale, N. 2008. 'Metal sources for Early Bronze Age Troy and the Aegean'. In H. Erkanal, H. Hauptmann, V. Şahoğlu, and R. Tuncel, eds., *The Aegean in the Neolithic, Chalcolithic and Early Bronze Age*. Ankara, Turkey: Ankara Üniversitesi Basımevi, pp. 203–222.

Garasanin, M. 2000. 'Zum begriff des Balkanisch-Anatolischen Komplexes des Späten Neolithikums'. In S. Hiller and V. Nikolov, eds., *Karanovo III: Beiträge zum Neolithikum in Südosteuropa*. Wien, Austria: Phoibos Verlag, pp. 343–347.

Garfinkel, Y. 1998. 'Dancing and the beginning of art scenes in the early village communities of the Near East and southeast Europe'. *Cambridge Archaeological Journal* **8**:207–237.

Garstang, J. 1953. *Prehistoric Mersin, Yümük Tepe in Southern Turkey: The Neilson Expedition in Cilicia*. Oxford, England: Clarendon Press.

Gatsov, I. 2001. 'Epipalaeolithic/Mesolithic, Neolithic periods chipped-stone assemblages from southern Bulgaria and northwest Turkey: Similarities and differences'. *Türkiye Bilimler Akademisi – Arkeoloji Dergisi (TUBA-AR)* **4**:101–112.

2003a. 'Chipped stone assemblages from Pendik: Technological and typological analysis'. In M. Özdoğan, H. Hauptmann, and N. Başgelen, eds., *Köyden Kente, Yakındoğu'da ilk Yerleşimler – Ufuk Esin'e Armağan*. Istanbul, Turkey: Arkeoloji ve Sanat Yayınları, pp. 283–292.

2003b. 'The latest results from the technological and typological analysis of chipped stone assemblages from Ilıpınar, Pendik, Fikirtepe and Menteşe, NW Turkey'. *Documenta Praehistorica* **30**:153–158.

2008. 'Chipped stone assemblages from Ilıpınar, Part 1: A techno-typological study'. In J. Roodenberg and S. Alpaslan-Roodenberg, eds., *Life and Death in a Prehistoric Settlement in Northwest Anatolia: The Ilıpınar Excavations III, with Contributions on Hacılartepe and Menteşe*. Leiden: Nederlands Instituut voor het Nabije Oosten, pp. 227–268.

Gatsov, I., and Özdoğan, M. 1994. 'Some Epipalaeolithic sites from NW Turkey: Ağaçlı, Domali, and Gümüsdere'. *Anatolica* **20**:97–120.

Gatsov, I., and Schwarzberg, H., eds. 2006. *Aegean, Marmara, Black Sea: The Present State of Research on the Early Neolithic*. Langenweissbach, Germany: Beier and Beran.

Gell, A. 1992. *The Anthropology of Time: Cultural Constructions of Temporal Maps and Images*. Oxford, England: Berg.

Georgiadis, M. 2008. 'The obsidian in the Aegean beyond Melos: An outlook from Yali'. *Oxford Journal of Archaeology* **27**:101–118.

Gérard, F. 2001. 'Stratigraphy and architecture on the southwest flank of Ilıpınar'. In J. Roodenberg and L. Thissen, eds., *The Ilıpınar Excavations II*. Leiden: Nederlands Instituut voor het Nabije Oosten, pp. 177–221.

2002. 'Transformations and societies in the Neolithic of Central Anatolia'. In F. Gérard and L. Thissen, eds., *The Neolithic of Central Anatolia: Internal Developments and External Relations during the 9th–6th Millennia cal. BC*. Istanbul, Turkey: Ege Yayınları, pp. 105–117.

Gérard, F., and Thissen, L., eds. 2002. *The Neolithic of Central Anatolia: Internal Developments and External Relations during the 9th–6th Millennia cal. BC*. Istanbul, Turkey: Ege Yayınları.

Gerber, C. 2006. 'Zur Stratigraphie der Fürstengräber von Alaca Höyük: Neue Einsichten in ein altes Problem'. In A. Erkanal-Öktü, E. Özgen, S. Günel, A. Tuba Ökse, H. Hüryılmaz, H. Tekin, N. Çınardalı-Karaaslan, B. Uysal, F. A. Karaduman, A. Engin, R. Spieß, A. Aykurt, R. Tuncel, U. Deniz, and A. Rennie, eds. *Studies in Honor of Hayat Erkanal: Cultural Reflections*. Istanbul, Turkey: Homer, pp. 379–388.

Gibson, C., and Last, J. 2003. 'West Mound excavations'. *Çatalhöyük Archive Reports*. Available at http://www.catalhoyuk.com/archive_reports/.

Gibson, C., Last, J., Raszick, T., and Frame, S. 2002. 'Çatalhöyük West mound study season 2002'. *Çatalhöyük Archive Reports*. Available at http://www.catalhoyuk .com/archive_reports/.

Gillespie, S. D. 2000. 'Maya "nested houses": The ritual construction of place'. In R. A. Joyce and A. S. Gillespie, eds., *Beyond Kinship: Social and Material Reproduction in House Societies*. Philadelphia: University of Pennsylvania Press, pp. 135–160.

Gimbutas, M. 1991. *The Civilization of the Goddess: The World of Old Europe*. San Francisco: Harper.

Godon, M. 2005. 'New results and remarks about Neolithic pottery in Central Anatolia: A view from Tepecik-Çiftlik'. *Colloquium Anatolicum* 4:91–103.

Goffart, W. A. 2006. *Barbarian Tides: The Migration Age and the Later Roman Empire*. Philadelphia: University of Pennsylvania Press.

Gökçek, L. G. 2006. 'The use of wagons (eriqqum) in ancient Anatolia according to the texts from Kültepe'. *Zeitschrift für Assyriologie und Vorderasiatischen Archäologie* **96**:185–199.

Göktürk, E. H., Hillegonds, D. J., Lipschutz, M. E., and Hodder, I. 2002. 'Accelerator mass spectrometry dating at Çatalhöyük'. *Radiochimica Acta* **90**:407–410.

Goldman, H. 1956. *Excavations at Gözlü Kule, Tarsus II: From the Neolithic through the Bronze Age*. Princeton, NJ: Princeton University Press.

Goodman, M. 1999. 'Temporalities of prehistoric life: Household development and community continuity'. In J. Brück and M. Goodman, eds., *Making Places in the Prehistoric World*. London, England: University College London Press, pp. 145–159.

Gorny, R. L. 1996. 'Viticulture and ancient Anatolia'. In P. E. McGovern, S. J. Flemming, and S. H. Katz, eds., *The Origins and Ancient History of Wine*. Amsterdam, the Netherlands: Gordon and Breach, pp. 133–174.

Görsdorf, J. 2005. '14C-Datierungen aus Aşağı Pınar'. In H. Parzinger and H. Schwarzberg, eds., *Aşağı Pınar II, Die mittel – und spätneolithische Keramik*. Mainz am Rhein, Germany: Philipp von Zabern, pp. 417–422.

Gourichon, L., and Helmer, D. 2008. 'Etude de la faune neolithique de Menteşe'. In J. Roodenberg and S. Alpaslan-Roodenberg, eds., *Life and Death in a Prehistoric Settlement in Northwest Anatolia: The Ilıpınar Excavations III, with Contributions on Hacılartepe and Menteşe*. Leiden: Nederlands Instituut voor het Nabije Oosten, pp. 435–448.

Govedarica, B. 2002. 'Die Majkop-Kultur zwischen Europa und Asien: Zur Entstehung einer Hochkultur im Nordkaukasus während des 4. Jts v. Chr'. In R. Aslan, S. Blum, G. Kastl, F. Schweizer, and D. Thumm, eds., *Mauerschau: Festschrift für Manfred Korfmann*. Remshalden-Grunbach, Germany: Bernhard Albert Greiner, pp. 781–797.

Gratuze, B. 1999. 'Obsidian characterization by laser ablation ICP-MS and its application to Prehistoric trade in the Mediterranean and the Near East: Sources and distribution of obsidian within the Aegean and Anatolia'. *Journal of Archaeological Science* **26**:869–881.

Gratuze, B., Barrandon, J. N., Al Isa, M., and Cauvin, M.-C. 1994. 'Nondestructive analysis of obsidian artifacts using nuclear techniques: Investigation of the provenance of Near Eastern artifacts'. *Archaeometry* **35**:1–11.

Gülçür, S. 1995. 'Some unknown aspects of Western Cappadocia: Results of the 1993 survey'. In G. Arsebük, M. J. Mellink, and W. Schirmer, eds., *Readings in Prehistory: Studies Presented to Halet Çambel*. Istanbul, Turkey: Graphis Yayınları, pp. 149–174.

1997. 'Güvercinkayası; Eine vorgeschichtliche Felsrückensiedlung in Zentralanatolien'. *Anatolica* **23**:85–110.

2000. 'Norşuntepe: Die chalcolithische Keramik (Elazığ/Ostanatolien)'. In C. Marro and H. Hauptmann, eds., *Chronologies des pays du Caucase et de l'Euphrate aux IVe – IIIe millenaires*. Paris, France: De Boccard, pp. 375–418.

2004. 'Güvercinkayası: The black burnished pottery: A general overview'. *Türkiye Bilimler Akademisi – Arkeoloji Dergisi (TUBA-AR)* **7**:141–164.

Gülçur, S., and Firat, C. 2005. 'Spatial analysis of Güvercinkayası, a Middle Chalcolithic hilltop settlement in northwestern Cappadocia: A preliminary report'. *Anatolia Antiqua* **13**:41–52.

Güldoğan, E. 2003. 'Aşıklı Höyük sürtmetaş endüstrisi buluntulaından bir grup (öğütücü ve ezici aletler)'. In M. Özdoğan, H. Hauptmann, and N. Başgelen, eds., *Köyden kente, Yakıdoğu'da ilk yerleşimler – Ufuk Esin'e Armağan*. Istanbul, Turkey: Arkeoloji ve Sanat Yayınları, pp. 415–427.

Günel, S. 2006a. 'New contributions to Western Anatolian cultural history: Aydin region survey project'. *Prähistorische Zeitschrift* **81**:153–174.

2006b. 'Çine-Tepecik Höyüğü 2004 yılı kazıları'. *Kazı Sonuçları Toplantisi* **27**/1:19–28.

2007. 'Çine-Tepecik Höyüğü 2005 yılı kazıları'. *Kazı Sonuçları Toplantisi* **28**/1:231–246.

2008. 'Çine-Tepecik Höyük 2006 yılı kazıları'. *Kazı Sonuçları Toplantisi* **29**/1:73–90.

Gürkan, G., and Seeher, J. 1991. 'Die frühbronzezeitlichen Nekropole vom Küçükhüyük bei Bozüyük'. *Istanbuler Mitteilungen* **41**:39–96.

Gürsan-Salzmann, A. 1992. 'Alaca Hoyuk: A reassessment of the excavation and sequence of the Early Bronze Age settlement'. Unpublished PhD thesis, University of Pennsylvania.

Güterbock, H. G. 1969. 'Ein neues Bruchstück der Sargon-Erzählung <<König der Schlacht>>'. *Mitteilungen der Deutschen Orientgesellschaft* **101**:14–26.

Hakyemez, H. Y., Erkal, T., and Göktas, F. 1999. 'Quarternary evolution of the Gediz and Büyük Menderes grabens, western Anatolia, Turkey'. *Quarternary Science Reviews* **18**/1:549–554.

Hall, M. E., and Steadman, S. R. 1991. 'Tin and Anatolia: Another look'. *Journal of Mediterranean Archaeology* **4**/1:217–234.

Halstead, P. 1999. 'Neighbours from hell? The household in Neolithic Greece'. In P. Halstead, ed., *Neolithic Society in Greece*. Sheffield, England: Sheffield University Press, pp. 77–95.

Hamilton, N. 1996. 'Figurines, clay balls, small finds and burials'. In I. Hodder, ed., *On the Surface: Çatalhöyük 1993–5*. Cambridge, England: MacDonald Institute, pp. 215–264.

1998. 'Re-thinking burial and society at Çatalhöyük'. *Neo-Lithics* **1998**/3:7–8.

2005a. 'The figurines'. In I. Hodder, ed., *Changing Materialities at Çatalhöyük: Reports from the 1995–1999 Seasons*. Cambridge, England: MacDonald Institute, pp. 187–214.

2005b. 'The beads'. In I. Hodder, ed., *Changing Materialities at Çatalhöyük: Reports from the 1995–1999 Seasons*. Cambridge, England: MacDonald Institute, pp. 325–332.

2005c. 'Social aspects of burial'. In I. Hodder, ed., *Inhabiting Çatalhöyük: Reports from the 1995–1999 Seasons*. Cambridge, England: MacDonald Institute, pp. 301–306.

Harding, A. F. 2000. *European Societies in the Bronze Age*. Cambridge, England: Cambridge University Press.

Harmankaya, S. 1983. 'Pendik kazısı 1981'. *Kazı Sonuçları Toplantısı* **4**:25–30.

Harmankaya, S., and Erdoğu, B. 2002. *Türkiye Arkeolojik Yerleşmeleri 4: Ilk Tünç*. Istanbul, Turkey: TASK.

Harris, D. R. 2002. 'The expansion capacity of early agricultural systems: A comparative perspective on the spread of agriculture'. In P. Bellwood and C. Renfrew, eds., *Examining the Farming/Language Dispersal Hypothesis*. Cambridge, England: MacDonald Institute, pp. 31–39.

Hauptmann, H. 1969. 'Die Grabungen in der prähistorischen Siedlung auf Yarıkkaya'. In K. Bittel, ed., *Boğazköy IV: Funde aus den Grabungen 1967 und 1968*. Berlin, Germany: Gebr. Mann Verlag, pp. 66–69.

1993. 'Ein Kultgebäude in Nevali Çori'. In M. Frangipane, H. Hauptmann, M. Liverani, P. Matthiae, and M. Mellink, eds., *Between the Rivers and Over the Mountains: Archaeologica Anatolica et Mesopotamica, Alba Palmieri Dedicata*. Rome, Italy: Universita di Roma 'La Sapienza', pp. 37–69.

1999. 'The Urfa region'. In M. Özdoğan and N. Başgelen, eds., *Neolithic in Turkey*. Istanbul, Turkey: Arkeoloji ve Sanat Yayınları, pp. 65–86.

Hayden, B. 1990. 'Nimrods, piscators, pluckers, and planters: The emergence of food production'. *Journal of Anthropological Archaeology* **9**:31–69.

Heinrich, E., and Seidl, U. 1969. 'Zur Siedlungsform von Çatal Hüyük'. *Archäologischer Anzeiger* **84**:113–119.

Helbaek, H. 1963. 'Textiles from Çatal Hüyük'. *Archaeology* **16**:39–46.

1964. 'First impressions of the Çatal Hüyük plant husbandry'. *Anatolian Studies* **14**:120–123.

1970. 'The palaeoethnobotany'. In J. Mellaart, ed., *Excavations at Hacılar*. Edinburgh, Scotland: Edinburgh University Press, pp. 188–242.

Henrickson, E. F., and Thuessen, I., eds. 1989. *Upon This Foundation: The 'Ubaid' Reconsidered*. Copenhagen, Denmark: Carsten Nieburh Institute.

Henry, D. O. 1989. *From Foraging to Agriculture: The Levant at the End of the Ice Age*. Philadelphia: University of Pennsylvania Press.

Herling, L., Kasper, K., Lichter, C., and Meriç, R. 2008. 'Im Westen nichts Neues? Ergebnisse der Grabungen 2003 und 2004 in Dedecik-Heybelitepe'. *Istanbuler Mitteilungen* **58**:13–65.

Hiebert, F. T., Ballard, R. D., Coleman, F. D., Ward, C., Torre, F., Miller, N., and Woods, W. 2002. 'Deepwater archaeology of the Black Sea'. *Türkiye Bilimler Akademisi – Arkeoloji Dergisi (TUBA-AR)* **5**:95–117.

Higgs, E. S., and Jarman, M. R. 1972. 'The origins of animal and plant husbandry'. In E. S. Higgs, ed., *Papers in Economic Prehistory*. Cambridge, England: Cambridge University Press, pp. 3–13.

Hillman, G. 1978. 'On the origin of domestic rye, *Secale cereale*: The finds from Aceramic Can Hasan III in Turkey'. *Anatolian Studies* **28**:157–174.

——— 1996. 'Late Pleistocene changes in wild plant foods available to hunter-gatherers of the northern Fertile Crescent: Possible preludes to cereal cultivation'. In D. R. Harris, ed., *The Origins and Spread of Agriculture and Pastoralism in Eurasia*. London, England: University College London Press, pp. 159–203.

Hodder, I. 1982. 'Theoretical archaeology: A reactionairy view'. In I. Hodder, ed., *Symbolic and Structural Archaeology*. Cambridge, England: Cambridge University Press, pp. 1–16.

——— 1987. 'Contextual archaeology: An interpretation of Çatal Hüyük and a discussion of the origins of agriculture'. *Bulletin of the Institute of Archaeology of the University of London* **24**:43–56.

——— 1990. *The Domestication of Europe: Structure and Contingency in Neolithic Societies*. Oxford, England: Blackwell.

——— 1998. 'Çatalhöyük, Turkey: A summary of some recent results'. *Documenta Praehistorica* **25**:71–80.

——— 2004. 'Women and men at Çatalhöyük'. *Scientific American* **290**:66–73.

——— 2005. 'Peopling Çatalhöyük and its landscape'. In I. Hodder, ed., *Inhabiting Çatalhöyük: Reports from the 1995–1999 Seasons*. Cambridge, England: MacDonald Institute, pp. 1–30.

——— 2006a. *The Leopard's Tale: Revealing the Mysteries of Çatalhöyük*. London, England: Thames and Hudson.

——— 2006b. 'Memory'. In I. Hodder, ed., *Çatalhöyük Perspectives: Themes from the 1995–1999 Seasons*. Cambridge, England: MacDonald Institute, pp. 183–196.

——— 2009. 'Upper stories at Çatalhöyük'. *Anatolian Archaeology* **15**:19–20.

Hodder, I., and Cessford, C. 2004. 'Daily practice and social memory at Çatalhöyük'. *American Antiquity* **69**:17–40.

Hole, F. 2000. 'Is size important? Function and hierarchy in Neolithic settlements'. In I. Kuijt, ed., *Life in Neolithic Farming Communities: Social Organization, Identity, and Differentiation*. New York: Kluwer Academic, pp. 191–209.

——— 2004. 'Nature's role in the origins of agriculture'. *Türkiye Bilimler Akademisi – Arkeoloji Dergisi (TUBA-AR)* **7**:13–19.

Hood, S. 1981. *Excavations in Chios 1938–1955: Prehistoric Emporio and Ayio Gala I*. London, England: British School of Archaeology at Athens/Thames and Hudson.

Horne, L. 1994. *Village Spaces: Settlement and Society in Northeastern Iran*. Washington, DC, and London, England: Smithsonian Institute Press.

Hütteroth, W.-D. 1968. *Ländliche Siedlungen im südlichen Inneranatolien in den letzten vierhundert Jahren*. Göttingen, Germany: Geographisches Institut des Universitäts Göttingen.

——— 1982. *Türkei*. Darmstadt, Germany: Wissenschaftliche Buchgesellschaft Darmstadt.

Ilhan, E. 1971a. 'The structural features of Turkey'. In A. S. Campbell, ed., *Geology and History of Turkey*. Tripoli, Italy: Petroleum Exploration Society of Libya, pp. 159–170.

——— 1971b. 'Earthquakes in Turkey'. In A. S. Campbell, ed., *Geology and History of Turkey*. Tripoli, Italy: Petroleum Exploration Society of Libya, pp. 431–442.

Isbell, W. H. 2000. 'The "imagined community" and the "natural community"'. In M. A. Canuto and J. Yaeger, eds., *The Archaeology of Communities: A New World Perspective*. London, England: Routledge, pp. 243–266.

Jablonka, P. 2003. 'The link between the Black Sea and the Mediterranean since the end of the last Ice Age: Archaeology and geology'. In G. A. Wagner, E. Penicka, and H.-P. Uerpmann, eds., *Troia and the Troad: Scientific Approaches*. Berlin, Germany: Springer, pp. 77–94.

Johnson, G. A. 1982. 'Organizational structure and scalar stress'. In C. Renfrew, M. Rowlands, and B. Segraves, eds., *Theory and Explanation in Archaeology: The Southampton Conference*. New York: Academic, pp. 389–421.

Joukowsky, M. S. 1986. *Prehistoric Aphrodisias I: An Account of the Excavation and Artefact Studies*. Providence, RI: Brown University Press.

   1996. *Early Turkey: An Introduction to the Archaeology of Anatolia from Prehistory through the Lydian Period*. Dubuque, IA: Kendall Hunt.

Kamil, T. 1982. *Yortan Cemetery in the Early Bronze Age of Western Anatolia*. Oxford, England: British Archaeological Reports International Series.

Kansu, S. A. 1944. 'Anadoluda Mezolitik Kültür Buluntuları'. *Dil ve Tarih-Coğrafya Fakültesi Dergisi* 2/5:673–683.

   1945. 'Isparta, Burdur Illeri Çevresinde T. T. K. Adına 1944 Haziranında Yapılan Prehistorya Araştırmalarına Dair ilk Raporu'. *Belleten* 9:277–287.

   1947. 'Stone Age Cultures in Turkey'. *American Journal of Archaeology* 51/3:227–232.

   1963. 'Marmara bölgesi ve Trakya'da Prehistorik Iskan bakımından araştırmalar'. *Belleten* 27:657–705.

Kansu, S. A., and Ozansoy, F. 1948. 'Ankara Cıvarında Paleolitik Yeni Buluntular'. *Türk Tarih Kongresi* 4:381–390.

Kaptan, E. 1986. 'Ancient mining in the Tokat Province, Anatolia: New finds'. *Anatolica* 13:19–36.

   1995. 'Tin and ancient mining in Turkey'. *Anatolica* 21:197–203.

Karajian, H. A. 1920. *Mineral Resources of Armenia and Anatolia*. New York: Armen Technical Books.

Kartal, M. 2003. 'Anatolian Epi-Paleolithic period assemblages: Problems, suggestions, evaluations and various approaches'. *Anadolu (Ankara Üniversitesi Dil ve Tarih-Coğrafya Fakültesi Arkeoloji Bölümü Dergisi)* 24:45–61.

Karul, N. 2003. 'Die Architektur von Aşağı Pınar'. In N. Karul, Z. Eres, M. Özdoğan, and H. Parzinger, eds., *Aşağı Pınar I, Einführung, Forschungsgeschichte, Stratigraphie und Architektur*. Mainz am Rhein, Germany: Philipp von Zabern, pp. 42–125.

   2006. 'Kuzeybatı Anadolu'da Neolitik ve Kalkolitik Cağ yerleşimlerinin sınırlandırılması'. In A. Erkanal-Öktü, E. Özgen, S. Günel, A. Tuba Ökse, H. Hüryılmaz, H. Tekin, N. Çınardalı-Karaaslan, B. Uysal, F. A. Karaduman, A. Engin, R. Spieß, A. Aykurt, R. Tuncel, U. Deniz, and A. Rennie, eds., *Studies in Honor of Hayat Erkanal: Cultural Reflections*. Istanbul, Turkey: Homer, pp. 479–486.

   2007. 'Aktopraklik: Kuzeybatı Anadolu'da Gelişkin Bir Köy'. In M. Özdoğan and N. Başgelen, eds., *Anadolu'da Uygarlığın Doğuşu Avrupaya Yayılımı Türkiye'de Neolitik Dönem, Yeni Kazılar, Yeni Bulgular*. Istanbul, Turkey: Arkeoloji ve Sanat Yayınları, pp. 387–392.

Karul, N., and Bertram, J.-K. 2005. 'From Anatolia to Europe: The ceramic sequence of Hoca Çeşme in Turkish Thrace'. In C. Lichter, ed., *How Did Farming Reach Europe? Anatolian–European Relations from the Second Half of the 7th through the First Half of the 6th Millennium BC.* Istanbul, Turkey: Ege Yayınları, pp. 117–129.

Kashima, K. 2000. 'The geo-archaeological program for palaeoenvironmental reconstruction during the Late Quarternary in Central Anatolia, 1995–1999'. *Anatolian Archaeological Studies/Kaman-Kalehöyük* 9:177–192.

2003. 'The geo-archaeological research project at Kaman-Kalehöyük and surroundings in 2001 and 2002'. *Anatolian Archaeological Studies/Kaman-Kalehöyük* 12:103–107.

Kayacan, N. 2003. 'Chipped stone industries of the Neolithic site of Musular (Cappadocia): Preliminary results'. *Anatolia Antiqua* 11:1–10.

Kayan, I. 1995. 'The geomorphological environment of the Ilıpınar mound'. In J. Roodenberg, ed., *The Ilıpınar Excavations I.* Istanbul, Turkey: Nederlands Historisch Archaeologisch Istituut te Istanbul, pp. 17–34.

1999. 'Holocene stratigraphy and geomorphological evolution of the Aegean coastal plains of Anatolia'. *Quaternary Science Reviews* 18/1:541–548.

Keller, J., and Seifried, C. 1990. 'The present status of obsidian source identification in Anatolia and the Near East'. *Revue du groupe europeén d'études pour les techniques physiques, chimiques, biologiques et mathématiques appliquées à l'archaeologie – Conseil de l'Europe (PACT)* 25:57–87.

Kenyon, K. 1956. 'Jericho and its setting in Near Eastern history'. *Antiquity* 30:184–196.

Kirch, P. V. 2000. 'Temples as "holy houses": The transformation of ritual architecture in traditional Polynesian societies'. In R. A. Joyce and S. D. Gillespie, eds., *Beyond Kinship: Social and Material Reproduction in House Societies.* Philadelphia: University of Pennsylvania Press, pp. 103–114.

Kislev, M. E. 1999. 'Agriculture in the Near East in the seventh millennium BC'. In P. C. Anderson, ed., *Prehistory of Agriculture: New Experimental and Ethnographic Approaches.* Los Angeles: Institute of Archaeology, pp. 51–55.

Kobayashi, K., Mochizuki, A. Z., and Mochizuki, A. 2003. 'Classification of obsidian sources in Turkey (II): Classification of obsidian sources in eastern Anatolia'. *Anatolian Archaeological Studies/Kaman-Kalehöyük* 12:109–112.

Kökten, K. 1952. 'Anadolu'da Prehistorik Yerleşme Yerlerinin Dağılışı Üzerini Bir Araştırma'. *Dil ve Tarih-Coğrafya Fakültesi Dergisi* 10:167–207.

Kökten, K., Özgüç, N., and Özgüç, T.. 1945. '1940 ve 1941 yılında Türk Tarih Kurumu adına yapılan Samsun bölgesinde kazıları hakkında ilk kısa rapor'. *Belleten* 9:361–400.

Korfmann, M. O. 1988. 'Beşik-Tepe, Vorbericht über die Ergebnisse der Grabungen von 1985 und 1986, Grabungen am Beşik-Yassıtepe und im Beşik-Gräberfeld'. *Archäologischer Anzeiger* 391–404.

Korfmann, M. O., ed. 1983. *Demircihüyük, Die Ergebnisse der Ausgrabungen 1975–1978, Band I: Architektur, Stratigraphie und Befunde.* Mainz am Rhein, Germany: Phillip von Zabern.

2006. *Troia: Archäologie eines Siedlungshügels und seiner Landschaft.* Mainz am Rhein, Germany: Philipp von Zabern.

Korfmann, M. O., Girgin, C., Mörçöl, C., and Kılıç, S. 1995. 'Kumtepe 1993: Bericht über die Rettungsgrabung'. *Studia Troica* 5:237–289.

Korfmann, M. O., and Kromer, B. 1993. 'Demircihöyük, Beşiktepe, Troia – Eine Zwischenbilanz zur Chronologie dreier Orte in Westanatolien'. *Studia Troica* 3:135–146.

Koşay, H. Z. 1934. 'Türkiye Cümhuriyeti maarıf vekaletince yaptırılan Ahlatlibel hafrıyatı'. *Türk Tarih, Arkeologya ve Etnografya Dergisi* 2:1–100.

    1951. *Türk Tarih Kurumu tarafından yapılan Alaca Höyük kazısı: 1937–1939 dakı calışmalara ve keşiflere ait ilk rapor.* Ankara: Türk Tarih Kurumu Basımevi.

    1976. *Keban projesi: Pulur kazısı, 1968–1970.* Ankara: Türk Tarih Kurumu Basımevi.

Koşay, H. Z., and Akok, M. 1944. *Ausgrabungen von Alaca Höyük: ein Vorbericht über die im Auftrage der Türkischen Geschichtskommission im Sommer 1936 durchgeführten Forschungen und Entdeckungen.* Ankara: Türk Tarih Kurumu Basımevi.

    1950. 'Amasya Mahmatlar köyü definesi'. *Belleten* 14:481–487.

    1957. *Türk Tarik Kurumu tarafından yapılan Büyük Güllücek kazısı 1947 ve 1949 dakı çalışmalar hakkında ilk rapor.* Ankara: Türk Tarih Kurumu Basımevi.

    1966. *Türk Tarih Kurumu tarafından yapılan Alaca Höyük kazısı : 1940-1948 dakı ççalışmalara ve keşiflere ait ilk rapor.* Ankara: Türk Tarih Kurumu Basımevi.

Kosse, K. 1990. 'Group size and social complexity: Thresholds in the long-term memory'. *Journal of Anthropological Archaeology* 9:275–303.

Kotsakis, K. 2005. 'Across the border: Unstable dwellings and fluid landscapes in the earliest Neolithic of Greece'. In D. Bailey, A. Whittle, and V. Cummings, eds., *Unsettling the Neolithic.* Oxford, England: Oxbow, pp. 8–15.

Kozlowski, S. K. 2002. *Nemrik: An Aceramic Neolithic Village in Northern Iraq.* Warsaw, Poland: Warsaw University Press.

Kozlowski, S. K., and Aurenche, O. 2005. *Territories, Boundaries, and Cultures in the Neolithic Near East.* Oxford, England: British Archaeological Reports International Series.

Kristiansen, K., and Larson, T. 2005. *The Rise of Bronze Age Society: Travels, Transmissions, and Transformations.* Cambridge, England: Cambridge University Press.

Kuhn, S. L. 2002. 'Paleolithic archeology in Turkey'. *Evolutionary Archaeology* 11:198–210.

Kuijt, I. 2000. 'Keeping the peace: Ritual, skull caching, and community integration in the Levantine Neolithic'. In I. Kuijt, ed., *Life in Neolithic Farming Communities: Social Organization, Identity, and Differentiation.* New York: Kluwer Academic, pp. 137–164.

Kuijt, I., and Chesson, M. S. 2005. 'Lumps of clay and pieces of stone: Ambiguity, bodies and identity as portrayed in Neolithic figurines'. In S. Pollock and R. Bernbeck, eds., *Archaeologies of the Middle East: Critical Perspectives.* Oxford, England: Blackwell, pp. 152–183.

Kuniholm, P., and Newton, M. 2002. 'Radiocarbon and dendrochronology'. In F. Gérard and L. Thissen, eds., *The Neolithic of Central Anatolia: Internal Developments and External Relations during the 9th–6th Millennia cal. BC.* Istanbul, Turkey: Ege Yayınları, pp. 275–277.

Kuzucuoğlu, C. 2002. 'The environmental frame in Central Anatolia from the 9th to the 6th millennia cal BC: An introduction to the study of relations between environmental conditions and the development of human societies'. In F. Gérard and L. Thissen, eds., *The Neolithic of Central Anatolia: Internal Developments and*

External Relations during the 9th–6th Millennia cal. BC. Istanbul, Turkey: Ege Yayınları, pp. 33–58.

Kuzucuoğlu, C., Marro, C., Özdoğan, A., and Tibet, A. 1997. 'Prospection archeologique Franco-Turque dans la region de Kastamonu (Mer Noire): Deuxieme rapport preliminaire'. *Anatolia Antiqua* **5**:275–306.

Kuzucuoğlu, C., and Roberts, N. 1997. 'Évolution de l'environment en Anatolie de 20,000 à 6000 BP'. *Paleorient* **23**/2:7–24.

Lamb, W. 1936. *Excavations at Thermi in Lesbos.* Cambridge, England: Cambridge University Press.

Lambeck, K. 1996. 'Sea-level change and shore-line evolution in Aegean Greece since Upper Palaeolithic time'. *Antiquity* **70**:588–622.

Lamberg-Karlovsky, C. C. 2002. 'Archaeology and language: The Indo-Iranians'. *Current Anthropology* **43**:63–88.

Lambrianides, K. 1995. 'Present-day Chora on Amorgos and prehistoric Thermi on Lesbos'. In N. Spencer, ed., *Time, Tradition and Society in Greek Archaeology: Bridging the 'Great Divide'.* London, England: Routledge, pp. 64–88.

Larsen, C. S. 1995. 'Biological changes in human populations with agriculture'. *Annual Review of Anthropology* **24**:185–213.

Larsen, M. T. 1987. 'Commercial networks in the Ancient Near East'. In M. Rowlands, M. T. Larsen, and K. Kristiansen, eds., *Centre and Periphery in the Ancient World.* Cambridge, England: Cambridge University Press, p. 47–56.

Last, J. 1996. 'Surface pottery at Çatalhöyük'. In I. Hodder, ed., *On the Surface: Çatalhöyük 1993–5.* Cambridge, England: MacDonald Institute, pp. 115–172.

——— 1998. 'A design for life: Interpreting the art of Çatalhöyük'. *Journal of Material Culture* **3**:355–378.

——— 2000. 'West Mound pottery'. *Çatalhöyük Archive Reports.* Available at http://www.catalhoyuk.com/archive_reporter/.

——— 2005. 'Pottery from the east mound'. In I. Hodder, ed., *Changing Materialities at Çatalhöyük: Reports from the 1995–1999 Seasons.* Cambridge, England: MacDonald Institute, pp. 101–138.

——— 2006. 'Art'. In I. Hodder, ed., *Çatalhöyük Perspectives: Themes from the 1995–1999 Seasons.* Cambridge, England: MacDonald Institute, pp. 209–230.

Last, J., and Gibson, C. 2006. 'Ceramics and society in the Early Chalcolithic of Central Anatolia'. In A. Gibson, ed., *Prehistoric Pottery: Some Recent Research.* Oxford, England: Archaeopress, pp. 39–49.

Le Mière, M., and Picon, M. 1998. 'Les débuts de la céramique au Proche-Orient'. *Paleorient* **24**:5–26.

Leotard, J. M., and López Bayón, I. 2002. 'La grotte d'Öküzini: Etude du materiel lithique'. In I. Yalcinkaya, M. Otte, J. Kozlowski, and O. Bar-Yosef, eds., *La Grotte d' Öküzini: Evolution du Palaeolithique Final du sud-ouest de l'Anatolie.* Liege, France: Universite de Liege, pp. 109–234.

Lévi-Strauss, C. 1973. *Anthropologie structurale deux.* Paris, France: Plon.

——— 1983. *The Way of the Maks* (translated from the French by Sylvia Modelski). London, England: Jonathan Cape.

——— 1991. 'Maison'. In P. Bonte and M. Izard, eds., *Dictionaire de l'Ethnologie et de l'Anthropologie.* Paris: Presses Universitaires de France, pp. 434–436.

Lewis-Williams, D. 2004. 'Constructing a cosmos: Architecture, power and domestication at Çatalhöyük'. *Journal of Social Archaeology* **4**:28–59.

Lewis-Williams, D., and Pearce, D. 2005. *Inside the Neolithic Mind: Consciousness, Cosmos and the Realm of the Gods*. London, England: Thames and Hudson.

Lichter, C. 2005. 'Western Anatolia in the Late Neolithic and Early Chalcolithic: The actual state of research'. In C. Lichter, ed., *How Did Farming Reach Europe? Anatolian–European Relations from the Second Half of the 7th through the First Half of the 6th Millennium BC*. Istanbul, Turkey: Ege Yayınları, pp. 59–74.

Lichter, C., ed. 2005. *How Did Farming Reach Europe? Anatolian–European Relations from the Second Half of the 7th through the First Half of the 6th Millennium BC*. Istanbul, Turkey: Ege Yayınları.

Lichter, C., and Meriç, R. 2007. 'Dedecik-Heybelitepe'. In M. Özdoğan and N. Başgelen, eds., *Anadolu'da Uygarlığın Doğuşu Avrupaya Yayılımı Türkiye'de Neolitik Dönem, Yeni Kazılar, Yeni Bulgular*. Istanbul, Turkey: Arkeoloji ve Sanat Yayınları, pp. 385–386.

Littauer, M. A., and Crouwel, J. H. 1979. *Wheeled Vehicles and Ridden Animals in the Ancient Near East*. Leiden, the Netherlands: Brill.

Lloyd, S. 1956. *Early Anatolia*. London, England: Penguin Books.

1962a. 'The Late Chalcolithic period'. In S. Lloyd and J. Mellaart, eds., *Beycesultan Volume I: The Chalcolithic and Early Bronze Age Levels*. London, England: British Institute of Archaeology at Ankara, pp. 17–26.

1962b. 'The Early Bronze Age levels: First phase'. In S. Lloyd and J. Mellaart, eds., *Beycesultan Volume I: The Chalcolithic and Early Bronze Age Levels*. London, England: British Institute of Archaeology at Ankara, pp. 27–35.

1962c. 'The Early Bronze Age levels: Second phase'. In S. Lloyd and J. Mellaart, eds., *Beycesultan Volume I: The Chalcolithic and Early Bronze Age Levels*. London, England: British Institute of Archaeology at Ankara, pp. 36–57.

1962d. 'The Early Bronze Age levels: Third phase'. In S. Lloyd and J. Mellaart, eds., *Beycesultan Volume I: The Chalcolithic and Early Bronze Age Levels*. London, England: British Institute of Archaeology at Ankara, pp. 58–70.

Lloyd, S., and Mellaart, J. 1962. *Beycesultan Volume I: The Chalcolithic and Early Bronze Age Levels*. London, England: British Institute of Archaeology at Ankara.

Loy, T. H., and Wood, A. R. 1989. 'Blood residue analysis at Çayönü Tepesi, Turkey'. *Journal of Field Archaeology* **16**:451–460.

Macqueen, J. G. 1978. 'Secondary burial at Çatal Hüyük'. *NUMEN, International Review for the History of Religions* **25**/3:226–239.

Makkay, J. 1993. 'Pottery links between late neolithic cultures of the NW Pontic and Anatolia, and the origins of the Hittites'. *Anatolica* **19**:117–128.

Malinowsky, B. 1922. *Argonauts of the Western Pacific: An Account of Native Enterprise and Adventure in the Archipelagoes of Melanesian New Guinea*. London: Routledge.

Mallory, J. P. 1989. *In Search of the Indo-Europeans: Language, Archaeology and Myth*. London, England: Thames and Hudson.

1997. 'The homelands of the Indo-Europeans'. In R. Blench and M. Spriggs, eds., *Archaeology and Language I: Theoretical and Methodological Orientations*. London, England: Routledge, pp. 93–121.

Manning, S. W. 1995. *The Absolute Chronology of the Aegan Early Bronze Age: Archaeology, Radiocarbon and History*. Sheffield, England: Sheffield Academic Press.

Mansfeld, G. 2001. 'Die Kontroll-Ausgrabung des "Pinnacle E415" im Zentrum der Burg von Troia'. *Studia Troica* **11**:51–308.

Marciniak, A., and Czerniak, L. 2007. 'Social transformations in the Late Neolithic and the Early Chalcolithic periods in Central Anatolia'. *Anatolian Studies* **57**:115–130.

Maréchal, A. 1985. 'The riddle of Çatalhüyük'. *Hali* **26**:6–11.

Marro, C., Özdoğan, A., and Tibet, A. 1996. 'Prospection archeologique Franco-Turque dans la region de Kastamonu (Mer Noire): Premier rapport preliminaire'. *Anatolia Antiqua* **4**:273–290.

1998. 'Prospection archeologique Franco-Turque dans la region de Kastamonu (Mer Noire): Troisieme rapport preliminaire'. *Anatolia Antiqua* **6**:317–335.

Marsh, B. 1999. 'Alluvial burial of Gordion: An Iron Age city in Anatolia'. *Journal of Field Archaeology* **26**:163–175.

2005. 'Physical geography, land use, and human impact at Gordion'. In L. Kealhofer, ed., *The Archaeology of Midas and the Phrygians*. Philadelphia: University of Pennsylvania Museum of Archaeology and Anthropology, pp. 161–171.

Martin, L., and Russel, N. 2000. 'Trashing rubbish'. In I. Hodder, ed., *Towards Reflexive Method in Archaeology: The Example at Çatalhöyük*. Cambridge, England: MacDonald Institute, pp. 51–69.

Martin, L., Russel, N., and Carruthers, D. 2002. 'Animal remains from the Central Anatolian Neolithic'. In F. Gérard and L. Thissen, eds., *The Neolithic of Central Anatolia: Internal Developments and External Relations during the 9th–6th Millennia cal. BC*. Istanbul, Turkey: Ege Yayınları, pp. 193–216.

Martinoli, D. 2002. 'Les macrorestes botaniques de la grotte d'öküzini'. In I. Yalçınkaya, M. Otte, J. Kozlowski, and O. Bar-Yosef, eds., *La grotte d'Öküzini: Evolution du Paleolithique Final du sud-ouest de l'Anatolie*. Liege, France: Universite de Liege, pp. 91–94.

2004. 'Plant food use, temporal changes and site seasonality at Epipalaeolithic Öküzini and Karain B caves, southwest Anatolia, Turkey'. *Paleorient* **30**:61–80.

2005. 'Plant food economy and environment during the Epipalaeolithic in Southwest Anatolia: An investigation of the botanical macroremains from Öküzini and Karain B'. Unpublished PhD thesis, University of Basel, Switzerland.

Martinoli, D., and Jacomet, S. 2004. 'Identifying endocarp remains and exploring their use at Epipalaeolithic Öküzini in southwest Anatolia, Turkey'. *Vegetation History and Archaeobotany* **13**:45–54.

Martinoli, D., and Nesbitt, M. 2003. 'Plant stores at Pottery Neolithic Höyücek, southwest Turkey'. *Anatolian Studies* **53**:17–33.

Matthews, R. 1996. 'Surface scraping and planning'. In I. Hodder, ed., *On the Surface: Çatalhöyük 1993–5*. Cambridge, England: MacDonald Institute, pp. 79–100.

2000. 'Time with the past in Paphlagonia'. In P. Matthiae, A. Enea, L. Peyronel, and F. Pinnock, eds., *Proceedings of the First International Congress of the Archaeology of the Ancient Near East*. Rome, Italy: Università degli studi di Roma 'La Sapienza', pp. 1013–1027.

2003. *The Archaeology of Mesopotamia: Theories and Approaches*. London: Routledge.

2004. 'Salur North: An Early Bronze Age cemetery in North-Central Anatolia'. In A. Sagona, ed., *A View from the Highlands: Archaeological Studies in Honour of Charles Burney*. Herent, Belgium: Peeters, pp. 55–66.

Matthews, W. 2005. 'Micromorphological and microstratigraphic traces of uses and concepts of space'. In I. Hodder, ed., *Inhabiting Çatalhöyük: Reports from the 1995–1999 Seasons*. Cambridge, England: MacDonald Institute, pp. 355–398.

2006. 'Life-cycle and course of buildings'. In I. Hodder, ed., *Çatalhöyük Perspectives: Themes from the 1995–1999 Seasons*. Cambridge, England: MacDonald Institute, pp. 125–150.

McGeehan-Liritzis, V., and Taylor, J. W. 1987. 'Yugoslavian tin deposits and the Early Bronze Age industries of the Aegean region'. *Oxford Journal of Archaeology* **6**:287–300.

McGovern, P. E. 2003. *Ancient Wine: The Search for the Origins of Viniculture*. Princeton, NJ: Princeton University Press.

Meece, S. 2006. 'A bird's eye view – of a leopard's spots: The Çatalhöyük "map" and the development of cartographic representation in prehistory'. *Anatolian Studies* **56**:1–16.

Mellaart, J. 1955. 'Some prehistoric sites in north-western Turkey'. *Istanbuler Mitteilungen* **6**:53–88.

1958. 'The end of the Early Bronze Age in Anatolia and the Aegean'. *American Journal of Archaeology* **62**:9–33.

1959. 'Notes on the architectural remains of Troy I and II'. *Anatolian Studies* **9**:131–162.

1960. 'Anatolia and the Balkans'. *Antiquity* **34**:270–278.

1961. 'Early cultures of the South Anatolian Plateau'. *Anatolian Studies* **11**:159–184.

1962a. 'Excavations at Çatal Hüyük: First preliminary report, 1961'. *Anatolian Studies* **12**:41–65.

1962b. 'The Late Chalcolithic pottery'. In S. Lloyd and J. Mellaart, eds., *Beycesultan Volume I: The Chalcolithic and Early Bronze Age Levels*. London, England: British Institute of Archaeology at Ankara, pp. 71–115.

1962c. 'Pottery of the Early Bronze 1 period'. In S. Lloyd and J. Mellaart, eds., *Beycesultan Volume I: The Chalcolithic and Early Bronze Age Levels*. London, England: British Institute of Archaeology at Ankara, pp. 116–134.

1963a. 'Excavations at Çatal Hüyük: Second preliminary report, 1962'. *Anatolian Studies* **13**:43–103.

1963b. 'Early cultures of the South Anatolian Plateau, II: The Late Chalcolithic and Early Bronze Ages in the Konya Plain'. *Anatolian Studies* **13**:199–236.

1964. 'Excavations at Çatal Hüyük: Third preliminary report, 1963'. *Anatolian Studies* **14**:39–119.

1965. 'Çatal Hüyük West'. *Anatolian Studies* **15**:135–156.

1966a. 'Excavations at Çatal Hüyük: Fourth preliminary report, 1965'. *Anatolian Studies* **16**:165–191.

1966b. *The Chalcolithic and Early Bronze Ages in the Near East and Anatolia*. Beirut, Lebanon: Khayats.

1967. *Çatal Hüyük: A Neolithic Town in Anatolia*. London, England: Thames and Hudson.

1970. *Excavations at Hacılar*. Edinburgh, Scotland: Edinburgh University Press.

1971. 'Anatolia, c. 4000–2300 B.C.'. In I. E. S. Edwards, C. J. Gadd, and N. G. L. Hammond, eds., *The Cambridge Ancient History, I:2: Early History of the Middle East*. Cambridge, England: Cambridge University Press, pp. 363–416.

1972. 'Anatolian Neolithic settlement patterns'. In P. J. Ucko, W. Dimbledy, and R. Tringham, eds., *Man, Settlement, and Urbanism*. London, England: Duckworth, pp. 279–284.

1975. *The Neolithic of the Near East*. London, England: Thames and Hudson.

1984. 'Anatolian kilims: New insights and problems'. *Anatolian Studies* **34**:87–95.

2000. 'Çatal Hüyük: The 1960s seasons'. In R. Matthews, ed., *Ancient Anatolia: Fifty Years' Work of the British Institute of Archaeology at Ankara*. London, England: British Institute of Archaeology at Ankara, pp. 35–41.

Mellaart, J., Hirsch, U., and Balpınar, B. 1989. *The Goddess from Anatolia I–IV*. Milan, Italy: Eskenazı.

Mellars, P. 2004. 'Stage 3 climate and the Upper Paleolithic revolution in Europe: Evolutionary perspectives'. In J. Cherry, C. Scarre, and S. Shennan, eds., *Explaining Social Change: Studies in Honour of Colin Renfrew*. Cambridge, England: MacDonald Institute, pp. 27–43.

Mellink, M. J. 1956. 'The royal tombs at Alaca Hüyük'. In S. S. Weinberg, ed., *The Aegean and the Near East: Studies Presented to Hetty Goldman on the Occasion of Her Seventy-Fifth Birthday*. New York: Augustin, pp. 39–58.

1965. 'Anatolian chronology'. In R. W. Ehrich, ed., *Chronologies in Old World Archaeology*. Chicago: University of Chicago Press, pp. 101–132.

1986. 'The Early Bronze Age in West Anatolia'. In G. Cadogan, ed., *The End of the Early Bronze Age in the Aegean*. Leiden, the Netherlands: Brill, pp. 139–152.

1998. 'Anatolia and the bridge from east to west in the Early Bronze Age'. *Türkiye Bilimler Akademisi – Arkeoloji Dergisi (TUBA-AR)* **7**:1–8.

Meskell, L. 1998a. 'Twin peaks: The archaeologies of Çatalhöyük'. In L. Goodison and C. Morris, eds., *Ancient Goddesses: The Myths and the Evidence*. London, England: British Museum Press, pp. 46–62.

Meskell, L., Nakamura, C., King, R., and Farid, S. 2008. 'Figured lifeworlds and deposited practices at Çatalhöyük'. *Cambridge Archaeological Journal* **18**:139–161.

Metcalf, P., and Huntington, R. 1991. *Celebrations of Death: The Anthropology of Mortuary Ritual*. Cambridge, England: Cambridge University Press.

Metz, H. C. 1996. *Turkey: A Country Study*. Washington, DC: Federal Research Division, Library of Congress.

Molleson, T., and Andrews, P. 1996. 'Trace element analysis of bones and teeth from Çatalhöyük'. In I. Hodder, ed., *On the Surface: Çatalhöyük 1993–95*. Cambridge, England: MacDonald Institute, pp. 271–300.

Molleson, T., Andrews, P., and Boz, B. 2005. 'Reconstruction of the Neolithic people of Çatalhöyük'. In I. Hodder, ed., *Inhabiting Çatalhöyük: Reports from the 1995–1999 Seasons*. Cambridge, England: MacDonald Institute, pp. 279–300.

Moore, A. M. T., Hillman, G. C., and Legge, A. J. 2000. *Village on the Euphrates: From Foraging to Farming at Abu Hureyra*. Oxford, England: Oxford University Press.

Moorey, P. R. S. 1994. *Ancient Mesopotamian Materials and Industries: The Archaeological Evidence*. Oxford, England: Clarendon Press.

Mortenson, P. 1970. 'Chipped stone industry'. In J. Mellaart, ed., *Excavations at Hacılar*. Edinburgh, Scotland: Edinburgh University Press, pp. 153–157.

Muhly, J. D. 1985. 'Tin and the beginnings of bronze metallurgy'. *American Journal of Archaeology* **89**:275–291.

1993. 'Early Bronze Age tin and the Taurus'. *American Journal of Archaeology* **97**:239–253.

Naroll, R. 1962. 'Floor area and settlement population'. *American Antiquity* **27**:587–589.

Naruse, T., Kashima, K., Ishimura, K., and Sayan, S. 2002. 'Sedimentary environmental changes over the past 60,000 years at Karayazı alluvial fan, Anatolian Plateau, Turkey'. *Anatolian Archaeological Studies/Kaman-Kalehöyük* **11**:153–157.

Nesbitt, M. 2002. 'When and where did domesticated cereals first occur in Southwest Asia?' In R. T. J. Cappers and S. Bottema, eds., *The Dawn of Farming in the Near East*. Berlin, Germany: Ex Oriente, pp. 113–132.

2004. 'Can we identify a centre, a region, or a supra-region for Near Eastern plant domestication?' *Neo-Lithics* 2004/01:38–40.

Nichols, J. 1998. 'The Eurasian spread zone and the Indo-European dispersal'. In R. Blench and M. Spriggs, eds., *Archaeology and Language II: Correlating Archaeological and Linguistic Hypotheses*. London, England: Routledge, pp. 220–266.

Nieuwenhuyse, O. 2007. *Plain and Painted Pottery: The Rise of Late Neolithic Ceramic Styles on the Syrian and Northern Mesopotamian Plains*. Turnhout, Belgium: Brepols.

Nikolov, V. 1998. 'The Circumpontic cultural zone during the 6th millennium BC'. *Documenta Praehistorica* **25**:81–89.

Ormerod, H. A. 1913. 'Prehistoric remains in south-western Asia Minor – III'. *Annual of the British School at Athens* **19**:48–60.

Orthmann, W. 1963. *Die Keramik der Frühen Bronzezeit aus Inneranatolien*. Berlin, Germany: Gebr. Mann Verlag.

1967. 'Zu den Standarten aus Alaca'. *Istanbuler Mitteilungen* **17**:34–54.

Osten, H. H. von der 1927. 'Explorations in Hittite Asia Minor'. *The American Journal of Semitic Languages and Literatures* **43**/2:73–176.

1937. *The Alishar Hüyük, Seasons of 1930–32: Part I*. Chicago: University of Chicago Press.

Otte, M. 2008. 'Turkey: Paleolithic cultures'. In D. M. Pearson, ed., *Encyclopedia of Archaeology*. New York: Academic Press, pp. 904–908.

Otte, M., Yalçınkaya, I., Leotard, J.-M., Kartal, M., Bar-Yosef, O., Kozlowski, J., Bayon, I. L., and Marshack, A. 1995. 'The Epipalaeolithic of Öküzini Cave (SW Anatolia) and its mobiliary art'. *Antiquity* **69**:931–944.

Özbal, H., Pehlivan, N., and Gedik, B. 2002. 'Metallurgy at İkiztepe'. In Ü. Yalçın, ed., *Anatolian Metal II*. Bochum: Deutschen Bergbau-Museum, pp. 39–48.

Özbal, R., Gerritsen, F., Diebold, B., Healey, E., Aydin, N., Loyet, M., Nardulli, F., Ekstrom, H., Sholts, S., Mekel-Bobrov, N., and Lahn, B. 2004. 'Tell Kurdu excavations 2001'. *Anatolica* **30**:37–107.

Özbaşaran, M. 1995. 'The historical background of researches at the caves of Yarımburgaz'. In H. Çambel, ed., *Readings in Prehistory: Studies Presented to Halet Çambel*. Istanbul, Turkey: Graphis Yayınları, pp. 27–39.

1998. 'The heart of a house: The hearth'. In G. Arsebük, M. J. Mellink, and W. Schirmer, eds., *Light on Top of the Black Hill: Studies Presented to Halet Çambel*. Istanbul, Turkey: Ege Yayınları, pp. 555–566.

1999. 'Musular: A general assessment on a new Neolithic site in Central Anatolia'. In M. Özdoğan and N. Başgelen, eds., *The Neolithic of Turkey*. Istanbul, Turkey: Arkeoloji ve Sanat Yayınları, pp. 147–155.

2000. 'The Neolithic site of Musular, Central Anatolia'. *Anatolica* **26**:129–151.

Özbaşaran, M., and Buitenhuis, H. 2002. 'Proposal for a regional terminology for Central Anatolia'. In F. Gérard and L. Thissen, eds., *The Neolithic of Central Anatolia: Internal Developments and External Relations during the 9th–6th Millennia cal. BC*. Istanbul, Turkey: Ege Yayınları, pp. 67–77.

Özbaşaran, M., Duru, G., Kayacan, N., Erdoğu, B., and Buitenhuis, H. 2007. 'Musular 1996–2004: Genel Değerlendirme'. In M. Özdoğan and N. Başgelen, eds., *Anadolu'da Uygarlığın Doğuşu Avrupaya Yayılımı Türkiye'de Neolitik Dönem, Yeni Kazılar, Yeni Bulgular*. Istanbul, Turkey: Arkeoloji ve Sanat Yayınları, pp. 273–284.

Özbek, M. 1998. 'Human skeletal remains from Aşıklı, a Neolithic village in near Aksaray, Turkey'. In G. Arsebük, M. J. Mellink, and W. Schirmer, eds., *Light on Top of the Black Hill: Studies Presented to Halet Çambel*. Istanbul, Turkey: Ege Yayınları, pp. 567–579.

Özbek, O. 2008. 'Kaynarca: A Neolithic mound in Gelibolu Peninsula'. *Anatolia Antiqua* **16**:1–12.

Özdemir, A. 2003. '"Hayali Geçmiş": Arkeoloji ve Milliyetçilik, 1923–1945 Türkiye Deneyimi'. In O. Erdur and G. Duru, eds., *Arkeoloji: Niye? Nasıl? Ne için?* Istanbul, Turkey: Ege Yayınları, pp. 7–26.

Özdoğan, A. 1999. 'Çayönü'. In M. Özdoğan and N. Başgelen, eds., *The Neolithic of Turkey*. Istanbul, Turkey: Arkeoloji ve Sanat Yayınları, pp. 35–63.

Özdoğan, M. 1982. 'Tilkiburnu: A Late Chalcolithic site in eastern Thrace'. *Anatolica* **9**:1–26.

1983. 'Pendik: A Neolithic site of Fikirtepe culture in the Marmara Region'. In R. M. Boehmer and H. Hauptmann, eds., *Beiträge zur Altertumskunde Kleinasiens: Festschrift für Kurt Bittel*. Mainz am Rhein, Germany: Philipp von Zabern, pp. 401–411.

1985. 'The Chalcolithic pottery of Yarımburgaz Cave'. In M. Liverani, A. Palmieri, and R. Peroni, eds., *Studi di Paletnologia in Onore di Salvatore M. Pugliesi*. Rome, Italy: Universita di Roma 'La Sapienza', pp. 177–18.

1993. 'Vinča and Anatolia: A new look at a very old problem'. *Anatolica* **19**:173–193.

1994. 'Obsidian in Anatolia: An archaeological perspective on the status of research'. In S. Demirçi, A. M. Özer, and G. D. Summers, eds., *Archaeometry 94: The Proceedings of the 29th International Symposium on Archaeometry*. Ankara, Turkey: Tübitak, pp. 423–431.

1995 'Neolithic in Turkey: The status of research'. In H. Çambel, ed., *Readings in Prehistory: Studies Presented to Halet Çambel*. Istanbul, Turkey: Graphics Yayınları, pp. 41–59.

1996. 'Pre–Bronze Age sequence of Central Anatolia: An alternative approach'. In U. Magen and M. Rashad, eds., *Vom Halys zum Euphrat: Thomas Beran zu Ehren*. Münster, Germany: Ugarit Verlag, pp. 185–202.

1997a. 'Anatolia from the last Glacial Maximum to the Holocene climatic optimum: Cultural formations and the impact of the environmental setting'. *Paleorient* **23**/2:25–38.

1997b. 'The beginning of Neolithic economies in southeastern Europe: An Anatolian perspective'. *Journal of European Archaeology* **5**:1–33.

1998. 'Ideology and archaeology in Turkey'. In L. Meskell, ed., *Archaeology under Fire: Nationalism, Politics and Heritage in the Eastern Mediterranean and Middle East*. London, England: Routledge, pp. 111–123.

1998b. 'Hoca Çeşme: An early Neolithic Anatolian colony in the Balkans?' In P. Anreiter, L. Bartowiescz, E. Jerem, and W. Meid, eds., *Man and the Animal World: Studies in Archaeozoology, Anthropology and Paleolinguistics in Memorian Sandor Bökönyi*. Budapest, Hungary: Archaeolingua, pp. 435–451.

1999a. 'Northwestern Turkey: Neolithic cultures in between the Balkans and Anatolia'. In M. Özdoğan and N. Başgelen, eds., *The Neolithic of Turkey*. Istanbul, Turkey: Arkeoloji ve Sanat Yayınları, pp. 203–224.

1999b. 'Concluding remarks'. In M. Özdoğan and N. Başgelen, eds., *The Neolithic of Turkey*. Istanbul, Turkey: Arkeoloji ve Sanat Yayınları, pp. 225–236.

2001. *Türk Arkeolojisinin Sorunları ve Koruma Politikaları*. Istanbul, Turkey: Arkeoloji ve Sanat Yayınları.

2002. 'Defining the Neolithic of Central Anatolia'. In F. Gérard and L. Thissen, eds., *The Neolithic of Central Anatolia: Internal Developments and External Relations during the 9th–6th Millennia cal. BC*. Istanbul, Turkey: Ege Yayınları, pp. 253–261.

2003. 'The Black Sea, the Sea of Marmara and Bronze Age archaeology: An archaeological predicament'. In G. A. Wagner, E. Pernicka, and H.-P. Uerpmann, eds., *Troia and the Troad: Scientific Approaches*. Berlin, Germany: Springer, pp. 105–120.

2005. 'Westward expansion of the Neolithic way of life: What we know and what we do not know'. In C. Lichter, ed., *How Did Farming Reach Europe? Anatolian–European Relations from the Second Half of the 7th through the First Half of the 6th Millennium BC*. Istanbul, Turkey: Ege Yayınları, pp. 13–27.

2006. 'Yakındoğu kentleri ve batı anadolu'da kentleşme süreci'. In A. Erkanal-Öktü, E. Özgen, S. Günel, A. Tuba Ökse, H. Hüryılmaz, H. Tekin, N. Çınardalı-Karaaslan, B. Uysal, F. A. Karaduman, A. Engin, R. Spieß, A. Aykurt, R. Tuncel, U. Deniz, and A. Rennie, eds., *Studies in Honor of Hayat Erkanal: Cultural Reflections*. Istanbul, Turkey: Homer, pp. 571–577.

2007a. 'Marmara Bölgesi Neolitik Çağ Kültürleri'. In M. Özdoğan and N. Başgelen, eds., *Anadolu'da Uygarlığın Doğuşu Avrupaya Yayılımı Türkiye'de Neolitik Dönem, Yeni Kazılar, Yeni Bulgular*. Istanbul, Turkey: Arkeoloji ve Sanat Yayınları, pp. 401–426.

2007b. 'Coastal changes of the Black Sea and Sea of Marmara in archaeological perspective'. In V. Yanko-Hombach, A. S. Gilbert, N. Panin, and P. M. Dolukhanov, eds., *The Black Sea Flood Question: Changes in Coastline, Climate and Human Settlement*. Dordrecht, the Netherlands: Springer, pp. 651–669.

Özdoğan, M., and Başgelen, N., eds. 1999. *The Neolithic of Turkey*. Istanbul, Turkey: Arkeoloji ve Sanat Yayınları.

Özdoğan, M., and Dede, Y. 1998. 'An anthropomorphic vessel from Toptepe, eastern Thrace'. In M. Stefanovich, H. Todorova, and H. Hauptmann, eds., *James Harvey Gaul – In Memoriam*. Sofia, Turkey: James Harvey Gaul Foundation, pp. 143–152.

2007. *Anadolu'da Uygarlığın Doğuşu ve Avrapa'ya Yayılımı Türkiye'de Neolitik Dönem: Yeni Kazılar, Yeni Bulgular*. Istanbul, Turkey: Arkeoloji ve Sanat Yayınları.

Özdoğan, M., and Gatsov, I. 1998. 'The Aceramic Neolithic period in western Turkey and in the Aegean'. *Anatolica* **24**:209–232.

Özdoğan, M., Mitake, Y., and Özbaşaran, N. D. 1991. 'An interim report on excavations at Yarımburgaz and Toptepe in eastern Thrace'. *Anatolica* **17**:59–121.

Özdoğan, M., and Parzinger, H. 2000. 'Aşağı Pınar and Kanlıgeçit excavations: Some new evidence on early metallurgy from eastern Thrace'. In Ü. Yalçın, ed., *Anatolian Metal I*. Bochum: Deutsche Bergbau Museum, pp. 83–91.

Özdoğan, M., Parzinger, H., and Karul, N. 2003. 'Der Siedlungshügel von Aşağı Pınar'. In N. Karul, Z. Eres, M. Özdoğan, and H. Parzinger, eds., *Aşağı Pınar I: Einführung, Forschungsgeschichte, Stratigraphie und Archiktektur*. Mainz am Rhein, Germany: Philipp von Zabern, pp. 14–38.

Özgen, E. 1986. 'A group of terracotta wagon models from Southeastern Anatolia'. *Anatolian Studies* **36**:165–171.

Özgüç, N. 1973. 'Haberler – kazılar. Niğde Tepe Bağları Höyüğü kazısı'. *Belleten* **38**:442–443.

Özgüç, T. 1945. 'Öntarihte Anadolu Kronolojisi'. *Belleten* **9**:341–360.

1956. 'Das prähistorischen Haus beim Felsrelief von Fraktın'. *Anatolia* **1**:65–70.

1964. 'New finds from Horoztepe'. *Anatolia* **8**:1–17.

1986. 'New observations on the relationship of Kültepe with Southeast Anatolia and North Syria during the third millennium B.C'. In J. V. Canby, E. Porada, B. S. Ridgway, and T. Stech, eds., *Ancient Anatolia: Aspects of Change and Cultural Development: Essays in Honor of Machteld J. Mellink*. Madison: University of Wisconsin Press, pp. 31–47.

2003. *Kültepe Kaniş/Nesa: The Earliest International Trade Center and the Oldest Capital City of the Hittites*. Istanbul, Turkey: Middle Eastern Culture Center in Japan.

Özgüç, T., and Akok, M. 1958. *Horoztepe: An Early Bronze Age Settlement and Cemetery*. Ankara: Türk Tarih Kurumu Basımevi.

Özgüç, T., and Temizer, R. 1993. 'The Eskiyapar treasure'. In M. J. Mellink and E. Porada, eds., *Aspects of Art and Iconography: Anatolia and its Neighbours. Studies in Honor of Nimet Özgüç*. Ankara: Türk Tarih Kurumu Basımevi, pp. 613–628.

Özsait, M. 2003. 'Les fouilles du cimetiere de Göndürle Höyük a Harmanören'. *Anatolica* **29**:87–102.

Öztan, A. 2002. 'Köşk Höyük: Anadolu Arkeolojisine yeni katkılar'. *Türkiye Bilimler Akademisi – Arkeoloji Dergisi (TUBA-AR)* **11**:55–69.

2003. 'A Neolithic and Chalcolithic settlement in Anatolia: Köşk Höyük'. *Colloquium Anatolicum* **2**:69–86.

2007. 'Köşk Höyük: Niğde-Bor Ovasında Bir Neolitik Yerleşim'. In M. Özdoğan and N. Başgelen, eds., *Anadolu'da Uygarlığın Doğuşu Avrupaya Yayılımı Türkiye'de Neolitik Dönem, Yeni Kazılar, Yeni Bulgular*. Istanbul, Turkey: Arkeoloji ve Sanat Yayınları, pp. 223–236.

Öztan, A., and Faydalı, E. 2003. 'An Early Chalcolithic building from Köşk Höyük'. *Belleten* **67**/248;45–75.

Öztan, A., and Özkan, S. 2003. 'Çizi ve nokta bezekli Köşk Höyük seramikleri'. In M. Özdoğan, H. Hauptmann, and N. Başgelen, eds., *Köyden kente, Yakındoğu'da ilk yerleşimler – Ufuk Esin'e Armağan*. Istanbul, Turkey: Arkeoloji ve Sanat Yayınları, pp. 447–458.

Parzinger, H. 1993. 'Zur Zeitstellung der Büyükkaya-Ware, Bemerkungen zur vorbronzezeitlichen Kulturfolge Zentralanatoliens'. *Anatolica* **19**:211–229.

2005. 'Die mittel – und spätneolithischen Keramik aus Aşağı Pınar, Grabungen 1993–1998'. In H. Parzinger and H. Schwarzberg, eds., *Aşağı Pınar II, Die mittel – und spätneolithische Keramik*. Mainz am Rhein, Germany: Philipp von Zabern, pp. 1–246.

Pasinli, A., Uzunoğlu, E., Atakan, N., Girgin, Ç., and Soysal, M. 1994. 'Pendik kurtarma kazısı'. *Müze Kurtarma Kazıları Semineri* 147–163.

Patzek, B. 1990. 'Schliemann und die Geschichte der Archäologie im Neunzehnten Jahrhundert: Von der Entstehung einer Wissenschaft zur archäologischer Sensation'. In W. M. Calder and J. Cobet, eds., *Heinrich Schliemann nach Hundert Jahren*. Frankfurt, Germany: Vittorio Klosterman, pp. 31–55.

Payne, S. 1972. 'Can Hasan III: The Anatolian Aceramic and the Greek Neolithic'. In E. S. Higgs, ed., *Papers in Economic Prehistory*. Cambridge, England: Cambridge University Press, pp. 191–194.

1985. 'Animal bones from Aşıklı Hüyük'. *Anatolian Studies* **35**:109–122.

Pecorella, P. E. 1984. *La cultura preistorica di Iasos in Caria*. Rome, Italy: Giorgi Bretschneider.

Peltenburg, E., ed. 2003. *The Colonisation and Settlement of Cyprus: Investigations at Kissonerga-Mylouthkia 1976–1996*. Sävedalen, Sweden: Paul Aström Förlag.

Peltenburg, E., Colledge, S., Croft, P., Jackson, A., McCartney, C., and Murray, M. A. 2001. 'Neolithic dispersals from the Levantine Corridor: A Mediterranean perspective'. *Levant* **33**:35–64.

Peltenburg, E., and Wasse, A., eds. 2004. *Neolithic Revolution: New Perspectives on Southwest Asia in Light of Recent Discoveries on Cyprus*. Oxford, England: Oxbow.

Perkins, D. 1969. 'Fauna of Çatal Hüyük: Evidence for early cattle domestication in Anatolia'. *Science* **64**:177–179.

Perkins, D., and Daly, P. 1968. 'A hunter's village in Neolithic Turkey'. *Scientific American* **219**:96–106.

Perlès, C. 2001. *The Early Neolithic in Greece*. Cambridge, England: Cambridge University Press.

2005. 'From the Near East to Greece, let's reverse the focus: Cultural elements that didn't transfer'. In C. Lichter, ed., *How Did Farming Reach Europe? Anatolian–European Relations from the Second Half of the 7th through the First Half of the 6th Millennium BC*. Istanbul, Turkey: Ege Yayınları, pp. 275–290.

Pernicka, E. 1998. 'Die Ausbreitung der Zinnbronze im 3. Jahrtausend'. In H. Hänsel, ed., *Mensch und Umwelt in der Bronzezeit Europas*. Kiel, Germany: Oetker-Voges, pp. 135–147.

2006. 'Metalle machen epoche: Bronze und Eisen als Werkstoffe und Handelsware'. In M. O. Korfmann, ed., *Troia: Archäologie eines Siedlungshügels und seiner Landschaft*. Mainz am Rhein, Germany: Philipp von Zabern, pp. 349–352.

Pernicka, E., Wagner, G. A., Muhly, J. D., and Öztunali, Ö. 1992. 'Comments on the discussion of ancient tin sources in Anatolia'. *Journal of Mediterranean Archaeology* **5**:91–98.

Perrot, J. 2001. 'Réflexions sur l'état des recherches concernant la Préhistoire récente du Proche et du Moyen-Orient'. *Paleorient* **26**:5–28.

Peschlow-Bindokat, A. 1996a. *Der Latmos: eine unbekannte Gebirgslandschaft an der türkischen Westküste*. Mainz am Rhein, Germany: Phillip von Zabern.

1996b. 'Vorländige Bericht über die Prähistorische Forschungen im Latmos'. *Archäologischer Anzeiger* 161–173.

Peters, E. 1972. 'Lehmziegelhäuser in der Altinova'. *METU – Keban Publications* **3** (1970):173–182.

　1982. 'Ländliche bauweisen im Keban-Gebiet'. *METU – Keban Publications* **7** (1974–1975): 217–232.

Peters, J., Helmer, D., von den Driesch, A., and Saña Segui, M. 1999. 'Early animal husbandry in the northern Levant'. *Paleorient* **25**:27–47.

Pinhasi, R., and Pluciennik, M. 2004. 'A regional biological approach to the spread of farming in Europe'. *Current Anthropology* **45**(supplement): 59–82.

Podzuweit, C. 1979. *Trojanische Gefäßforme der Frühbronzezeit in Anatolien, der Agäis und angrezenden Gebieten, Ein Beitrag zur vergleichende Stratigraphie*. Mainz am Rhein, Germany: Phillip von Zabern.

Powell, M. A. 1996. 'Wine and the vine in ancient Mesopotamia: The cuneiform evidence'. In P. E. McGovern, S. J. Flemming, and S. H. Katz, eds., *The Origins and Ancient History of Wine*. Amsterdam, the Netherlands: Gordon and Breach, pp. 97–122.

Price, T. D. 1996. 'The first farmers of southern Scandinavia'. In D. R. Harris, ed., *The Origins and Spread of Agriculture and Pastoralism in Eurasia*. London, England: University College of London Press, pp. 346–362.

Pulhan, G. 2003. 'Türkiye Cumhuriyeti Geçmişini Arıyor: Cumhuriyet'in Arkeoloji Seferberliği'. In O. Erdur and G. Duru, eds., *Arkeoloji: Niye? Nasıl? Ne için?* Istanbul, Turkey: Ege Yayınları, pp. 139–147.

Pullen, D. 2009. 'The Early Bronze Age in Greece'. In C. W. Shelmerdine, ed., *The Cambridge Companion to the Aegean Bronze Age*. Cambridge, England: Cambridge University Press, pp. 19–46.

Pustovoytov, K., Schmidt, K., and Taubauld, H. 2007. 'Evidence for Holocene environmental changes in the northern Fertile Crescent provided by pedogenic carbonate coatings'. *Quarternary Research* **67**:315–327.

Redman, C. L. 1978. *The Rise of Civilization: From Early Farmers to Urban Society in the Ancient Near East*. San Francisco: W. H. Freeman.

Reed, J. M., Roberts, N., and Leng, M. J. 1999. 'An evaluation of the diatom response to Late Quaternary environmental change in two lakes in the Konya Basin, Turkey, by comparison with stable isotope data'. *Quaternary Science Reviews* **18**:631–646.

Reingruber, A. 2005. 'The Argissa Magoula and the beginning of the Neolithic in Thessaly'. In C. Lichter, ed., *How Did Farming Reach Europe? Anatolian–European Relations from the Second Half of the 7th through the First Half of the 6th Millennium BC*. Istanbul, Turkey: Ege Yayınları, pp. 155–171.

Renfrew, C. 1986. 'Varna and the emergence of wealth in Prehistoric Europe'. In A. Appadurai, ed., *The Social Life of Things: Commodities in Cultural Perspective*. Cambridge, England: Cambridge University Press, pp. 141–168.

　1987. *Archaeology and Language: The Puzzle of Indo-European Origins*. London, England: Penguin Books.

　1996. 'Language families and the spread of farming'. In D. R. Harris, ed., *The Origins and the Spread of Agriculture and Pastoralism in Eurasia*. London, England: University College of London Press, pp. 70–92.

　2000. '10,000 or 5000 years ago? Questions of time depth'. In C. Renfrew, A. McMahon, and L. Trask, eds., *Time Depth in Historical Linguistics*. Cambridge, England: MacDonald Institute, pp. 413–439.

Renfrew, C., Cann, J. R., and Dixon, J. E. 1965. 'Obsidian in the Aegean'. *Annual of the British School at Athens* **60**:225–247.

Renfrew, C., Dixon, J. E., and Cann, J. R. 1966. 'Obsidian and early cultural contact in the Near East'. *Proceedings of the Prehistoric Society* **32**:30–72.

1968. 'Further analysis of Near Eastern obsidians'. *Proceedings of the Prehistoric Society* **34**:319–331.

Renfrew, J. M. 1968. 'A note on the Neolithic grain from Can Hasan'. *Anatolian Studies* **18**:55–56.

1996. 'Palaeoethnobotanical finds of Vitis from Greece'. In P. E. McGovern, S. J. Flemming, and S. H. Katz, eds., *The Origins and Ancient History of Wine*. Amsterdam, the Netherlands: Gordon and Breach, pp. 255–267.

Richards, M. P., Pearson, J. A., Molleson, T. I., Russell, N., and Martin, L. 2003. 'Stable isotope evidence of diet at Neolithic Çatalhöyük, Turkey'. *Journal of Archaeological Science* **30**:67–76.

Ritchey, T. 1996. 'Note on the building complexity'. In I. Hodder, ed., *On the Surface: Çatalhöyük 1993–95*. Cambridge, England: MacDonald Institute, pp. 7–18.

Robb, J. E., and Farr, R. H. 2005. 'Substances in motion: Neolithic Mediterranean "Trade"'. In E. Blake and A. B. Knapp, eds., *The Archaeology of Mediterranean Prehistory*. Oxford, England: Blackwell, pp. 24–45.

Roberts, N. 1990. 'Human-induced landscape change in south and southwest Turkey during the Later Holocene'. In S. Bottema, G. Entjes-Nieborgh, and W. Van Zeist, eds., *Man's Role in the Shaping of the Eastern Mediterranean Landscape*. Rotterdam, the Netherlands: A. A. Balkema, pp. 53–67.

2002. 'Did Prehistoric landscape management retard the Post-Glacial spread of woodland in Southwest Asia?' *Antiquity* **76**:1002–1010.

Roberts, N., Black, S., Boyer, P., Eastwood, W. J., Griffiths, H. I., Lamb, H. F., Leng, M. J., Parish, R., Reed, J. M., Twigg, D., and Yiğitbaçioğlu, H. 1999. 'Chronology and stratigraphy of Late Quatenary sediments in the Konya Basin, Turkey: Results from the KOPAL Project'. *Quatenary Science Reviews* **18**:611–630.

Roberts, N., Boyer. P., and Parish, R. 1996. 'Preliminary results of geoarchaeological investigations at Çatalhöyük'. In I. Hodder, ed., *On the Surface: Çatalhöyük 1993–95*. Cambridge, England: MacDonald Institute, pp. 19–40.

Roberts, N., Reed, J. M., Leng, M. J., Kuzucuoğlu, C., Fontugne, M., Bertaux, J., Woldring, H., Bottema, S., Black, S., Hunt, E., and Karabıyıkoğlu, M. 2001. 'The tempo of Holocene climatic change in the eastern Mediterranean region: New high-resolution crater-lake sediment data from central Turkey'. *The Holocene* **11**:721–736.

Roberts, N., and Wright, H. E. 1993. 'Vegetational, lake-level, and climatic history of the Near East and southwest Asia'. In H. E. Wright, J. E., Kutzbach, T. Webb, W. F. Ruddiman, F. A. Street-Perrott, and P. J. Bartlein, eds., *Global Climates Since the Last Glacial Maximum*. Minneapolis: University of Minnesota Press, pp. 194–220.

Robin, C. 2003. 'New directions in Classic Maya household archaeology'. *Journal of Archaeological Research* **11**:307–336.

Rollefson, G. O. 2004. 'The character of LPPNB social organization'. In H. D. Bienert, H. G. K. Gebel, and R. Neef, eds., *Central Settlements in Neolithic Jordan*. Berlin, Germany: Ex Oriente, pp. 145–156.

Rollefson, G. O., and Gebel, H. G. K. 2004. 'Towards new frameworks: Supra-regional concepts in Near Eastern Neolithization'. *Neo-Lithics* 2004/**1**:21–52.

Roodenberg, J. 1995a. 'Chronologies and conclusion'. In J. Roodenberg, ed., *The Ilıpınar Excavations I*. Istanbul, Turkey: Nederlands Historisch Archaeologisch Istituut te Istanbul, pp. 167–174.

1995b. 'Stratigraphy and architecture: The "biq square"'. In J. Roodenberg, ed., *The Ilıpınar Excavations I*. Istanbul, Turkey: Nederlands Historisch Archaeol-ogisch Istituut te Istanbul, pp. 35–76.

1999. 'Ilıpınar: An early farming village in the Iznik Lake basin'. In M. Özdoğan and N. Başgelen, eds., *The Neolithic of Turkey*. Istanbul, Turkey: Arkeoloji ve Sanat Yayınları, pp. 193–202.

2001. 'Miscellaneous'. In J. Roodenberg and L. Thissen, eds., *The Ilıpınar Exca-vations II*. Istanbul, Turkey: Nederlands Instituut voor het Nabije Oosten, pp. 223–255.

2008a. 'The inhabitants'. In J. Roodenberg and S. Alpaslan-Roodenberg, eds., *Life and Death in a Prehistoric Settlement in Northwest Anatolia: The Ilıpınar Exca-vations III, with Contributions on Hacılartepe and Menteşe*. Leiden: Nederlands Instituut voor het Nabije Oosten, pp. 69–90.

2008b. 'Stratigraphy and architecture: The basal occupation levels (phases X and IX)'. In J. Roodenberg and S. Alpaslan-Roodenberg, eds., *Life and Death in a Prehistoric Settlement in Northwest Anatolia: The Ilıpınar Excavations III, with Contributions on Hacılartepe and Menteşe*. Leiden: Nederlands Instituut voor het Nabije Oosten, pp. 1–34.

2008c. 'The Late Chalcolithic cemetery'. In J. Roodenberg and S. Alpaslan-Roodenberg, eds., *Life and Death in a Prehistoric Settlement in Northwest Anatolia: The Ilıpınar Excavations III, with Contributions on Hacılartepe and Menteşe*. Leiden: Nederlands Instituut voor het Nabije Oosten, pp. 315–334.

Roodenberg, J., and S. Alpaslan 2007. 'Ilıpınar ve Menteşe: Doğu Marmara'da Neolithik Döneme Ait Iki Yerleşme'. In M. Özdoğan and N. Başgelen, eds., *Anadolu'da Uygarlığın Doğuşu Avrupaya Yayılımı Türkiye'de Neolitik Dönem, Yeni Kazılar, Yeni Bulgular*. Istanbul, Turkey: Arkeoloji ve Sanat Yayınları, pp. 393–400.

Roodenberg, J., and Schier, W. 2001. 'Radiocarbon determinations'. In J. Rooden-berg and L. Thissen, eds., *The Ilıpınar Excavations II*. Istanbul, Turkey: Ned-erlands Historisch Archaeologisch Istituut te Istanbul, pp. 257–278.

Roodenberg, J., Thissen, L., and Buitenhuis, H. 1990. 'Preliminary report on the archaeological investigations at Ilıpınar in NW Anatolia'. *Anatolica* **16**:61–144.

Roodenberg, J., van As, A., and Alpaslan-Roodenberg, S. 2008. 'Barcın Hüyük in the plain of Yenişehir (2005–2006): A preliminary note on the fieldwork, pottery and human remains of the prehistoric levels'. *Anatolica* **34**:53–60.

Roodenberg, J., van As, A., Jacobs, L., and Wijnen, M. H. 2003. 'Early settlement in the plain of Yenişehir (NW Anatolia): The basal occupation of Menteşe'. *Anatolica* **29**:17–59.

Rosen, A. 2005. 'Phytolith indicators of plant and land use at Çatalhöyük'. In I. Hod-der, ed., *Inhabiting Çatalhöyük, Reports from the 1995–1999 Seasons*. Cambridge, England: MacDonald Institute, 203–212.

2007. *Civilizing Climate: Social Responses to Climate Changes in the Ancient Near East*. Lanham, MD: Altamira Press.

Rosen, A., and Roberts, N. 2006. 'The nature of Çatalhöyük: People and their changing environments on the Konya Plain'. In I. Hodder, ed., *Çatalhöyük Perspectives: Themes from the 1995–1999 Seasons*. Cambridge, England: Mac-Donald Institute, pp. 39–53.

Rosenberg, M., and Peasnall, B. L. 1998. 'A report on soundings at Demirköy Höyük: An Aceramic Neolithic site in Eastern Anatolia'. *Anatolica* **24**:195–207.

Rosenstock, E. 2005. 'Höyük, Toumba and Mogila: A settlement form in Anatolia and the Balkans and its ecological determination 6500–5500 cal BC'. In C. Lichter, ed., *How Did Farming Reach Europe? Anatolian–European Relations from the Second Half of the 7th through the First Half of the 6th Millennium BC*. Istanbul, Turkey: Ege Yayınları, pp. 221–237.

Rossignol-Strick, M. 1993. 'Late Quarternary climate in the eastern Mediterranean region'. *Paleorient* **19**/1:135–152.

1995. 'Sea–land correlation of pollen records in the eastern Mediterranean for the Glacial–Interglacial transition: Biostratigraphy versus radiometric time-scale'. *Quarternary Science Review* **14**:893–915.

1997. 'Paléoclimat de la Méditerranée Orientale et de l'Asie du Sud-Ouest de 15,000 à 6000 BP'. *Paleorient* **23**/2:175–186.

Rountree, K. 2001. 'The past is a foreigners' country: Goddess feminists, archaeologists, and the appropriation of Prehistory'. *Journal of Contemporary Religion* **16**:5–27.

Runnels, C., and Hansen, J. 1986. 'The olive in the Prehistoric Aegean: The evidence for domestication in the Early Bronze Age'. *Oxford Journal of Archaeology* **5**:299–308.

Runnels, C., and Özdoğan, M. 2001. 'The Palaeolithic of the Bosphorus region, NW Turkey'. *Journal of Field Archaeology* **28**:69–92.

Runnels, C., Papagopoulou, E., Murray, P., Tsartsidou, G., Allen, G., Mullen, K., and Tourloukis, E. 2005. 'A mesolithic landscape in Greece: Testing a site-location model in the Argolid at Kandia'. *Journal of Mediterranean Archaeology* **18**:259–285.

Russell, N. 2005. 'Çatalhöyük worked bone'. In I. Hodder, ed., *Changing Materialities at Çatalhöyük: Reports from the 1995–1999 Seasons*. Cambridge, England: MacDonald Institute, pp. 339–368.

Russell, N., and Martin, L. 2005. 'The Çatalhöyük mammal remains'. In I. Hodder, ed., *Inhabiting Çatalhöyük: Reports from the 1995–1999 Seasons*. Cambridge, England: MacDonald Institute, pp. 33–98.

Russell, N., Martin, L., and Buitenhuis, H. 2005. 'Cattle domestication at Çatalhöyük revisited'. *Current Anthropology* **46**:101–108.

Russell, N., and McGowan, K. 2005. 'Çatalhöyük bird bones'. In I. Hodder, ed., *Inhabiting Çatalhöyük: Reports from the 1995–1999 Seasons*. Cambridge, England: MacDonald Institute, pp. 99–110.

Russell, N., and Meece, S. 2006. 'Animal representation and animal remains at Çatalhöyük'. In I. Hodder, ed., *Çatalhöyük Perspectives: Themes from the 1995–1999 Seasons*. Cambridge, England: MacDonald Institute, pp. 209–230.

Ryan, W. B. F., and Pitman, W. 1999. *Noah's Flood: The New Scientific Discoveries about the Event That Changed History*. New York: Simon & Schuster.

Ryan, W. B. F., Pitman, W. C., Major, O. C., Shimkus, K., Moskalenko, V., Jones, G. A., Dimitrov, P., Goriir, N., Saking, M., and Yiice, H. 1997. 'An abrupt drowning of the Black Sea shelf'. *Marine Geology* **138**:119–126.

Ryder, M. L. 1965. 'Report of textiles from Çatal Hüyük'. *Anatolian Studies* **15**:175–176.

Sağlamtimur, H. 2007. 'Ege Gübre Neolitik Yerlişimi'. In M. Özdoğan and N. Başgelen, eds., *Anadolu'da Uygarlığın Doğuşu Avrupaya Yayılımı Türkiye'de Neolitik Dönem, Yeni Kazılar, Yeni Bulgular*. Istanbul, Turkey: Arkeoloji ve Sanat Yayınları, pp. 373–376.

Sagona, A. 2004. 'Social boundaries and ritual landscapes in Late Prehistoric Trans-Caucasus and highland Anatolia'. In A. Sagona, ed., *A View from the Highlands: Archaeological Studies in Honour of Charles Burney*. Herent, Belgium: Peeters, pp. 475–538.

Sagona, A., and Zimansky, P. 2009. *Ancient Turkey*. London, England: Routledge.

Şahoğlu, V. 2008a. 'Crossing borders: The Izmir region as a bridge between the east and the west during the Early Bronze Age'. In C. Gillis and B. Sjöberg, eds., *Crossing Borders*. Sävedalen, Sweden: Paul Aström Förlag, pp. 153–173.

Şahoğlu, V. 2008b. 'Liman Tepe and Bakla Tepe: New evidence for the relations between the Izmir region, the Cyclades, and the Greek mainland during the late fourth and third millennia BC'. In H. Erkanal, H. Hauptmann, V. Şahoğlu, and R. Tuncel, eds., *The Aegean in the Neolithic, Chalcolithic and Early Bronze Age*. Ankara, Turkey: Ankara Üniversitesi Basımevi, pp. 483–501.

Saidel, B. A. 2008. 'The Bedouin tent: An ethno-arachaeological portal to antiquity or a modern construct?' In H. Barnard and W. Wendrich, eds., *The Archaeology of Mobility: Old World and New World Nomadism*. Los Angeles: Cotsen Institute of Archaeology, pp. 465–486.

Sazcı, G. 2005. 'Troia I-III, die Maritime und Troia IV-V, die Anatolische Troia-Kultur: eine Untersuchung der Funde und Befunde im mittleren Schliemanngraben (D07, D08)'. *Studia Troica* **15**:33–98.

Sazcı, G., and Treister, M. 2006. 'Troias Gold, Die Schätze des dritten Jahrtausend vor Christus'. In M. O. Korfmann, ed., *Troia: Archäologie eines Siedlungshügels und seiner Landschaft*. Mainz am Rhein, Germany: Philipp von Zabern, pp. 209–218.

Schirmer, W. 1971. 'Überlegungen zu einige Baufragen der Schichten I und II in Troja'. *Istanbuler Mitteilungen* **21**:1–43.

1983. 'Drei Bauten des Çayönü Tepesi'. In R. M. Boehmer and H. Hauptmann, eds., *Beiträge zur Altertumskunde Kleinasiens: Festschrift für Kurt Bittel*. Mainz am Rhein, Germany: Phillip von Zabern, pp. 463–476.

2000. 'Some aspects of building at the "Aceramic Neolithic" settlement of Çayönü Tepesi'. *World Archaeology* **21**:363–387.

Schloen, D. J. 2001. *The House of the Father as Fact and Symbol: Patrimonialism in Ugarit and the Ancient Near East*. Winona Lake, IN: Eisenbrauns.

Schmidt, H. 1902. *Heinrich Schliemanns Sammlung trojanischer Altertümer*. Berlin, Germany: Königliche Museen zu Berlin.

Schmidt, K. 1998. 'Frühneolithische Tempel, Ein Forschungsbericht zum präkeramischen Neolithikum Obermesopotamiens'. *Mitteilungen der Deutschen Orientgesellschaft* **130**:17–49.

Schoop, U.-D. 1995. *Die Geburt des Hephaistos: Technologie und Kulturgeschichte neolithischer Metallverwendung im Vorderen Orient*. Espelkamp, Germany: Verlag Marie Leidorf.

2002. 'Frühneolithikum im südwestanatolischen Seengebiet? Eine kritische Betrachtung'. In R. Aslan, S. Blum, G. Kastl, F. Schweizer, and D. Thumm, eds., *Mauerschau: Festschrift für Manfred Korfmann*. Remshalden-Grunbach, Germany: Bernhard Albert Greiner, pp. 421–436.

2005a. *Das anatolische Chalkolithicum*. Remshalden, Germany: Albert Greiner Verlag.

2005b. 'The late escape of the Neolithic from the Central Anatolian Plain'. In C. Lichter, ed., *How Did Farming Reach Europe? Anatolian–European Relations from the Second Half of the 7th through the First Half of the 6th Millennium BC*. Istanbul, Turkey: Ege Yayınları, pp. 41–58.

2008. 'Ausgrabungen in Çamlibel Tarlası 2007'. *Archäologischer Anzeiger* 148–157.

2009. 'Ausgrabungen in Çamlibel Tarlası 2008'. *Archäologischer Anzeiger* 56–67.

Schwarzberg, H. 2005. 'Kultgefäße von Aşağı Pınar. "Kulttischen" und ihre Stellung im Neolitikum und Chalcolitikum Südosteuropas und Anatoliens'. In H. Parzinger and H. Schwarzberg, eds., *Aşağı Pınar II: Die mittel – und spätneolithische Keramik*. Mainz am Rhein, Germany: Philipp von Zabern, pp. 247–416.

Seeher, J. 1985. 'Vorläufiger Bericht über die Keramik des Beşik-Sivritepe'. *Archäologischer Anzeiger* 172–182.

1987a. *Demiricihüyük, Die Ergebnisse der Ausgrabungen 1975–1978 III*. Mainz am Rhein, Germany: Philipp von Zabern.

1987b. 'Prähistorische Funde aus Gülpınar/Chryse: Neue Belege für einen vor-Trojanischen Horizont and der Nordwestküste Kleinasiens'. *Archäologischer Anzeiger* 533–556.

1990. 'Coşkuntepe, Anatolisches Neolithikum am Nordostufer der Ägäis'. *Istanbuler Mitteilungen* **40**:9–15.

1992. 'Die kleinasiatischen Marmorstatuetten vom Typ Kiliya'. *Archäologischer Anzeiger* 153–170.

2000. *Die bronzezeitlichen Nekropole von Demircohöyük – Sariket*. Tübingen, Germany: Ernst Wasmuth Verlag.

Sherratt, A. 1983. 'The secondary exploitation of animals in the Old World'. *World Archaeology* **15**:90–104.

2004. 'Fractal farmers: Patterns of Neolithic origin and dispersal'. In J. Cherry, C. Scarre, and S. Shennan, eds., *Explaining Social Change: Studies in Honour of Colin Renfrew*. Cambridge, England: MacDonald Institute, pp. 53–63.

Silistreli, U. 1984. 'Pınarbaşı ve Köşk Höyükleri'. *Kazı Sonuçları Toplantısı* **5** (1983): 81–85.

1985. '1984 Kösk Höyüğü'. *Kazı Sonuçları Toplantısı* **7** (1985): 129–141.

Simmons, A. 2007. *The Neolithic Revolution in the Near East: Transforming the Human Landscape*. Tucson: University of Arizona Press.

Singh, P. 1976. *Neolithic Cultures of Western Asia*. London, England: Seminar Press.

Slimak, L., and Giraud, Y. 2007. 'Circulations sur plusieurs centaines de kilométres durant le Paléolithique Moyen'. *Palevol* **6**:359–368.

Sperling, J. W. 1976. 'Kum Tepe in the Troad: Trial excavations, 1934'. *Hesperia* **45**/4:305–364.

Steadman, S. R. 1994. 'Prehistoric sites on the Cilician coastal plain: Chalcolithic and Early Bronze Age pottery from the 1991 Bilkent University survey'. *Anatolian Studies* **44**:85–103.

1995. 'Prehistoric interregional interaction in Anatolia and the Balkans: An overview'. *Bulletin of the American Society of Oriental Studies* **299**/300:13–32.

Steadman, S. R., McMahon, G., and Ross, J. C. 2007. 'The Late Chalcolithic at Çadır Höyük in central Anatolia'. *Journal of Field Archaeology* **32**:515–558.

Steadman, S. R., Ross, J. C., McMahon, G., and Gorny, R. L. 2008. 'Excavations on the north-central plateau: The Chalcolithic and Early Bronze Age occupation at Çadır Höyük'. *Anatolian Studies* **58**:47–86.

Stech, T. 1999. 'Aspects of early metallurgy in Mesopotamia and Anatolia'. In V. C. Pigott, ed., *The Archaeometallurgy of the Asian Old World*. Philadelphia: Museum, University of Philadelphia, pp. 59–72.

Steel, L. 2004. *Cyprus Before History: From the Earliest Settlers to the End of the Bronze Age*. London, England: Duckworth.

Stein, G. J., ed. 2005. *The Archaeology of Colonial Encounters: Comparative Perspectives*. Santa Fe, NM: School of American Research Press.

Stein, G., and Özbal, R. 2007. 'A tale of two Oikumenai: Variation in the expansionary dynamics of Ubaid and Uruk Mesopotamia'. In E. C. Stone, ed., *Settlement and Society: Essays Dedicated to Robert McCormick Adams*. Los Angeles: Cotsen Institute of Archaeology, pp. 329–342.

Steinhauer, F., ed. 1970. *Climatic Atlas of Europe*. Geneva, Switzerland: World Meteorological Organization.

Stevanovic, M. 1997. 'The age of clay: The social dynamics of house destruction'. *Journal of Anthropological Archaeology* **16**:334–395.

Stordeur, D., and Abbès, F. 2002. 'Du PPNA au PPNB, Mise en lumière d'une phase de transition à Jerf el Ahmar (Syrie)'. *Bulletin de la Société Préhistorique Française* **99**:563–595.

Süel, M. 1989. 'Balıbağı 1988 kurtarma kazısı'. *Türk Arkeoloji Dergisi* **28**:145–163.

Summers, G. D. 1991. 'Chalcolithic pottery from Kabakulak (Niğde) collected by Ian Todd'. *Anatolian Studies* **41**:125–131.

___ 2002. 'Concerning the identification, location and distribution of the Neolithic and Chalcolithic settlements in Central Anatolia'. In F. Gérard and L. Thissen, eds., *The Neolithic of Central Anatolia: Internal Developments and External Relations during the 9th–6th Millennia cal. BC*. Istanbul, Turkey: Ege Yayınları, pp. 131–137.

Swiny, S., ed. 2001. *The Earliest Prehistory of Cyprus: From Colonization to Exploitation*. Boston: American Schools of Oriental Research.

Takaoğlu, T. 2002. 'Chalcolithic marble working at Kulaksızlar in Western Anatolia'. *Türkiye Bilimler Akademisi Arkeoloji Dergesi* **5**:71–93.

___ 2004. 'Interactions in the fifth millennium BC eastern Aegean: New evidence'. *Anatolia Antiqua* **12**:1–6.

___ 2005. *A Chalcolithic Marble Workshop at Kulaksızlar in Western Anatolia: An Analysis of Production and Craft Specialization*. Oxford, England: Archaeopress.

___ 2006. 'The Late Neolithic in the eastern Aegean: Excavations at Gülpınar in the Troad'. *Hesperia* **75**:289–315.

Talalay, L. E. 2004. 'Heady business: Skulls, heads, and decapitation in Neolithic Anatolia'. *Journal of Mediterranean Archaeology* **17**:139–163.

Taşkıran, H. 1996. 'Karain Mağarası Çevresi ile Antalya Sahil Şeridi Arasında Paleolitik iskan Acısından iliskiler'. *Yılı Anadolu Medeniyetleri Müzesi Konferansları* 1995 94–114.

Taşman, C. E. 1937. 'Salt domes of Central Anatolia'. *Maden Tetkik ve Arama Dergisi* **9**:45–47.

Tchernov, E. 1991. 'Biological evidence for human sedentism in southwest Asia during the Natufian'. In O. Bar-Yosef and F. R. Valla, eds., *The Natufian Culture in the Levant*. Ann Arbor: University of Michigan Press, pp. 315–340.

1998. 'An attempt to synchronize the faunal changes with the radiometric dates and the cultural chronology in Southwest Asia'. In H. Buitenhuis, L. Bartosiewicz, and A. M. Choyke, eds., *Archaeozoology of the Near East 3*. Groningen, the Netherlands: ARC, pp. 7–44.

Thissen, L. 1993. 'New insights in Balkan–Anatolian connections in the Late Chalcolithic: Old evidence from the Turkish Black Sea littoral'. *Anatolian Studies* **43**:207–237.

2000. 'Early village communities in Anatolia and the Balkans, 6500–5500 cal BC: Studies in chronology and culture contact'. Unpublished PhD thesis, Leiden University, the Netherlands.

2001. 'The pottery of Ilıpınar: Phases X to VA'. In J. Roodenberg and L. Thissen, eds., *The Ilıpınar Excavations II*. Istanbul, Turkey: Nederlands Historisch Archaeologisch Istituut te Istanbul, pp. 3–154.

2002. 'Appendix I: The CANeW 14C databases: Anatolia 10,000–5000 cal BC'. In F. Gérard and L. Thissen, eds., *The Neolithic of Central Anatolia: Internal Developments and External Relations during the 9th–6th Millennia cal. BC*. Istanbul, Turkey: Ege Yayınları, pp. 299–337.

2005. 'Coming to grips with the Aegean in Prehistory: An outline of the temporal framework, 10,000 to 5500 cal BC'. In C. Lichter, ed., *How Did Farming Reach Europe? Anatolian–European Relations from the Second Half of the 7th through the First Half of the 6th Millennium BC*. Istanbul, Turkey: Ege Yayınları, pp. 29–40.

2008. 'The pottery of phase VB'. In J. Roodenberg and S. Alpaslan-Roodenberg, eds., *Life and Death in a Prehistoric Settlement in Northwest Anatolia: The Ilıpınar Excavations III*. Leiden: Nederlands Instituut voor het Nabije Oosten, pp. 91–116.

Todd, I. A. 1966. 'Aşıklı Höyük: A Protoneolithic site in Central Anatolia'. *Anatolian Studies* **16**:139–163.

1968a. 'The dating of Aşıklı Höyük in Central Anatolia'. *American Journal of Archaeology* **12**:157–158.

1968b. 'Preliminary report on a survey of Neolithic sites in Central Anatolia'. *Türk Arkeoloji Dergisi* **15** (1966): 103–107.

1976. *Çatal Hüyük in Perspective*. Menlo Park, CA: Cummings.

1980. *The Prehistory of Central Anatolia I: The Neolithic Period*. Göteborg, Germany: Paul Åström Förlag.

Todorova, H. 1998. 'Der balkano-anatolische Kulturbereich vom Neolithikum bis zur Frühbonzezeit'. In M. Stefanovich, H. Todorova, and H. Hauptmann, eds., *James Harvey Gaul – In Memoriam*. Sofia, Turkey: James Harvey Gaul Foundation, pp. 27–54.

Tomkins, P., Day, P. M., and Kilikoglu, V. 2004. 'Knossos and the earlier Neolithic landscape of the Herakleion basin'. In G. Cadogan, E. Hatzaki, and A. Vasilakis, eds., *Knossos: Palace, City, State*. Athens, Greece: British School at Athens, pp. 51–74.

Topbaş, A., Efe, T., and Ilaslı, A. 1998. 'Salvage excavations of the Afyon archaeological museum, part 2: The settlement of Karaoğlan Mevkii and the Early Bronze Age cemetery of Kaklik Mevkii'. *Anatolia Antiqua* **6**:21–94.

Trigger, B. G. 1994. 'Childe's relevance to the 1990's'. In D. R. Harris, ed., *The Archaeology of V. Gordon Childe*. Chicago: University of Chicago Press, pp. 9–34.
    1998. *Sociocultural Evolution: Calculation and Contingency*. Oxford, England: Blackwell.
    2003. *Understanding Early Civilisations: A Comparative Study*. Cambridge, England: Cambridge University Press.
Tschora, N. 2004. 'Les rites funérarires d'Alaca Hüyük au Bronze Ancien: Étude comparative'. In O. Pelon, ed., *Studia Aegeo-Anatolica*. Lyon, France: Maison de L'orient et de la Mediterranée – Jean Pouilloux, pp. 187–222.
Tuna, C. 2008. *Orta Karadeniz Bölgesi Sahil Kesiminde Geleneksel Mimari*. Istanbul, Turkey: Arkeoloji ve Sanat Yayınları.
Türkcan, A. U. 2005. 'Some remarks on Çatalhöyük stamp seals'. In I. Hodder, ed., *Changing Materialities at Çatalhöyük: Reports from the 1995–1999 Seasons*. Cambridge, England: MacDonald Institute, pp. 175–186.
Twiss, K. C., Bogaard, A., Bogdan, D., Carter, T., Charles, M. P., Farid, S., Russell, N., Stevanovic, M., Yalman, E. N., and Yeomans, L. 2008. 'Arson or accident? The burning of a Neolithic house at Çatalhöyük, Turkey'. *Journal of Field Archaeology* **32**:41–57.
Umurtak, G. 2000. 'A building type of the Burdur region from the Neolithic period'. *Belleten* **64**:683–716.
    2005. 'A study on the dating of new groups of pottery from Bademağacı Höyük and some reflections on the Late Chalcolithic cultures of southwestern Anatolia'. *Anatolia Antiqua* **13**:53–69.
Ünal, A. 1966. 'Çengeltepe (Yozgat) sondaji önraporu'. *Türk Arkeoloji Dergisi* **15/1**:119–142.
Ünlüsoy, S. 2006. 'Vom Reihenhaus zum Megaron – Troia I bis Troia III'. In M. O. Korfmann, ed., *Troia: Archäologie eines Siedlungshügels und seiner Landschaft*. Mainz am Rhein, Germany: Philipp von Zabern, pp. 133–144.
Urbin-Choffray, T. 1987. 'Triade divine, Prémisses à Çatal Hüyük au VIIe millénaire'. *Hethitica* **7**:255–266.
Van Andel, T. H. 2005. 'Coastal migrants in a changing world? An essay on the Mesolithic in the eastern Mediterranean'. *Journal of the Israel Prehistoric Society* **35**:381–397.
Van Beek, G. W. 2008. *Glorious Mud! Ancient and Contemporary Earthen Design and Construction in North Africa, Western Europe, the Near East, and South Asia*. Washington, DC: Smithsonian Institute Press.
Verhoeven, M. 1999. *An Archaeological Ethnography of a Neolithic Community: Space, Place and Social Relations in the Burnt Village at Tell Sabi Abyad, Syria*. Istanbul, Turkey: Nederlands Instituut voor het Nabije Oosten.
    2000. 'Death, fire and abandonment: Ritual practice at neolithic Tell Sabi Abyad, Syria'. *Archaeological Dialogues* **7**:46–83.
    2002. 'Ritual and ideology in the Pre-Pottery Neolithic B of the Levant and Southeast Anatolia'. *Cambridge Archaeological Journal* **12**:233–258.
    2006. 'Megasites in the Jordanian Pre-Pottery Neolithic B: Evidence for "proto-urbanism"'? In E. B. Banning and M. Chazan, eds., *Domesticating Space: Construction, Community, and Cosmology in the Late Prehistoric Near East*. Berlin, Germany: Ex Oriente, pp. 75–80.
    2007. 'Losing one's head in the Neolithic: On the interpretation of headless figurines'. *Levant* **39**:175–183.

Vigne, J. D., Buitenhuis, H., and Davis, S. 1999. 'Les premiers pas de la domestica-
    tion animale à l'ouest de l'Euphrate, Chyphre et l'Anatolie Centrale'. *Paleorient*
    25:49–62.
Vigne, J. D., and Guilaine, J. 2004. 'Les premiers animaux de compagnie, 8500 ans
    avant notre ère? Ou comment j'ai mangé mon chat, mon chien et mon renard'.
    Anthropozoologica **39**:249–273.
Vogelsang-Eastwood, G. M. 1988. 'A re-examination of the fibres from the Çatal
    Hüyük textiles'. *Oriental Carpet and Textile Studies* **3**/1:15–19.
Voigt, M. M. 2000. 'Çatal Hüyük in context: Ritual at Early Neolithic sites in central
    and eastern Turkey'. In I. Kuijt, ed., *Life in Neolithic Farming Communities:
    Social Organization, Identity, and Differentiation*. New York: Kluwer Academic,
    pp. 253–293.
Wagner, F., Aaby, B., and Visscher, H. 2002. 'Rapid atmospheric CO_2 changes
    associated with the 8,200-years-B.P. cooling event'. *Proceedings of the National
    Academy of Sciences* **99**/19;12011–12014.
Wagner, G. A., Pernicka, E., and Uerpmann, H. P., eds. 2003. *Troia and the Troad:
    Scientific Approaches*. Berlin, Germany: Springer.
Wagner, G. A., and Weiner, K. L. 1987. 'Spaltspurenanalysen an Obsidianproben'.
    In M. Korfmann, ed., *Demircihüyük: Die Ergebnisse der Ausgrabungen 1975–1978
    II; Naturwissenschaftliche Untersuchungen*. Mainz am Rhein, Germany: Philipp
    von Zabern, pp. 24–29.
Warner, J. L. 1994. *Elmalı – Karataş II: The Early Bronze Age Village of Karataş*. Bryn
    Mawr, PA: Bryn Mawr College Archaeological Monographs.
Warren, P., and Hankey, V. 1989. *Aegean Bronze Age Chronology*. Exeter, England:
    Bristol Classical Press.
Waterson, R. 1990. *The Living House: An Anthropology of Architecture in South-East
    Asia*. New York: Whitney Library of Design.
    1995. 'Houses and hierarchies in island Southeast Asia'. In J. Carsten and S. Hugh-
    Jones, eds., *About the House: Lévi-Strauss and Beyond*. Cambridge, England:
    Cambridge University Press, pp. 47–68.
    2003. 'The immortality of the house in Tana Toraja'. In S. Sparkes and S. Howel,
    eds., *The House in Southeast Asia: A Changing Social, Economic and Political
    Domain*. London, England: Routledge Curzon, pp. 34–52.
Watkins, T. 1990. 'The origins of house and home'. *World Archaeology* **21**:336–347.
    1996. 'Excavations at Pınarbaşı: The Early Stages'. In I. Hodder, ed., *On the Sur-
    face: Çatalhöyük 1993–95*. Cambridge, England: MacDonald Institute, pp. 47–
    58.
    2004. 'Building houses, framing concepts, constructing worlds'. *Paleorient* **30**:5–
    24.
    2006. 'Neolithisation in southwest Asia: The path to modernity'. *Documenta Prae-
    historica* **33**:71–88.
Weisgerber, G., and Cierny, J. 2002. 'Tin for ancient Anatolia?' In Ü. Yalçın, ed.,
    Anatolian Metal II. Bochum: Deutschen Bergbau-Museum, pp. 179–186.
Weiss, H., and Bradley, R. S. 2001. 'Archaeology: What drives societal collapse?'
    Science **291**/5504:609–610.
Wendrich, W. 2005. 'Çatalhöyük basketry'. In I. Hodder, ed., *Changing Material-
    ities at Çatalhöyük: Reports from the 1995–1999 Seasons*. Cambridge, England:
    MacDonald Institute, pp. 333–338.

Wengrow, D. 2006. *The Archaeology of Early Egypt: Social Transformations in North-East Africa, 10,000 to 2650 BC*. Cambridge, England: Cambridge University Press.

Westley, B. 1970. 'The mammalian fauna'. In J. Mellaart, ed., *Excavations at Hacılar*. Edinburgh, Scotland: Edinburgh University Press, pp. 245–247.

Wheeler, T. S. 1974. 'Early Bronze Age burial customs in Western Anatolia'. *American Journal of Archaeology* **78**:415–425.

Whittemore, T. 1943. 'Archaeology during the Republic in Turkey'. *American Journal of Archaeology* **47**/2:164–170.

Wilk, R. R., and Rathje, W. L. 1982. 'Household archaeology'. *American Behavioral Scientist* **25**/6:617–639.

Wilkinson, T. J. 2003. *Archaeological Landscapes of the Near East*. Tucson: University of Arizona Press.

Williams-Thorpe, O. 1995. 'Obsidian in the Mediterranean and the Near East: A provenancing success story'. *Archaeometry* **37**:217–248.

Willies, L. 1992. 'Reply to Pernicka et al., "Comment on the discussion of ancient tin sources in Anatolia"'. *Journal of Mediterranean Archaeology* **5**:99–103.

Wirth, E. 2000. *Die orientalische Stadt im islamischen Vorderasien und Nordafrika, Städtische Bausubstanz und räumliche Ordnung, Wirtschaftleben and soziale Organisation*. Mainz, Germany: Philipp von Zabern.

Wobst, H. M. 1974. 'Boundary conditions for Paleolithic social systems: A simulation approach'. *American Antiquity* **39**:147–178.

Woldring, H., and Bottema, S. 2001/2002. 'The vegetation history of East-Central Anatolia in relation to archaeology: The Eski Acıgöl pollen evidence compared with the Near Eastern environment'. *Palaeohistoria* **43**/44:1–34.

Wright, G. A. 1969. *Obsidian Analyses and Prehistoric Near Eastern Trade*. Ann Arbor: University of Michigan Press.

Wunn, I. 2001. *Götter, Mütter, Ahnenkult: Religionsentwicklung in der Jungsteinzeit*. Rahden, Germany: Verlag Marie Leidorf.

Yakar, J. 1975. 'Northern Anatolia in the Early Bronze Age'. *Tel Aviv* **2**:133–145.

1985. *The Later Prehistory of Anatolia: The Late Chalcolithic and Early Bronze Age*. Oxford, England: British Archaeological Reports – International Series.

1991. *Prehistoric Anatolia: The Neolithic Transformation and the Early Chalcolithic Period*. Tel Aviv, Israel: Tel Aviv University Press.

1994. *Prehistoric Anatolia: The Neolithic Transformation and the Early Chalcolithic Period, Supplement I*. Tel Aviv, Israel: Tel Aviv University Press.

Yalçınkaya, I., Otte, M., Bar-Yosef, O., Kozlowski, J., Léotard, J.-M., and Taskiran, H. 1993. 'The excavations at Karain Cave, southwestern Turkey: An interim report'. In D. I. Olszewski and H. L. Dibble, eds., *The Palaeolithic Prehistory of the Zagros-Taurus*. Philadelphia: University of Pennsylvania Press, pp. 101–118.

Yanko-Hombach, V. 2007. 'Controversy over Noah's flood in the Black Sea: Geological and foraminiferal evidence from the shelf'. In V. Yanko-Hombach, A. S. Gilbert, N. Panin, and P. M. Dolukhanov, eds., *The Black Sea Flood Question: Changes in Coastline, Climate and Human Settlement*. Dordrecht, the Netherlands: Springer, pp. 149–203.

Yasin, S. A. 1985. *The Ubaid Period in Iraq: Recent Excavations in the Hamrin Region*. Oxford, England: British Archaeological Reports.

Yeğingil, Z., Bigazzi, G., Poupeau, G., and Bellot-Gurlet, L. 1998. 'The Aceramic Neolithic of Central Anatolia: Recent finds in the chipped stone industry'. In G. Arsebük, M. J. Mellink, and W. Schirmer, eds., *Light on Top of the Black Hill: Studies Presented to Halet Çambel*. Istanbul, Turkey: Ege Yayınları, pp. 823–844.

Yener, K. A. 2000. *The Domestication of Metals: The Rise of Complex Metal Industries in Anatolia*. Leiden, the Netherlands: Brill.

Yener, K. A., Geçkinli, E., and Özbal, H. 1994. 'A brief survey of Anatolian metallurgy prior to 500 BC'. In S. Demirci, A. M. Özer, and G. D. Summers, eds., *Archaeometry 94: The Proceedings of the 29th International Symposium on Archaeometry*. Ankara, Turkey: Tübitak, pp. 375–390.

Yener, K. A., and Goodway, M. 1992. 'Response to Mark E. Hall and Sharon R. Steadman, "Tin and Anatolia: Another look"'. *Journal of Mediterranean Archaeology* **5**:77–90.

Yener, K. A., and Özbal, H. 1987. 'Tin in the Turkish Taurus Mountains: The Bolkardağ mining district'. *Antiquity* **61**:220–226.

Yener, K. A., and Vandiver, P. B. 1993a. 'Tin processing at Göltepe: An Early Bronze Age site in Anatolia'. *American Journal of Archaeology* **97**:207–238.

1993b. 'Reply to J. D. Muhly, "Early Bronze Age tin and the Taurus"'. *American Journal of Archaeology* **97**:255–264.

Yildirim, B., and Gates, M. H. 2007. 'Archaeology in Turkey, 2004–2005'. *American Journal of Archaeology* **111**:275–356.

Yilmaz, Y. 2003. 'Seismotectonics and geology of Troia and surrounding areas: Northwest Anatolia'. In G. A. Wagner, E. Pernicka, and H.-P. Uerpmann, eds., *Troia and the Troad: Scientific Approaches*. Berlin, Germany: Springer, pp. 55–75.

Young, T. C., Smith, E. L., and Mortensen, P. 1983. 'Introduction'. In T. C. Young, E. L. Smith, and P. Mortensen, eds., *The Hilly Flanks: Essays on the Prehistory of Southwestern Asia Presented to Robert J. Braidwood*, Chicago: Oriental Institute, pp. 1–7.

Zambello, M. 2004. 'The use of obsidian and flint at Prehitoric Yumuktepe: An overview'. In I. Caneva and V. Sevin, eds., *Mersin-Yumuktepe: A Reppraisal*. Lecce, Italy: Congedo Editore, pp. 143–151.

Zeder, M. A. 2009. 'The Neolithic macro-(r)evolution: Macrorevolutionairy theory and the study of culture change'. *Jounal of Archaeological Research* **17**:1–63.

Zeist, W. van, and Bottema, S. 1991. *Late Quarternary Vegetation of the Near East*. Wiesbaden, Germany: Dr. Ludwig Reichert Verlag.

Zeist, W. van, and Buitenhuis, H. 1983. 'A palaeobotanical study of Neolithic Erbaba, Turkey'. *Anatolica* **10**:47–89.

Zeist, W. van, and De Roller, G. J. 1995. 'Plant remains from Aşıklı Höyük: A Pre-Pottery Neolithic site in Central Anatolia'. *Vegetation History and Archaeobotany* **4**:179–185.

Zeist, W. van, Woldring, H., and Stapert, D. 1975. 'Late quarternary vegetation and climate of southwestern Turkey'. *Palaeohistoria* **17**:53–143.

Zimmermann, T. 2006a. 'Zu den sogenannten "Pilznaufkeulen" der anatolischen Frühbronzezeit, Zeremonialgerät zwischen Halysbogen und Kuban'. *Eurasia Antiqua* **12**:127–135.

2006b. 'Kalinkaya: A Chalcolithic–Early Bronze Age settlement in northern Central Anatolia, first preliminary report: The burial evidence'. *Anadolu Medeniyetleri Müzesi Konferansları* 2005 yilliği: 271–311.

2007. 'Anatolia as a bridge from north to south? Recent research in the Hatti heartland'. *Anatolian Studies* **57**:65–75.

Zohary, D. 1973. *Geobotanical Foundations of the Middle East*. Stuttgart, Germany: Gustav Fischer Verlag.

1989. 'Domestication of the southwest Asian Neolithic crop assemblages of cereals, pulses, and flax: The evidence from the living plants'. In D. R. Harris and G. C. Hillman, eds., *Foraging and Farming: The Evolution of Plant Exploitation*. London, England: Unwin Hyman, pp. 358–373.

Zohary, D., and Hopf, M. 1993. *Domestication of Plants in the Old World: The Origins and Spread of Cultivated Plants in West Asia, Europe, and the Nile Valley*. Oxford, England: Clarendon Press.

Zürcher, E. J. 2004. *Turkey: A Modern History*. London, England: I. B. Tauris.

Zvelebil, M. 1996. 'The agricultural frontier and the transition to farming in the circum-Baltic region'. In D. R. Harris, ed., *The Origins and Spread of Agriculture and Pastoralism in Eurasia*. London, England: University College of London Press, pp. 323–345.

2001. 'The agricultural transition and the origins of Neolithic society in Europe'. *Documenta Praehistorica* **28**:1–26.

INDEX